# Artifact and Artifice

# Artifact

Classical Archaeology and the Ancient Historian

# & Artifice

Jonathan M. Hall

The University of Chicago Press  ::  Chicago and London

Jonathan M. Hall is the Phyllis Fay Horton Distinguished Service
Professor in the Humanities and professor in the Departments of
History and Classics and the College at the University of Chicago.
He is the author of three books, most recently *A History of the
Archaic Greek World, ca. 1200–479 BCE.*

The University of Chicago Press, Chicago 60637
The University of Chicago Press, Ltd., London
© 2014 by The University of Chicago
All rights reserved. Published 2014.
Printed in the United States of America

23  22  21  20  19  18  17  16  15  14        1  2  3  4  5

ISBN-13: 978-0-226-31338-2 (cloth)
ISBN-13: 978-0-226-09698-8 (paper)
ISBN-13: 978-0-226-08096-3 (e-book)
DOI: 10.7208/chicago/9780226080963.001.0001

Library of Congress Cataloging-in-Publication Data
Hall, Jonathan M.
Artifact and artifice : classical archaeology and the ancient historian /
Jonathan M. Hall.
pages cm
Includes bibliographical references and index.
ISBN 978-0-226-31338-2 (cloth : alk. paper) — ISBN 978-0-226-09698-8 (paper) —
ISBN 978-0-226-08096-3 (e-book)
1. Archaeology and history—Greece. 2. Archaeology and history—Rome.
3. Greece—Antiquities. 4. Greece—Historiography. 5. Rome—Antiquities.
6. Rome—Historiography. 7. Christian antiquities. 8. Church history—Primitive
and early church, ca. 30–600. I. Title.
DE59.H35 2014
938—dc23

2013018750

♾ This paper meets the requirements of ANSI/NISO Z39.48-1992
(Permanence of Paper).

# Contents

# Illustrations

# Abbreviations

| | |
|---|---|
| AA | Archäologischer Anzeiger |
| AAEA | Anejos di Archivio Español de Arqueología |
| ABSA | Annual of the British School at Athens |
| AC | L'Antiquité Classique |
| ActaArch | Acta Archaeologica |
| AE | Αρχαιολογική Εφημερίς |
| AEHE V | Annuaire de l'École Pratique des Hautes Études, Ve section: Sciences Religieuses |
| AEMT | Το Αρχαιολογικόν Έργον στη Μακεδονία και Θράκη |
| AJA | American Journal of Archaeology |
| AK | Antike Kunst |
| AmerAnt | American Antiquity |
| AnalRom | Analecta Romana Instituti Danici |
| AncPhil | Ancient Philosophy |
| AncW | Ancient World |
| Antiquity | Antiquity: A Quarterly Review of World Archaeology |
| AR | Archaeological Reports |
| ARC | Archaeological Review from Cambridge |
| ArchClass | Archeologia Classica: Rivista della Scuola Nazionale di Archeologia, Università di Roma |
| ArchRel | Archiv für Religionwissenschaft |
| ArtB | The Art Bulletin |
| ASAA | Annuario della Scuola Archeologica di Atene |
| ASNSP | Annali della Scuola Normale Superiore di Pisa |

| | |
|---|---|
| *Athenaeum* | *Athenaeum: Studi di Letteratura e Storia dell'Antichità* |
| *AttiPontAcc* | *Atti della Pontificia Accademia Romana di Archeologia* |
| *AWE* | *Ancient West and East* |
| *BA* | *Bollettino d'Arte del Ministero per i Beni Culturali e Ambientali* |
| *BAR* | *British Archaeological Reports* |
| *BASOR* | *Bulletin of the American Schools of Oriental Research* |
| *BCH* | *Bulletin de Correspondance Hellénique* |
| *BibArch* | *The Biblical Archaeologist* |
| *BMCRev* | *Bryn Mawr Classical Review* |
| *BollArch* | *Bollettino di Archeologia* |
| *BPI* | *Bollettino di Paleontologia Italiana* |
| *BullCom* | *Bullettino della Commissione Archeologica Comunale di Roma* |
| *CAH* | *Cambridge Ancient History* |
| *CAJ* | *Cambridge Archaeological Journal* |
| *CI* | *Critical Inquiry* |
| *CIL* | *Corpus Inscriptionum Latinarum* (Berlin, 1863–) |
| *ClAnt* | *Classical Antiquity* |
| *CPh* | *Classical Philology* |
| *CQ* | *Classical Quarterly* |
| *CRAI* | *Comptes Rendus de l'Académie des Inscriptions et Belles-Lettres* |
| *CT* | *Clinical Toxicology* |
| *DArch* | *Dialoghi di Archeologia* |
| *DHA* | *Dialogues d'Histoire Ancienne* |
| *Eranos* | *Eranos: Acta Philologica Suecana* |
| *Ergon* | Τὸ Ἔργον τῆς Ἀρχαιολογικῆς Ἑταιρείας |
| *FGrH* | F. Jacoby, *Die Fragmente der griechischen Historiker* (Berlin and Leiden, 1923–; this work is now being updated, with English translations, as Brill's New Jacoby: online version at http://www.brill.nl /publications/online-resources/jacoby-online) |
| *GHI* | M. N. Tod, *A Selection of Greek Historical Inscriptions*, 2 vols. (Oxford, 1948–51) |
| *GRBS* | *Greek, Roman, and Byzantine Studies* |
| *Gymnasium* | *Gymnasium: Zeitschrift für Kultur der Antike und humanistische Bildung* |
| *Hermes* | *Hermes: Zeitschrift für klassische Philologie* |
| *Hesperia* | *Hesperia: Journal of the American School of Classical Studies at Athens* |
| *Historia* | *Historia: Zeitschrift für alte Geschichte* |
| *HSCP* | *Harvard Studies in Classical Philology* |
| *HTR* | *Harvard Theological Review* |
| *IG* | *Inscriptiones Graecae* (Berlin, 1873–) |
| *ILLRP* | A. Degrassi, *Inscriptiones Latinae Liberae Rei Publicae* (Florence, 1957–63) |
| *ILS* | H. Dessau, *Inscriptiones Latinae Selectae* (Berlin, 1892–1916) |
| *Inscr.It* | *Inscriptiones Italiae* (Rome, 1931–) |
| *IJMS* | *International Journal of Medical Sciences* |
| *IstMitt* | *Istanbuler Mitteilungen* |
| *JAOS* | *Journal of the American Oriental Society* |
| *JAS* | *Journal of Archaeological Science* |
| *JBL* | *Journal of Biblical Literature* |
| *JBR* | *Journal of Bible and Religion* |
| *JDAI* | *Jahrbuch des Deutschen Archäologischen Instituts* |

| | |
|---|---|
| *JGS* | *Journal of the Geological Society* |
| *JHS* | *Journal of Hellenic Studies* |
| *JJS* | *Journal of Jewish Studies* |
| *JMGS* | *Journal of Modern Greek Studies* |
| *JRA* | *Journal of Roman Archaeology* |
| *JRS* | *Journal of Roman Studies* |
| *JSAH* | *Journal of the Society of Architectural Historians* |
| *JThS* | *Journal of Theological Studies* |
| *Kadmos* | *Kadmos: Zeitschrift für vor- und frühgriechische Epigraphik* |
| *Klio* | *Klio: Beiträge zur alten Geschichte* |
| *LCM* | *Liverpool Classical Monthly* |
| *LGPN* | *A Lexicon of Greek Personal Names* (Oxford, 1987–; online version at http://www.lgpn.ox.ac.uk/) |
| *LRB* | *London Review of Books* |
| *MDAI(A)* | *Mitteilungen des Deutschen Archäologischen Instituts: Athenische Abteilung* |
| *MDAI(R)* | *Mitteilungen des Deutschen Archäologischen Instituts: Römische Abteilung* |
| *MEFRA* | *Mélanges d'Archéologie et d'Histoire de l'École Française de Rome: Antiquité* |
| ML | R. Meiggs and D. Lewis, *A Selection of Greek Historical Inscriptions to the End of the Fifth Century BC*, rev. ed. (Oxford, 1988) |
| *NBKI* | S. Langdon, *Die neubabylonischen königsinschriften* (Leipzig, 1912) |
| *Numen* | *Numen: International Review for the History of Religions* |
| *NYSJM* | *New York State Journal of Medicine* |
| *OCD*[3] | *Oxford Classical Dictionary*, 3rd ed., ed. S. Hornblower and A. Spawforth (Oxford, 1996) |
| *ORom* | *Opuscula Romana* |
| *Paideia* | *Paideia: Rivista Letteraria di Informazione Bibliografica* |
| *Phoenix* | *Phoenix: The Journal of the Classical Association of Canada* |
| *PMG* | D. Page, *Poetae Melici Graeci* (Oxford, 1962) |
| *POxy* | *Oxyrhyncus Papyri* (London, 1898–) |
| *PP* | *La Parola del Passato: Rivista di Studi Antichi* |
| *Praktika* | *Πρακτικά της εν Αθήναις Αρχαιολογικής Εταιρείας* |
| *REG* | *Revue des Études Grecques* |
| *RPAA* | *Rendiconti della Pontificia Accademia Romana di Archeologia* |
| *ScAnt* | *Scienze dell'Antichita: Storia, Archeologia, Antropologia* |
| *SEG* | *Supplementum Epigraphicum Graecum* (Leiden, 1923–) |
| *SHT* | *Studia Humaniora Tartuensia* |
| *StudRom* | *Studi Romani: Rivista Bimestrale dell'Istituto di Studi Romani* |
| *TAPhA* | *Transactions of the American Philological Association* |
| *WA* | *World Archaeology* |
| *WACPCR* | *Workshop di Archeologia Classica: Paesaggi, Costruzioni, Reperti* |
| *WACQ* | *Workshop di Archeologia Classica: Quaderni* |
| *ZKG* | *Zeitschrift für Kirchengeschichte* |
| *ZNTW* | *Zeitschrift für die Neutestamentliche Wissenschaft und die Kunde der älteren Kirche* |
| *ZPE* | *Zeitschrift für Papyrologie und Epigraphik* |

# Preface

This book has grown out of a course, entitled "Archaeology and the Ancient Historian," which I have offered from time to time at the University of Chicago. As both the course title and the subtitle of this book indicate, this is not intended as an introduction to classical archaeology. Rather, it is directed, in the first instance, at advanced undergraduate and graduate students of ancient history as well as a more general, informed readership, although I hope that at least some classical archaeologists will find something of interest here. The core of the book is represented by a series of nine case studies, or "cautionary tales," which explore how previous scholars have juxtaposed literary and material evidence in their reconstructions of the past. Most of these, which typically revolve around historical individuals and events, should be familiar—not least because they continue to generate controversy both inside and outside scholarly circles. Ultimately, however, this book represents something of a sequel to my *History of the Archaic Greek World, ca. 1200–479 BCE* (Malden, MA, 2007; 2nd ed., 2014), in the sense that its underlying concern is with historical method. The case studies are designed to illustrate the broader methodological problems involved with correlating textual and material evidence rather than to offer definitive solutions to the subjects with which they are concerned.

At first sight, the title *Artifact and Artifice* might suggest a distinction between objective "facts" and subjective interpretations whereby the traditional centrality of the artifact within the archaeologist's primary materials could be taken to imply a mapping of this objective-subjective dichotomy onto the distinction between archaeological and literary evidence. But the currently popular definition of "artifice" as something involving cunning or trickery is a comparatively recent development, obscuring the fact that both "artifact" and "artifice" share the same Latin etymological derivation and simply mean an object or product created by art or skill. Indeed, historical texts have sometimes been defined as "literary artifacts" while some recent approaches to the archaeological record employ metaphors of reading and textuality. The juxtaposition of these terms in my title is intended to signal that both material objects and written texts are created "artfully" by knowledgeable agents and that both need to be interpreted with art and skill.

The gestation of this book has been lengthy, and I have incurred many debts of gratitude in the course of its development. I am especially grateful to Clifford Ando, Eugene Borza, Alain Bresson, Christopher Faraone, Margaret Mitchell, James Romm, Susan Rotroff, Peter Wiseman, and the anonymous referees for the University of Chicago Press for reading, and offering invaluable comments on, earlier drafts of various chapters. I have greatly benefitted from discussions concerning individual points with numerous friends and colleagues, especially Gabriël Bakkum, Hans Beck, Anna Maria Bietti Sestieri, John Camp, Helma Dik, Alexander Fatalkin, Ann Kuttner, Jeremy McInerney, Margaret Miles, Richard Neer, Harm Pinkster, James Redfield,

Nicola Terrenato, Jennifer Tobin, and Pietro Vannicelli. Various chapters have been delivered in front of audiences at the University of Pennsylvania, San Francisco State University, the University of Illinois at Chicago, Stanford University, Duke University, the University of Minnesota, McGill University, and the Rockford Chapter of the Archaeological Institute of America, as well as students and alumni of the University of Chicago, and I am grateful to all those who offered comments and feedback on those occasions. I owe the decision to include a chapter on the Delphic Oracle to the suggestion of Amanda Reiterman, while the "new" interpretation tentatively offered in the Vergina chapter builds on a suggestion that my friend Daniel Richter made during a visit to the site thirteen years ago.

For assistance with the illustrations, I am grateful to John Prag and Sally Thelwell (Manchester Museum), Natalia Vogeikoff-Brogan (American School of Classical Studies at Athens), Jan Jordan (Agora Excavations), Konstantinos Kontos (Photostock/Kontos Studios), Calliopi Christophi (École Française d'Athènes), Daria Lanzuolo (Deutsches Archäologisches Institut at Rome), and Shabnam Moshfegh Nia (University of Köln), as well as to Kevin Schuhl, who patiently redrew the maps and plans. From the University of Chicago Press, I would like to thank Anthony Burton, Erik Carlson, and especially Susan Bielstein for her steadfast support and faith. Finally, the patient encouragement of my wife, Ilaria Romeo, has continued to be indispensable.

## Note on the Spelling of Greek Names and Translations

In line with a growing trend among Greek historians, I generally prefer direct transliterations from Greek proper names to their Latinized equivalents (e.g., Perikles, rather than Pericles; Herodotos, rather than Herodotus). There are, however, some names that still appear relatively unfamiliar when transcribed according to these rules, so I have made exceptions based on how the names are typically *pronounced* in the classroom—thus, Thucydides (rather than Thoukudides), Plutarch (Ploutarkhos), Mycenae (Mykenai), Corinth (Korinthos), or Crete (rather than the disyllabic Krētē). That is a consistency of sorts; for the orthographic purists, I can only offer my apologies in advance. All translations are my own.

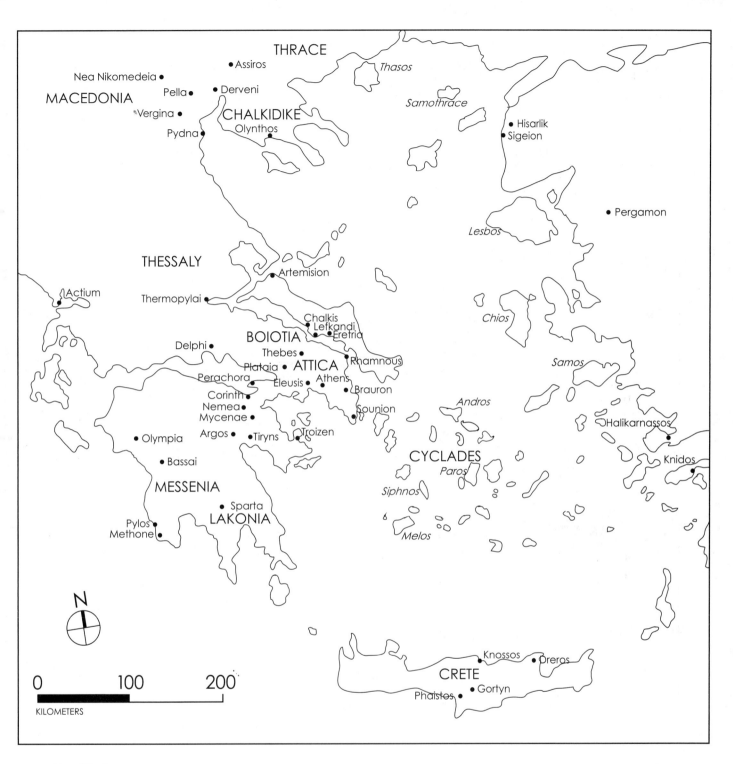

THRACE

Nea Nikomedeia •
• Assiros
*Thasos*

MACEDONIA
Pella •
• Derveni
*Samothrace*

•Vergina •
CHALKIDIKE
Pydna •
Olynthos •
• Hisarlik
• Sigeion

• Pergamon

*Lesbos*

THESSALY
Artemision

•Actium

Thermopylai •
*Chios*

Chalkis
Delphi •
Lefkandi
• Eretria
*Samos*

BOIOTIA
Thebes •
Rhamnous •
Plataia
ATTICA
Perachora •
Eleusis •
Athens
*Andros*
•Halikarnassos
Corinth •
Braurón
Nemea •
Sounion
Mycenae •
CYCLADES
Knidos
Olympia •
Argos •
• Tiryns
Troizen
*Paros*

• Bassai
*Siphnos*

MESSENIA
• Sparta
LAKONIA
*Melos*

Pylos •
Methone •

N

0      100      200

KILOMETERS

Knossos •
• Dreros
CRETE
Phaistos •
• Gortyn

Map of the Aegean

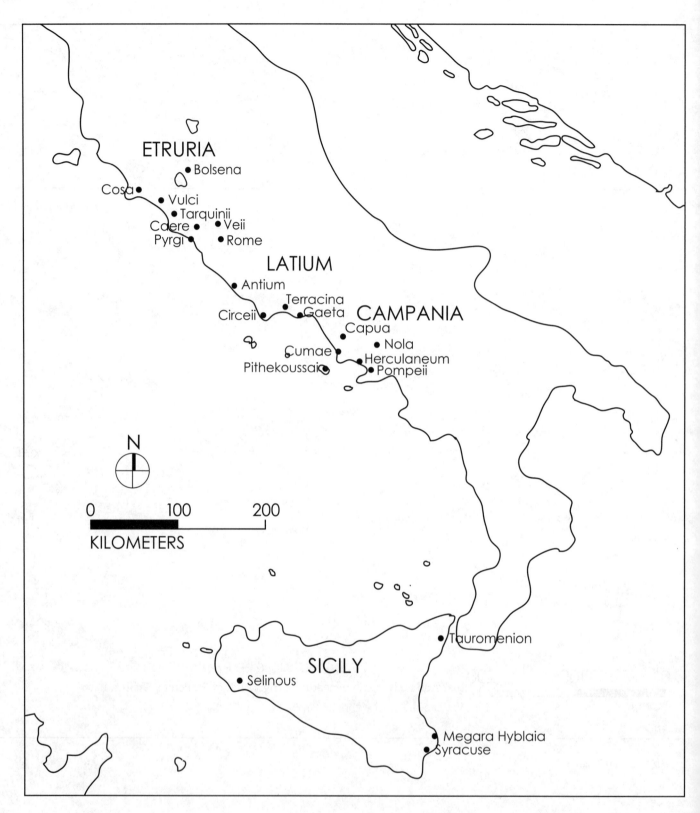

ETRURIA

• Bolsena

Cosa •

• Vulci

• Tarquinii

Caere • • Veii

Pyrgi • • Rome

LATIUM

• Antium

Terracina
Circeii • • Gaeta

CAMPANIA

• Capua

Cumae • • Nola

Pithekoussai • • Herculaneum
• Pompeii

N

0    100    200

KILOMETERS

SICILY

• Tauromenion

• Selinous

• Megara Hyblaia
• Syracuse

Map of Italy

# 1

# Classical Archaeology:

## The "Handmaid of History"?

Can the geology and geochemistry of the Delphi region offer clues to why the oracle of Apollo was so highly regarded in the ancient world? Should the proposed redating of a single temple cause us to revise the chronology we assign to Classical art? Why did the Athenians wait so long before repairing their temples after the Persian invasion of 480–479 BCE? Can we trace the footprints of the historical Sokrates in the Athenian agora? Are the human remains discovered in a Macedonian tomb at Vergina those of Philip II, the father of Alexander the Great? Was there a historical individual named Romulus and did he found Rome in 753 BCE? Are the literary accounts of the fall of the Roman monarchy and the establishment of the Republic reflected in the construction of the temple of Jupiter Capitolinus? Have we discovered the Palatine residence of the emperor Augustus? And is the tomb beneath the High Altar of St. Peter's Basilica in the Vatican that of the apostle Peter?

These are the questions that are examined over the course of the next nine chapters. They are all cases that continue to generate scholarly disagreement, and many of them have also attracted recent attention in the popular media—not infrequently because of the political issues that are involved. To the degree that they tend to revolve around specific individuals or events, they are, of course, only a subset of the sorts of questions that ancient historians and classical archaeologists ask. Since the late 1950s, many historians have increasingly eschewed traditional political or military narratives for more social, economic, or cultural approaches to the past, and "idealist" histories, centred around "great men," have yielded in many quarters to more materialist analyses. The last few decades have, for example, witnessed detailed studies of topics such as the ancient economy, social organization and class, literacy, gender and sexuality, ethnicity, or religion, even if much of this has been conducted on the basis of epigraphy or papyrology, rather than archaeology, or through comparisons with better-documented societies. Conversely, many classical archaeologists have turned to more processual readings of the past that display little or no dependence upon literary texts to illuminate themes such as trade and interaction, urbanization, settlement patterns, and the exploitation of the landscape or technology. A new battery of scientific techniques now allows us to answer questions about the organization of production, food preparation and dietary habits, demography, and pathology which we would never have guessed from literary sources alone.

Above all else, however, the choice of these specific case studies has been guided by the fact that they should be relatively familiar to the reader because, ultimately, this is a book about historical method—that is, how the practitioner evaluates archaeological evidence against the textual documents that have traditionally dominated the field of ancient history. It thus subscribes to the view that history is not simply a matter of memorizing and synthesizing an immense amount of disparate, but seemingly self-evident, data—a consequence, perhaps, of the fact that we often use the word "history" as a synonym for "the past."[1] Rather, history is an active, forensic *practice*, which involves engaging with, testing and interrogating the fragmentary

clues that have survived from the past.[2] There are no hard and fast "rules" for how one undertakes this practice—which is why I generally avoid offering definitive resolutions to the cautionary tales that follow, preferring to leave it to the reader to draw his or her own conclusions. But there are, I believe, "more" and "less" methodologically sound ways to proceed, and this ultimately depends on the degree of self-critical awareness we bring to the project. In this sense, the route that we take is just as important and rewarding as the destination to which we are headed, since, in confronting our own assumptions and value judgements, we inevitably have to engage in a profoundly humanistic project of self-knowledge.

In some of the cases that follow, archaeologists have turned to literary texts for help in interpreting material remains. More commonly, however, ancient historians have turned to the archaeological record for confirmation or refutation of information furnished by ancient authors. In both cases, there is an assumption—latent or otherwise—that the two types of evidence represent two sides of the same coin. The assumption is not necessarily flawed, but today it is probably accepted more by ancient historians than it is by classical archaeologists, many of whom react, perhaps correctly, against the characterization of archaeology as "the handmaid of history"—ironically, a phrase that seems to have been coined not by a historian but by the president of the Archaeological Institute of America.[3] The relationship between history and archaeology will be explored further in chapter 11, but, for now, it may be worth tracing very briefly how classical archaeology arrived at its presumptively ancillary role.

:::  1. Hall 2014: 8–11.

2. Cf. Carr (1987: 30), who defines history as a "continuous interaction between the historian and his facts, an unending dialogue between the present and the past." Indeed, this definition comes close to the term's Greek origins (from *historia*, meaning "inquiry").

3. James Egbert, in the Annual Report of the Archaeological Institute of America (1925: 7); cited in Dyson 1998: 159. See Wiseman 1980: 279; Dyson 1981: 8; Snodgrass 1987: 37.

Anthony Snodgrass has argued that there are four competing—though not necessarily mutually exclusive—views of classical archaeology as it is practised today. According to the first, classical archaeology is a branch of archaeology and therefore amenable to the sorts of methods employed in archaeology at large. The second regards classical archaeology as a branch of classics that employs material evidence to shed light on other—largely textual—testimony. The third view sees classical archaeology as a branch of art history. The fourth considers it to be an autonomous field with aims that are significantly different from those of other disciplines, including other fields within both classics and archaeology.[4] The first and last of these are largely developments of the nineteenth and, especially, twentieth centuries, and we shall return to them shortly. The second and third, by contrast, are inherent in the very origins of classical archaeology, which emerged by means of a triangulation process between, on the one hand, art history and connoisseurship and, on the other, interests that were more philological or literary.

With the collapse of the Roman Empire and the expurgation of "pagan" rites and culture that accompanied the triumph of Christianity, the monuments of the ancient world were transformed into vestiges of an obsolete past.[5] Some were allowed to fall into decay, subject to looting or serving as sources for building materials. Others were appropriated by the new order and endowed with a Christian significance in order to obliterate their heretical pedigree: thus, the Parthenon in Athens was converted into the church of the Parthenos Theotokos (Maiden Mother of God) in the 480s CE, while the Pantheon in Rome was handed over to Pope Boniface IV by the Byzantine emperor Phocas and consecrated as a church to St. Mary of the Martyrs

in 609 CE.[6] It is not that the denizens of medieval cities were entirely indifferent to the traces of antiquity that were everywhere visible: in 1162, the Senate of Rome decreed that anybody caught damaging or vandalizing Trajan's Column was liable to execution and confiscation of property.[7] By and large, however, a true enthusiasm for the classical past had to wait until the Renaissance.

For the humanists of the Renaissance, antiquity—and especially Roman antiquity—presented an exemplary, if ultimately unattainable, model to be followed. Most, such as Francesco Petrarca (Petrarch) who first discovered Cicero's letters to Atticus, were guided by newly discovered manuscripts of ancient authors. But Petrarch was also a fervent supporter of the self-proclaimed consul of Rome, Cola di Rienzo, whose collection of antique inscriptions bolstered his aspirations to establish a popular government along the lines of the ancient Roman Republic—ultimately leading to his violent assassination in 1354.[8] Typical of the Renaissance spirit was the series of volumes on the historical topography of Rome and its monuments, written in the 1440s and 1450s by Flavio Biondo, who believed that the Eternal City could serve as a "speculum, exemplar, imago omnis virtutis" (mirror, paradigm and image of all virtue).[9] At about the same time, Ciriaco (Cyriac) dei Pizzicolli, a merchant from Ancona who had been sent to the Aegean to win back markets for the west ahead of a possible renewed crusade against the Turks, described, drew, and measured a number of Greek monuments, including the Parthenon and the temple of Olympian Zeus in Athens. Unusually for his time, Cyriac had learnt both Greek and Latin but was of the opinion that monuments and inscriptions possessed more faith (*fides*) than texts.[10] With the capture of Constantinople in May 1453 and the annexation of much

---

4. Snodgrass 2012: 13–14.
5. Schnapp 1996: 80–87.
6. For the Christian Parthenon, see Kaldellis 2009.
7. Weiss 1988: 10.

8. Bengtson 1970: 708; Weiss 1988: 30–42.
9. Weiss 1988: 66–70; Schnapp 1996: 122–23.
10. Weiss 1988: 137–42; Eisner 1991: 47–49.

of the former Byzantine Empire by the Ottoman Turks, Cyriac would be one of the last westerners to visit Greece for at least a couple of centuries: the German scholar Martin Kraus, writing in 1554, described Greece as a "terra incognita."[11]

By the end of the sixteenth century, artists and architects were flocking to Italy to seek inspiration for their designs. Inigo Jones, often credited with having introduced renaissance architecture to Britain, made his first visit to Rome in 1598, while, in 1666, Louis XIV founded the Académie de France à Rome to allow artists to work in the presence of classical masterpieces.[12] There was, however, another side to this. The instructional value that the humanists invested in the vestiges of the past was inevitably converted into a pecuniary value whereby ancient objects were appreciated in their own right rather than for the information they could yield about the past or the lessons they could teach for the future. By the early seventeenth century, Rome and Italy had become the prime destinations for aristocrats embarking on the Grand Tour. This exposure to the sites and antiquities of Italy had profound consequences for the appreciation of classical culture in Western Europe but it also fostered a mania for collecting. On Jones's second visit to Rome in 1613–14, he was accompanied by Thomas Howard, 2nd Earl of Arundel, who used his position as a foreign envoy of Charles I to build up a collection of ancient sculpture, mostly from Italy, for his townhouse just off the Strand in London.[13] The tendency to furnish stately homes with objets d'art acquired abroad picked up pace in the eighteenth century. On his return from Rome in 1718, Thomas Coke, 1st Earl of Leicester, brought with him a large assemblage of manuscripts and sculpture which formed the kernel of the collection that he installed at Holkham Hall in Norfolk. Two years later, Thomas Herbert, 8th Earl of Pembroke, acquired 1,300 pieces from

the vast collection of paintings and statues that had been assembled in Rome by Vincenzo and Benedetto Giustiniani,[14] while the group of marbles, bronzes, and terracottas acquired by Charles Townley in the 1770s now forms the core of the British Museum's collection of Greek and Roman sculpture.[15]

The realization that excavation might satisfy the growing demand for antiquities on the part of collectors probably arose in 1560, with Pirro Ligorio's topographical study of Hadrian's Villa near Tivoli, ahead of the construction of a new villa for his patron, Cardinal Ippolito d'Este. In 1711, Charles VII, king of the Two Sicilies and heir to the Spanish throne, appropriated a plot of land at Resina, on the Bay of Naples, in the expectation of finding objets d'art to adorn the new royal palace he was constructing at nearby Portici. A year or two earlier, digging at the site had revealed the remains of the theatre of ancient Herculaneum, a Roman town buried under a pyroclastic flow when Mount Vesuvius erupted in 79 CE. Under the direction of a Spanish military engineer, Rocque Joaquin de Alcubierre, a series of subterranean tunnels was constructed to explore the remains that had been buried beneath some 20 metres of volcanic debris. When Karl Jakob Weber, Alcubierre's Swiss assistant, proposed a reorientation of the tunnels to understand better the urban fabric of the town, he was severely reprimanded by Alcubierre for concentrating more on streets than on antiquities. In 1748, attention shifted to another site near Torre Annunziata, to the southeast of Herculaneum, where excavations brought to light ancient Pompeii—a victim of the same volcanic eruption though buried beneath a thinner level of ash, thus allowing for an open excavation by which sculpture and paintings might be retrieved more easily.[16]

:::    11. Etienne, Müller, and Prost 2000: 6.
12. Dyson 2006: 20.
13. Chaney 1998: 208; Medwid 2000: 161–62.

14. Dyson 2006: 8.
15. Medwid 2000: 287–88; Wallace-Hadrill et al. 2001: 13.
16. Parslow 1995: 19–24, 31, 44–45, 126–32.

## The Opening Up of Greece

The Ottoman conquest of Crete in 1669 led to a more stable environment for travel in the Aegean, and some antiquarians and collectors were quick to exploit it. In 1674, Charles-François Olier, marquis de Nointel, was dispatched as French ambassador to Constantinople with the express purpose of acquiring antiquities for the collections of Louis XIV and Cardinal Mazarin. In his company was the young painter Jacques Carrey, whose detailed drawings of the sculptures on the Parthenon were to prove invaluable when, thirteen years later, the central part of the structure was blown out by a Venetian cannonball, causing considerable damage to the sculptural decoration.[17] In 1676, the French antiquarian Jacob Spon and the English botanist George Wheler began their own tour of Greece, publishing detailed descriptive accounts and engravings of the monuments that they saw, including the temple of Athena Nike on the Athenian acropolis, the Tower of the Winds (a hydraulic clock) in the Roman agora, and the choregic monument of Lysikrates in the Street of the Tripods.[18] At this stage, Italy continued to attract more visitors than Ottoman-controlled Greece: the earliest studies in English of Greek architecture were actually based on the ruins of temples in southern Italy and Sicily.[19] In the middle of the eighteenth century, however, the Society of Dilettanti, founded in London by Grand Tour alumni in 1734 to promote the study of Greek and Roman culture, extended its interest to Greece and sponsored the visits between 1751 and 1753 of the painter James Stuart and the architect Nicholas Revett.[20] *The Antiquities of Athens*, which appeared in three volumes between 1762 and 1794, contained detailed descriptions, measurements, and drawings of Athenian monuments and was to prove immensely influential in inspiring Greek Revival architecture such as William Wilkins's design for Downing College, Cambridge, and Thomas Jefferson's plan for the University of Virginia at Charlottesville.

Johann Joachim Winckelmann, often credited as the founding father of Greek archaeology, never visited Greece, but, in his capacity as prefect of antiquities for Pope Clement XIII, he had access to hundreds of pieces of Greek art in the vast collections of the Vatican.[21] In his monumental *Geschichte der Kunst der Alterthums* (*History of Ancient Art*), first published in 1764, Winckelmann set out—for the first time—a stylistically based, four-part chronological scheme for the development of Greek art which still, with various modifications, forms the basis of stylistic dating today.[22] The first phase was termed "Archaic" and is roughly equivalent to what is now termed the "severe style" of the early fifth century. The second, "Sublime," phase, which, for Winckelmann, signalled the apogee of Greek sculpture, was associated with the sculptor Pheidias and his successors in the later fifth and early fourth centuries. This was followed in turn by a "Beautiful" phase (from Praxiteles to Lysippos in the second half of the fourth century) and, finally, a "Decadent" phase (the art of the later Hellenistic and Roman periods).[23] This schema was actually based on Joseph Justus Scaliger's four-age model for the development of Greek poetry, published in 1608,[24] but—unlike Scaliger—Winckelmann was more interested in universal truths than in historical particularities. His aim was to uncover the "essence" of art (*das Wesen der Kunst*), and, in line with contemporary Enlightenment thought, he entertained a unitary conception of culture as a transnational march towards rationality and perfection in which

⋮⋮⋮   17. Etienne, Müller, and Prost 2000: 8–9; Beard 2003: 77–81.

18. Eisner 1991: 56–58; Shanks 1996: 55–56; Etienne, Müller, and Prost 2000: 6.

19. Chaney 1998: 5–12, 24–33.

20. Eisner 1991: 71–72; Dyson 2006: 4–5.

21. Marchand 1996: 7; Dyson 2006: 2.

22. This in spite of the fact that most of the pieces Winckelmann studied were not, as he supposed, Greek originals but

Roman "copies" of Greek originals: Bianchi Bandinelli 1985: xvi, 13–14; Schnapp 1996: 263.

23. Bianchi Bandinelli 1985: 14; Whitley 2001: 20–23.

24. Bernal 1987: 212; Grafton 1993: 619. As Pollitt (1990: 3–5) points out, the idea of a "life cycle" to Greek art had already been proposed by Pliny the Elder, even if Winckelmann's framework is actually closer to that of the first-century CE rhetorician Quintilian.

all human societies participated, albeit at different paces. If the Greeks had arrived at that goal early on, it was because their defeat of the Persians in 479 BCE had ushered in a "freedom which gave birth to great events, political changes, and jealousy . . . [and] planted, as it were in the very production of these effects, the germ of noble and elevated sentiments."[25]

Winckelmann's work met with an enthusiastic reception—especially in his homeland. The Germans had never really shared the nostalgia for ancient Rome that had been so fervent in many other European countries, not least because much of Germany had not only escaped incorporation into the Roman Empire but had even offered spirited resistance to Roman imperialist designs.[26] Such sentiments were exacerbated further by Martin Luther's opposition to the Roman church and his insistence that a proper understanding of the New Testament required knowledge of Greek to study the scriptures in their original language rather than through the filter of Latin commentaries.[27] Among the more important thinkers influenced by Winckelmann's study of Greek art were Johann Gottfried Herder, the father of German romanticism, and Karl Wilhelm von Humboldt, who, as Prussian minister of education, presided over important educational reforms which promoted the study of classical antiquity in schools and universities.[28] As hostilities with France, which was proclaiming itself the "New Rome," became ever more acute, the tendency of German scholars to look toward ancient Greece only increased: von Humboldt, for example, made an explicit comparison between German and Greek as being "pure" and "uncontaminated" languages.[29] Enthusiasm for Greek art also spread to Britain: in 1772, the British Museum paid eight thousand guineas for a collection of Attic red-figure vases that had been procured in Italy by Sir William Hamilton, British ambassador to the Kingdom of the Two Sicilies.[30]

The looting of artistic masterpieces was still rife at the onset of the nineteenth century. Napoleon's domination of Rome, following the Treaty of Tolentino of 1797, allowed for the transportation of Roman antiquities to France while excavations were conducted around the Arches of Septimius Severus, Titus, and Constantine, the Pantheon, the Colosseum, the Forum Boarium, and Trajan's Forum.[31] With Rome off limits to the Grand Tourists for almost a generation, collectors set their sights on Greece. Among the most infamous examples is Thomas Bruce, 7th Earl of Elgin and British ambassador to Constantinople. In 1801, armed with a *firman* (mandate) from the Ottoman authorities to conduct limited investigations on the Athenian acropolis, Elgin's agents set about removing one of the caryatid columns from the Erechtheion and sawing through frieze blocks of the Parthenon to dismantle its cornice and remove architectural sculptures that might adorn Elgin's family home in Fife, Scotland. More than fifty slabs of the carved frieze that ran inside the colonnade of the Parthenon and fifteen metopes of the external frieze as well as seventeen figures from the pediments were packed up and dispatched to Britain, though one of the consignments sank in a shipwreck off the southern Peloponnese and was only recovered after a difficult three-year salvage operation. Eventually, beset by mounting debts, Elgin was forced to sell his collection to the British Museum in 1816 for the sum of thirty-five thousand pounds—far less than he had expended on removing and transporting the marbles.[32]

---

:::    25. Winckelmann 1880: 293; cited in Schnapp 1996: 263. See Bianchi Bandinelli 1985: 12–15. For Enlightenment and Romantic views of culture, see Hall 2004: 35–37.

26. The rediscovery of the manuscript of Tacitus's *Germania* offered a model of heroic resistance to Rome that was enthusiastically adopted by German humanists from the late fifteenth century onward. See Marchand 1996: 156–57; Schnapp 1996: 114–15.

27. Morris 1994: 16.

28. Bernal 1987: 282–88; Dyson 2006: 29–30.

29. Humboldt 1903: 266; see Bernal 1987: 288.

30. Morris 1994: 24; Medwid 2000: 135–37. For the dubious provenance of much of Hamilton's collection, see Ramage 1992: 658–60.

31. MacKendrick 1962: 265; Packer 1989: 138; Dyson 2006: 21–28.

32. See generally St. Clair 1998. For the ongoing controversy about the Parthenon marbles: Hitchens 1987; Beard 2003; Hamilakis 2007: 243–86.

As notorious as they have become, Elgin's actions were hardly unusual in this period. When, in 1784, the French painter Louis François Sébastien Fauvel was dispatched to Athens as vice-consul, he was instructed to "remove all you can. Don't neglect any opportunity to pillage all that is pillageable in Athens and its territory."[33] Indeed, had it not been for the resistance of the Turkish garrison commander who lived on the acropolis, the Parthenon sculptures might well have ended up in Paris. In 1811, an Anglo-German team excavated the temple of Aphaia on Aigina and removed, at the behest of King Ludwig of Bavaria, the pedimental sculpture of the temple, which was taken away to be displayed, after some heavy restoration by the Danish sculptor Bertel Thorwaldsen, in the Munich Glyptothek.[34] The same team, joined by archaeologists from Denmark, Estonia, and Würtemburg, also excavated the temple of Apollo at Bassai in Arkadia, where they removed the 31-metre-long sculpted frieze, which was sold to the British Museum in 1814 for nineteen thousand pounds. Meanwhile, the French acquired the famed Venus de Milo from the island of Melos in 1822 and the Winged Nike of Samothrace (still under Ottoman control) in 1863.[35]

## Philological Archaeology

The 1820s mark a crucial period in the development of classical archaeology, with two events in particular serving to weaken the almost exclusive hold that antiquarian connoisseurship had exercised over the study of material remains. The first was a law, passed in 1827 by the provisional government of a newly independent Greece, banning the exportation of antiquities.[36] As a consequence, foreign archaeologists were invited to establish research centres in Greece and to study antiquities "on location." The first to take advantage of this were the French, who established the École Française d'Athènes in 1846 to promote the archaeological interests of French scholars in Greece. Other foreign institutes of archaeology followed in subsequent decades, with the foundation of the Deutsches Archäologisches Institut in 1874, the American School of Classical Studies in 1881, the British School in 1886, the Österreichisches Archäologisches Institut in 1898 and the Italian Scuola Archeologica in 1909. Since 1928, it has been impossible for foreign archaeologists to work in Greece without securing prior approval from the relevant national institute of archaeology.[37] In Rome too, foreign schools were established or re-instituted: in 1874, the Imperial Archaeological Institute of Berlin established a permanent base in the city, while in 1875–76, the École Française de Rome replaced the earlier French Academy;[38] the British School at Rome was founded in 1900 and the American Academy of Rome in 1912.[39] The liberation of Greece in the 1820s and the unification of Italy in 1861 fostered in those countries a new focus on a national history that could not but influence how foreign archaeologists approached the past.

The second event was the foundation, in 1829, of the German Institut für archäologische Korrespondenz—a forerunner to the Imperial Institute—in the Palazzo Caffarelli on Rome's Campidoglio hill. Already, in the 1670s, Spon had regarded the study of antiquities as primarily a textual matter and his treatment of inscriptions and coins to that end did much to establish epigraphy and nu-

:::
33. Cited in Shanks 1996: 71.
34. Dyson 1998: 123; 2006: 134.
35. Etienne, Müller, and Prost 2000: 9; Dyson 2006: 137, 142.
36. Voudouri 2008. As a consequence, the attention of collectors began to shift to Turkey, where, in 1878–79, Carl Humann excavated, and transported back to Berlin, the Great Altar of Pergamon: Dyson 2006: 115, 145.

37. Etienne, Müller, and Prost 2000: 10.
38. Marchand 1996: 41; Schnapp 1996: 306–7; Wallace-Hadrill et al. 2001: 15; Dyson 2006: 86.
39. Dyson 1998: 114; Wallace-Hadrill et al. 2001: 14–16, 21–51.

mismatics, respectively, as "positive sciences" in their own right.[40] But this belief was taken further by Eduard Gerhard, who helped to launch the first systematic collection of Greek inscriptions (the *Corpus Inscriptionum Graecarum*) and was also one of the founders of the Institut. Gerhard was critical of the "dependence of the archaeologist on the amateurs of antiquities and the artists which has often led to the reprehensible development of what one might call antiquarian dilettantism," and, in distancing himself from the world of collectors and artists, he sought sanctuary with more literary scholars, arguing that archaeology "must be founded on a close relation with philological teaching in its entirety."[41] It is hard not to see here the influence of his teacher, Friedrich August Wolf, who distinguished between "first-class disciplines" (linguistics, prosody, and grammar) and "second-class disciplines" (numismatics, history, geography, and archaeology), even if Gerhard aspired to a less dependent status for archaeology.[42] The alignment of classical archaeology with philology was to prove decisive in the future development of the discipline, but it also served effectively to isolate classical archaeology from the theories and methods that were being developed at the time in European prehistory—especially in Scandinavia.[43]

Within a few decades, other countries were following the trail blazed by German scholars and were similarly confronted with defining the problematic relationship between archaeology and aesthetics. In the 1870s and 1880s, classical archaeology was added to the undergraduate classics curriculum at Harvard University and the University of Cambridge; the newly established Johns Hopkins University began to offer graduate instruction in the field, soon followed by Bryn Mawr College; and the Sorbonne appointed its first professor of Greek

archaeology in 1876.[44] This was also, however, the era of the grand museums: the Boston Museum of Fine Arts opened in 1876 and the Metropolitan Museum of Art in 1880, and both relied heavily on the antiquities market—in particular, the collection of Luigi Palma di Cesnola, who, as American consul on Cyprus, had acquired a large number of antiquities on the island under somewhat dubious circumstances.[45] The tensions between those who were interested in research and those who were more concerned with collecting were particularly apparent at the first meeting of the Archaeological Institute of America in May 1879—not least because many of the institute's founders were also involved in launching the Boston Museum of Fine Arts.[46]

Such tensions were also evident in the excavations that the Germans initiated at Olympia in 1875. One of the first of the so-called big digs, it was to have a profound effect on how classical archaeology would be practised in the twentieth century. The German authorities which backed the campaign at Olympia were interested primarily in works of art—limited excavations by the French in 1829 had already recovered five sculpted metopes belonging to the great temple of Zeus—and when, after only a few months, the pedimental sculptures of the Zeus temple and the fifth-century Nike of Paionios were discovered, the originally provisional funding for the dig was guaranteed.[47] However, the concerns of Ernst Curtius, the director of the excavations, with close links to the ruling house of Prussia, were driven more by philology: a noted historian, he wished to understand the spatial relationship between various buildings on the site, using, as a guide, the detailed description of the sanctuary offered by the second-century CE author Pausanias.[48] Within the first six years, and employing up to five hundred labourers, Curtius had laid bare the

:::     40. Schnapp 1996: 182–85.

41. Gerhard 1850: 204; cited in Schnapp 1996: 304. See also Marchand 1996: 41; 2007: 256–57; Dyson 2006: 30–36.

42. Marchand 1996: 21.

43. Morris 1994: 11, 26. In the late seventeenth century, the Swedish naturalist Olof Rudbeck was conducting stratigraphic investigations of a tumulus at Uppsala, roughly a century before Thomas Jefferson excavated indigenous American mounds in Virginia: Schnapp 1996: 200–201; MacKendrick 1962: 8–9; Biers 1992: 17; Renfrew and Bahn 2007: 14–15.

44. Etienne, Müller, and Prost 2000: 11.

45. Dyson 1998: 132; Medwid 2000: 57–59.

46. Dyson 1998: 38–42.

47. Marchand 1996: 84–85.

48. Bianchi Bandinelli 1985: 80.

Temples of Zeus and Hera and a terrace supporting eleven small treasury buildings.

In the course of the excavations, however, thousands of small terracotta and bronze dedications were found in the ash layers that covered much of the sanctuary, and these were published in meticulous detail, eventually prompting unfavourable contrasts back in Germany between the "rubbish" that was being excavated at Olympia and the fine works of Hellenistic sculpture that were being recovered from the German excavations at Pergamon.[49] Employing a typological-chronological classification that was novel for its day, the Olympia excavations created a new genre of nonnarrative archaeological writing, concerned overwhelmingly with cataloguing and classifying classes of objects.[50] Although not dependent upon literary texts, this approach has also been described as "philological" to the extent that it applied analytical methods akin to those of textual criticism.[51] The person charged with the responsibility for publishing most of these small finds was Adolf Furtwängler, whose keen eye for detail and attentive observation of similarities and parallels between various artifacts drew him also to other categories of material—including, eventually, works of art. In 1893, he published his *Meisterwerke der griechischen Plastik*, which sought to identify the "artistic personalities" behind various works of Greek sculpture, and, in the last seven years of his life, he turned to Greek vase painting. This study, in turn, was to have a profound influence on the work of John Beazley, Lincoln Professor of Classical Art and Archaeology at the University of Oxford from 1925 to 1956, who applied to thousands of Attic black-figure and red-figure vases analytical techniques borrowed from the Italian art historian Giovanni Morelli in order to identify individual artists, workshops, "circles," "groups," and "schools."[52]

The German excavations at Olympia prompted equally ambitious hopes among other foreign archaeologists. The École Française and the American School of Classical Studies vied with each other to secure the rights to excavate Delphi, the other great sanctuary of the Greek world. The concession was eventually awarded to the French, largely in return for an agreement by the French government to waive customs duties on the importation of Greek currants. In 1891 the modern village of Kastrí was physically transplanted to its current site, west of the sanctuary, and, in a five-year campaign from 1892 to 1897, much of Apollo's sanctuary had been cleared.[53] Almost immediately, the French also commenced excavations on Delos. The Americans, instead, had to content themselves with digging the sanctuary of Hera outside Argos, although rights to excavate Corinth were granted in 1895, and, in 1925, the American School of Classical Studies secured the concession to dig the Athenian agora.[54] The Greek Archaeological Service was particularly infuriated that the rights to dig Delphi had been ceded to outsiders, and, despite major Greek excavations on the Athenian acropolis and at Sounion, Eleusis, and Eretria, there was—and, in some quarters, remains—considerable indignation that, in the period prior to the Second World War, ever more sites were handed over to foreign archaeologists.[55] In postunification Italy, by contrast, foreign archaeologists were prohibited from excavating, fostering the rise of a more "nationalist" archaeology. So, at about the time that the Americans began digging the Athenian agora, a similar operation was being launched in Rome, under the orders of Benito Mus-

:::     49. Marchand 1996: 95–96; Dyson 2006: 84.

50. Morris 1994: 27; Whitley 2001: 34. Schnapp (1996: 188–93) attributes the development of the typological-chronological system to the English scholar John Aubrey (1626–97), who employed this scheme to classify artifacts such as architecture, blazons and clothing.

51. Bianchi Bandinelli 1985: 37.

52. Whitley 1997; 2001: 36–41; Medwid 2000: 31–33, 109–11; Etienne, Müller, and Prost 2000: 166–68; Wallace-Hadrill et al. 2001: 29. In the United States, a similar approach was applied to Archaic sculpture by Gisela Richter (e.g., Richter 1970): see Dyson 1998: 148. For Furtwängler: Marchand 2007.

53. Dyson 1998: 73–74.

54. Lord 1947: 244; Dyson 1998: 83–87, 179–81; Tung 2001: 260–65; Sakka 2008; Camp 2010: 30.

55. The Americans also dug at Nemea and Olynthos; the British at Perachora and Sparta; the French at Thasos and Argos; the Germans at the Samian Heraion, the Athenian Kerameikos, and Tiryns; the Austrians at Samothrace; and the Italians at Gortyn and Phaistos.

solini, to clear the Imperial Fora in order to "liberate the trunk of the great oak from everything that still overshadows it."[56] It was not until after the Second World War that foreign excavation resumed in Italy, with the French initiating digs at Bolsena and Augusta (ancient Megara Hyblaia) on Sicily and the Americans at Ansedonia (ancient Cosa).[57]

Needless to say, the "big digs" recovered countless works of art, but that was not their primary rationale. Thanks to the immense programme of cataloguing at Olympia, fragments of decorated pottery, metalwork, and terracottas were employed chiefly to answer questions concerning the date and function of buildings. Above all else, however, these large-scale excavations were designed to bring to life the ancient world of the texts, and most of the sites were chosen—and often identified—on the basis of accounts by literary authors. For example, one of the early volumes devoted to the American excavations in the Athenian agora sought to reconstruct the route that Pausanias followed around the agora,[58] and it is still not uncommon for newly enrolled students in the foreign schools to make their first visits to sites with a volume of Pausanias's *Description of Greece* in hand. The continuing dominance of a philologically oriented approach to antiquity is illustrated by the fact that, even today, graduate students who wish to be admitted as regular students to the American School of Classical Studies—a virtual prerequisite for professional inculcation into classical archaeology—are still expected to sit examinations in Greek unseen translation.

## The Birth of Prehistory

It has been suggested that the "big digs" can be seen as a reaction, on the part of the academic establishment, to what it viewed as an alarming new trend of dilettantism, embodied in the figure of the self-made and self-educated German businessman Heinrich Schliemann.[59] After meeting with a British consular official named Frank Calvert, who had unearthed ancient remains at a mound named Hisarlik in northwest Turkey, Schliemann became convinced that this was the site of ancient Troy and began conducting excavations there in 1870.[60] In the course of four campaigns that lasted until his death in 1890, Schliemann discovered a series of superimposed settlements dating from the Early Bronze Age through to the Classical period. He was particularly impressed by the second city on the site (Troy II), which he tentatively identified as Homer's Troy—especially after the "discovery" in 1873 of a large cache of cups, weapons, and jewellery made from electrum, gold, silver, bronze, and copper, which is colloquially known as Priam's Treasure. It was only towards the end of his life that he realized that this settlement was much older than the Late Bronze Age and that a subsequent settlement (Troy VI) was a more likely candidate for the city described by ancient sources.[61] Schliemann supplemented his investigations at Troy with excavations conducted on the Greek mainland—at Mycenae, in 1876, where he brought to light a funerary enclosure (Grave Circle A) just inside the monumental Lion Gate, and at Tiryns in 1884–85.[62]

Until very recently, it has been fashionable to denigrate Schliemann as an unscrupulous charlatan whose wrongheaded convictions and clumsy excavation techniques did much to damage the reputation of classical archaeology in its early days.[63] That he was a publicity-seeking egoist is undeniable; that his reports were "economical with

:::      56. Cited in Manacorda and Tamassia 1985: 69. See generally MacKendrick 1962: 146, 156; Packer 1989: 139; Barbanera 1998: 144–47; Dyson 2006: 177–79; Millett 2012: 35.

57. Dyson 2006: 98, 228–31.

58. Wycherley 1957: plate IV.

59. Snodgrass 2012: 17–18.

60. Allen 1999.

61. McDonald and Thomas 1990: 14–46.

62. McDonald and Thomas 1990: 46–76; Medwid 2000: 266–71.

63. E.g., Calder and Traill 1986; Traill 1995.

the truth" is irrefutable, to judge from close examination of his publications, biographical materials, and excavation notebooks; and although suspicions that he had fabricated Priam's Treasure are probably exaggerated, there is some evidence to suggest that the recovery of the trove was "staged."[64] He frequently flouted the terms of his permit and certainly smuggled some of the more sensational finds from Troy out of Turkey. And it is true that, in his zeal to uncover as much of Troy II as possible, he removed a great deal of valuable evidence from the later settlements that covered the mound of Hisarlik. On the other hand, Schliemann, along with Giuseppe Fiorelli at Pompeii, was one of the first Mediterranean excavators to appreciate the importance of stratigraphy—that is, the principle that human and natural activity will deposit discrete, superimposed "strata" on a site that is inhabited over a long period of time, so that material recovered from lower strata will generally be earlier than that found in overlying strata.[65] As such, despite inevitable mistakes, he was responsible for pioneering new methods and techniques of excavation. He recognized the importance of painted pottery for dating archaeological levels, and he was meticulous in drawing and photographing the objects he retrieved and recording the depth at which they were found. And he was punctilious in publishing the results of his excavations: the publication of Tiryns appeared only a year after the dig.

Schliemann's archaeological interests were driven primarily by philological imperatives: his excavation of Troy was conducted to challenge the then-prevailing consensus among German scholars that the Homeric epics were works of fiction with no historical foundation, while the unearthing of Grave Circle A at Mycenae was guided by Pausanias's description (2.16.6) of the grave of Agamemnon and his companions. Nevertheless, with his discovery of the "Mycenaean" civilization, which had flourished in mainland Greece between the sixteenth and twelfth centuries BCE, he unwittingly became the founding father of Aegean prehistory—a field of study in which, in the absence of contemporary literary texts, philological concerns would soon become of tangential importance.[66] Instead, narratives had to be constructed on the basis of careful typological, chronological, and stratigraphic analysis—a technique with which Schliemann's assistant, Wilhelm Dörpfeld, had become familiar due to his apprenticeship on the Olympia excavations.

Schliemann's work was received with particular enthusiasm in Britain, where, in contrast to the professionalization of the study of antiquity in Germany, a certain dilettantesque character permitted greater freedom for archaeologists. Among those influenced by his discoveries was Arthur Evans, who, in 1884, was appointed keeper of antiquities at the Ashmolean Museum in Oxford. In 1900, Evans bought a plot of land at Knossos, near Iraklio on Crete, where, almost two decades earlier, some digging had revealed rooms with red-plastered walls standing to a height of six or seven feet in some places. Within just one year, a vast area of more than two hectares had been opened up, revealing a sprawling palatial complex whose layout reminded Evans of the myths that told of the labyrinth constructed by the legendary King Minos. Excavation down to Neolithic levels confirmed that the great heyday of the palace dated to the first half of the second millennium BCE, and Evans argued—wrongly, as it turned out—that the Mycenaean culture was, in fact, a late offshoot of the "Minoan"

::: 64. Schliemann's diaries, papers, and correspondence have been made available by the American School of Classical Studies and can be found online at http://www.ascsa.edu.gr/index.php /archives/heinrich-schliemann-finding-aid (last accessed July 26, 2012). For the controversy over the so-called Mask of Agamemnon, see Dickinson 2005.

65. Daniel 1975: 165–68; 1981: 85–86, 124–25; Greene and Moore 2010: 39–41. The science of stratigraphy, initially developed by geologists, was first applied to archaeological excavation in Sweden and Denmark: see Fagan 2005: 51–55; Balme and Paterson 2006: 98–104.

66. Shanks 1996: 98–101. Several Mycenaean sites—especially, Pylos, Knossos, and Thebes—have yielded hundreds of tablets inscribed in the Linear B script, eventually deciphered in 1952 by Michael Ventris and John Chadwick, but the documents are primarily concerned with inventory and accounting procedures and do not constitute a true literature.

culture of Crete.[67] Evans had never held much enthusiasm for classical antiquity—when he was appointed to a professorial chair in Oxford in 1909, it was in prehistoric archaeology—but he had good relations with the British School at Athens and initiated a continuing trend among British archaeologists in Greece to focus on prehistoric—and, from the 1950s, protohistoric—sites.[68] Interest in Aegean prehistory was not, of course, limited to British scholars: the German Archaeological Institute assumed control of the excavations at Troy and Tiryns in the 1890s; the Italians began campaigns at a number of Minoan sites on Crete from the beginning of the twentieth century; and, for the American School, Carl Blegen dug at Troy between 1932 and 1938 and at Pylos in Messenia between 1952 and 1964.[69] For all this, however, there was a lingering sentiment among more philologically inclined classical archaeologists that prehistoric archaeology was somehow devoid of humanism.

Nowhere was this more true than in Germany, where the highly professionalized field of *Altertumswissenschaft* (the science of antiquity) emphasized an integrated approach to the study of the ancient world, employing philological, historical, and archaeological evidence—even if philology remained dominant. In the late nineteenth and early twentieth centuries, many American institutions of higher education self-consciously adhered to the German model. Indeed, many professors at universities in the United States had, in fact, been trained in Germany: Charles Waldstein, the excavator of the Argive Heraion, earned his PhD at Heidelberg, while Harold North Fowler, coauthor of one of the first American textbooks on Greek archaeology, received his doctorate from the University of Bonn.[70]

In the wake of the Second World War, however, an anti-German attitude set in and American classicists aligned themselves more with their counterparts in British universities, where classical archaeology had never enjoyed the same prestige.[71] Although the connoisseur tradition pioneered by Beazley for Greek art remained strong, the British enthusiasm for prehistory had served to isolate further many Greek archaeologists from their classicist colleagues. The irony is that, just as Anglophilia was sweeping through classics departments in the United States, the reputation in Britain of classics itself was ebbing rapidly. This was due, in part, to a new postwar climate of "utilitarianism" but also to the fact that a classical education had formerly been a prerequisite for the administrators of the now-discredited British Empire. At the same time, mainstream archaeology grew in popularity as university education opened up and as rapid economic redevelopment fuelled a rise in the number of rescue excavations. For the first time, the classical—and especially Roman—world began to attract the interest of British students who had been educated in archaeology, not classics, departments and classical archaeologists began searching for common ground with their archaeological colleagues.[72]

Partly as a consequence of this rapprochement between classical and mainstream archaeology, new techniques of archaeological investigation such as aerial photography, geophysical prospection, and, perhaps most notably, intensive field survey were adopted.[73] In 1953, for example, the University of Minnesota embarked on a systematic field survey of Messenia in southwestern Greece, followed, a year later, by the British School at Rome's survey of road systems and settlement

: : :    67. McDonald and Thomas 1990: 113–69; Medwid 2000: 103–6; MacGillivray 2000.

68. Examples include Mycenae, Nea Nikomedeia in Macedonia, Phylakopi on Melos, Emborio on Chios, and Lefkandi on Euboia. See MacKendrick 1981: 47–49; Waterhouse 1986.

69. MacKendrick 1962: 10; McDonald and Thomas 1990: 217–43; Petricioli 1990: 3–26; Barbanera 1998: 92–95; Medwid 2000: 38–41.

70. Dyson 1998: 56, 104. Waldstein later fled the United States due to anti-Semitism and was appointed Slade Professor of Fine

Arts at the University of Cambridge; he was eventually knighted under the title Sir Charles Walston.

71. Dyson 1998: 218.

72. Millett 2012: 37–39.

73. For field survey in the Mediterranean, see Lloyd and Barker 1981; Greene 1986: 98–141; Cherry 1983; Snodgrass 1987: 93–131; Alcock, Cherry, and Davis 1994; Jameson, Runnels, and Van Andel 1994; Wilkinson 2001; Bintliff, Howard, and Snodgrass 2007.

patterns in southern Etruria.[74] Furthermore, classical archaeologists soon started to realize the potential of scientific techniques that had been applied in other branches of archaeology such as radiocarbon dating, dendrochronology, physical and chemical analysis, archaeobotany, zooarchaeology, and

palaeoanthropology: in 1974, the British School at Athens instituted the Fitch Laboratory for scientific analysis, while the Wiener Laboratory at the American School of Classical Studies was inaugurated in 1992.[75]

## Theory Wars

In 1971, Moses Finley, Regius Professor of Ancient History at the University of Cambridge, wondered "whether current trends in archaeology are departing so far from the kinds of questions historians have traditionally put to archaeologists that the gap between the two will soon be widened rather than narrowed."[76] The "current trends" to which he was referring were the emergence of what was termed "New" or "Processual" Archaeology, advocated by Lewis Binford in the United States and David Clarke in Britain.[77] New Archaeology was not a reaction to classical archaeology as such;[78] rather, it took aim at what it regarded as the uncritical and atheoretical "culture historical" approaches to the material record, practised by classical and nonclassical archaeologists alike, by which recurring complexes of artifacts were interpreted as the material traces of historical populations and change was explained by reference to "exogenous" (external) factors such as invasion and migration.[79] Drawing on approaches from cultural ecology, on the other hand, the New Archaeologists preferred to view cultures in systemic terms as adaptive responses to the environment and favoured "endogenous" (internal) explanations for culture change such as shifts in tech-

nology, trade, or demography.[80] Advocating for a more systematic and rigorous body of theory modelled on the hard sciences, they argued for the employment of quantitative and statistical approaches and the generation of "covering laws" regarding the material reflexes of human behaviour by proposing hypotheses that could be tested against the material evidence.[81] Above all else, however, they rejected historicizing approaches to the past in favour of anthropological ones, summarized by Gordon Willey and Philip Phillips's often-cited dictum that "American archaeology is anthropology or it is nothing" or Clarke's warning that "[a]rchaeological data are not historical data and consequently archaeology is not history."[82]

New Archaeology had more of an impact in the United States, where nonclassical archaeology was typically taught in anthropology departments.[83] In Britain, it probably would have gone all but unnoticed by classical archaeologists had it not been for Colin Renfrew, an early enthusiast of New Archaeology and an Aegean prehistorian with close links to the British School at Athens. In an address during the centennial celebrations of the Archaeological Institute of America, Renfrew highlighted what

:::     74. McDonald and Rapp 1972; Potter 1979. See Dyson 1998: 248–50; 2006: 237; Wallace-Hadrill et al. 2001: 107.

75. See further Bowkett et al. 2001; Brothwell and Pollard 2001; Fagan 2005; Balme and Paterson 2006; Renfrew and Bahn 2007; Cunliffe, Gosden, and Joyce 2009; Greene and Moore 2010.

76. Reprinted in Finley 1975: 88.

77. The landmark publications are Binford and Binford 1968 and Clarke 1968.

78. Snodgrass 1985: 33.

79. For discussion of the "culture historical" approach, see Childe 1956: 123; 1929: v–vi; Renfrew 1984: 33; Veit 1989: 35–37; Hall

1997: 129; 2004: 38. Johnson (2010: 21) points out that the New Archaeologists often promoted their agenda through an exaggerated caricature of what "normative" archaeologists practised.

80. E.g., Renfrew 1972. See Trigger 1989: 294–312; Hodder 1991: 19–34; Hall 2004: 39–40; Greene and Moore 2010: 265.

81. For discussion: Courbin 1988: 45–46; Shanks and Hodder 1995: 3–4; Renfrew and Bahn 2007: 255; Greene and Moore 2010: 265.

82. Willey and Phillips 1958: 2; Clarke 1968: 12.

83. Renfrew 1980: 292; Hodder 1991: 10; Thomas 1995: 343.

he saw as a "Great Divide" between the "Great Tradition" of classical archaeology and other branches of the discipline.[84] In part, the divide was geographical: although the original charter of the Archaeological Institute of America emphasized the promotion of archaeological studies in the United States as well as foreign countries, interest soon dwindled in studying "monuments of a race that never attained to a high degree of civilization, and that has left no trustworthy records of continuous history."[85] As a consequence, archaeological study of the Americas was largely left to organizations such as the Society for American Archaeology, while the Archaeological Institute of America focused its attention more on the older civilizations of the Mediterranean and the Near East.[86] More importantly, however, Renfrew argued that classical archaeology had fallen behind "in the development of new ideas and in that acute awareness of the need for coherent and explicit theory."[87] While extolling the rich and meticulously published databases available from Old World sites, he mildly chided classical archaeologists for their inductive and essentially descriptive approaches, whereby an "adequate explanation of events is seen as flowing rather naturally from their full description."[88] The remedy, Renfrew suggested, was for classical archaeologists to adopt the sorts of theoretical approaches that were being pioneered within New Archaeology.

There were essentially three responses from classical archaeologists to Renfrew's clarion call. Some, like Stephen Dyson and Anthony Snodgrass, were broadly receptive.[89] Although Snodgrass pointed out that classical archaeology was not, in fact, the target of the New Archaeologists' attack on "normative" archaeology, he agreed with Renfrew that New Archaeology had considerable benefits to offer—specifically in terms of a greater critical awareness of method, the employment of quantita-

tive techniques, and a particular focus on the meaning of the archaeological record—and that classical archaeologists had an incomparably rich set of data on which to test explicitly formulated hypotheses. Indeed, within a decade, two of Snodgrass's students had published important works on the burial practices and material culture of Early Iron Age Athens while a third collaborated with an Aegean prehistorian on an article about state formation in the Argive Plain: all three appealed explicitly to contemporary archaeological theory and employed quantitative techniques, albeit within a historicizing framework.[90]

The second response was essentially negative, heralded most famously by the publication, in 1982, of *Qu'est-ce que l'archéologie?* (*What Is Archaeology?*) by Paul Courbin, professor at the École des Haute Etudes en Sciences Sociales at Paris. Courbin criticized the New Archaeologists for failing to practise what they preached and characterized them as arrogant charlatans and intellectual terrorists with a penchant for infantile graphics.[91] For Courbin, not only anthropology but also history were frivolous diversions: "[T]he archaeologist can—if he is of a mind to—play very well at being a historian or an anthropologist. . . . The important thing is that he be aware that, in doing this, he is acting not as an archaeologist but as an anthropologist or a historian. He is no longer doing 'archaeology,' but something else."[92] In this sense, Courbin was staking a claim to classical archaeology as an autonomous field with aims and procedures that are significantly different from those in related disciplines—the fourth of Snodgrass's definitions (see above, p. 3).

By far the most widespread reaction, however, was one of studied indifference.[93] For many classical archaeologists, Courbin had demolished the rude intrusion of theory so effectively that there was not even a need to engage more deeply with his

:::     84. Renfrew 1980.
85. Renfrew 1980: 291, citing the first annual report of the Archaeological Institute of America (1880: 18–21).
86. Cf. Dyson 1981: 7.
87. Renfrew 1980: 292.
88. Renfrew 1980: 290.

89. Dyson 1981; Snodgrass 1985.
90. Morris 1987; Whitley 1991; Morgan and Whitelaw 1992.
91. Courbin 1988, esp. 160–61.
92. Courbin 1988: 155.
93. Snodgrass 1987: 6–11; Morris 2004: 262.

arguments. The influence that the German tradition of *Altertumswissenschaft* had exercised on the field, together with the fact that classical archaeology had traditionally been taught in classics departments, prescribed a rigorous curriculum in artifact identification and typological classification in which explicit theoretical reflection found little space. To those committed to the mastery of minute detail, theory was considered a luxury that could only be afforded by those not similarly blessed with such a plethora of primary data.[94]

The 1970s saw a flurry of archaeological theory building in mainstream archaeology as practitioners experimented with approaches drawn from Marxism, structuralism, and the symbolic anthropology of Clifford Geertz. This was due in no small measure to a dwindling confidence in the explanatory power of universalizing covering laws unless they operated at so self-explanatory a level as to be banal—what Kent Flannery, an early adherent to New Archaeology, famously described as "Mickey Mouse Laws."[95] The publication, in 1986, of the first edition of Ian Hodder's *Reading the Past* represents the culmination of these diverse theoretical influences and set out a new agenda for a "postprocessual" or "interpretive" archaeology.[96] Criticizing what they view as arbitrary dichotomies between theory and data, structure and process, and materialism and idealism, the postprocessualists are concerned with the production of meaning in the archaeological record, which they argue can only be recognized by means of close contextual analysis rather than appealing to universal, generalizing "laws" regarding the material reflection of human behaviour.[97]

Most significantly for the current discussion, the postprocessualists have turned back to history. Hodder himself appealed to the concept of the "his-

torical imagination," as outlined by Robin Collingwood in *The Idea of History* (first published in 1946), whereby "the historian must re-enact the past in his own mind."[98] Although Hodder was thinking of a historical *process* that might be applied even in the absence of documentary records, there is at least a growing acceptance now that "many of the most exciting and fruitful 'postprocessual' case studies have been done in historical archaeology, where there is plenty of documentary and ethnohistoric data to bring to bear on questions of mentality."[99] A case in point is Flannery and Marcus's examination of the religious beliefs of the Zapotec culture of central Mexico, considered by many to be one of the most successful attempts to apply the precepts of cognitive archaeology to a past society, which was largely facilitated by access to eyewitness accounts written in the sixteenth century CE.[100] The notion that "context matters" or that there might be a natural alliance between archaeology and history must have struck many classical archaeologists as a revelation akin to the reinvention of the wheel.[101] But the point is that, if many classical archaeologists were de facto already practising what the postprocessualists preached, it was often not in any conscious or self-critical way that might contribute to more constructive dialogues with other archaeologists.

The foregoing, necessarily brief, survey has sought to explain how it is that classical archaeology came to be so closely aligned with ancient history. Born from a largely aesthetic appreciation in which the past was of interest only to the extent that it might serve as a utopian model for the present, the study of material remains was wrested away from the stranglehold of connoisseurs and collectors by subordinating it to the newly professionalized sciences of antiquity, in which philology commanded pride of place and where ancient his-

::: 94. See Boardman 1973: 67; cited in Finley 1985: 19.

95. Flannery 1973: 51.

96. For the theoretical influences on postprocessual archaeology: Hodder 1991: 35–79; Barrett 2001; Renfrew and Bahn 2007: 253–59; Johnson 2010: 94–98; Greene and Moore 2010: 273–80.

97. Hodder 1991: 156–81; Shanks and Hodder 1995; Johnson 2010: 105–11.

98. Collingwood 1993: 282. See Hodder 1991: 80–106.

99. Johnson 2010: 120; cf. Hodder 1991: 145–46.

100. Flannery and Marcus 1993. See Hodder 1991: 30. For "cognitive archaeology," see Renfrew 2001; Renfrew and Bahn 2007: 262–63; Hodder 2001: 3; Johnson 2010: 99–101.

101. Hall 1991.

torians were seen as a natural ally: objects could be studied to illustrate, explain, or be explained by the world that was described by ancient authors. Although the discovery of prehistory offered a possible emancipation through finding common ground with practitioners of other branches of archaeology, mainstream archaeology itself has long been marked by a strongly historicizing tendency which has persisted—and even been reinvented—notwithstanding the efforts of the New Archaeologists. For all that, however, history and archaeology remain quite different discourses with their own distinctive objectives and methodologies.[102] The rules that one applies to the interpretation of literary documents are not necessarily those that are appropriate to understanding material culture and vice versa. In the nine case studies that follow, we will explore some of the possibilities, limitations, and pitfalls that confront the historian who employs archaeological evidence in the reconstruction of the past.

:::     102. Dyson 1981: 10.

# 2

# Delphic Vapours

## The Triumph of Science?

It has become something of a self-congratulatory pastime for professors of ancient history to stage screenings of Zack Snyder's 2006 film *300* merely to discredit it for its lack of attention to historical detail (or, to be more precise, to Herodotos's account of events during the Persian invasion of Greece in 480–479 BCE, which is not quite the same thing). Yet the motion picture—as much as Frank Miller's graphic novel, on which it is based—offers a valuable barometer for popular perceptions of Sparta and ancient Greece more generally. In one early scene, the Spartan Ephors, depicted as lecherous, leprosy-ridden inbreds, consult the "oracle" on the advisability of King Leonidas's plan to meet the Persians at Thermopylai. Amidst wafting plumes of vapours, the young, seminude mantic writhes in ecstasy, penetrated by the divine spirit, while her unintelligible moans are inventively "interpreted" by her loathsome Ephor guardians. The scene is not so far removed from Lewis Richard Farnell's description of the Pythian priestess at Delphi, who "ascended into the tripod, and, filled with the divine afflatus which at least the later ages believed to ascend in vapour from a fissure in the ground, burst forth into wild utterance, which was probably some kind of inarticulate speech, and which the 'holy ones,' who with the prophet sat around the tripod, knew well how to interpret."[1]

:::  1. Farnell 1907: 189; cited in Fontenrose 1978: 196.

Just as Farnell was writing these words, however, a more mundane and far less sensational picture was beginning to emerge from the French excavations at Delphi, which commenced in 1892 (see p. 00). Despite their initial and excited expectations, the excavators of the temple of Apollo found no evidence of a fissure or gas exhalations, just a rather unassuming depression towards the southwest corner of the *cella*. Already in 1904, Adolph Paul Oppé, a lecturer in ancient history at the University of Edinburgh, adduced the disappointing results to support his contention that the chasm and its prophetic vapours were an invention of later authors. While allowing for the slight possibility that gaseous emissions might have arisen from a fault line in the general area of Delphi, he maintained that "such vapours, like all others which issue from the earth, do nothing more to those who inhale them than suffocate and choke."[2] This more sceptical position was converted into an academic orthodoxy in Pierre Amandry's *La mantique apollinienne à Delphes*, which argued that a nonvolcanic area such as Delphi could not have produced toxic gases and that the popular image of an intoxicated Pythia was a product of early Christian authors who were intent on discrediting traditional religious practices and beliefs.[3] By the second half of the twentieth century, it was almost universally accepted that geological factors played no part in the functioning of the oracle: "[T]his account is wholly fanciful. There was no vapor and no chasm."[4]

There was, then, something of a stir when, at the 1997 Joint Annual Meeting of the American Philological Association and the Archaeological Institute of America in Chicago, John Hale delivered a paper entitled "Chasm and Vapor at Delphi," in which he argued that the temple of Apollo stood above an intersection of fault lines, from which issued natural emissions of ethylene—a gas known for its ability to induce euphoric-like trances. Hale, a professor of ancient history and archaeology at the University of Louisville, based his findings on a two-year collaboration with a geologist named Jelle de Boer, whose initial investigations of the Delphi area had been prompted by a United Nations survey of seismic activity in Greece. Joined, in 1998, by a geochemist (Jeffrey P. Chanton) and, two years later, by a toxicologist (Henry A. Spiller), the team produced a series of articles that seemed to rescue the popular image of the ecstatic Pythia from the dry sobriety of unimaginative academics.[5] As William J. Broad, a Pulitzer-winning writer for the *New York Times*, triumphantly exclaims: "Remarkably, the men who made the skepticism so fashionable knew astonishingly little about the fundamental aspects of science that supposedly informed their hypotheses and conclusions—little of geology, faults, volcanoes, rocky strata, hydrology, and the evolution of the earth's crust over billions of years. They were archaeologists or classicists or men of letters who were out of their depth, dilettantes [sic] who professed to know more than they really did."[6]

Anybody who has waded through the published reports of the French excavations at Delphi might be a little surprised to find the site's archaeologists branded as dilettantes. In reality, however, it is somewhat misleading to draw a distinction between "men of letters" and "men of science," given that, subsequent to the publications of de Boer and his collaborators, two separate teams of Greek and Italian geologists independently concluded that there was little solid evidence for ethylene emissions at Delphi.[7] Yet, even if the results were sound, what exactly would they contribute to our understanding of how the Delphic Oracle functioned in antiquity?

:::     2. Oppé 1904: 233–34.
3. Amandry 1950: 196–230.
4. Fontenrose 1978: 196; cf. Dodds 1951: 73; Parke and Wormell 1956: 22; Whittaker 1965: 23; Price 1985: 140; Morgan 1990: 151.

5. De Boer, Hale, and Chanton 2001; Spiller, Hale, and de Boer 2002; Hale et al. 2003.
6. Broad 2006: 106.
7. Etiope et al. 2006; Piccardi et al. 2008.

## The Delphic Oracle

There is some doubt as to whether a large quantity of Mycenaean terracotta female figurines, almost certainly redeposited in fill designed to form a terrace in the lower sanctuary of Athena Pronaia, indicates the existence of ritual activity in the Late Helladic period (ca. 1600–1200 BCE).[8] In any case, the area seems to have been abandoned ca. 1200 BCE and not reoccupied until ca. 875, with evidence for cult—primarily pottery and bronze tripods and figurines—commencing around 800.[9] Fragments of Corinthian roof tiles and tufa column drums, built into a nearby springhouse, are generally thought to belong to the first stone temple of Apollo, constructed some time in the second half of the seventh century; this may have been the structure that, according to Pausanias (10.5.5), was destroyed by fire in 548 BCE.[10] After about thirty-five years, a new peripteral temple was constructed in tufa with a marble architrave and roof tiles. According to Herodotos (5.62.2–3), contributions towards the expense were solicited by the Delphic Amphiktyony, the league of central Greek states which administered the sanctuary, and the Athenian family of the Alkmaionidai accumulated considerable symbolic capital by constructing the eastern façade in Parian marble rather than tufa, as originally contracted.[11] The tufa temple which dominates the site today (fig. 2.1) was built, again from contributions levied by the Amphiktyony, in the third quarter of the fourth century—probably because its "Alkmaionid" predecessor had been damaged in a devastating earthquake that occurred in 373 BCE.[12]

Quite how early the oracle entered into service is impossible to establish with any certainty. Consultation of the Delphic Oracle is a common—though by no means universal—feature of some of the traditions that told of the foundation of Greek colonies in the west from the later eighth century onwards. Since, however, these accounts generally took shape only in the course of the fifth century and conform to the same broad formulaic patterns, it is doubtful how valuable such testimony is.[13] That said, the identity of the states that are said to have consulted Delphi at an early date (Corinth, Chalkis, Sparta, and perhaps Messenia) does seem to be paralleled in the archaeological record of the site—at least in terms of the provenance of eighth- and seventh-century votives.[14] The eighth century was a critical period in the history of the Greek world, with the expansion of urban settlements, the reorganization of social structures, and the re-establishment of long-distance communications, and Catherine Morgan has suggested that this climate of instability and the need to establish consensus and seek legitimation for new initiatives would have made divination an attractive resource for community leaders.[15] Furthermore, the oracle at Delphi would have been a popular choice for seeking divine sanction because of its marginal geographical position, removed from "the direct control of any single interested party."[16] Once established, the oracle functioned at least down to the third quarter of the third century CE, and possibly down to

*[Margin handwritten note: written or oral passed down history]*

---

:::   8. Amandry 1950: 212–14; Morgan 1990: 107, 148. Those who believe in a Mycenaean cult often appeal to Pausanias's comment (10.5.3) that the sanctuary at Delphi had originally belonged to the earth goddess Ge, or Gaia, but many modern scholars dismiss this testimony: Fontenrose 1978: 1; Sourvinou-Inwood 1987.

  9. Morgan 1990: 137–46; Bommelaer and Laroche 1991: 15–16.

  10. A frieze block and part of a marble sima (roof gutter), both dated to the sixth century, may indicate either a repair of or a successor to the seventh-century temple: see Billot 1977; Bommelaer and Laroche 1991: 183.

  11. The story seems to be verified by the fact that the eastern pedimental figures, depicting Apollo's arrival at Delphi, are of marble, while those from the western pediment, which rep-

resented a Gigantomachy, are of tufa. See de la Coste-Messelière 1946. For the Delphic Amphiktyony: Sánchez 2001.

  12. Homolle 1896: 687; Bommelaer and Laroche 1991: 176–81. See, however, Courby (1915–27: 112–13), who attributed the destruction to flood damage. The earthquake of 373 triggered a tsunami that buried the Achaian city of Helike on the opposite side of the Corinthian gulf: Polybios 2.41; Strabo 8.7.2; Pausanias 7.24.6.

  13. Hall 2008: 388–402. Fontenrose (1978: 137–44) doubts the authenticity of most of the colonization oracles; see, however, Forrest 1957.

  14. Morgan 1990: 161.

  15. Morgan 1990: 154–55.

  16. Morgan 1990: 183.

2.1    The *adyton* of the fourth-century temple of Apollo at Delphi, April 18, 1894. (Photo courtesy of the École Française d'Athènes.)

391 CE, when Theodosius I closed pagan temples and outlawed divination.[17]

Unfortunately, almost all of our information about the working of the oracle derives from late authors and especially Plutarch, who was himself a priest at the sanctuary (*Moralia* 792f). Among the personnel who serviced the oracle, by far the most important was the Pythia, the priestess of Apollo. Her absence from the *Homeric Hymn to Apollo*, often—though not unproblematically—dated to the early sixth century, has suggested to some that she was not the original mouthpiece for Apollo's prophecies.[18] Her earliest literary appearance is in the *Elegies* attributed to Theognis (805–10), though

: : :    17. Fontenrose 1978: 5.
18. Fontenrose 1978: 204; Johnston 2008: 39. On the basis of

the *Homeric Hymn to Apollo* (393–96), Fontenrose (1978: 215) suggests that it was originally the Cretan priests of the sanctuary

this is a composite work with some elements dating back to the seventh century and others to the early fifth.[19] She was selected from among the local women of Delphi, and Diodoros's notice (16.26.6) that she was around fifty years of age certainly accords with the description of the Pythia in Aischylos's *Eumenides* (38).[20] Plutarch (*Moralia* 405c) implies that, in his own day, the Pythia was selected from undistinguished families and that, during the oracle's heyday, there had been as many as three priestesses appointed simultaneously (414b).[21] He notes further (292d) that the Pythia was assisted by five *Hosioi* (Holy Ones), also recruited from the local community, as well as two *Prophētai* or *Hiereis* (437a), appointed—like the *Hosioi*—for life.[22]

On the day of consultation, which normally seems to have taken place only once a month (Plutarch, *Moralia* 292e–f, 398a),[23] the Pythia prepared herself by washing in the waters of the nearby Kastalia spring, from which she may also have drunk. After burning bay leaves and barley meal on an altar (397a), she mounted the oracular tripod, crowned with a wreath of bay leaves.[24] The consultation session itself took place in the temple of Apollo: Pindar (*Olympian Odes* 7.32) and Herodotos (7.141.2) refer to an *adyton*, a word that literally means "inaccessible" and is often thought to refer to a subterranean chamber within the *cella* of the temple. But Herodotos (5.72.3) also uses the term in reference to the temple of Athena Polias on the Athenian acropolis, where no such feature is attested either by literary sources or by archaeological investigations. In fact no early author refers explicitly to a subterranean chamber in connection with the oracle: the word *muchos* simply means a "recess," with no necessary vertical connotations,[25] while Euripides' mention of a "cave" (*Phoenician Women* 232) refers to the abode of the dragon Python, whom Apollo is supposed to have killed to win sovereignty over Delphi, and has nothing to do with the oracle itself.[26]

It is not until the first century BCE that we start to find references to a chasm. Strabo (document 2.1 at the end of this chapter) says that the oracle was situated in a cave, and Diodoros (document 2.2) specifies that the *adyton* was constructed over a chasm.[27] The tradition was followed by the first-century CE author of *On the Sublime* (document 2.3) and the third-century Neoplatonist author Iamblichos (documents 2.4; 2.5), from where it was picked up by the church fathers and scholarly commentators. However, although Strabo (document 2.1) associates the bronze tripod on which the Pythia sat with an opening in the earth,[28] Iamblichos appears to dissociate the two (document 2.5). Interestingly enough, Plutarch himself does not refer to a chasm, although he does refer to the Pythia "descending" (*katabē*) to the oracle (document 2.6).[29]

The popular belief that the Pythia's responses were uttered in a frenzied state is not supported by the literary testimony and probably owes much to representations of the Pythia in tragedy—and especially portrayals of the Trojan prophetess Kassan-

---

::: who received Apollo's inspiration. Janko (1982: 119–21) dates the *Homeric Hymn* to ca. 590 BCE, but Parke and Wormell (1956: 102–3) assign it to the late seventh century and Robertson (1978: 49) to the second half of the sixth.

19. Cobb-Stevens, Figueira, and Nagy 1985: 2.

20. Amandry 1950: 115–18; Johnston 2008: 40–41. Diodoros says that the Pythia had originally been an unmarried virgin, until she was raped by a certain Echekrates of Thessaly at some unknown date, though this is probably a mythologized attempt to explain why the Pythia dressed as a virgin.

21. Bowden 2005: 16; Ustinova 2009: 123–24.

22. Amandry 1950: 118–25; Maurizio 1995: 83–84. The term *prophētēs* appears only in earlier literature and is probably equivalent to the *hiereus*, attested in inscriptions after ca. 200 BCE; cf. Amandry 1950: 118–23; Fontenrose 1978: 218.

23. Regular consultations were held on the seventh day of the month for each of the nine months (excluding winter) during which Apollo was thought to reside at Delphi; during winter, conversely, Dionysos was believed to rule the sanctuary. See Amandry 1950: 82; Bowden 2005: 17; Ustinova 2009: 124.

24. Fontenrose 1978: 224 with references to the (almost invariably late) literary testimony on which this reconstruction is based.

25. E.g., Pindar, *Pythian Odes* 5.68; Aischylos, *Eumenides* 38).

26. Cf. Klearchos fr. 64 Wehrli. See Oppé 1904: 216–17, 223–25, 239–40.

27. As Ustinova (2009: 126) points out, the phrase "they say" in the Strabo passage means that this is not an eyewitness account.

28. Cf. Diodoros 16.26.5.

29. Oppé 1904: 217–20, 225–30; Fontenrose 1978: 227.

dra.[30] Plutarch (document 2.6) does describe a session during which the Pythia became crazed, but he seems to indicate that this was an exceptional occurrence.[31] Lucan (*Pharsalia* 5.75-236) also depicts a frenzied Pythia, but it has been suggested that his representation is heavily influenced by traditions concerning Aeneas's consultation of the Sybil at Cumae.[32] As far as we can tell from the limited literary testimonia at our disposal, the Pythia uttered Apollo's oracular responses while in a trancelike state, desensitized to external stimuli and automatic reactions.[33] Plato (*Apology* 22c) compares poets to prophets and those who pronounce oracles because all are *enthousiazontes*—literally, "filled with the god."[34] It was commonly believed that, when the Pythia made her pronouncements, she was "possessed" by the god Apollo, though the notion that this possession was sexual in nature or that the Pythia was, in some respects, the "bride" of Apollo is probably a product of early Christian propaganda.[35] Authors vary, however, as to whether Apollo acted through some animate or inanimate intermediary. Plutarch (*Moralia* 431c-432c) notes the theory that Apollo sent *daimones*, or disembodied spirits, whose souls mingled with that of the Pythia to communicate the god's prophecy, while Iamblichos (document 2.5) hypothesizes that Apollo came upon the Pythia in the form of a divine light.[36] Pausanias (10.24.7), by contrast, states that the Pythia's faculty for prophecy derived from the waters of the Kassotis spring, near the temple of Apollo.[37]

One word that is often mentioned in connection with the Delphic oracle is *pneuma*—literally, "breath" or "wind." When it is found in those later authors who mention a chasm in the *adyton*, it seems to refer to some sort of vapour or exhalation (e.g., documents 2.1, 2.5) and may be used inter-changeably with other terms such as *atmos* or *epipnoia* (e.g., document 2.4). Although Diodoros (document 2.2) does not refer specifically to a vapour, it seems to be implied in his account of how the oracle was originally discovered by goats, which became intoxicated when they approached the chasm. In Plutarch, however, the word *pneuma* seems to denote more a kind of spirit—that is, a divine, rather than geochemical, agent (document 2.6).[38] In a section of the *Moralia*, entitled "On the Obsolescence of Oracles," Plutarch does mention an exhalation (*anathymiasis*), which he describes as sweet odoured, but he does not associate it with a chasm (document 2.7); indeed, his comment that it seems "as if the source of its propulsion is the *adyton*" ought to suggest that this was not, in fact, the origin of the vapour at all. As far back as the fifth century BCE, Pindar (document 2.8) talks about the sweetly fragrant *adyton* at Delphi, but he too fails to specify the origin of the odour—it could, presumably, refer to incense—and makes no mention of a fissure in the ground.

What emerged, then, from the French excavations of the 1890s was nothing short of disappointing. The remains of the fourth-century temple (figs. 2.1, 2.2), which included reused masonry from its sixth-century predecessor, were extremely disturbed, though M. F. Courby suggested that the foundations of the southern interior colonnade were interrupted by a construction, of which only some limestone blocks remained in the southwest part of the *cella*.[39] Adjacent to this was an unpaved area, sunken into the foundations to a depth of a little over 2 metres. Together, the two components measured approximately 3 by 5 metres and were identified as constituting the *adyton* of the temple. Immediately to the south was a water channel,

:::     30. Bowden 2005: 14, 21; Ustinova 2009: 125-27.

31. Amandry 1950: 41-56; Fontenrose 1978: 197, 208; Maurizio 1995: 69-70. Plutarch (*Moralia* 437b-c) implies that a nonreaction on the part of the sacrificial victim meant that Apollo was not in residence.

32. Oppé 1904: 218; Amandry 1950: 19-24; Fontenrose 1978: 210. Ustinova (2009: 140-41) thinks otherwise.

33. Maurizio 1995: 73.

34. Cf. Plato, *Ion* 533e. See Maurizio 1995: 77.

35. Origen (*Against Celsus* 7.3-4) tells how the God entered the Pythia, and John Chrysostom (*Homilies on the First Epistle to the Corinthians* 29.12.1) says that the Pythia sat on the tripod with her legs apart, so that she could be penetrated by the evil spirit. See Johnston 2008: 40-42.

36. Johnston 2008: 46-47.

37. Fontenrose 1978: 202.

38. Cf. Fontenrose 1978: 197.

39. Courby 1915-27: 47-69.

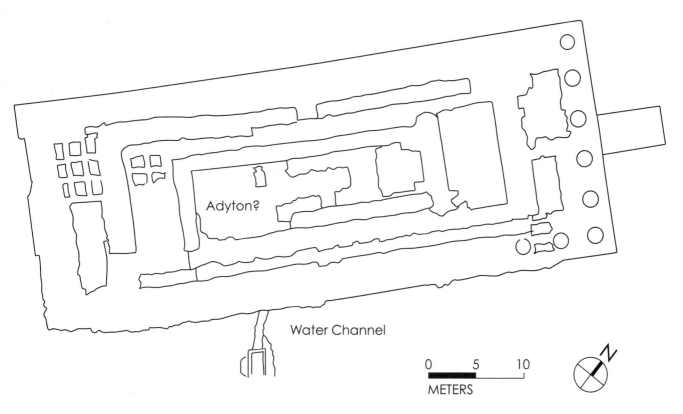

2.2   Plan of the fourth-century temple of Apollo at Delphi. (After Bommelaer and Laroche 1991: plate 3.)

which seems to have served drainage purposes in the fourth century, though it has tentatively been connected with the Kassotis spring at an earlier date.[40] Courby was unable, however, to detect any fissure, be it natural or artificial, in the rock beneath the *adyton*.

## The Geology of the Site

Delphi stands on the northern flank of the Corinth rift zone, caught between the African, Anatolian, and Eurasian plates; as each new episode of crustal extension widens the Corinthian Gulf, the Peloponnese is pulled ever further away from central Greece, and these long periods of gradually increasing strain are consequently punctuated by major seismotectonic events.[41] Initially invited to join a geological survey designed to test the feasibility of constructing nuclear power stations in Greece, Jelle de Boer conducted a series of field surveys of the region around Delphi in the 1980s, during which he identified an east-west-running fault line (the "Delphi" fault) that seemed to transect the sanctuary of Apollo, even though it was partly obscured by artificial terracing and erosional fill (fig. 2.3).[42] In 1995, de Boer initiated a joint geological and archaeological investigation, which incorporated not only field

:::   40. See also Bommelaer and Laroche 1991: 182; Spiller, Hale, and de Boer 2002: 190; Hale et al. 2003: 70.
      41. De Boer, Hale, and Chanton 2001: 707–8.
      42. De Boer, Hale, and Chanton 2001: 708; Hale et al. 2003: 69.

By contrast, Piccardi (2000) hypothesizes that the Delphi fault runs south of the sanctuary of Apollo, beneath the sanctuary of Athena Pronaia.

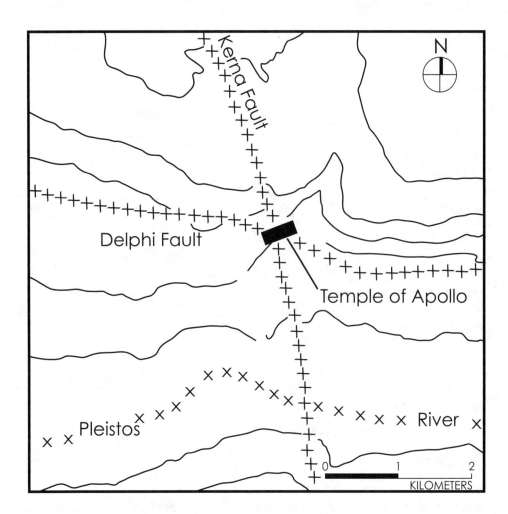

2.3　The proposed intersection of the Delphi and Kerna faults. (After De Boer, Hale, and Chanton 2001: 708, fig. 2.)

survey but also a chemical analysis of spring waters and mineral deposits. A second fault line, named the "Kerna" fault, was now identified, marked by the sites of five springs—of which only one is still active—and running in a roughly north-south direction; based on its trajectory, de Boer suggested that it intersected with the Delphi fault in the approximate location of the temple of Apollo.[43]

Familiar with the ancient traditions concerning Delphi and gaseous emissions, de Boer and Hale formulated the hypothesis that this intersection between two major faults would have allowed rising springwater and hydrocarbon gases to rise to the surface. The hydrocarbon gases themselves would have been created by the heating and vaporizing of lighter constituents in the deep layers of bituminous limestone in the area—itself a consequence of friction along fault planes. Furthermore, ground deposits of snow and ice would mean that the gases would be released less in winter, when the oracle was said not to have functioned, while gradual calcite sedimentation would eventually clog the exit pathways for the gases until they were released by further seismic activity, which might also account for the waning popularity of the oracle in Plutarch's day as well as his observation (document 2.7) that the strength of the exhalation fluctuated.[44]

The hypothesis was tested by analysing samples of springwater, taken from the Kerna spring high above the sanctuary, and travertine deposits from

: : :　43. De Boer, Hale, and Chanton 2001: 708; Hale et al. 2003: 70; Broad 2006: 171. The Kerna fault had already been identified by Michael and Reynold Higgins (1996: 80–81).

44. De Boer, Hale, and Chanton 2001: 709; Spiller, Hale, and de Boer 2002: 192; Hale et al. 2003: 72; Broad 2006: 157.

the Kerna spring and from various locations within and around the foundations of the temple of Apollo. The results tested positive for the hydrocarbon gases methane and ethane, but the sample of water taken from the Kerna spring also yielded evidence for the presence of ethylene (also known as ether) in concentrations of 0.3 nM/L.[45] Characterized by its sweet smell, ethylene was widely used in general anaesthesia from the 1930s down to the 1970s, when it was replaced due to isolated fires and explosions that had been reported from operating rooms. In low doses, the gas provokes a feeling of euphoria and a reduced sense of inhibition. Experiments conducted by Isabella Herb in the 1950s found that within two minutes, subjects could maintain a seated position, respond to questions, and write answers but would also display altered speech patterns and utter random thoughts; recovery was complete within fifteen minutes, though subjects would have no memory of what had transpired while under the influence of the gas. In concentrations higher than 20 percent, however, ethylene can cause unconsciousness or even death, and this is what de Boer and his associates speculate happened during the disastrous oracular consultation that is reported by Plutarch (document 2.6).[46]

Convinced that the intersection of the Delphi and Kerna faults could account for the emission of gaseous vapours and that the documented presence of ethylene was consistent with descriptions of the Pythia's demeanour during oracular consultations, de Boer and his colleagues re-examined the published reports of the excavation of the temple of Apollo. Although the French had discovered nothing that was immediately identifiable with a chasm in the earth, a photograph taken during the excavations did seem to show "subvertical extensional fractures in the bedrock below the temple foundation" together with the presence of rising springwater.[47] The yawning chasm may have been the

product of an overactive literary imagination, but could the fissures and the springwater have been the vehicles for the transmission of the hydrocarbon gases that intoxicated the Pythia?[48]

The ethylene hypothesis has recently been challenged from within the scientific community by two new reports, each published independently of the other in the first decade of the twenty-first century. The first, by a team of geologists and geophysicists from the National Institute of Geophysics and Vulcanology in Rome and the University of Patras, reports the results of a more complete gas-geochemical survey of the area and questions the presence of ethylene in significant amounts at the site. Noting that ethylene is normally present in natural biogenic gases only in very low amounts and that it seldom persists for enough time to accumulate because it is readily reduced to paraffin by the presence of hydrogen, the authors note that, for ethylene to be the sweet-smelling odour described by Pindar (document 2.8) and Plutarch (2.7), it would have to be present in concentrations higher than the odour threshold of 290 ppmv—far in excess of the comparatively negligible concentration that de Boer's team tested from the Kerna spring. Recording relatively high concentrations of carbon dioxide—together with methane and ethane—in samples taken from the Kerna and Kastalia springs, the authors suggest that a better explanation for the Pythia's trance might be attributed to oxygen depletion, due to the exhalation of carbon dioxide and methane. If the effects of this oxygen depletion were further accelerated by the use of a coal burner with essential oils, perfumes, or drugs, then carbon monoxide could have been produced.[49]

The second report, written by scientists from the National Institute of Geosciences and Earth Resources in Florence, the University of Florence, the University of Athens, and the National Observatory of Athens, casts doubt even on the presence of the

:::    45. De Boer, Hale, and Chanton 2001: 709; Spiller, Hale, and de Boer 2002: 192; Broad 2006: 193–98.
    46. De Boer, Hale, and Chanton 2001: 709; Spiller, Hale, and de Boer 2002: 193; Hale et al. 2003: 73.

    47. De Boer, Hale, and Chanton 2001: 709; cf. Hale et al. 2003: 70, 72; Broad 2006: 90, 141, 145–47; Ustinova 2009: 144.
    48. The hypothesis is accepted in Ustinova 2009: 146–50.
    49. Etiope et al. 2006.

Kerna fault.[50] Disputing that an alignment of five springs is necessarily evidence for the presence of a fault, the authors argue that two of the co-ordinates mapped by de Boer's team are not, in fact, in alignment and may not even belong to the same fault. On the basis of further geochemical measurements, the team concluded that "[h]igh concentrations of ethylene . . . are thermodynamically impossible and are unrealistic in non-volcanic areas."[51] The authors argued, however, that literary accounts of gas exhalations and chasms were not complete invention but rather "true physical elements connected with earthquake faulting."[52] During such "events," there could well have been "episodic anomalous gas releases," but the gases involved are far more likely to have been hydrogen sulphide and carbon dioxide—the latter capable of causing dizziness and confusion together with aural and visual dysfunction.

The fact that both teams concluded that carbon dioxide was more likely than ethylene to be the gas described by some of our literary sources is not without interest, because Michael and Reynold Higgins had already made the same conjecture, based in part on the documented presence of lethal carbon dioxide emissions at the oracle of Apollo Kareios in Phrygian Hierapolis (modern Pamukkale in Turkey).[53] Strabo (document 2.9) describes how the fumes from the so-called Ploutonion could kill not only sparrows but also bulls and goes on to relate that the Galloi (eunuch priests normally associated with the cult of Cybele, or the "Great Mother") would regularly descend into the chasm while holding their breath.[54] Geophysical research has identified a fault line that runs beneath the temple of Apollo Kareios, while chemical studies have demonstrated how carbon dioxide emissions issue from the hot springs of the Pammukale area, which are rich in calcium carbonate.[55] Indeed, an arched shaft beneath the temple has been walled up due to asphyxiation fatalities on the part of injudiciously curious visitors in the past (fig. 2.4),[56] although it now appears that the entrance to the Ploutonion that Strabo describes should be situated further to the west, by the Temple Nymphaeum.[57] Now, admittedly, one could argue that there is a distinct difference between the fumes at Hierapolis and the vapours at Delphi, since the gas at the former "was not so much intoxicating as toxic."[58] But this only begs the question as to how, exactly, intoxicating gases—be they ethylene or carbon dioxide—are supposed to have functioned within the oracular process. No truly solemn or prophetic pronouncements were issued when, in August 2002, Spiller attempted to replicate the Delphic oracle by pumping ethylene into his converted garden shed, recruiting as his Pythia the vice president of a southern Indiana beer appreciation society.[59] According to Broad, de Boer himself admitted that "the chemical stimulus in no way explained the Oracle's cultural and religious power, her role as a font of knowledge, her liberation of hundreds of slaves, her encouragement of personal morality, her influence in helping the Greeks invent themselves, or—by extension—whether she really had psychic powers."[60]

## Inspired Mantic or Fraudulent Puppet?

In Broad's view, the findings of de Boer and his colleagues served to recuperate the respectability of the Pythia, restoring "the Oracle's air of mystery and spirituality, perhaps even some of her repute

---

50. Piccardi et al. 2008. The possibly phantomatic presence of the Kerna fault had already been flagged in Etiope et al. 2006: 821.

51. Piccardi et al. 2008: 15.

52. Piccardi et al. 2008: 15.

53. Higgins and Higgins 1996: 80–81.

54. Cf. Apuleius, *On the World* 17.

55. Cross and Aaronson 1988; Negri and Leucci 2006.

56. D'Andria 2003: 142–44.

57. Ismaelli 2009. For this reason, it is unclear that the temple of Apollo and the Ploutonion were as directly connected as Ustinova (2009: 154) supposes.

58. Hale et al. 2003: 70.

59. Broad 2006: 214–20.

60. Broad 2006: 241.

2.4    Bricked-up doorway to what used to be considered the entrance to the Ploutonion at Hierapolis. (Photo by author.)

for navigating all time and space, for exploring the hidden powers of the mind."[61] In truth, as de Boer seems to have recognized, the ethylene hypothesis is ultimately just one in a long line of reductive explanations, designed to strip away the sort of mysticism and superstition that so embarrasses the modern Western mind and replace it with something that makes cold, rational sense.[62] For all its potential verification through geological investigation, as an explanation for how the oracle functioned, it is not so different from those theories that attributed the Pythia's trance to her chewing bay or laurel leaves.[63]

Needless to say, no modern scholar believes that Apollo really spoke through the Pythia, or that the

:::    61. Broad 2006: 249.

62. See, for example, Vernant (1991: 306–8), who argues that oracles were "pre-rational" institutions that were eventually superseded by the *polis*.

63. Fontenrose (1978: 225) attributes this belief to a mis-

reading of a satirical rant by Lucian (*The Double Indictment* 1). As Bowden (2005: 18) points out, bay leaves are not known for their hallucinogenic properties, while laurel leaves are poisonous; cf. Amandry 1950: 128–29; Whittaker 1965: 23; Price 1985: 138–39.

Pythia was endowed with a genuine gift for predicting the future. For some, it was Delphi's role as an interregional sanctuary, attracting visitors from far afield, that allowed it to serve as a "clearing-house for information," offering knowledge of the world that extended beyond the parochial boundaries of the polis.[64] At its most extreme, the sceptical view regards the entire oracular process as a sham, perpetrated on credulous suppliants by a manipulative coterie of temple officials and prophets, eager to please whichever state or individual was willing to invest in the sanctuary.[65] Noting the fact that many of the early oracular responses are recorded in hexameter verse, sceptics have questioned whether a local woman from an undistinguished family is likely to have had the improvisational or cultural skills to issue poetic predictions and have therefore assumed that it was the priests and prophets who "interpreted"—or manipulated—the responses of the Pythia and recast inarticulate prose into verses, if they did not compose them outright.[66]

Proponents of this critique often point to what they see as the oracle's deliberate ambiguity.[67] Herodotos provides us with a number of examples, of which two are related to oracular consultations of Delphi by Kroisos, king of Lydia, in the mid-sixth century. On the first occasion (1.53), Kroisos asked the oracle whether he should declare war on Persia, to which the Pythia replied that, if he marched against the Persians, he would destroy a great empire. On the second (1.55), he asked if his rule would be long lived and received the response that he had nothing to worry about until a mule became king of the Persians. As the Pythia later explained to the now-ousted Lydian ruler, the "mule" was Cyrus the Great, son of a Persian father and a Median mother, while the "great empire" destined to be destroyed was, of course, Kroisos's own: "[A]nd he, when he

heard this, realized that the fault had been his own and not the god's" (1.91). The employment of deliberately ambiguous language, it is often argued, kept all options open so as to defend the integrity of the oracle.

It is within the same sceptical and rationalist spirit that attempts have been made to gauge the authenticity of the more than six hundred Delphic responses that have been preserved in literary texts and inscriptions. So, for example, Herbert William Parke and Donald Ernest Wilson Wormell arranged responses chronologically, according to nine periods of the oracle's history, and subdivided the entire corpus into those they considered "historical" and those they deemed "fictitious."[68] Along somewhat similar lines, Joseph Fontenrose classified the responses according to four source-critical categories: historical, quasi-historical, legendary, and fictional.[69] A historical response—which need not necessarily be genuine—is one that was delivered within the lifetime of the writer who recorded it, while quasi-historical responses are those that were given in historical times, but only recorded later; legendary responses are those purportedly given before the oracle began to function in the eighth century, and fictional responses are those that are invented by poets and dramatists. Fontenrose found that the majority of "historical" responses were "simple commands and statements, none requiring uncommon foresight or cleverness"; about three-quarters of them concerned religious instructions, while most of the remainder related to civic affairs.[70] A statistical analysis of "quasi-historical" responses, on the other hand, seemed to show more affinities with legendary than with historical responses. In the end, Fontenrose concluded that barely more than one hundred recorded Delphic responses were genuine.[71]

:::     64. Eg. Snodgrass 1980: 63; cf. Forrest 1957: 174; Whittaker 1965: 25–26.

65. Maurizio (1995: 70) and Broad (2006: 105–6) seem to attribute this position to—among others—Parke and Wormell, though the latter actually argue (1956: 36–37) that the long-lived prestige of Delphi belies suspicions of political manipulation.

66. E.g., Amandry 1950: 168; Parke and Wormell 1956: 38. Whittaker (1965: 38–42) notes the control that the priest exercises

over "the voice" at Mwari in Zimbabwe and compares the situation to Delphi, though he is careful to avoid levelling charges of charlatanism.

67. E.g., Nilsson 1951: 125–27; Parke and Wormell 1956: 94.

68. Parke and Wormell 1956.

69. Fontenrose 1978: 7–9.

70. Fontenrose 1978: 22, 26–27.

71. Fontenrose 1978: 88.

In the last two decades, there has been something of a reaction against the rationalist-sceptical position—and especially the question of authenticity, which is insensitive to issues of genre and medium (e.g., the differences between literary texts and inscriptions) and fails to consider adequately the circumstances of the transmission of oracular responses.[72] The fact is that the Greeks never seem to have doubted the efficacy of the oracle: even though Delphi urged the Greeks to side with the Persian invaders in 480 BCE, there is no evidence that this advice discredited the oracle in subsequent decades.[73] If the reconstruction of the Pythia as a passive pawn of political opportunists is so patent to the modern sceptical historian, why did the Greeks themselves fail to recognize it?[74] If it was the priests or the prophets who "transcribed" the unintelligible rantings of the Pythia, then surely at least one eyewitness would have spoken up. Instead, the Pythia is always described as communicating directly and articulately with the consultor.[75] Indeed, the occasional charges that were levelled against individuals accused of trying to bribe the Pythia would seem to imply that she spoke in her own voice.[76] Nor do ancient writers characterize the oracle as ambiguous—at least not deliberately so.[77] Plutarch (*Moralia* 408e-f) actually describes the responses as "simple and direct," without ambiguity (*amphibolia*). It may be, as Julia Kindt suggests, that the seemingly opaque speech of the Pythia was thought to reflect the alterity of divine—as opposed to human—utterances rather than serve as a deliberate tactic of deception.[78]

The question of whether the Pythia issued her responses in prose or poetry is a little more intrac-

table. A large number of the oracular responses that are reported by Herodotos, or in late collections such as the *Palatine Anthology*, are in hexameter verse, and Plutarch implies that the Pythia had once prophesied in verse but no longer did so in his own day (e.g., *Moralia* 402b). In the fourth century, Demosthenes (*Against Meidias* 51-52) cites an oracle that is both in verse and prose, though Plato's juxtaposition of the mantic priestesses at Delphi and Dodona with poets (*Phaidros* 244a) ought to imply that the Pythia was thought to speak in verse.[79] It could be that the medium varied from Pythia to Pythia, or from occasion to occasion, but it is just as likely to be a consequence of transmission.

Although alphabetic writing is attested from the early eighth century, Greece remained a predominantly oral culture down to as late as the fourth century.[80] That oracular responses were generally circulated and transmitted in the oral domain is strongly suggested by an incident reported by Thucydides (document 2.10). In the midst of the deadly plague that devastated Athens in 430 BCE, the older Athenians remembered an oracle that told how pestilence would accompany a "Dorian war"—the Peloponnesian War between the Athenians and the "Dorians" of Sparta had broken out the previous year. But, as Thucydides notes, there was some disagreement as to whether the oracle had specified a pestilence (*loimos*) or a famine (*limos*), and the historian mischievously ventures the suggestion that the oracle would be told rather differently were a future war with Sparta to be accompanied by a famine.[81]

Once the oral character of Delphic responses is recognized, two important consequences follow. The first concerns versification, because the met-

72. E.g., Maurizio 1997, esp. 310-11. For an argument against political or cynical manipulation, see Bonnechère 2010.

73. Price 1985: 151-53; cf. Bowden 2005: 26-27. Contra Nilsson 1951: 127.

74. Parke and Wormell 1956: 36-37; Price 1985: 141-43.

75. Amandry 1950: 120-21; Fontenrose 1978: 197, 212; Maurizio 1995: 71-72; Bowden 2005: 22.

76. According to Herodotos (5.63, 90-91), the Pythia ordered the Spartans to expel the tyrant Hippias from Athens because she had been bribed by the Alkmaionidai, after their benefactions at the sanctuary (see above, p. 19). King Kleomenes of Sparta is also said to have bribed the Pythia to declare his coruler, Demaratos,

illegitimate (6.66, 75.3). See Johnston 2008: 44, 50-51; cf. Maurizio 1995: 84.

77. Fontenrose 1978: 236; Morgan 1990: 156-57; Bonnechère 2008-9: 389.

78. Kindt 2006: 36-37.

79. Maurizio 1995: 78-79; Bowden 2005: 33-34.

80. Thomas 1989: 45-60.

81. Maurizio 1997: 317-18. There is some dispute concerning the pronunciation of ancient Greek—see Petrounias 2007—though it is worth noting that in Modern Greek, *loimos* and *limos* would be pronounced, though not spelled, exactly the same.

rical qualities of verse provide useful mnemonic cues that facilitate the oral transmission of material, whether or not that material was originally composed in prose or poetry. The second concerns the inherent adaptability—and mutability—of orally transmitted material. Once the Pythia had made her pronouncement, with or without interpretative glosses from the prophets and priests, it fell to the consultor (*theōros*) to convey her message to the community that had dispatched him. Theognis (*Elegies* 805-10) tells his addressee that the *theōros* must be "straighter than a compass, a set square or the marker on a sundial," neither adding to—nor subtracting from—the sacred oracles of the god. The fact that such correct comportment needs to be spelled out reveals the underlying anxiety that not all *theōroi* were so honest. Even then, however, the conveyed response was subject to debate and the interpretation of the community. Indeed, ultimately it was the community that conferred authority on the oracular response and the person who conveyed it, and it is hard to believe that this "dialogue" had no effect on the subsequent oral transmission of the response.[82] The example of the "wooden wall" oracle may clarify the point.

In 480 BCE, with the Persian army of Xerxes on their doorstep, the Athenians consulted the oracle at Delphi and were told to "flee to the ends of the earth" (Herodotos 7.140). Dismayed by the response, the Athenians were advised to adopt the guise of suppliants and seek a second oracle; this time, although the prognosis was not significantly more encouraging than before, they were at least told that a "wooden wall" would provide protection (document 2.11). Fontenrose casts doubt on the authenticity of the two oracles on the grounds that their long, unclear predictions, together with spontaneous utterances, suggest more affinities with legendary and nongenuine quasi-historical—than with histori-

cal—responses.[83] This criticism is only valid, however, if we assume that the responses preserved by Herodotos represent the font, rather than the culmination, of the oracular transmission. If, instead, they stand at the end of a protracted process of oral performances, which included communal discussion and competing interpretations that sought to negotiate between the oracular prediction and the various opinions and suggestions of political leaders (for instance, Themistokles, who interpreted the "wooden wall" to signify the Athenian navy), then the general gist behind both oracular responses seems less fantastic and we can begin to get a glimpse of how the oracle may have functioned within communal decision making.[84]

That, of course, makes it more difficult to reconstruct the precise character of the initial response, but cross-cultural comparisons may offer some clues.[85] One oracle in particular that is often cited in connection with Delphic divination is the so-called poison oracle among the Azande of Sudan, first described by the anthropologist Edward Evans-Pritchard. Like Delphi, the oracle was marginally situated with regard to population centres and, like Delphi, it was consulted on matters regarding natural disasters, affairs of war, the appointment of officials, and questions of religious protocol, as well as on more personal subjects such as marriage, childlessness, pregnancy, and the advisability of making journeys. The oracle was consulted only after considerable communal discussion and the drafting, by community leaders, of alternative or "binary" scenarios, which would be adjudicated by administering poison to a chicken and seeing whether it lived or died.[86] Responding to his more sceptical critics, Evans-Pritchard himself noted: "I always kept a supply of poison for the use of my household and neighbours and we regulated our affairs in accordance with the oracle's decisions. I may remark

:::     82. Fontenrose 1978: 93–94, 119; Parker 1985: 301–2; Morgan 1990: 158; Maurizio 1997: 312–22; Johnston 2008: 51.

83. Fontenrose 1978: 124–28.

84. Maurizio 1997: 312, 322; cf. Morgan 1990: 154.

85. See especially Whittaker 1965.

86. Evans-Pritchard 1937. See Whittaker 1965: 36; Morgan 1990: 152–53; Bowden 2005: 29–30.

that I found this as satisfactory a way of running my house and my affairs as any other I know of."[87]

On this basis, it is widely assumed that consultations of the Delphic oracle were framed in terms of a binary question—that is, "a simple statement for confirmation or refutation, or alternatives requiring the expression of a preference."[88] Thucydides (1.118.3) may provide a hint of the sort of formula adopted when, on the eve of the Peloponnesian War in 431 BCE, he has the Spartans ask the oracle "if it would be better to go to war."[89] Alternatively, the oracle might be asked to choose between alternatives. According to the author of the Aristotelian *Constitution of Athens* (21.6), when, in the last decade of the sixth century, Kleisthenes reorganized the Athenian citizen body into ten new tribes, the tribal names were selected by the Pythia from a submitted list of one hundred.[90] Similarly, when, in 352 BCE, the Athenians were trying to decide whether to lease out a meadow near Eleusis that was sacred to Demeter and Kore, they randomly placed a "positive" and a "negative" tablet into a gold and silver jar and asked the Pythia to choose between them.[91]

A similar procedure is known from Hierapolis, where the oracle was asked to choose one of twenty-four lots, one for each letter of the alphabet; the lot chosen was then matched to a prescribed response, in either hexameters or iambic trimeters. For example, the response corresponding to the letter theta instructed the consultor to "[u]ndertake your enterprise resolutely and see it through to completion," while the extraction of the letter pi sagely advised that "tortoises run ahead of crows, even if the latter have wings."[92] Amandry speculated that a lot oracle existed alongside the more famous mantic rite at Delphi.[93] Either way, the hypothesis that consultations were phrased in terms of alternatives or preferences need not, of course, exclude more inventive and extemporizing proclamations on the part of the Pythia.

## Conclusion

For more than a millennium, Greeks—and non-Greek rulers—sought the advice of Apollo, secure in the belief that the Pythia at Delphi revealed the truth, as even Kroisos was forced to admit. The oracle was neither prescriptive nor proscriptive: it did not spontaneously initiate action, but rather served as a tool in deciding between policy alternatives that had already been formulated by the community's leaders.[94] Nor, to judge from the "wooden wall" oracle, was it necessarily the last word on an issue; rather, it contributed to an ongoing debate that was ultimately reconciled at the human level.

The Pythia's responses conveyed authority to decision making, but that authority was further guaranteed through transmission and circulation among an ever wider audience—especially in those happy circumstances when events seem to have confirmed the oracular prediction.

There is no compelling reason to doubt the testimony that the Pythia delivered her pronouncements while in a trance. Gases, be they ethylene or carbon dioxide, may have contributed to the atmosphere of the occasion—alongside light deprivation, the scent of burning perfumes, and, perhaps,

:::    87. Evans-Pritchard 1937: 126; cited in Price 1985: 146.

88. Morgan 1990: 155; cf. Bowden 2005: 19; Johnston 2008: 49; Bonnechère 2008–9: 389.

89. Price 1985: 154.

90. Amandry 1950: 33–34.

91. *IG* II² 204. See Amandry 1950: 151–53; Whittaker 1965: 27; Bowden 2005: 24; Johnston 2008: 53.

92. The prefabricated responses were found on two inscriptions, one from the sanctuary of Apollo and the other from the Martyrion of St. Philip. See D'Andria 2003: 228–31; Ritti 2006: 167–71; Ismaelli 2009: 160. Interestingly enough, very few of the responses are negative or discouraging.

93. Amandry 1950: 29–36; cf. Parke and Wormell 1956: 18; Whittaker 1965: 27; Johnston 2008: 54–55; Fontenrose (1978: 219–21), by contrast believes that there was only one mantic rite at Delphi.

94. Morgan 1990: 154.

even percussion instruments—but they cannot be the primary explanation for the Pythia's trance. Firstly, there would have been marked fluctuations in the emission of such gases, both in the long and short terms, and secondly, the intoxicating effects of such vapours would presumably not be limited to the Pythia alone. At Hierapolis, where the existence of carbon dioxide emissions is undeniable, it is far from clear that they were integral to—let alone indispensable for—the functioning of the oracle.[95] Rather, they seem to have been taken more as the physical indication of a divine presence, and that is perhaps how we should best understand their role at Delphi also.

## DOCUMENTS FOR CHAPTER 2

**2.1**   They say that the oracle is a deep, hollow cave with a narrow entrance and from it arises a divinely inspired vapour (*pneuma*); over its mouth is placed a high tripod which the Pythia climbs to receive the vapour and give the prophecy in verse or prose. Prose responses are adapted to verse by certain poets who work in the sanctuary. (Strabo 9.3.5)

**2.2**   For it is said that in ancient times, goats discovered the oracle, which is why even to this day the Delphians use goats to consult the oracle. They say that the manner of its discovery occurred like this. There is a chasm in the place where now is situated the part of the sanctuary called the *adyton*, around which goats used to graze in the days when Delphi was not yet occupied. And when a goat would approach the chasm and gaze into it, it would leap about in a wondrous way and issue a sound different from that which it was formerly accustomed to emit. The goatherd, amazed at this astonishing sight, approached the chasm, and, looking down to see what it was, he experienced the same effect as the goats, for they started acting like those who are possessed by the god while he began predicting the future. After this, as word spread among the locals concerning what happened to those who approached the chasm, more people converged on the spot, and those who made a test of it because of its miraculous character became inspired as soon as they came near to the place. For this reason, the oracle became the object of wonder and was considered to be the oracle of the goddess Ge. And for a time, those who wished to consult the oracle visited the chasm and made their oracular pronouncements to each other. But later, after many had fallen into the chasm due to their trancelike state and had all disappeared, the inhabitants of the region, in order to eliminate risks, decided to appoint one woman as prophetess for everyone and to administer oracular responses through her. (Diodoros 16.26.1–4)

**2.3**   For many acquire divine inspiration through an extraneous spirit (*pneuma*), in the same way as speech holds the Pythia when she approaches the tripod, where they say there is a chasm in the earth that breathes divine vapour (*atmos*); pregnant with the divine force, she straightaway pronounces oracles on account of the exhalation (*epipnoia*). ([Longinus], *On the Sublime* 13.2)

**2.4**   But another well-known and highly visible type of divination, that of oracles, is variegated, on which one declares such things: "[S]ome are inspired when drinking water, like the priest of [Apollo] Klarios at Kolophon; others, while sitting over openings in the earth, like the women who de-

---

:::     95. Contra Ustinova 2009: 84–86. Strabo (document 2.9) makes no connection between the fumes and the oracular pronouncements. Apuleius, *On the World* 17, describes the Ploutonion in a passage that, a few lines earlier, refers to prophecy but makes no explicit link between oracular pronouncements and the noxious fumes at Hierapolis. In any case, like Strabo, he notes that the only beings who could tolerate the fumes were the Galloi—priests not of Apollo, but of Cybele.

liver oracles at Delphi; and others, when overpowered by vapours from waters, like the prophets at Branchidai." (Iamblichos, *On the Mysteries* 3.11)

**2.5**   However, the prophetess at Delphi, whether she gives oracles to humans from a subtle, fire-like spirit/vapour (*pneuma*) that wafts up from somewhere through an opening in the earth, or whether she prophesies sitting in the *adyton*, either on the bronze tripod-throne or the four-legged throne which is sacred to the god, she gives herself up entirely to the divine spirit/vapour (*pneuma*) and is shined upon by the ray of divine fire. And when the fire, dense and abundant, wafts up from the aperture, it encircles her completely and she is filled with the divine ray; and when she sits down on the throne of the god, she is at one with the unwavering oracular force of the god; from both such preparations, she is wholly given over to the god. (Iamblichos, *On the Mysteries* 3.11)

**2.6**   So, whenever the imaginative and prophetic power is well adapted to the constitution of the spirit (*pneuma*), just as to a drug, inspiration will, by necessity, come to those who prophesy; when this is not the case, it will not come, or else it will come but in a manner that is deviated, not uncontaminated and disturbed, as we know from the case of the Pythia who died recently. For it is said that a delegation from abroad was present to consult the oracle but that, during the preliminary libations, the sacrificial victim remained unmoved and insensitive. The priests, however, persevered, driven to excess by ambition, and when the victim was inundated and nearly drowned, it finally gave in. And what happened to the priestess? Well, she went down (*katabē*) into the oracle, unwilling—as they say— and without any enthusiasm, and right from her first responses it was evident from the harshness of her voice that her reaction was not right and that, like a labouring ship, she was filled with a mute and evil spirit. Finally, thoroughly crazed, she uttered an unintelligible and frightful scream, ran towards the exit, and threw herself down on the ground, so that not only the delegation but also the *prophētēs*

Nikandros and those of the *Hosioi* who were present fled. After a little while, however, they re-entered and picked her up, still conscious, and she survived for a few days. (Plutarch, *Moralia* 438a–b)

**2.7**   So I think that the exhalation (*anathymiasis*) is not always in the same state, but that sometimes it is weak while again at other times it gains in strength. I base my proof on the testimony of many strangers and all those who serve in the sanctuary. For the room (*oikos*) in which they seat those who consult the god is filled—not frequently or with any regularity but, as it happens, from time to time— with a sweet odour and a breeze (*pneuma*) such as are emitted by the sweetest and most costly of perfumes, and it is as if the source of its propulsion is the *adyton*. Probably, its florescence is due to heat or some other latent force there. But if this does not seem likely to you, you will at least agree that the Pythia herself is subject to different influences which vary over time with regard to that part of her soul to which the spirit (*pneuma*) comes close, and that she does not always maintain just one temperament, harmonious, as it were, and unchanged on every occasion. (Plutarch, *Moralia* 437c–d)

**2.8**   But he [Tlepolemos] went to the god and consulted the oracle. And to him the Golden-Haired God [Apollo] spoke from the sweetly fragrant *adyton*. (Pindar, *Olympian Odes* 7.31–32)

**2.9**   But the Ploutonion, below the small brow of a mountain range that lies above it, is an opening of modest proportions, just large enough to admit a man, though it is very deep, and it is surrounded by a rectangular precinct, about half a plectrum in circumference. And this place is filled with a darkness that is so foggy and dense that one can barely see the ground. The air is harmless to those who come close to the precinct, because in fair weather the area is free of the darkness because it remains inside the circuit. But instant death awaits any living being that enters into it. At least, bulls that are led in fall to the ground and are dragged out dead, while we cast in sparrows, which immediately fell and expired. But the Gallic eunuchs go inside without suffering anything, so that they even go up close to the opening and bend over it and descend to a certain depth, while holding their breath as much as they can (for we saw from their face that they were exhibiting some sort of asphyxiation attack). I do not know whether this immunity is one that is shared by all who are mutilated in this way, or just to those around the temple, or whether it is through some divine foresight, as would be reasonable in the case of those possessed by the god, or due to certain strengths that are the antidotes to what happens. (Strabo 13.4.14).

2.10    And among the things that they reasonably enough remembered in the midst of their hardship was a verse, which the older men said had been chanted a long time ago:

> A Dorian war shall come, and along with it pestilence (*loimos*).

Then a dispute arose among the men to the effect that it was not "pestilence" (*loimos*) that was stated in the verse but "famine" (*limos*), but in the present circumstances, naturally the "pestilence" interpretation prevailed. I daresay that if another Dorian war were to occur after this and there were to be a famine, then famine will be what was originally chanted. (Thucydides 2.54.2–3)

2.11    Pallas [Athena] is unable to propitiate Olympian Zeus
Though she beseeches him with many words and dense craft.
But once more I will approach and say this word to you, untamed as you are:
All else will be captured that the boundaries of Kekrops
Hold within, along with the recesses of divine Kithairon.
Yet far-seeing Zeus grants to Tritogeneia [Athena] a wooden wall,
The only thing to be unravaged; but it will benefit your children.
Do not await peacefully the coming cavalry and foot-army,
The great army from the continent; no, retreat,
Turn your back. There will be future conflict to come.
O godlike Salamis, you will destroy women's children
When the gifts of Demeter are either sowed or harvested.
(Herodotos 7.141.3–4)

# 3

# The Persian Destruction of Eretria

Situated on the southern coast of the island of Euboia, about a half hour's ferry ride from the Attic port of Skala Oropou, Eretria is a little off the tourist trail. The museum, on the western outskirts of the town, receives its fair share of Greek children on school trips, but as one wanders through the quiet and somewhat characterless streets of modern Eretria, it is easy to forget that this was one of the most prosperous and dynamic settlements in Greece during the eighth century BCE. Credited by Strabo (5.4.9) with the joint foundation—along with neighbouring Chalkis—of Pithekoussai, the first permanent Greek settlement in Italy, Eretrians also established new settlements in the Chalkidike peninsula of northern Greece.[1] The evidence of grave goods and votives shows that its elites were in contact not only with Attica, Boiotia, Thessaly, and the Cyclades but also Cyprus and North Syria.

The centrepiece of the museum is a pedimental group, whose extant fragments depict the goddess Athena and the Athenian hero Theseus carrying off a female figure who has been identified as Antiope, the queen of the Amazons (fig. 3.1). The group is considered pivotal within the history of Greek art because, while there are some lingering Archaic-style features such as the isolated and somewhat static detachment of the Athena figure, other traits—for example, the naturalistic drapery that the goddess wears, together with the squarish skull of Theseus and

::: 1. Thucydides 4.123.1; Plutarch, *Moralia* 293b.

3.1    Statue group from the west pediment of the temple of Apollo Daphnephoros at Eretria, Eretria Archaeological Museum (formerly Chalkis Archaeological Museum). *Left*, Athena. *Right*, Theseus and Antiope. (Photo courtesy of the American School of Classical Studies: Alison Frantz Photographic Collection.)

the fact that the figures are carved virtually in the round—anticipate in many respects the art of the Early Classical period.[2] The pediment is thus commonly regarded as dating to a transitional phase between Archaic and Classical art. For reasons that will become clearer below, the conventional date attributed to the pediment is roughly 500–490 BCE.[3]

The pediment was discovered among the ruins of the temple of Apollo Daphnephoros, situated in the centre of the ancient (and modern) town and

first excavated by the Greek archaeologist Konstantinos Kourouniotis in 1899 and then again from 1962 by the Swiss School of Archaeology. The more recent Swiss excavations have revealed that, from the first half of the eighth century, the site of the later temple was occupied by a series of small, apsidal, ovoid and rectilineal buildings, while the earliest recognizably cultic building is a long apsidal structure, dated to ca. 725, in front of which was constructed a square altar.[4] It is, however, the remains

: : :      2. For a re-evaluation of the beginnings of the Classical style of art, see Stewart 2008 and, along somewhat different lines, Neer 2010.

3. Touloupa 1983: 93–103; Stewart 1990: 137; 2008.
4. Kahil 1980; 1981; Drerup 1985; Mazarakis-Ainian 1987; Verdan 2000; 2001; 2002; 2012; Huber 2003; Ducrey 2004: 22, 92.

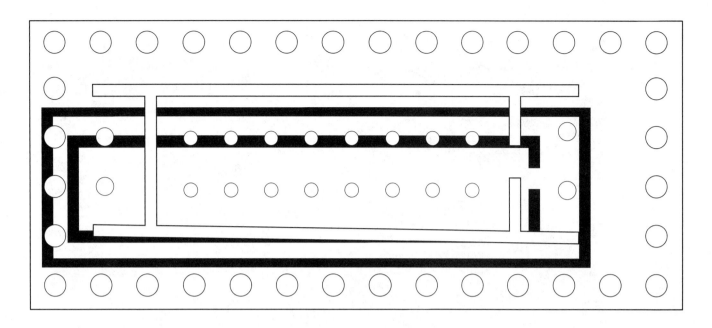

METERS

3.2 Plan of the first (*in black*) and second rectilineal temples of Apollo Daphnephoros at Eretria. (After Auberson 1968: plates II–III.)

of the two subsequent rectilinear temples that will occupy us in this chapter.

The earlier of these temples (fig. 3.2) measured 34 by 7 metres and was oriented southeast-northwest. Its foundations of undressed grey limestone probably supported a superstructure of mud brick and a timber gabled roof. The presence of a stylobate indicates that the temple was "peripteral" (i.e., it had an external colonnade), but its modest width and depth suggest that the columns were of wood.[5] Kourouniotis believed that this temple dated to the late sixth century and therefore attributed to it the Theseus pediment, but the Swiss excavators found pottery dating to the early seventh century in the fill below the *cella*. Parallels between the plan of the Apollo temple at Eretria and Hekatompedon II at Samos suggest that this earlier temple dates to 670–650 BCE.[6]

The second temple (fig. 3.3) adopted almost the

same orientation as its predecessor, on whose ruins it was constructed, though, at 46.4 by 19.15 metres, it was much larger. Its foundations of pseudopolygonal local blue limestone supported a superstructure of fine-grain poros blocks and a peristyle of Doric columns, whose capitals exhibit profiles which seem to fit within a series between those of the sixth-century temple to Apollo at Corinth and those of the "Alkmaionid" temple to Apollo at Delphi (see p. 19). On this basis, the second temple has been dated to ca. 530–520 BCE.[7] Although this is approximately a generation earlier than the pedimental sculpture which is assumed to have occupied the temple's west pediment, the apparent disparity can be reasonably explained by supposing that the pediments would have been the last elements of the temple to be completed.[8]

The dating of the pedimental sculpture is not, however, based entirely on stylistic considerations.

5. Auberson 1968: 13–14.

6. Kourouniotis 1900; Auberson 1968: 15.

7. Auberson 1968: 19–20. Measurements of the ratio between the height and diameter of columns as well as the angle of capital

profiles allow archaeologists to establish a relative chronological sequence for architecture that can then be pegged to the more precisely dated ceramic series.

8. Auberson 1968: 9.

3.3 The foundations of the second rectilineal temple of Apollo Daphnephoros at Eretria from the west. (Photo by author.)

Herodotos (document 3.1) recounts how, in vengeance for the support that the Eretrians had earlier lent to the Ionian revolt, the Persians attacked the city in 490 BCE and burned its sanctuaries.[9] Although he does not explicitly list the temple of Apollo Daphnephoros—or any other temple, for that matter—among the casualties of the Persian attack, most have assumed that the apparent importance of the Apollo temple within the cultic landscape of Archaic Eretria makes it unlikely that it was spared.[10]

According to the reconstruction of the Swiss excavators, those Eretrians who escaped summary execution or enforced exile would have dismantled the charred ruins of the temple and carefully buried the pedimental scupture as an act of veneration. Furthermore, the absence of architectural elements or blocks that can be securely dated to the fifth or fourth centuries indicates that the Eretrians never rebuilt or restored the temple that the Persians had destroyed.[11]

## A Tale of Two Temples

Classical archaeologists tend to assign different classes of material—especially painted pottery—to relative chronological sequences on the principle of stylistic evolution (the employment of scientific techniques will be discussed further below). In the case of pottery and smaller metal items these rela-

:::    9. In 499 BCE, at the outset of the Ionian revolt, Eretria had dispatched five triremes to join twenty Athenian pentekonters in aiding the rebels: Herodotos 5.97. See, however, Walker (2004: 277–78), who attempts to argue, on the basis of a citation from the historian Lysanias of Mallos in Plutarch, *Moralia* 861c, that the Eretrian naval contingent was actually much larger.
10. Bérard 1971; Reber, Hansen, and Ducrey 2004: 654–55.
11. Auberson 1968: 10.

tive sequences can be checked against stratigraphic excavations, where later artifacts will typically appear in strata that overlie those in which earlier ones are found. Furthermore, different classes of artifacts can be correlated with one another: so, for example, sculptural styles can be pegged to the style of architecture with which they are associated, while architectural styles can themselves be matched to ceramic sequences by means of pottery sherds found in foundation trenches.

"Fixed points" are historical dates provided by independent sources that serve to anchor these "floating" relative chronological sequences to absolute dates.[12] Particularly informative here are settlement destructions that are recorded and dated by historical sources. For example, the Assyrian king Sargon II is said to have sacked the Syrian city of Hama in a year that corresponds roughly to 720 BCE. If this is the destruction that caused a burnt level at Hama, in which were found fragments of an Attic Middle Geometric II *kratēr* (a mixing bowl for wine), then 720 offers an approximate *terminus ante quem* (literally, the date *before which*) for Attic Middle Geometric pottery and a *terminus post quem* (the date *after* which) for any material found in levels above the destruction horizon. Similarly, the latest pottery found in the destruction horizon of the Palestinian city of Ashkelon is identified as "transitional" Corinthian; since Babylonian records inform us that King Nebuchadnezzar sacked Ashkelon in 604 BCE, this provides a *terminus ante quem* for the transition from Protocorinthian to Corinthian styles (table 3.1). Other important destruction dates are the Persian sack of Athens in 480 and 479 BCE, Philip II's destruction of Olynthos in 348 BCE, and the eruption of Mount Vesuvius in 79 CE: in all three cases, the latest material found among the destruction debris must predate the disaster.

Documented foundations also provide a set of fixed points. At the beginning of his account of the Sicilian Expedition of 415 BCE, Thucydides (6.1–5) describes the Greek settlements in Sicily, dated by reference to the foundation of Megara Hyblaia in 728 BCE. At both Megara and Syracuse, supposedly founded five years earlier, the earliest pottery found is of the Late Geometric and Protocorinthian styles, meaning that the introduction of Protocorinthian should date roughly to the last quarter of the eighth century. At Selinous, on the other hand, which—again, according to Thucydides—was founded in 628 BCE, the absence of Protocorinthian pottery should indicate that the transition from Protocorinthian to Corinthian styles happened a little ahead of this date. Similarly, the absolute chronology of the *terra sigillata* sequence, which was widely used in the Roman world from the first century BCE, was anchored in part by its discovery in Roman forts on the German and British frontiers, whose period of use can be dated by historical sources such as Tacitus.[13]

Individual "fixed points" are not immune from controversy. We cannot always be absolutely certain that archaeological destruction levels at Near Eastern sites equate with the precise hostile actions that are recorded in documentary sources, while some have cast doubt on the value of Thucydides' dates for the Sicilian foundations—not least because he does not inform us as to the method by which he obtained them.[14] It is, rather, the cumulative results of multiple "fixed points" that lend some confidence to the absolute dates that are assigned to our relative chronological sequences.

Herodotos's description of the Persian destruction of the temples at Eretria has come to serve as one of these "fixed points," but how secure is it? The fact is that the sanctuary of Apollo Daphnephoros did not cease to function as a cultic site in 490 BCE, because it is specifically named in inscriptions that date to the fourth century (documents 3.2 and 3.3). This provided the starting point for an explicit challenge to the Eretrian temple's conventionally assigned date, launched by Michael Vickers and the late E. D. Francis as part of a more systematic attempt to lower our standard chronologies for the

:::    12. See Biers 1992: 25–78; Whitley 2001: 61–71; Hall 2014: 33–39.
13. Greene 1986: 158.

14. For Near Eastern sites: Forsberg 1995. For the Sicilian dates: Snodgrass 1987: 54–56.

TABLE 3.1 Ceramic chronology for Attica and Corinthia, ca. 1200–480 BCE

| Fixed point | Attica | Corinthia | Time (BCE) |
|---|---|---|---|
| | Late Helladic IIIC | Late Helladic IIIC | 1200 |
| | | | 1150 |
| | | | 1100 |
| End of XX Dynasty in Egypt (1070) | Submycenaean | Submycenaean | |
| | | | 1050 |
| | | | 1000 |
| | Early Protogeometric | Early Protogeometric | |
| | Middle Protogeometric | Middle Protogeometric | |
| | | | 950 |
| | Late Protogeometric | Late Protogeometric | |
| | | | 900 |
| | Early Geometric I | | |
| | Early Geometric II | Early Geometric | |
| | | | 850 |
| | Middle Geometric I | | |
| | | Middle Geometric I | |
| | | | 800 |
| | Middle Geometric II | Middle Geometric II | |
| | Late Geometric Ia | | 750 |
| Foundation of Syracuse (733) | Late Geometric Ib | Late Geometric | |
| Destruction of Hama (720) | Late Geometric IIa | | |
| Bokkhoris Scarab (718–712) | Late Geometric IIb | Early Protocorinthian | |
| Destruction of Tarsus? (696) | | | 700 |
| | Early Protoattic | | |
| | | Middle Protocorinthian I | |
| | Middle Protoattic | Middle Protocorinthian II | |
| | | | 650 |
| | Late Protoattic | Late Protocorinthian | |
| Foundation of Selinus (628) | | Transitional | |
| | | Early Ripe Corinthian | |
| Destruction of Ashkelon (604) | Black Figure | | 600 |
| | | Middle Ripe Corinthian | |
| | | | 550 |
| | | Late Ripe Corinthian | |
| | Red Figure | | |
| | | Red Figure | 500 |
| Persian sack of Athens (480) | | | 480 |

Late Archaic and Early Classical period. According to Francis and Vickers, the continuation of the sanctuary of Apollo Daphnephoros throughout the Classical period, together with the absence of obvious signs of burning on the pedimental sculpture, should mean that it was the earlier, and not the later, of the two rectilinear temples that was destroyed by the Persians. The second, and larger, stone temple would then have been constructed once the Persian threat had subsided—perhaps in the 470s. Some support for this position can be found in another study of the Doric capitals, which associated them more closely with the those of the temple of Zeus at Olympia, begun in the 470s BCE, than with the Archaic temples at Corinth or Delphi.[15] Furthermore, Francis and Vickers believe that this later temple was constructed as a victory monument after the final expulsion of the Persians from Greece, with Theseus's rape of the Amazon Antiope symbolizing the Athenian and Eretrian sack of the Lydian capital Sardis in 498 BCE.[16]

Livy (document 3.4) describes how Eretria was attacked in 198 BCE by the Roman naval commander Lucius Quinctius Flamininus. Francis and Vickers note that among the spoils carried off by Flamininus were antique works of art (signa tabulae priscae artis), which they interpret as the—to Roman eyes—slightly old-fashioned fifth-century pedimental sculpture of the Apollo temple.[17] As further support, they point to an Amazon, discovered in the Villa Ludovisi at Rome in 1888 and now in the Museo Centrale Montemartini, which is generally believed to have originated from the same pedimental group at Eretria.[18] This, in their view, provides further evidence that the temple foundations and associated pedimental sculpture which the Swiss excavators dated to the late sixth and early fifth centuries should, in fact, belong to a temple that was constructed no earlier than the 470s and that remained

a significant location for Eretrian cult down to its dismantling by Flamininus in 198 BCE.

The issue regards not simply the dating of a single building. If the pedimental sculpture of the temple of Apollo Daphnephoros is not transitional Archaic-Classical but rather Early Classical, then this has knock-on consequences for how we date all Late Archaic sculpture and, as a consequence, much of the material culture of the late sixth and early fifth centuries. It is for this reason that the Francis-Vickers hypothesis quickly drew attack from the archaeological establishment and especially John Boardman, Lincoln Professor of Classical Art and Archaeology at the University of Oxford from 1978 to 1994. Boardman attaches little significance to the apparent absence of fire damage to the pedimental sculpture because a fire set inside a temple, causing the roof to collapse, need not inflict much visible damage to exterior surfaces.[19] He also finds it difficult to believe that Eretria would have been in much of a position in the 470s to fund the construction of a major public building such as the temple of Apollo: Herodotos (document 3.1) claims that the town's inhabitants were enslaved after the Persian assault, and, although Eretria contributed forces at the battles of Artemision and Salamis in 480 BCE and Plataia in 479 BCE, their reduced numbers hint at the difficulties the city was facing.[20] As to the works of art that Flamininus is supposed to have plundered, it should be noted that Livy does not specify that they were sent to Rome—even if that is a likely proposition—while the term priscae (old, early, former) offers no chronological precision that would enable us to date it to the Early Classical period alone. In fact, strictly speaking, Livy does not actually mention antique sculpture at all. He lists three categories of plundered material: signa, which might refer to sculpture; tabulae, which are probably painted panels; and ornamenta, which are

---

:::       15. Coulton 1979: 102–4.

16. Francis and Vickers 1983: 53. Herodotos (5.102.1) tells how, during the sack of Sardis, the temple of Artemis-Cybele—the patron goddess of the Amazons—was torched, while Pindar (fr. 74 Snell) attributes the foundation of the Ionian cities of Smyrna and Ephesos to eponymous Amazons. See La Rocca 1985: 52.

17. Francis and Vickers 1983: 51.

18. Konstantinou 1954–55; Touloupa 1983: 62.

19. Boardman 1984: 162.

20. For Eretrian participation in the Persian War, see Herodotos 8.46; 9.28.31; ML no. 27.

ornaments of some kind, but it is only the *tabulae* that are described as being "in the old style" (*priscae artis*).[21] And if Flamininus was responsible for the transportation of the Ludovisi Amazon to Rome, it is perhaps odd that he would have left behind the more iconographically significant parts of the pediment for archaeologists to discover more than two millennia later.[22]

As we have seen, Francis and Vickers's case was largely built on the unlikelihood that the Apollo temple stood in ruins for centuries after the Persian attack and on its attestation in fourth-century inscriptions as a functioning cult centre. As Boardman points out, however, all but one of these inscriptions refer to a *hieron* (e.g., document 3.2), which technically means a sanctuary rather than a temple.[23] In fact, temples, which served primarily as a shelter for the cult statue, were not absolutely essential to Greek ritual practices, which demanded merely an altar within a demarcated area.[24] This is why at many sanctuaries in the Greek world, temples postdate—sometimes by several centuries—the earliest attested evidence for cultic practice, as indicated by votive dedications and sacrificial debris. But Boardman also points to the so-called Oath of Plataia, by which the Greeks swore not to repair those cultic installations that had been destroyed by the Persians but to leave them as a permanent memorial to barbarian impiety (see chap. 4). No source explicitly says that the Eretrians swore the oath, but, given that Eretria was one of the earliest and most severe casualties of Persian aggression, it is certainly true that it would have had particular cause to commemorate the disaster it suffered.[25] This conclusion is not necessarily invalidated by the one inscription (document 3.3) that does appear to refer to a temple (*naos*). Quite apart from the fact that the phrase "in front of the temple of" is an editor's restoration,[26]

it is not entirely impossible that part of the temple remained standing after the conflagration and that it was deliberately left in ruins as a poignant memorial within a sanctuary that continued to function.[27]

Two further observations should be made. The first is that, with the exception of part of a male head, found on the eastern side of the temple and tentatively assigned to a gigantomachy scene, there is no sculpture that can be definitively attributed to the east pediment. One possibility is that Flamininus removed only the sculpture from the front of the building,[28] though why he should have spared the rest is a mystery. But another possibility—especially for those who favour a construction date shortly before 490 BCE—is that only the sculpture in the west pediment had been completed by the time of the Persian sack and this was carefully buried immediately after the destruction, thus sparing it from Flamininus's depredations. Admittedly, it is somewhat surprising to find the Eretrians adorning the back of the temple before the front,[29] but the temple of Aphaia on Aigina and the Siphnian treasury at Delphi offer parallel instances where the sculpture on the back of the building was completed before that on the principal façade.[30]

The second involves the iconography of the pedimental group. Despite Francis and Vickers's attempts to view Theseus as a symbol of Eretria, he was a decidedly and almost uniquely Athenian hero, and, unless the Eretrians were particularly keen to fawn on their more powerful neighbour in the early years of the Delian League, it is hard to account for why they would have chosen to mount Theseus on the west pediment of their most important temple in the 470s BCE. If the higher dating of the temple is accepted, however, a different scenario emerges. The Athenian tyrant Peisistratos had very close connections with Eretria: one of his wives was said to

::: 21. Boardman 1984: 162.
22. Boardman 1984: 162.
23. Cf. *IG* XII.9 208.23–24; 210.28–29; 212.23; 215.12–13; 216.14–15; 220.20–21; 225.7–8; 229.4–5; 230.5.
24. Boardman 1984: 161; Bruit Zaidman and Schmitt Pantel 1997: 58.
25. Boardman 1984: 162.
26. Wilhelm 1892: 134.

27. A similar situation has been argued for the Archaic temple of Athena Polias on the Athenian acropolis: see Ferrari 2002. For a modern parallel, consider the ruins of the old Coventry Cathedral in England, bombed by the Lufwaffe in 1940 and left standing next to the newly constructed cathedral.
28. Ducrey 2004: 227.
29. Touloupa 1983: 91–92; following Delivorrias 1974: 179.
30. Stewart 1990: 128, 137.

be an aristocratic Eretrian named Koisyra (Scholiast to Aristophanes, *Clouds* 48) while Eretria served as a base for Peisistratid operations immediately before their victorious battle at Pallene in the mid 540s BCE (Herodotos 1.61.2). Since the Swiss dating of the second temple places it well before the Peisistratid dynasty fell in 510 BCE, it is entirely possible that it was partly funded by the Peisistratids in gratitude for the support they had received from their allies in Eretria and that the appearance of Theseus on the west pediment reflects the close relationship between the ruling parties of the two cities.[31]

An added complication arises with two passages of Strabo. In his description of Eretria (document 3.5), the geographer records that the "ancient city" (*archaian polin*) was destroyed by the Persians and that the locals still point out the ruined foundations at a place that is called Old Eretria (*palaian Eretrian*).[32] But earlier, in his geographical overview of the Greek coastline (document 3.6), he seems to distinguish between Old Eretria, which he says is opposite Delphinion in Attica, and Modern Eretria (*hē nun Eretria*), opposite Oropos, which he locates twenty stades from Delphinion. A natural reading would suppose that Old Eretria and Modern Eretria were two distinct geographical locations, with the latter being founded at some point after the Persian invasion. Yet the area in which the sanctuary

of Apollo Daphnephoros is situated was inhabited continuously down to Strabo's own day.[33] Logically, then, this would be Modern Eretria, meaning that Old Eretria and the destroyed "ancient city" should be located elsewhere, thus potentially severing any link between the Daphnephoros site and literary accounts of the Persian sack.[34]

The difficulty with this interpretation, however, is that the area in which the sanctuary of Apollo is located dates back archaeologically at least as far as the ninth century, long before the Persian sack of the city. This might suggest, then, that Old and Modern Eretria are not distinct localities but rather that the former constitutes a particular zone or "neighbourhood" within the latter: in fact, while the verb Strabo uses to indicate the relationship between the two (*epektistai*) is often translated as "is a new foundation," it means more literally "is built on top of." In this case, the apparent confusion in document 3.6 might arise from the fact that Strabo is synthesizing *two* earlier but independent accounts of the geography of the Attic/Euboian coastline—one that referred to the Archaic city of Eretria in connection with Delphinion and one that discussed its Classical successor by reference to Oropos. Indeed, now that the harbour of Delphinion has probably been located at the modern location of Kamaraki, 5 kilometres east of Oropos, Strabo's calculations turn out to be approximately correct.[35]

## Yet Another Temple?

In his publication of the temple of Apollo Daphnephoros, the Swiss excavator Paul Auberson stressed that there was no evidence for fifth- or fourth-century building materials that might indicate that the large stone temple was ever repaired.[36] Yet, in a

coauthored guide to the site, published four years later, reference is made to a small fragment from the upper frame of a window, which is tentatively attributed to a fifth-century temple of Apollo.[37] No argument is offered as to why this fragment

:::     31. Hall 2014: 252.

32. Although Strabo claims he owes his information to Herodotos, Herodotos makes no mention of the Persians "netting" the Eretrians.

33. Bérard 1970; Ducrey 1993, 2004: 49; Reber 1998; Schmid 1999.

34. Boardman (1957: 22–24) suggested that Old Eretria is to be located at Nea Psara; Popham, Sackett, and Themelis (1980: 323–

24) and Walker (2004: 73–87), on the other hand, identify it with Lefkandi. Earlier objections that Lefkandi was abandoned ca. 700 BCE may now need to be qualified in light of ongoing excavations on the Xeropolis hill: see http://lefkandi.classics.ox.ac.uk/.

35. Cosmopoulos 2001: 90–91.

36. Auberson 1968: 10.

37. Auberson and Schefold 1972: 121.

3.4   The temple of Apollo Sosianus at Rome. (Photo by author.)

should belong to the temple of Apollo—or, indeed, a temple at all—and it begs the obvious question: if the temple of Apollo really was rebuilt in the fifth century, where is the rest of it? In 1985, Eugenio La Rocca, professor of classical archaeology at the University of Rome "La Sapienza" and former archaeological superintendent for the city of Rome, offered a surprising answer to this question.

Beneath the western flank of Rome's Campi-doglio (Capitoline) hill, immediately north of the Theatre of Marcellus, stand the three surviving (though re-erected) columns of the temple of Apollo Sosianus (fig. 3.4). The first temple on the site had been dedicated to Apollo Medicus (Apollo the Doctor) by the consul Cnaeus Iulius in 431 BCE, in the wake of a devastating plague that had hit Rome, and had been reconstructed in 179 BCE by the censor Marcus Fulvius Nobilior.[38] It was, however, re-

::: 38. Livy 4.29.7; 40.51.3.

3.5   Statue group from the temple of Apollo Sosianus at Rome, Capitoline Museums. *Left to right*: fallen Greek, mounted Amazon, kneeling Greek, Herakles, Hippolyte, Athena, Nike, Theseus, mounted Amazon. (Photo courtesy of the Cologne Digital Archaeology Laboratory [www.arachne.uni-koeln.de]; negative number Ma11290_0_4.)

dedicated in the late 30s BCE by Caius Sosius, who had originally served in Mark Antony's fleet at Actium but had been one of the few enemy combatants to be pardoned by the victorious Octavian/Augustus—perhaps, as Ronald Syme conjectures, because he had betrayed Antony during the battle.[39] According to Pliny (*Natural History* 13.11; 36.28), the temple had, since that time, commonly been known as that of Apollo Sosianus.

The area around the temple of Apollo Sosianus was cleared shortly before the Second World War. Among the finds recovered were fragments of sculpture in Parian marble, thought to originate from the pediment of the temple, which included

representations of Athena, Herakles, the goddess Nike, the Amazon queen Hippolyte, and a young male who was originally thought to be Apollo but was later identified as Theseus on the basis of his hairstyle and the fact that he was being crowned by Nike (fig. 3.5).[40] The identification of the figures suggests that they formed part of an amazonomachy scene, while a stylistic analysis of the surviving fragments concluded that they dated to around the third quarter of the fifth century BCE and were the product of a Greek—and, more precisely, an Ionicizing—workshop.[41] La Rocca hypothesized that the sculpture was originally commissioned for a fifth-century rebuilding of the temple of Apollo Daphne-

:::     39. Cassius Dio 50.14.1; 51.2.4; Velleius Paterculus 2.86.2. See Syme 1939: 297.

40. La Rocca 1988: 131; Cook 1989a: 522.
41. La Rocca 1985: 59-72.

phoros at Eretria and that the temple was deliberately dismantled block by block and its sculptural adornment transported to Rome.[42] The argument is based on three observations. The first is that the vertical dimensions of the Athena figure from Eretria and that from the Apollo Sosianus temple are practically the same (between 2.1 and 2.2 metres). For La Rocca, the close correlation arises from the fact that any Classical temple to Apollo at Eretria would have respected the foundations and dimensions of its predecessor.[43]

Secondly, there is a marked similarity of theme between the Late Archaic/Early Classical pediment of the Apollo temple at Eretria and that of the Apollo Sosianus temple. There is no strong evidence to suggest that Herakles was represented on the earlier Eretria pediment: in sixth-century vase painting, Herakles' labour to steal the girdle of Hippolyte and Theseus's abduction of Antiope are represented independently of each other, suggesting that the two myths had not yet been conflated.[44] But in Euripides' *Herakleidai* (214–18), probably first performed ca. 430 BCE, Theseus participates in Herakles' venture, and, according to Pausanias (5.11.4), both heroes were represented in the amazonomachy that adorned the throne of Pheidias's chryselephantine statue of Zeus at Olympia, dated to around the same time.[45] La Rocca suggests that the decision to include Herakles in an amazonomachy decorating a fifth-century Eretrian temple might have been intended to lend the portrayal a more panhellenic, less parochial, perspective, but he points out that Theseus is still the most significant figure in the group because it is he, not Herakles, who is being crowned by Nike and that this therefore indicates that the sculpture comes from a temple with very close links to Athens.[46] The suitability of reusing the amazonomachy theme for the Apollo Sosianus temple, on the other hand, might reside in the fact that it could have been read as an allegory for Octavian's victory in 31 BCE over Antony and Cleopatra—a motif that Augustan poets cast in terms of an epic struggle between the civilized west and the decadent east, much as Athenian dramatists had represented the Greek defeat of the Persians five centuries earlier.[47]

Thirdly, La Rocca proposes a transmission route for the cult of Apollo Medicus from Eretria to Rome via Cumae on the Campanian coast. It was not uncommon for Greek foundations in Italy to "import" cults from their mother city, and, according to Dionysios of Halikarnassos (*Roman Antiquities* 7.3.1), Cumae had been founded by the Eretrians. Quite how an Eretrian cult of Apollo at Cumae might have made its way to Rome is less obvious, but we do know that the last king of Rome, Tarquinius Superbus, is said to have consulted the Sibylline Books—thought to be the oracular utterances of Apollo issued through an aged woman named the Sibyl who, in many traditions, is located at Cumae—and that he was commanded to establish the *Ludi Tauri* in precisely the area where the Theatre of Marcellus was later to be built. Furthermore, Livy (4.25.5) tells us that the establishment of cult to Apollo Medicus in the fifth century coincided with the dispatch of an embassy to Cumae to request grain.[48]

If La Rocca is right, an elegant solution presents itself which goes a long way in answering the objections of both Francis and Vickers, on one side, and Boardman, on the other (table 3.2). According to this reconstruction, the temple that the Persians destroyed in 490 BCE would have been the second—perhaps still unfinished—rectangular structure. The pedimental sculpture from the west end

---

::: 42. La Rocca 1985: 76; 1988: 134. There are certainly recorded instances of the Romans' dismantling Greek temples and transporting them elsewhere (see Camp 2001: 189–92), though there is no suggestion that the architectural members of the Apollo Sosianus temple were reused blocks from a fifth-century Greek structure.

43. La Rocca 1985: 76; 1988: 133–34.

44. Herakles' amazonomachy appears in vase painting from the second quarter of the sixth century, while Theseus's rape of Antiope is first represented towards the end of the sixth century. See La Rocca 1985: 49.

45. La Rocca 1985: 49, 53. For the dating of the Zeus statue: Mallwitz and Schiering 1964: 272.

46. La Rocca 1985: 27–32.

47. La Rocca 1988: 137. This interpretation is doubted in Hafner 1992: 20 and Gurval 1995: 116–17 n. 73.

48. La Rocca 1985: 16, 80, 129. For the Sibylline Books, see Frederiksen 1984: 161.

TABLE 3.2    The dates of the Eretria temples according to Boardman, Francis and Vickers, and La Rocca

|  | Temple 1 | Temple 2 | Temple 3 |
|---|---|---|---|
| Boardman | 670/650-ca. 530/520 | Ca. 530/520-490 | X |
| Francis and Vickers | 670/650-490 | 490-198 | X |
| La Rocca | 670/650-ca. 530/520 | Ca. 530/520-490 | Ca. 440-198/187 |

of the temple, which may have fallen as a result of the conflagration, would have been carefully buried while the rest of the building could have been left in ruins as a permanent monument of barbarian impiety. The decision not to rebuild, however, might have been reversed in the 440s BCE—as we shall see in chapter 4, a similar reconstruction has been proposed for Attica. A new amazonomachy composition would have adorned the west pediment while the sculptures of the east pediment may have represented the destruction of Niobe's children by Apollo and Artemis. It would have been this temple that was subsequently plundered by the Romans—its Classical sculpture appearing decidedly "quaint" to Romans more familiar with Hellenistic art. Unfortunately, as satisfying as this solution is, it is not without its difficulties.[49]

We need not spend too much time on the question of whether the Greek sculptures were really displayed on the pediments of the temple of Apollo Sosianus, as opposed to elsewhere in the precinct. Doubts have been expressed on this matter in two respects. Firstly, Greek pediments were of a different shape from Roman ones: the dimensions of the pediment to which the sculptural group at Eretria belonged has been calculated at around 2.1 metres high and 20 metres long, whereas that of the Apollo Sosianus temple was approximately 3 metres by 16 metres, so any group transferred from the former to the latter would have had plenty of headroom

but would have been crowded along its horizontal baseline.[50] Secondly, it is unlikely that any statuary placed in the pediments of the Apollo Sosianus temple would have been visible from ground level, because of the close proximity of the Theatre of Marcellus.[51] Neither objection, however, affects the hypothesis that the sculpture originally adorned a fifth-century temple at Eretria.

More problematic from a methodological point of view is the inherent assumption that the fifth-century sculpture found in association with the temple of Apollo Sosianus must have originated from one of the handful of Greek temples whose remains have survived down to the present day rather than from one of the hundreds of cultic structures that have never been—and may never be—recovered. The Ionicizing style of the sculpture may narrow down the options, and the preeminence accorded Theseus similarly suggests an origin within the orbit of Athenian influence, but that still leaves dozens of possibilities, many of which are now simply unknown. Eretria certainly fell under Athenian domination after Perikles' suppression of the Euboian revolt in 446 BCE (Thucydides 1.114), but the most obvious explanation for why Theseus would be represented in a pedimental group would be that it originally belonged to a temple in Attica, which certainly witnessed a boom in religious building during the 440s and 430s BCE (see pp. 68-72). The case for a rebuilding of Apollo's

49. See generally Cook 1989a.

50. La Rocca 1985: 24; Hafner 1992: 23.

51. Hafner 1992: 20-21, who suggest that the statues were therefore displayed at ground level, either inside or in the immediate vicinity of the temple. That said, the issue of visibility

may not be very significant because the same could be said of the elaborate Ionic frieze inside the *peristasis* of the Parthenon at Athens or the detailed historical reliefs that snake their way up Trajan's column at Rome: see Osborne 1987; Brilliant 1984: 90-94.

temple at Eretria in this period would certainly be strengthened if architectural elements from such a structure could be positively identified—either at Eretria or elsewhere—but, for now, the mere fragment of a window frame hardly provides grounds for much confidence.

Nor are Cumae's Eretrian origins entirely beyond reproach. In fact, Dionysios of Halikarnassos is the only author who attributes the colony's foundation to Eretria; every single other author claims, instead, that Cumae was founded by Chalkis, Eretria's neighbour and bitterest enemy.[52] In short, while it is certainly possible that the Apollo Sosianus sculptures originally decorated a fifth-century temple at Eretria, the evidence is not yet compelling enough for us to assume the existence of a third stone temple that would obviate most of Francis and Vickers's conclusions.

## Unmooring "Fixed Points"

Francis and Vickers's attempt to downdate the pedimental sculpture of the temple of Apollo Daphnephoros at Eretria was part of a more systematic project that sought to lower, by some sixty years or so, many previously accepted "fixed points" in the stylistic chronology of Late Archaic and Early Classical art. It is, therefore, worth examining their argument concerning the treasury of the Siphnians at Delphi—a building that they explicitly compare, in the same article, to the Eretria temple.

The treasury, 8.41 by 6.04 metres, is situated on the southern side of the lower stretch of the Sacred Way. Its attribution to the Cycladic island of Siphnos is virtually guaranteed by its location with regard to Pausanias's description of Delphi and by the use of Siphnian marble for the walls, although the decoration of the entablature was of Naxian marble while the sculpture was carved from Parian marble. The entrance to the treasury was on the western side, via a porch flanked by two caryatids (female figures serving the function of supporting columns [fig. 3.6]). Above the entrance was a pediment depicting the struggle between Apollo and Herakles for the prophetic tripod of Delphi—the composition of the east pediment is unknown—while around the top of the exterior walls ran a frieze portraying the judgement of Paris, the abduction of a woman (probably Helen), the Trojan war, a council of the gods, and a gigantomachy.[53]

Our sole independent evidence for the dating of the building comes from Herodotos (3.57–58), who tells us that the Siphnians had recently dedicated a treasury at Delphi from the proceeds of gold and silver mining on the island when a contingent of Samians arrived on Siphnos seeking support against the Samian tyrant Polykrates. We know from both Herodotos (3.125) and Thucydides (1.13.6) that Polykrates held the tyranny at Samos during the reign of the Persian king Kambyses, who ruled from ca. 529 to 522 BCE. Furthermore, Herodotos (3.57.1) tells us that the Samian dissidents appealed to the Siphnians because they had just been abandoned by the Spartans, whose own expedition against Polykrates took place during Kambyses' invasion of Egypt (3.39.1). Since Kambyses overthrew Psammetichos III, last ruler of the Egyptian Twenty-Sixth Dynasty, in 525 BCE, this provides us with an approximate date for the construction of the Siphnian treasury. That, however, constitutes a problem for Francis and Vickers, because it opens up a gap of roughly half a century between the date of the Siphnian treasury and their revised date for the temple of Apollo at Eretria—two buildings whose sculptural decoration is normally presumed, on stylistic

::: 52. Thucydides 6.4.5; Strabo 5.4.4; Livy 8.22.6; Velleius Paterculus 1.4.1; pseudo-Skymnos 238–39; Statius, *Silvae* 4.4.78; Virgil, *Aeneid* 6.17; Aulus Gellius, *Attic Nights* 10.16.8; Pliny, *Natural History* 3.61; Stephanos of Byzantium, s.v. *Chalkis*.

53. Bommelaer and LaRoche 1991: 124–25. For the symbolism of the iconography of the treasury: Neer 2003.

grounds, to be within a generation at most of one another. It is, therefore, critical to their argument that Herodotos's testimony should be deemed unreliable.

To do this, Francis and Vickers turn instead to the architectural treatise of Vitruvius, writing under the Roman emperor Augustus, who observed that the use of female figures called caryatids in weight-bearing positions commemorated the punishment meted out to the Peloponnesian town of Karyai for having sided with the Persians in 480 BCE. According to Vitruvius, the male population was executed while the married women were led off into slavery, dressed in all their finery, so that they should provide an eternal example of slavery (*On Architecture* 1.1.5).[54] By making the Siphnian treasury a product of the post–Persian War period, Francis and Vickers are able to suggest that the frieze representing the Trojan war can be viewed as a "mythical antetype of the Persian Wars."[55]

This, however, requires them to counter a possible objection. There are three fragments of caryatids discovered by the excavators of Delphi that are generally agreed to be stylistically earlier than the Siphnian examples. Two of these have been tentatively assigned to the treasury of the Knidians, which, according to Francis and Vickers, "is conventionally dated to the 540s, mainly on the historical argument that the Cnidians would have been unable to erect a treasury at Delphi once they had fallen under Persian sway."[56] But by claiming that Pausanias (document 3.7) attributes the dedication of the Knidian treasury either to "some victory" or to "good fortune" (*eudaimonia*), they argue that this fortune was due not to economic prosperity in the sixth century, as is usually supposed, but to their liberation from Persian rule in 479 BCE.[57] Since, stylistically speaking, the Siphnian treasury should be

3.6 Caryatid from the Siphnian treasury, Archaeological Museum, Delphi. (Courtesy of the École Française d'Athènes/Ph. Collet [1986].)

: : :   54. Francis and Vickers 1983: 59–62.
55. Francis and Vickers 1983: 65.
56. Francis and Vickers 1983: 63. The Knidian treasury may have stood on foundations excavated just to the east of the treasury of the Athenians, though the identification is highly conjectural: Bommelaer and Laroche 1991: 141–43.
57. Francis and Vickers 1983: 62–65.

slightly later than the Knidian treasury, then it too would be a construction of the post–Persian War period, and this encourages Francis and Vickers to invert a standard orthodoxy concerning the decoration of the Siphnian treasury. An inscription on the treasury's frieze confirms what stylistic considerations would otherwise indicate—namely, that two different sculptors working in two different stylistic traditions were responsible for the reliefs. Typically, art historians regard the sculptor of the east and north friezes as more innovative and forward looking than the sculptor who took charge of the west and south friezes. For Francis and Vickers, on the other hand, the artist of the north and east friezes was merely reflecting the stylistic conventions of his time (the 470s) while it was his colleague who "retained his archaic style in an age more typically represented by that of his colleague."[58]

Needless to say, this last claim is entirely subjective and depends on the date one wishes to assign to the Siphnian treasury.[59] The argument concerning the Knidian treasury, on the other hand, is fundamentally flawed. For one thing, the dating of the Knidian treasury is not predicated solely on a historical argument that it must have preceded the city's capture by the Persians in the 540s; independent testimony is provided by the Archaic style of the letter forms in the dedicatory inscription of the treasury.[60] For another, Pausanias (document 3.7) does not actually say that the treasury was dedicated *either* to mark a victory *or* to signal good fortune. Rather, he professes absolute ignorance as to the reasons for its construction ("I do not know . . ."), in stark contrast to his professed knowledge that the Athenian and Theban treasuries were financed by the spoils of the battles of Marathon and Leuktra, respectively. Since it is the Siphnian, and not the Knidian, treasury for which a literary source provides a chronological attribution, it is method-

ologically erroneous to date the former on the basis of the latter. It is, in any case, by no means certain that the earlier caryatid fragments recovered at Delphi originated from the Knidian treasury, for which we have no literary descriptions. Everything, then, hangs on the testimony of Vitruvius.

In championing Vitruvius's information over that of Herodotos, Francis and Vickers join a long list of "Herodotos bashers" that stretches all the way back to Cicero (*On the Laws* 1.1.5), who pointed to the countless fairy tales (*fabulae*) in Herodotos's work, and to Plutarch, who devoted a whole section of his *Moralia* (854e–874c) to the prejudiced "malignity" of Herodotos.[61] Normally, the pejorative verdict is based on comparison with Thucydides—long regarded as the first truly "scientific" historian. In recent years, however, that hierarchy of credibility has weakened as scholars have both come to appreciate Thucydides' literary merits, which sometimes obfuscate if they do not compromise the seeming "transparency" of his historical information, and to comprehend better exactly what it is that Herodotos is up to.[62] True enough, few historians would take too literally Herodotos's computations of fighting forces—especially on the Persian side—during the Persian Wars, and there may be some indications that his "eyesight" testimony is sometimes either exaggerated or misremembered, or both, but his chronology—at least from the middle of the sixth century onwards—is not seriously doubted, and, in the cases where independent testimony exists, it is often confirmed. More to the point, it is difficult to see how he could have been so wrong about a building which, according to Francis and Vickers, was only constructed—or, at the very least, completed—during his lifetime at a sanctuary he clearly knew well.[63]

By contrast, Francis and Vickers go to a great deal of trouble to inflate Vitruvius's historical repu-

::: 58. Francis and Vickers 1983: 66.

59. Boardman 1984: 163.

60. Salviat 1977.

61. Other ancient writers who doubted Herodotos's historical reliability include Valerius Pollio, Harpokration, Dionysios of Halikarnassos, and Lucian. See Momigliano 1966a: 127–42.

62. For Herodotos's *Histories* as a "meditation on Hellenicity": Redfield 1985; Hall 2002: 189–94.

63. Boardman 1984: 162.

tation. They note that Vitruvius considers it essential that the architect know history—along with geometry, natural and moral philosophy, music, and physics—so that he can account for the uses of the ornaments that he might design (*On Architecture* 1.1.3–4). They also seek a plausible context in which the Lakonian city of Karyai might have been punished (though it is worth noting that Vitruvius does not specify to which Karyai in the Peloponnese he is referring). This, however, is entirely to miss the point. Vitruvius's account is an *aition*—an explanation as to *why* the name "caryatid" was given to this particular architectural form. In this sense,

the historical explanation is subordinate to the imperatives of etymology. In fact, Vitruvius is demonstrably wrong to suggest that the architectural feature was as much an invention of the fifth century as the name: in the seventh century, Lakonian craftsmen were producing marble *perirrhanteria* (water stands) supported by female figures while, in the sixth, ornate—if naked—female statuettes served as handles for the bronze mirrors which were so popular in Sparta.[64] In short, the evidence of Vitruvius on its own offers little credible reason for rejecting Herodotos's date of ca. 525 BCE for the Siphnian treasury.[65]

## Science to the Rescue?

Faced with a situation in which the conventional archaeological chronology of the Late Archaic and Early Classical periods runs the risk of being discredited on the basis of a single literary source, it is not unreasonable to hope for a resolution of the issue from scientific dating methods such as radiocarbon dating and dendrochronology. The latter, pioneered by the American astronomer Andrew Ellicott Douglass in the early decades of the twentieth century, is based on the principle that trees produce a new ring of wood each year, meaning that by counting the number of tree-rings in a cross-section of the trunk, one can determine the age of a tree. More importantly, annual climatic variations produce a patterning of rings with variable thicknesses that, much like a bar code on a supermarket product, offer a unique profile for a given chronological range. By piecing together samples with overlapping patterns, continuous sequences have been generated for bristlecone pines in the American Southwest stretching back to the seventh millennium BCE and for German oaks back to the eighth millennium. In practice, there are several limita-

tions to the technique for classical archaeologists. Firstly, wood does not typically survive well in the soil conditions of the Mediterranean, meaning that there is a shortage of usable samples. Secondly, timber may be trimmed prior to use in construction, thus removing the outer rings; in this case, timbers dated by reference to tree-rings could erroneously appear to be significantly earlier than the date at which they were felled. Alternatively, timber could be reused, meaning that a structure might be rather later than the dendrochronological dates assigned to its wooden material; this "old wood effect," as it is called, is a complicating factor especially in analyses of charcoal samples.[66]

Radiocarbon dating, pioneered by Willard Libby at the University of Chicago in 1949, operates on the principle that carbon is absorbed by all living organisms until the point of death. A technique known as accelerator mass spectrometry (AMS) counts the surviving atoms of carbon 14 in minute samples of organic materials and compares this to the half-life of the isotope to calculate the number of years BP (before present) from when the object ceased to

:::      64. Boardman 1984: 162.

     65. For a systematic critique of Francis and Vickers's other attempts to redate "fixed points" in the Late Archaic and Early Classical periods, see Cook 1989b.

     66. Bowkett, Hill, Wardle, and Wardle 2001: 123–24; Kuniholm

2001; Fagan 2005: 158; Renfrew and Bahn 2007: 108–11; Greene and More 2010: 164–67. For a cautionary tale in the dendrochonological dating of the Great Tumulus at Gordion, see Snodgrass 2006: 19–22.

exist. Subsequent to Libby's original report on the technique, it became clear that, due to fluctuations in the level of cosmic radiation, the concentration of carbon 14 in the atmosphere has not remained constant over time, and this occasioned a recalibration of the radiocarbon curve whereby radiocarbon dates derived from samples of oak and bristlecone pine were adjusted by reference to the series of their dendrochronological dates. Although subject to a "margin of error," indicated in terms of "standard deviations," the use of tree-ring sequences to "wiggle-match" the radiocarbon calibration curve has resulted in a higher level of resolution than was obtainable even a decade ago.[67]

The two techniques in combination have been employed with important results for the chronology of the Bronze Age and Early Iron Age Aegean.[68] Although a continuous tree-ring sequence, stretching back from living trees, currently extends only as far as the Byzantine period for the Aegean area, a "floating" 1,599-year sequence has been constructed for Anatolia, largely on the basis of juniper and pine tree-ring sequences from the Phrygian site of Gordion, and has been assigned absolute—if approximate—dates on the basis of high-precision radiocarbon measurements.[69] At Assiros, in Macedonia, four charcoal samples taken from Phases 3 and 2 of the Toumba site were cross-dated against this Anatolian sequence and independently dated by means of dendrochronological radiocarbon "wiggle-matching," with results that suggest that the beginning of the Protogeometric ceramic phase in southern Greece should be raised by about one hundred years to ca. 1100 BCE (cf. table 3.1).[70] These results conform broadly to studies, based on radiocarbon

tests, that argue in favour of raising absolute dates across the Mediterranean during the Late Bronze and Early Iron Ages.[71] There is, however, no overall scholarly consensus regarding this so-called High Chronology. A team of archaeologists and scientists from Tel Aviv University has criticized the results that favour the High Chronology on the grounds that the samples were "long-lived" (i.e., possibly subject to reuse) and selected from problematic archaeological contexts at sites that were largely unstratified, as well as being subjected to statistical analysis that they consider flawed. In their view, the results of testing "short-lived" samples from well-stratified sites with easily recognizable diagnostic pottery tend to support the Low Chronology of the southern Levant and the conventional chronology of the Aegean basin, as outlined in table 3.1.[72]

Yet, even if there were consensus about absolute dates in the Early Iron Age Aegean, that would offer little help for the chronology of the Late Archaic and Early Classical periods. This is due to a phenomenon known as the Hallstatt Plateau—a flattening of the radiocarbon calibration curve whereby "[r]adiocarbon dates of around 2450 BP always calibrate to ca. 800–400 BC, no matter the measurement precision."[73] In theory, wiggle-match dating with tree-ring sequences would, to a certain extent, offset this present gap in our measurements, but, at the present time, such sequences remain to be constructed. While there are good grounds for cautious optimism concerning the potential applicability, in the near future, of scientific dating approaches to the mid-first millennium BCE, for now we must remain content with more conventional methods of dating.

:::      67. Bowkett, Hill, Wardle, and Wardle 2001: 122–23; Taylor 2001; Fagan 2005: 180–81; Renfrew and Bahn 2007: 111–18; Pollard 2009: 152–57; Greene and More 2010: 167–76.

68. Recalibrated radiocarbon dates have, for example, suggested that the volcanic eruption on Thera (modern Santorini) occurred towards the end of the seventeenth century BCE—almost a century earlier than the conventional date derived from ceramic chronologies: see Manning et al. 2006.

69. Manning et al. 2001.

70. Newton, Wardle, and Kuniholm 2003.

71. E.g., Nijboer 2005; van der Plicht, Bruins, and Nijboer 2009; Bruins, Nijboer, and van der Plicht 2011. For the absolute chronology of Italy, see pp. 00–00.

72. See, most recently, Fantalkin, Finkelstein, and Piasetzky 2011; for an earlier defence of the conventional Aegean chronology, largely on the basis of its internal rhythm: Coldstream 2003.

73. van der Plicht 2004: 45.

## Conclusion

The question of a third rectilineal temple to Apollo Daphnephoros at Eretria must remain open for discussion. Its postulated existence dispenses with the need to offer special pleading for epigraphic references to a functioning sanctuary in the fourth century while satisfying those who find it difficult to believe that the Eretrians never restored one of their most important temples. In doing so, it also removes at a stroke the principal justification for Francis and Vickers's redating of the second temple. On the other hand, the complete absence of later architectural elements, save for the elusive fragment of the mysterious window frame, is nothing short of astonishing, and it is difficult to imagine how Flamininus—if it was him—could have been so thorough in his depredation of the site. The only purpose behind dismantling a temple block by block is presumably with a view to reconstructing it elsewhere, and for that, there is—up to now—no evidence.

The attempts by Francis and Vickers to downdate the chronology of Greek material culture by approximately half a century are certainly valuable in the sense that they remind us of the fragility of the absolute chronological system we all too often take for granted. Ultimately, however, the project has been pursued by resorting to exactly the same methodological procedures that have traditionally been employed in classical archaeology—namely, by reference to far-from-explicit (and, in this case, even dubious) literary testimony. Although Herodotos, Strabo, and Livy do not explicitly say that the temple of Apollo Daphnephoros was a casualty of the Persian sack of 490, this is a likelihood that, at present, accounts best for the archaeology of the site, thus offering some support for the conventional chronology of the Late Archaic and Early Classical periods.

### DOCUMENTS FOR CHAPTER 3

**3.1**  The attack on the walls [of Eretria] was strong, and over the course of six days many men fell on both sides. On the seventh day, Euphorbos, son of Alkimachos, and Philagros, son of Kyneas, men of high station among the citizens, betrayed [the city] to the Persians. The Persians entered the city and sacked and burned the sanctuaries, exacting vengeance for the sanctuaries that had been burned to the ground in Sardis. Then, in accordance with the orders of Darius, they enslaved the inhabitants. (Herodotos 6.101.2–3)

**3.2**  This [decree] is to be recorded on a stone *stēlē* [and set up in] the sanctuary [of Apollo] Daphne[phoros]. (*IG* XII.9 202, 10–14)

**3.3**  This *proxe*[*neia*] is to be recorded [in front of the temple of] Apol[lo Daphneph]oros. (*IG* XII.9 204, 7–9)

**3.4**  So long as [the Eretrians] entertained the hope of peace, they confronted the duties of war more sluggishly and they stationed armed guards at that part of the wall which had been destroyed while neglecting the other stretches. But Quinctius [Flamininus] launched a nighttime assault with ladders at a place where an attack was least expected and captured the city. A huge throng of townsmen together with their wives and children sought refuge on the acropolis, where they surrendered. There was certainly not much money, be it gold or silver; but statues, paintings in the old style, and ornaments were discovered in greater quantities than expected, given the size of the city and its other resources. (Livy 32.16)

**3.5**  The Persians razed the ancient city [of Eretria], netting—as Herodotos says—the men by virtue of their numbers, the barbarians being spread around the walls. And they still show the ruins today; they call it Old Eretria, while the current city is a new foundation [*or* is built on top of it]. (Strabo 10.1.10)

**3.6** [The coastline] begins at Oropos and the Sacred Harbour, which they call Delphinion, opposite which is Old Eretria on Euboia, the distance across being sixty stades. Oropos is twenty stades after Delphinion, and opposite it is the current city of Eretria, the distance across being forty stades. (Strabo 9.2.6)

**3.7** The treasury of the Thebans [at Delphi] was the consequence of a war, as was that of the Athenians. As for the Knidians, I do not know whether theirs was built to mark some victory or as a display of good fortune, but the Theban treasury was built from the spoils at Leuktra and the Athenian one from those who disembarked with Datis at Marathon. (Pausanias 10.11.5)

# 4

# Eleusis, the Oath of Plataia,
# and the Peace of Kallias

## *The* Archaios Neos *at Eleusis*

One of the most famous cult sites in Greece is the sanctuary of Demeter and Kore at Eleusis, situated on the Saronic coast approximately 22
kilometres northwest of Athens. At some point, Eleusis was incorporated within Attic territory, but the precise date is disputed. Thucydides
(2.15.1–2) implies that this happened with Theseus's unification of Attica
back in the dim and distant past,[1] but Plutarch (*Life of Solon* 8–10) narrates how the early-sixth-century poet and statesman Solon reinitiated
hostilities with the Megarians for the possession of the offshore island of
Salamis,[2] and it is often assumed that Eleusis, on the border of Attica and
the Megarid, was likewise an object of dispute.[3] The most that we can say
is that Eleusis was under Athenian control by the later sixth century—
it formed one of the Kleisthenic "demes"—though it is entirely possible
that its incorporation dates much earlier.[4]

The Eleusinian mysteries in honour of Demeter and Kore were cer-

1. Cf. Plutarch, *Life of Theseus* 10.4.
2. Cf. Solon fr. 1 West.
3. Mylonas 1961: 61; cf. Lavelle 2005: 32. Herodotos (1.30) also talks about hostilities between Athens and the Eleusinians but provides no precise chronological context.
4. Osborne (1994: 152–53; cf.) notes that, already in the eighth century BCE, there are no
marked distinctions in the use of material culture between Athens and Eleusis; cf. Parker
1996: 25; Sourvinou-Inwood 2003: 26. This, however, assumes a direct correlation between
political and cultural boundaries, which is not necessarily the case—especially given the
documented mobility of artisans.

tainly being celebrated at the time of the Persian invasion of Attica in 480 BCE, and many believe that the *Homeric Hymn to Demeter*, thought to have been composed towards the end of the seventh century, already presupposes their institution.[5] The earliest evidence for cult on the site seems to date to the later eighth century, indicated primarily by votives and, perhaps, a small apsidal shrine of the Late Geometric period (ca. 760–700 BCE).[6] It is, however, the sixth century that witnesses the construction of the first of a succession of buildings which lasted through to the suppression of the mysteries by the emperor Theodosius I in 391 CE.[7] The buildings were the consecutive phases of the Telesterion, or "initiation hall," which housed the most important rites of the mysteries and which contained within it an enclosed area known as the "anaktoron," constructed around a natural outcrop of the bedrock (fig. 4.1).

The phases that concern us here are the second, third, and fourth Telesteria. Telesterion II was a square hall, roughly twice the size of its rectangular predecessor, whose marble-tiled roof was supported by twenty-two interior Ionic columns. Access to the hall was from the southeast via three doors, indicated by thresholds still preserved in its foundations, and the building was fronted by a deep portico of ten Doric columns. Much of its superstructure, including cornice blocks, capitals,

and ornamental marble rams' heads, were found in foundation fills throughout the sanctuary or reused in later buildings.[8] Telesterion III is known only from beddings and foundations for its interior columns and from rock-cut steps along its northeastern side. None of its superstructure has survived, leading to the suggestion that its construction was interrupted at an early stage.[9] Telesterion IV, on the other hand, was a much larger structure, 51.6 by 51.2 metres, its roof supported by forty-two columns disposed in two tiers. Entrance to the hall was by six doorways, two on each side except for the northwest (fig. 4.2).[10]

Establishing the chronology of these three phases is not straightforward. It is generally agreed that Telesterion IV dates to the 440s BCE and should, therefore, be part of the so-called Periklean programme of monumentalization.[11] Telesterion II has often been dated to the reign of the tyrant Peisistratos (ca. 546–528) or that of his son Hippias (ca. 528–510), though there have recently been some attempts to shift the date of this building down to the last decade of the sixth century.[12] Herodotos (document 4.1) recounts how, in either 480 or—more probably—479 BCE, the Persians had set fire to the *anaktoron* at Eleusis, and it was long thought that it was Telesterion II that was the casualty of Persian sacrilege.[13] This would then mean that the unfin-

---

5. E.g., Burkert 1985: 285; 1987: 21; Parker 1996: 98. See, however, Clinton (1993), who argues that the cult celebrated in the *Homeric Hymn* is that of the Thesmophoria. For the celebration of the mysteries in 480: Herodotos 8.65.

6. Kourouniotis (1935) and Mylonas (1961: 38–49) believed that walls, dated to Late Helladic II (fifteenth century BCE) and lying beneath the later Telesterion, belonged to a Bronze Age temple, though Darcque (1981) assigned them to a larger residential complex. Cosmopoulos (2003) has argued against too sharp a segregation between cultic and residential uses at such an early date and considers cult activity on the site in Late Helladic II to be certain, although he recognizes that there appears to be no continuity of activity down to the eighth century. For a possible eighth-century temple: Mylonas 1961: 56–59; Evans 2002: 233–34 n. 7.

7. The first phase was originally assigned to the Early Archaic period and tentatively associated with Solon: Mylonas 1961: 64–76. More recently, similarities between the "Lesbian" polygonal masonry employed in its lower courses and the style of the precinct wall of the City Eleusinion on the northern slopes of the Athenian acropolis have been adduced to argue for a date closer to the middle of the sixth century: Miles 1998: 28 n. 12.

8. Mylonas 1961: 78–88; Shear 1982: 131–32.

9. Mylonas 1961: 111–13.

10. Mylonas 1961: 113–29. In the third quarter of the fourth century, an elaborate portico, supported by a high terrace wall, was added to the front of the Telesterion: see Mylonas 1961: 133–35.

11. Plutarch, *Life of Perikles* 12.1. For a discussion of the date on epigraphic grounds: Clinton 1986. Strabo (9.1.12) and Vitruvius (*On Architecture* 7.16) say that Iktinos, the architect of the Parthenon, was also responsible for the Telesterion at Eleusis, though Plutarch (*Life of Perikles* 13.5) credits Koroibos, Metagenes, and Xenokles. For discussion and an attempt to reconcile the evidence: Mylonas 1961: 113–15.

12. Peisistratid Telesterion: Noack 1927: 69; Mylonas 1961: 81–82; Boersma 1970: 24–25; Boardman 1975: 5; Shear 1982: 131; Hurwit 1985: 247; Morgan 1990: 12–13; Camp 2001: 38. In favour of a later dating: Hayashi 1992: 19–29; cf. Shapiro 1989: 68; Childs 1994; Clinton 1994: 162; Miles 1998: 28; Anderson 2003: 187. For a critique of this revisionist dating: Hall 2007: 339–42; 2014: 253–55.

13. Noack 1927: 93; Mylonas 1961: 88–90.

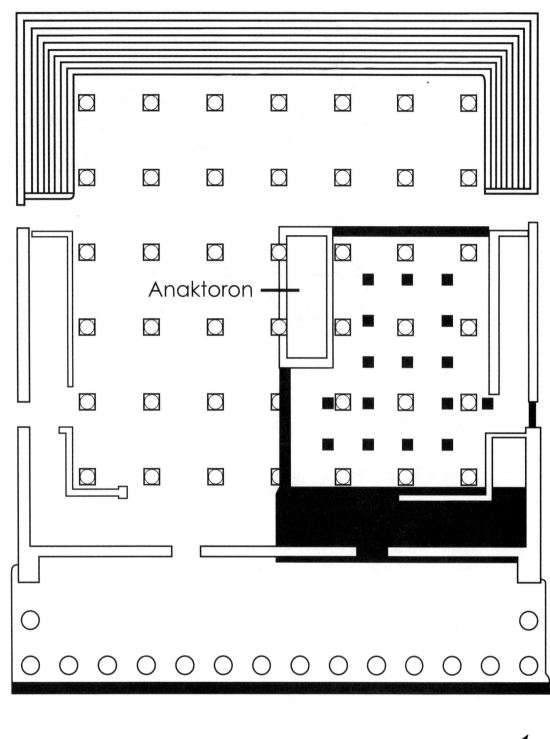

Anaktoron

METERS

4.1 Plan of the second (*in black*) and fourth Telesteria at Eleusis. (After Mylonas 1961: fig. 26.)

4.2    The fifth-century Telesterion at Eleusis from the northwest. (Photo by author.)

ished Telesterion III should be dated to the period between the 470s and 440s, and George Mylonas attributed its construction to the Athenian statesman Kimon, whose ostracism in 461 might therefore account for the building's incomplete state.[14] There is, however, no evidence for Kimon's involvement at Eleusis, and T. Lesley Shear, Jr., has challenged the very idea of a Kimonian Telesterion.[15]

Shear's argument is based on three inscriptions found at Eleusis. The first (document 4.2) is a decree of the Athenian Boule (council) and Demos (assembly), dated to 421/0 BCE, which authorizes the construction of a bridge along the Sacred Way that ran from Athens to Eleusis and specifies that it is to be built from reused blocks which had been "taken down from the Old Temple" (*Archaios Neos*). The second (document 4.3) and third (*IG* I[3] 387) are the inventories recorded by the overseers (*epistatai*) of the sanctuary at Eleusis in the years 408/7 and 407/6, respectively, which refer to material that has also been "taken down from the temple." Combining the information from the inscriptions, we seem to have a situation where material taken down from

an "old" temple has been stored in, or in proximity to, the sanctuary; and since the Telesterion served primarily as the temple of Demeter and Kore, it should be this structure that is intended. More specifically, the mention of "three pairs of doors" and a "portico" can only really refer to Telesterion II, which was fronted by a Doric porch and entered via three doorways. What is surprising, however, is the inclusion in the inventory of wooden epistyles and rafters, because it is scarcely credible that these could have survived the sort of conflagration that Herodotos imagines took place in the sanctuary. Furthermore, analysis of the architectural members of Telesterion II that were reused in later buildings in the sanctuary reveals no signs of the cracking or calcination that would be the natural consequence of fire damage. Shear concludes that Telesterion II must have been deliberately dismantled, perhaps after the fall of the Peisistratid tyranny, and that the building that was set alight by the Persians must have been the still incomplete Telesterion III. The fact that Herodotos specifies that it was the *anaktoron*—the "holy of holies"—that was destroyed

:::    14. Mylonas 1961: 111–13.

15. Shear 1982.

rather than the *neos* more generally might suggest that this was the only part of Telesterion III that was standing above ground level in 480–479.

This solution, compelling as it is, opens up a gap between the destruction of Telesterion III in 479 BCE and the construction of Telesterion IV in the 440s. That might appear problematic,[16] but there is a parallel in the case of the Parthenon. This building was constructed in the 440s and 430s above the foundations of a predecessor, initiated after the Athenian victory at Marathon in 490 but destroyed before completion by the Persians in 480. Some of the column drums of the Pre-Parthenon were incorporated into the northern fortifications of the acropolis shortly after the Persian retreat, but work on the Parthenon would not resume again for a further three decades.[17] The explanation often offered for this hiatus—though not explicitly adduced by Shear for the Telesterion at Eleusis—appeals to the so-called Oath of Plataia.

## The Oath of Plataia

In 331 BCE, the Athenian statesman Lykourgos prosecuted a man named Leokrates on the charge of treason. As part of a rhetorical strategy designed to contrast Leokrates' treacherous activity with the traditional bravery of Athenians, Lykourgos recalls an oath that the Greeks had sworn before the battle of Plataia in 479, including a provision not to rebuild any sanctuaries that the Persians had burnt and destroyed (document 4.4). Diodoros (11.29.2–3), generally thought to be following the account of the fourth-century historian Ephoros, also cites the oath in practically the same words, although he has it sworn not on the battlefield at Plataia but on the isthmus of Corinth some time prior to the battle. He also omits from this oath the clause about tithing the property of Greek cities that went over to the Persians, although he says elsewhere (11.3.3) that this provision had been pledged by the Greeks a year earlier, before the battle of Thermopylai.[18] Isokrates (document 4.5) also refers to an oath not to rebuild sanctuaries destroyed by the Persians but attributes it not to the Greeks at Plataia but to the Ionians of Asia Minor. Finally, a fourth-century inscription from the Attic deme of Acharnai (document 4.6) records the so-called Ephebic Oath—sworn by Athenian youths charged with defending the frontiers of Attica—as well as an oath "which the Athenians swore when they were about to fight against the barbarians." The oath on the Acharnai *stēlē* contains many of the provisions cited by Lykourgos, though the sanctuaries clause is absent.[19]

Does this combined literary and epigraphic testimony offer any guarantees that a genuine oath was sworn immediately before the battle of Plataia, including a provision not to restore the sanctuaries that had been destroyed by the Persians? There are three potential difficulties: (i) the lack of any corroboration from fifth-century sources, especially Herodotos; (ii) the negative appraisal of the testimonia by the fourth-century historian Theopompos of Chios; and (iii) the apparent inconsistencies between the fourth-century accounts of the oath.

According to Herodotos (9.86–88), after the Greeks had buried their dead at Plataia, they held a council at which it was decided to march to Thebes and to demand the surrender of those who had sided with the Persians but to destroy the city if these were not handed over. Plutarch (*Life of Aristeides* 21.1–2) also talks about a general assembly of the Greeks after the battle of Plataia, at which a resolution was passed establishing a festival to be celebrated every four years in honour of Zeus Eleu-

---

:::   16. See Mylonas (1961: 106–7), who doubts that so important a temple could have been left in ruins for three decades or so.

17. Hill 1912; Boersma 1970: 38–39; Hurwit 1999: 132–35, 142.

18. Krentz 2007: 734–35.

19. For a comparison of the Acharnai *stēlē* with other literary testimonia for the oath of Plataia: Siewert 1972.

therios. Diodoros (11.29.1) too mentions the decision to establish the festival of the Eleutheria, but he places the deliberative moment before the battle. Elsewhere (9.10.5), he refers to an oath of the Greeks at Plataia to bequeath "to their children's children hatred against the Persians so long as rivers run into the sea, humanity exists and the earth brings forth fruit."[20] Clearly, these authors are not presenting us with exactly the same information, but all assume that there was some formal meeting of the Greeks—either before or after the battle of Plataia—at which certain decisions were made, and the testimony of Herodotos demonstrates that the tradition of such a meeting does, in fact, go back to the fifth century. Furthermore, Herodotos's account of the siege of Thebes is not inconsistent with the oath, cited by Lykourgos, to "dedicate a tenth of the spoils from all those cities that chose the side of the barbarian."

It is also worth noting another incident that Herodotos (8.140–144) associates with the battle of Plataia. Learning that the Macedonian king Alexander I was attempting to win the Athenians over to the Persian side, the Spartans are supposed to have sent an embassy to dissuade the Athenians from breaking ranks. In their response to Spartan concerns, the Athenians proclaim that they will not betray *to Hellēnikon* (Greekness), which they define in terms of common blood, a common tongue, common cult places and sacrifices, and similar customs (8.144.2).[21] Yet this now-famous definition of Hellenicity is preceded by a more parochial imperative: it would be wrong, the Athenians tell the Spartans, to come to terms with an enemy that has burnt and destroyed our statues and temples (document 4.7). Although the speech itself is almost certainly fictionalized, the fact that Herodotos's Athenians can be so outraged about the destruction of their sanctuaries and that they express this shortly before the battle of Plataia is, at the least, highly suggestive. In the end, of course, we cannot rule out the possibility that additional resolutions were later attached to

this tradition of a panhellenic council in order to offer forged precedents for subsequent decisions, but the fact that different authors focus on different issues that were supposed to have been discussed in such a forum does not, in itself, argue in favour of fourth-century invention.

That, however, is precisely what Theopompos (document 4.8) is sometimes taken to affirm when he says that the oath the Athenians say the Greeks swore before the battle of Plataia was "spurious." The information presented here is preserved in a rather corrupt text known as the *Progymnasmata*, written by the first-century CE rhetorician Aelius Theon of Alexandria, and we simply cannot tell to what extent Theopompos's original words might have been paraphrased. The general gist is clear: Theopompos, apparently exiled from Chios due to his pro-Spartan sympathies and evidently no friend of Athens, is criticizing the Athenians' propagandistic recounting of their own history.[22] Three "historical" events are specifically mentioned. One is the battle of Marathon, whose historicity even Theopompos cannot deny, though he says that it did not happen in quite the way the Athenians describe in their "hymns." The other two are the Oath of Plataia and the Peace of Kallias (see "The Peace of Kallias" below), both of which are dismissed as "spurious." Quite what Theompompos means by the verb *katapseudetai* is unclear. It might simply mean "to be misrepresented," which would put the Oath of Plataia and the Peace of Kallias in the same category as the battle of Marathon—not so much inventions as exaggerations.[23] If the verb *alazoneuetai* in the final clause is interpreted in its primary sense as "to be bragged about" rather than "to be feigned," then this might refer back to the whole passage and thus give credibility to such a translation. But even if *katapseudetai* is translated in its stronger sense as "to be lied about," that could simply mean that certain details recounted in connection with the Oath of Plataia had been invented or embellished, not

:::     20. Raubitschek 1960.
21. For a discussion, see Hall 2002: 189–94.

22. For Theopompos's sympathies: 115 *FGrH* T2.
23. Walsh 1981: 14–15, 44–45.

**TABLE 4.1**   Comparison of sources for the Oath of Plataia

|  | Isokrates | Akharnai Stele | Lykourgos | Diodoros |
|---|---|---|---|---|
| People | Ionians | Athenians | Greeks | Greeks |
| Location | Asia Minor? | Unspecified | Plataia | Isthmus |
| To value freedom over life |  | √ | √ | √ |
| To not abandon |  | *Taxiarkhos* or *enômotarkhês* | Leaders | Leaders |
| To not retreat |  | √ |  |  |
| To bury allies |  | √ | √ | √ |
| To tithe |  | Thebes | Medizing cities |  |
| To not destroy |  | Athens, Sparta, Plataia or allies | Allied cities | Allied cities |
| To not allow allied cities to starve |  | √ |  |  |
| To not allow allied cities to have their water cut off |  | √ |  |  |
| To not restore sanctuaries destroyed by the Persians | √ |  | √ | √ |

that the oath itself was an utter fiction. Ultimately, it would be unwise to invest too much faith in this single, seemingly dissenting voice.

Table 4.1 tabulates the information about the oath that is provided by our principal fourth-century sources. Save for the location where the oath is supposed to have been sworn, the versions presented by Lykourgos and Diodoros are practically the same. The Acharnai *stēlē*, which is dated variously to the second or third quarters of the fourth century, is more detailed though it does not contain the provision concerning the restoration of sanctuaries.[24] By contrast, Isokrates, whose *Panegyrikos* was published around 380 BCE, mentions only the sanctuaries clause but, as already noted, attributes it to the Ionians. Peter Siewert argues that the Acharnai *stēlē* preserves the genuine oath that was taken by the Greeks before Plataia and that it was Diodoros's source, Ephoros, who "contami-

nated" the original oath with a formerly independent imprecation about sanctuaries that was made by the Ionians, as recorded by Ephoros's teacher Isokrates. Lykourgos would then have taken the Ephoran version but situated it at Plataia rather than the Corinthian isthmus.[25] For Siewert, then, the oath itself is historical but the sanctuaries clause is a later corruption.

Hans van Wees is similarly disinclined to see the oath on the Acharnai *stēlē* as a fourth-century forgery but is struck by the fact that it seems to lack the more civic-minded and democratic orientation of the Ephebic Oath, inscribed on the same stone.[26] Furthermore, while the *taxiarchos* is an officer known in the Athenian army, the *enomotarchēs* is unattested outside the Spartan army. The promise to "fight so long as I live" and to "not value living over freedom" conforms closely to the ideology of valour that is often associated with Sparta, especially

24. Robert (1938) and Rhodes and Osborne (2003: 447–48) date the *stēlē* to the third quarter of the fourth century; Daux (1965) and Krentz (2007: 740) prefer a date in the second quarter of the fourth century. See van Wees 2006: 152.

25. Siewert 1972.
26. van Wees 2006.

in the poetry of Tyrtaios. In van Wees's opinion, the Acharnai inscription ultimately derives from Late Archaic oaths that Spartans swore to their military officers—to which, perhaps, the clause concerning obedience to the generals was added at the time of the Persian War, to be sworn by Sparta's allies. By the fourth century, this originally Spartan oath had been "Atticized" for Athenian propaganda purposes, but its Spartan origins are betrayed by the prayer that the city be unravaged and by the absence of the sanctuaries clause (Sparta, unlike Athens, was never sacked by the Persians). The hypothesis is extremely suggestive, though is not without its problems. Firstly, it is legitimate to wonder whether the ideology of self-sacrifice for the *polis* was truly unique to Sparta in the Archaic period or is rather the product of the so-called Spartan Mirage by which later—largely non-Athenian and nondemocratic—authors sought to represent Sparta as especially distinctive from Athens. Secondly, it is not entirely clear why Dion of Acharnai, a priest of Ares and Athena, would have wanted to erect in his home community the copy of an oath that was as distinctively Spartan as van Wees supposes.

Like van Wees, Peter Krentz believes that the original oath recorded on the Acharnai *stēlē* predates, rather than postdates, the Persian War of 480–479 BCE but that it originates in an Athenian, not Spartan, context.[27] In fact, he believes that it transcribes an oath that the Athenians and their allies took eleven years earlier, before the battle of Marathon. Like the Spartans in 479, the Athenians in 490 had not yet experienced the destruction of their city, and it may not be coincidental that the only cities to be mentioned by name on the *stēlē*—Athens, Sparta, and Plataia—are the three states that had agreed to fight at Marathon, even if the Spartans were ultimately delayed.[28] The reference to the *enomotarchēs* would be due to the fact that the Spartans had also been expected to swear the oath,[29] while the promise to bury fallen allies "on the spot" reminds us of Thucydides' comment (2.34.5) that the Athenian war dead were normally interred in the *dēmosion sēma* (public tomb) in the Kerameikos, "save for those at Marathon," who were buried on the battlefield.[30] In Krentz's opinion, when Lykourgos says that the oath of Plataia was an imitation of the "oath that was customary among you [Athenians]," what he has in mind was the oath sworn by the Athenians and their allies before the battle of Marathon, as later recorded on the Acharnai *stēlē*. On the later occasion, the sanctuaries clause could have been added to take account of new contemporary realities, as perhaps suggested by the speech that Herodotos (document 4.7) puts into the mouths of the Athenian envoys.

## The Peace of Kallias

If the Athenians and their allies at Plataia did swear an oath not to rebuild their devastated temples, it is evident that, at some point, they no longer regarded themselves as bound by that promise. As we have seen, the Telesterion at Eleusis was restored, probably in the 440s, and a similar picture emerges in the case of sanctuaries throughout Attica (see "Restoring the Sanctuaries of Attica" below). What may account for this seeming perfidy was an agreement with Persia, known by modern scholars as the Peace of Kallias. Nevertheless, like the Oath of Plataia, the Peace of Kallias is only attested for the first time in fourth-century sources, without any solid corroboration from fifth-century authors—including Thucydides. And, again like the Oath of Plataia, its historicity seems to have been disputed by Theopompos.

The earliest extant notice about a peace treaty between Greece and the Persian Empire is offered, ca. 380 BCE, by Isokrates (document 4.9), who seeks

:::     27. Krentz 2007.
       28. Herodotos 6.106, 120.

29. Cf. Siewert 1972: 58–59.
30. See, however, the discussion in Hornblower 1991: 292–93.

to draw an evaluative distinction between an earlier peace, which kept the Persian navy beyond the city of Phaselis on the coast of southern Asia Minor, and a peace treaty "inscribed now." The latter is the so-called Peace of Antalkidas, or King's Peace, drawn up between the Spartans and the Persian king in 387 BCE, which guaranteed autonomy for the city-states of the Greek mainland at the expense of confirming the king's supremacy over the Greek cities of Asia Minor. In two later speeches (*Areopagitikos* 7; *Panathenaïkos* 59), Isokrates adds that while Persian ships did not sail west of Phaselis, the Persian army did not cross the River Halys, the easternmost boundary of Asia Minor. In 351, Demosthenes (*For the Liberty of the Rhodians* 29) also referred to two peace treaties with the Persian king, which he describes as "familiar" to all his listeners: the one, sponsored by the Athenians, was universally commended, while the other, contracted by the Spartans (the Peace of Antalkidas), was widely condemned. In 343, he attempted to discredit the attempts of his rival Aischines to negotiate peace with Philip II of Macedon by comparing the proposed terms unfavourably with those brokered by Kallias, son of Hipponikos, "who engineered the peace on everybody's lips, whereby the [Persian] king was not to come by foot within a day's horseride of the sea, nor to sail with a warship inside the Chelidonian islands and the Kyanean rocks."[31] It is clear that this Peace of Kallias equates with the "commendable" Athenian peace mentioned in the speech of 351.

Kallias, son of Hipponikos, also features in the most detailed account of the peace treaty with Persia—that of Diodoros, whose source was again almost certainly Ephoros (document 4.10). According to Diodoros, the Persian king Artaxerxes was forced to conclude peace after suffering defeat in Cyprus, ca. 450 BCE, at the hands of an Athenian

coalition commanded by Kimon. Under the terms of the treaty, the Athenians and their allies promised not to invade the king's territory provided that the Greek cities in Asia Minor retained their autonomy and that the king's army stayed more than three days' march from the Aegean sea while his navy remained east of Phaselis and the Kyanean rocks. Lykourgos presents similar information (document 4.11) but with one important difference—namely, that the peace was struck in the aftermath of the Athenian victory over the Persians at the battle of Eurymedon, again under the command of Kimon but rather earlier, in ca. 466.[32] Plutarch (document 4.12) also seems to place the peace brokered by Kallias in the context of the Persian defeat at Eurymedon, but he at least provides us with his source—an archive of copies of treaties that had been collected by Krateros. Since virtually all the details that Plutarch reports from the document he consulted in Krateros's archive match with the information that Demosthenes provides (see table 4.2), it is entirely possible that Demosthenes himself had seen this treaty and that, had he cared to give a date to the peace (which was not an immediate concern to him in the courtroom context in which he mentioned the treaty), he too would have placed it soon after the battle of Eurymedon.[33]

Was the treaty that Demosthenes saw, however, a recent forgery of the fourth century? In fact, it has been argued that the Peace of Kallias was one of a series of documents created shortly after the middle of the fourth century as part of anti-Macedonian propaganda, in which the role of the barbarian aggressor was now taken by Philip II.[34] Apparent support for a late forgery is provided by Theopompos (document 4.8), who, as we have seen, groups the peace together with the Oath of Plataia in the "spurious" category. This time, however, he offers

: : :     31. Demosthenes, *On the Embassy* 273–74. The Chelidonian islands lay off the coast of Phaselis. Wade-Gery (1940: 135–36) and Sealey (1954–55) argue that the Kyanean rocks also lay off the coast of southern Asia Minor, though Oliver (1957) believes, following Aelius Aristides (*Panathenaic Oration* 153), that they were situated near the mouth of the Thracian Bosphorus; cf. Mattingly 1965: 277.

    32. For the date: Badian 1993: 2–10.

    33. Murison 1971: 16, 21–22; Walsh 1981: 35–36.

    34. E.g., Habicht 1961: 25–26—though he does not dispute the reality of the peace itself, which he regards more as a verbal agreement—and Murison 1971. Among others who dispute the historicity of the Peace of Kallias are Sealey 1954–55; Stockton 1959; Mattingly 1965. To this list of supposedly forged documents is often added the so-called Decree of Themistokles, inscribed on a *stēlē* found at Troizen (ML 23). Jameson (1960), who first published the *stēlē*, dates it to the third century; cf. Robertson 1982.

**TABLE 4.2**    Comparison of sources for the Peace of Kallias

|  | Isokrates | Demosthenes | Ephoros | Lykourgos | Plutarch |
|---|---|---|---|---|---|
| Time |  |  | 449/448 | 460s | 460s |
| Autonomy for Greek cities of Asia Minor |  |  | √ | √ |  |
| Land limits | River Halys | 1 day from coast by horse | 3 days from coast |  | 1 day from coast by horse |
| Sea limits | Phaselis | Khelidonian Islands and Kyanean Rocks | Phaselis and Kyanean Rocks | Phaselis and Kyanean Rocks | Khelidonian Islands and Kyanean Rocks |

a reason for his scepticism: the inscription recording the peace, he says, is inscribed not in the Attic but in the Ionic script, which was only officially adopted by Athens at the very end of the fifth century (document 4.13).[35] Furthermore, according to Plutarch (document 4.12), Kallisthenes, the great-nephew of Aristotle and Alexander the Great's "official" historian, also denied the authenticity of the "well-known peace."

These objections may have been unduly exaggerated in modern scholarship. It is possible that what Kallisthenes denied was not the authenticity of the peace itself but rather the precise terms which Plutarch cites, presumably taken from the document in Krateros's collection.[36] As for Theopompos, it is entirely possible that the inscription he saw had been recut after the restoration of the Athenian democracy in 403 BCE or that it had been reinscribed in the Ionic script for dissemination throughout Ionia and the islands.[37] In any case, it is not the fact that the Ionic script is never used in Attic inscriptions prior to the end of the fifth century: in a decree (*IG* I[3] 36) regulating payment for the priestess of Athena Nike and dated to 424/3, Ionic lettering is used from the sixth line onwards.[38]

Interesting in this respect is that, in the citation preserved in Theon's *Progymnasmata*, Theopompos is said to have referred to the peace concluded "with king Darius." Since Darius did not accede to his father's throne until 424 BCE, the appearance of his name here has sometimes been regarded as a textual corruption.[39] But Andokides (*On the Peace with Sparta* 29) refers to a "permanent friendship" with the Great King of Persia which was brokered by his maternal uncle, Epilykos, and suspended after Athenian machinations with a Persian renegade caused the king to switch his support to Sparta. The alliance with Sparta dates to 412, while the Peace of Epilykos was presumably negotiated as soon as possible after Darius became king in 424.[40] Andokides does not specify that Epilykos renewed an earlier peace, brought about by Kallias, though this is what most scholars assume.[41] Since we have firm evidence from the decree concerning the priestess of Athena Nike that the Ionic script was already being employed in 424, it is not impossible that the Peace of Epilykos was also inscribed in Ionic characters and that it was this inscription that Theopompos saw.[42] Harold Mattingly, however, has gone further. Noting that the proposer of the Athena Nike decree was one Kallias, he has suggested that the same man was responsible for proposing the treaty of friend-

35. See, however, Stockton (1959: 62), who argues that this cannot have been the only reason why Theopompos denied the authenticity of the treaty.

36. Murison 1971: 15; Walsh 1981: 46; Bosworth 1990. On the other hand, Eddy (1970: 12) suggests that Kallisthenes willfully disparaged Greek efforts to make peace with the Persians in order to glorify the achievements of his patron, Alexander.

37. Meiggs 1972: 138; Badian 1993: 26.

38. Mattingly 1965 n. 13; cf. Santi Amantini 2005: 41.

39. Connor (1968: 78) defends the reading. For the date: Diodoros 12.71.1.

40. For the alliance with Sparta: Thucydides 8.58.1.

41. E.g., Badian 1993: 40: "We may take it that the 'Peace of Epilycus' was a renewal of the Peace of Callias"; cf. Andrewes 1961: 5.

42. Santi Amantini 2005: 40.

ship with Darius—notwithstanding Andokides' promotion of his uncle's part in the negotiations—and that later writers confused this Kallias with the earlier Kallias, son of Hipponikos.[43] In other words, the so-called Peace of Kallias was, in reality, nothing other than the Peace of Epilykos of 424/3.[44]

Be that as it may, it is difficult to square the hypothesis of a mid-fourth-century forged peace treaty with Isokrates' explicit injunction (document 4.9) to compare—indeed, literally "read side by side"—the Peace of Antalkidas with the earlier peace treaty between the Athenians and the Persians.[45] This strongly implies that the existence of the earlier peace treaty was a matter of common knowledge by 380 BCE, though it need not entail that Isokrates had actually consulted the written document himself or, if he had, that he remembered its details faithfully. In particular, the idea of the River Halys as the western limit for the Persian army's movements strains credulity and is at odds with our other authors, who tell us that the Persians had to stay three days' march—equalling a day's horseride—from the Aegean coast (table 4.2).[46] To be sure, the fact that so many documents purporting to date to the fifth-century Persian War and its aftermath suddenly attract the attention of Athenian orators in the decades immediately after the middle of the fourth century is striking.[47] But just because they found such documents useful for rallying public opinion against the growing power of Macedon does not, in itself, argue against their authenticity. Indeed, if the Peace of Kallias was a forgery of the fourth century, it is hard to believe that there was nobody at Athens who did not know better. And since both Demosthenes and Lykour-

gos referred to it in making their arguments for the prosecution of individuals whose actions were considered to have fallen well short of those of their ancestors, it is unlikely that they would have risked weakening the case for the prosecution by relying on rhetorical "benchmarks" whose authenticity was considered dubious. Similarly, in the *Panegyrikos*, which seems to have been a pamphlet intended for distribution throughout Greece to forge a sense of panhellenism among the warring city-states, it would not have been in Isokrates' interests to assume common knowledge of a treaty that he or his associates had invented.[48]

There remains, of course, the silence of Thucydides, which several commentators have considered decisive.[49] Mention of a peace concluded by Kallias, whether it occurred after the battle of Eurymedon or after Kimon's successes in Cyprus, should have appeared in the so-called *Pentekontaetia*—an account of the almost fifty years that intervened between the Persian and Peloponnesian Wars, during which the growing power of the Athenians eventually forced Sparta to initiate hostilities.[50] The *Pentekontaetia*, it is true, is far from comprehensive and lacks the details that are provided in Thucydides' account of the Peloponnesian War proper.[51] On the other hand, its purpose is—at least in part—to document how the Athenians attained their hegemony by dominating an alliance, the Delian League, that was formed to conduct "warfare against the barbarian," and it is odd that Thucydides should have neglected to mention a peace that technically put an end to those hostilities and removed the raison d'être for the league's existence.[52] That said, Thucydides makes no mention of either

: : :   43. Mattingly 1965.

44. See, however, Murison 1971: 25–26, who notes that we can only assume the historicity of the Peace of Epilykos if we are willing to take Andokides at his word. W. E. Thompson (1981: 167–68) argues that, Andokides excepted, fourth-century authors knew of only one fifth-century peace. There is, however, possibly confirmatory evidence for a peace treaty in 424/3 from an inscription (IG II² 8) which honours a man named Herakleides for his services in concluding a treaty with the Great King: see Wade-Gery 1958: 207–11.

45. Meiggs 1972: 598; W. E. Thompson 1981: 164–65; Badian 1993: 3.

46. Sealey 1954–55: 331; Oliver 1957: 255; W. E. Thompson 1981: 171–72. See, however, Andrewes 1961: 16–18 and Badian 1993: 53 with n. 65.

47. Habicht (1961) counts no fewer than nine such documents.

48. Walsh 1981: 43; W. E. Thompson 1981: 165.

49. E.g., Stockton 1959; Sealey 1976: 281–82.

50. Thucydides 1.89–117.

51. See, most recently, Bresson 2010.

52. Sealey 1976: 281–82.

a peace or reconfirmation of a peace in 424/3 BCE. It has been suggested that it was not until very late that he came to realize the importance of the "Persian factor" in deciding the eventual outcome of the war and that he was intending to revise earlier sections of his work to take account of this when he died.[53]

Herodotos (7.151), on the other hand, makes a passing comment that is of interest to this question. In support of the widespread suspicion that the Argives had come to an agreement with the Persian king Xerxes in 480 BCE, he notes that, "many years later," an Argive embassy was sent to Xerxes' son, Artaxerxes, at Susa to ask if the friendship that they had contracted with Xerxes was still in force. He implies that he knows this information because, at the same time, there were in Susa Athenian ambassadors, engaged "in another matter," among whom was Kallias, son of Hipponikos. Given the costs involved in sending ambassadors to Susa, it is difficult to imagine what Kallias's delegation might have been doing there if it was not for the purpose of negotiations with the Great King.[54] Herodotos provides no further details—which is not so surprising given that this is a "fast forward" to an event that falls well after his central narrative—but, imagined in the oral context in which the *Histories* were originally delivered, the seemingly allusive reference to "another matter" surely presumes familiarity on the part of his Athenian audience with the event to which he refers.[55]

Herodotos provides no date for Kallias's embassy, other than to say that it occurred many years after Xerxes' invasion, but if the Argives had wanted to know whether the treaty of friend- ship that they had brokered with Xerxes was still in effect under his successor, they are likely to have made the journey to Susa as soon as possible after Artaxerxes' accession in 465/4 BCE.[56] This would place Kallias's own embassy in the years immediately following Eurymedon, which is the period to which most of our sources date the Peace of Kallias (table 4.2).[57] Diodoros, however, dates it to 449/8— immediately after Kimon's campaign, and death, in Cyprus—and so too does the late antique chronicler Aristodemos (104 *FGrH* 1, 13.2) who, like Diodoros, is almost certainly following Ephoros. It is possible that Ephoros or Diodoros (or both) simply confused the two ventures: it has, for example, been noticed that the whole account of the Cyprus expedition seems to be "calqued" on that of the Eurymedon campaign.[58] Alternatively, it may be that Ephoros has "corrected" what he deemed to be an error, since he was well aware of continued hostilities between the Athenians and the Persians after the 460s.[59]

There is, however, a third possibility. The Suda (s.v. *Kallias*), a Byzantine encyclopaedia compiled in the tenth century CE but drawing on many documents now lost, says that when Kallias was general, he confirmed with Artaxerxes the boundaries that were prescribed by the peace drawn up at the time of Kimon, and he seems to associate this confirmation of an earlier peace with the Spartan invasion of Eleusis in 447/6 BCE. Furthermore, the Athenian Tribute Lists, which record on stone the one-sixtieth part of the annually assessed tribute that Athens's allies had to dedicate to Athena, appear to list no contributions for the year 449/8. This is sometimes taken to indicate a temporary cessation of tribute assessments in light of a peace that tech-

---

53. Andrewes 1961. Thucydides' *History* breaks off in 411, even though it is clear that he survived the end of the war in 404. Meiggs (1972: 141) is also troubled by Thucydides' silence on this matter but ultimately deems it not to be decisive in gauging the authenticity of the peace; cf. Badian 1993: 27–28.

54. Murison 1971: 27; Walsh 1981: 32, 41–42.

55. That Athenians constituted at least one of the audiences whom Herodotos addressed is clear from 1.98, where the longest wall at Ekbatana is said to be similar in length to the wall that surrounds Athens; from 4.99, where the boundaries of Scythia are

compared to those of Attica; and from 1.192, where a Persian measure of volume is translated into its Attic equivalent.

56. Badian 1993: 3–4.

57. Badian (1993: 11) suggests that peace was made with Xerxes immediately after Eurymedon, and then renewed with Artaxerxes shortly after his succession a couple of years or so later.

58. Gomme 1945: 286, 330; Walsh 1981: 36–37; Badian 1993: 21.

59. Kallisthenes' supposed objections to the Peace of Kallias could be due to a similar reason. See Eddy 1970: 10–11; Murison 1971: 22, 31; Badian 1993: 27.

nically rendered the Athenian alliance against Persia redundant.[60] It could, then, be that an original treaty, engineered by Kallias in the 460s and perhaps not strictly observed, was renewed in the early 440s after the Persian reversals in Cyprus, only to be renewed for a third time in 424/3 BCE by the embassy which is supposed to have included Andokides' uncle, Epilykos.[61] We do not know the precise terms of the earlier peaces, but the third peace, that of Epilykos, might have been recorded—in Ionic letters—on the inscription whose existence is attested by Isokrates and whose authenticity was questioned by Theopompos.

What, however, does all this have to do with the oath not to restore Attic sanctuaries? According to Plutarch (document 4.14), Perikles had proposed a decree in the Athenian assembly to invite representatives from the Greek cities to a congress at Athens where they might discuss rebuilding the sanctuaries destroyed by the Persians, along with making arrangements for common sacrifices and policing the seas. Needless to say, the authenticity of the "Congress Decree," as it is termed in modern scholarship, has also been doubted. This is partly on the basis of some of the provisions that Plutarch's version of it contains—which seem to suit better the context of the "common peaces" of the fourth century—and partly because it is only attested in a late source.[62] On the other hand, unlike the later rhetorical employment of the Oath of Plataia or the Peace of Kallias, which were contrasted favourably with recent fourth-century events, the Congress Decree was ultimately a failure: although invited, none of the cities actually attended, due to Spartan opposition. It is, then, difficult to imagine what purpose a fourth-century forger might have hoped to achieve.[63]

The injunction in the decree to "keep the peace" has often been taken to refer to the Peace of Kallias, while the provision to police the seas seems to presume a treaty that needed to be enforced.[64] The Athenians might also have reasoned that, with a formal cessation of hostilities, they were no longer bound by the terms of their earlier oath not to repair their sanctuaries. Unfortunately, Plutarch does not provide us with a date for the Congress Decree. The fact that it comes immediately before his account of the Battle of Koroneia and that Perikles is clearly in a dominant position within the state at the time of the decree's proposal would suggest a date in the early 440s, though Plutarch's specification that it took place "when the Spartans *began* to be bothered by the increasing power of the Athenians" might indicate a date in the late 460s, immediately before the outbreak of the so-called First Peloponnesian War.[65] Perhaps, here too there is a confusion between an original peace treaty and its renewal, and we cannot rule out the possibility that concerns with restoring desecrated sanctuaries and ensuring the continued maintenance of an Athenian-dominated alliance—which is surely the main purpose behind the decree—were voiced on both occasions. What, if anything, does the archaeology of fifth-century Attic sanctuaries have to contribute to the problem?

---

::: 60. Meritt, Wade-Gery, and McGregor 1939: 133; Wade-Gery 1945. Conversely, Dow (1942; 1943) and Sealey (1954-55) believe that the year in which no tribute was collected was 447/6—perhaps as a result of the Athenian defeat at the battle of Koroneia. Badian (1993: 60) is unconvinced that the missing tribute need have anything to do with renewal of the Peace of Kallias.

61. This is the view of Badian 1993: 2-26.

62. Seager (1969) thinks that it was invented for the purposes of anti-Macedonian propaganda. Bosworth (1971), by contrast, argues that it promotes an agenda in favour of Philip as a panhellenic unifier.

63. Among those who accept the authenticity of the Congress Decree: Accame 1956: 242; Stockton 1959: 71; Meiggs 1972: 512-15; Perlman 1976: 6-12; Walsh 1981: 49-59; MacDonald 1982; Badian 1993: 28-29.

64. See, however, Bosworth (1971), who argues that, notwithstanding the use of the definite article, the clause refers to peace more generally.

65. Walsh 1981: 49-59.

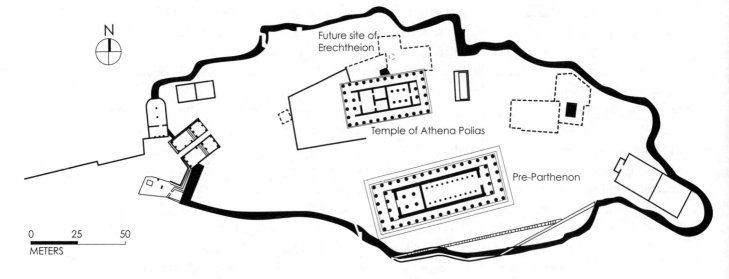

4.3   Plan of the Athenian acropolis ca. 480 BCE. (After Travlos 1971: fig. 71.)

## Restoring the Sanctuaries of Attica

On the Athenian acropolis, by far the most important cultic structure was the temple of Athena Polias, which stood on a set of poros foundations that lie to the north of the Parthenon (fig. 4.3).[66] It is widely agreed that it was one of the casualties of the Persian sack of the acropolis in 480 BCE.[67] Save for the southern "Caryatid" porch of the Erechtheion, initiated perhaps in the late 420s, no later building ever encroached on the foundations of the temple of Athena Polias.[68] It is not, however, certain that the Persians entirely destroyed the temple down to its foundations. A decree (*IG* I³ 207 14–15), dated prior to ca. 420, mandates the construction of a column "on the acropolis, behind the *opisthodomos* [back porch]," and later commentators tell us that the *opisthodomos* was "at the back of the temple of Athena known as Polias," which may mean that the western (back) porch of the temple—and, perhaps, part of the *cella* that housed the cult statue—

survived relatively unscathed.[69] It has often been supposed that the Erechtheion, to the north, was a multipurpose cult site, one of whose functions was to serve as the new temple of Athena Polias.[70] Part of the reasoning for this belief rests on an inscription (*IG* I³ 474), dated to 409/8, which gives an account of building work on the acropolis—including the construction of the Erechtheion—and is signed by the "*epistatai* [overseers] of the *naos* on the acropolis, in which is the ancient statue." But, as Gloria Ferrari has pointed out, the Erechtheion was still in an incomplete state in 409 and so is unlikely to have already housed the ancient cult statue of Athena Polias by this date. Furthermore, a decree (*IG* I³ 32 12–13), proposed by a certain Thespieus shortly after the middle of the fifth century, establishes a board of supervisors at Eleusis "along the lines of those who were supervising the works on the acropolis for the *naos* and the statue."[71]

:::   66. Dörpfeld 1885.

67. Herodotos 8.53. See Dinsmoor 1932: 310; Hurwit 1999: 136.

68. Mattingly (1965: 278) dates the Erechtheion's construction to 427–424 BCE. Hurwit (1999: 206) suggests that it may have been planned in the mid 430s but that construction did not begin until the later 420s and may have continued down to ca. 406; cf. Dinsmoor 1932: 324.

69. Scholiast to Aristophanes, *Wealth* 1193; cf. Scholiast to

Demosthenes 13.14; Harpokration, s.v. *opisthodomos*; Suidas, s.v. *opisthodomos*; Photios, s.v. *opisthodomos*. See Ferrari 2002: 15–16. Hurwit (1999: 143–44; cf. 2004: 76–77), on the other hand, identifies the *opisthodomos* with the western porch of the Parthenon.

70. E.g., Dinsmoor 1932: 310.

71. Ferrari 2002. See, however, Rhodes (2008: 505), who dates the decree to "432 or a little later."

It could be that the ancient image of Athena was housed in a temporary shelter while work on the Erechtheion proceeded,[72] but the hypothesis may be unnecessary. In Ferrari's view, the Archaic temple of Athena Polias, severely damaged but not levelled by the Persian attack, remained unrestored, with its ruins prominently incorporated within the re-design of the Athenian acropolis associated with Perikles.[73] This would certainly explain why there was enough of the "former" (palaios) temple for it to suffer further fire damage in 406 BCE and why Pausanias (1.26.5, 27.1) seems to draw a clear distinction between the "temple [naos] of Polias" and "the building called the Erechtheion."[74] Either way, there is little compelling evidence to support Dörpfeld's belief that the temple of Athena Polias was restored shortly after the Persians retreated from Attica.[75]

Another casualty of the Persian sack was the sanctuary of Athena Nike, perched on a high bastion at the southwest corner of the acropolis. According to the most recent detailed study of the sanctuary, the temple that the Persians destroyed was a small Doric structure of the sixth century. In its second phase, dated to after 479 BCE, the sanctuary had, at most, a simple altar with no temple. A third phase is marked by the construction of an irregularly shaped precinct wall, inside which stood a small poros shrine (naiskos), while to a fourth phase belongs the Ionic amphiprostyle temple of Pentelic marble, begun in the 420s.[76] Study of the masonry and mouldings of the naiskos belonging to the third phase suggests a terminus post quem of ca. 465 and a terminus ante quem of ca. 435, but Ira Mark has attempted to establish a more precise date of around the middle of the fifth century on the basis of a decree (IG I³ 35) that mandates the appointment of a priestess of Athena Nike and commissions a man named Kallikrates to build a new temple and stone altar to the goddess.[77] The decree has generally been dated to the mid-fifth century because it employs

a three-bar sigma—a letter form which was long thought to have become obsolete by ca. 445 BCE, when it was replaced by a four-bar sigma. That orthodoxy has, however, been overturned because of the appearance of the three-bar sigma in a treaty between Athens and the Sicilian city of Egesta (ML 37), which is now usually dated to 418/7.[78] The decree could be associated with the construction of the naiskos, which might therefore be as early as the late 460s, but it could equally well refer to the construction of the amphiprostyle temple of the fourth phase.

Fresh from their victory over the Persians at Marathon in 490 BCE, the Athenians levelled the southern area of the acropolis and began construction of a massive marble structure known as the Older Parthenon or Pre-Parthenon.[79] Work was cut short by the Persian invasion, and construction was not resumed until the Periklean building programme in 447–432. For those who believe in an Oath of Plataia and a Peace of Kallias—or its renewal—in ca. 449, the Parthenon and its predecessor seem to offer welcome corroboration. Ironically, however, the Parthenon may be something of a red herring, since it is by no means clear that it was, in fact, a temple and hence subject to the conditions of any oath not to rebuild sanctuaries. Unlike the priestesshoods of Athena Polias and Athena Nike, which are epigraphically attested, we hear of no priestess—or, indeed, cult—of Athena Parthenos. Nor is there any evidence for an altar in association with the Parthenon, unless sacrifices were offered to Athena Parthenos on the neighbouring altar of Athena Polias.[80]

Much depends on what we think stood on the site of the Parthenon prior to the construction of the post-Marathon building. An inscription (IG I³ 4), normally dated to 485/4 BCE, makes a clear distinction between the neos (presumably the temple of Athena Polias) and a hekatompedos—a term, liter-

---

72. Dinsmoor 1932: 318.
73. For doubts, see Hurwit 2004: 167.
74. For the fire: Xenophon, Hellenika 1.6.1.
75. Dörpfeld 1887.
76. See generally Mark 1993.

77. Mark 1993: 104–5, 115–22.
78. Mattingly 1961; Chambers, Gallucci, and Spanos 1990; cf. Rhodes 2008.
79. See Hurwit 1999: 130–35 with bibliography.
80. Hurwit 1999: 163–64.

ally meaning "100 feet long," that is often applied to temples and was certainly used to describe the principal chamber of the Classical Parthenon. The *hekatompedos* in question might possibly be the Older Parthenon, but, given the little that had been constructed of this by the time of the Persian invasion five years later, it has generally been assumed that the term referred to an older, Archaic construction. Many scholars believe that this was a temple and that two limestone pediments, dating to ca. 560, belonged to it.[81] One represents lions hunting a bull, Herakles wrestling with a sea creature, and a three-headed monster nicknamed Bluebeard on account of the traces of paint discovered on the sculpture. The other depicts another group of lions and a calf, together with at least two large serpents. If a large temple stood on the southern part of the acropolis in the sixth century, then this would obviously strengthen the case for those who see its successors—the Older Parthenon and the Periklean Parthenon—as temples.

Alternatively, it has been suggested that the "Bluebeard" pediments belonged to an earlier temple of Athena Polias and originally stood on the poros foundations identified by Dörpfeld to the north of the Parthenon; in the last quarter of the sixth century, the building would have been dismantled and replaced by a new temple—the one sacked by the Persians.[82] In this case, the *hekatompedos* of *IG* I³ 4 might designate not a temple but a large terrace, conceived to accommodate the numerous sixth-century treasuries whose existence is known from a series of small limestone pediments recovered from the acropolis. Indeed, the decree associates the *hekatompedos* with *oikēmata*—a term often applied to treasuries.[83] If this view is correct, then

continuity of function would argue for the identification of the successive Parthenons as treasuries—a case of the Athenian state usurping the function formerly exercised by the aristocratic families who can be assumed to have dedicated the Archaic treasuries.[84]

The buildings that stood in the Athenian agora in 480 BCE were not spared the Persian onslaught either. A small Archaic shrine in the sanctuary of Zeus Eleutherios seems to have been destroyed at this time, and a new temple was not constructed until the last third of the fifth century.[85] Its neighbour, the temple of Apollo Patröos, was not restored until the late fourth or early third century.[86] Construction on the Hephaisteion, often assigned to the 440s, may have begun as early as ca. 460, but it was, in any case, a new temple, not the restoration of a sacked predecessor.[87] On the northern slopes of the acropolis, foundations were laid for a temple in the City Eleusinion in the decade 500–490. It is unclear how far construction had proceeded by the time of the Persian invasion, but the most recent examination of the site suggests that the temple of Triptolemos was either set or rebuilt on top of the foundations in the second quarter of the fifth century—very possibly the 460s.[88]

Outside Athens in Attica, the picture is less clear. At Brauron, on the east coast, the late-sixth-century temple of Artemis seems to have been destroyed at about the time of the Persian War—Pausanias (3.16.8) says that Xerxes carried off its cult statue to Susa—and was only rebuilt in the 420s BCE.[89] At Sounion, on the southernmost tip of Attica, there are two sanctuaries. In the sanctuary of Athena, a small temple with two prostyle columns was probably built at the end of the sixth century. It is un-

---

: : :    81. E.g., Dinsmoor 1947.

82. This is the view of Plommer 1960 and Preisshofen 1977.

83. Tölle-Kastenbein 1993.

84. Hurwit 1999: 164. For a general discussion: Hurwit 1985: 238–45; 1999: 106–16.

85. Thompson and Wycherley 1972: 96–102; Camp 1990: 77–79; 2010: 75.

86. Lawall 2009; Camp 2010: 70–72—revising the earlier date given in Boersma (1970: 172), Thompson and Wycherley (1972: 136–39), and Camp (1990: 74–77).

87. Dinsmoor 1940: 47; Thompson and Wycherley 1972: 143; Mark 1993: 102 n. 47; Hurwit 1999: 158.

88. Miles 1998: 42–43.

89. Mylonopoulos and Bubenheimer 1996: 12. The dates are based on ceramic evidence and correct the earlier view of Papadimitriou (1959: 19) and Boersma (1970: 175) that the Classical temple dates to the second quarter of the fifth century.

4.4 Temple of Poseidon at Sounion, southern peristyle. The steps of the mid-fifth-century temple overlie the foundations of the unfinished earlier temple. (Photo by author.)

certain whether it suffered any damage during the Persian occupation, but a larger temple, with columns flanking only the east and south sides, was constructed immediately to the south in the decade 460–450. In the sanctuary of Poseidon, work began on a peripteral temple in the 480s, before it was halted by the Persians, and was not resumed until the 440s (fig. 4.4).[90] At Rhamnous, in northeast Attica, the Doric temple of Nemesis is generally agreed to be contemporary with the Poseidon temple at Sounion. It was probably the belated successor to a sixth-century shrine whose existence is attested by Lakonian rooftiles and architectural elements. A small temple, built with polygonal blocks of marble to the south, is dated, without further precision, to the fifth century and may have served as a temporary shelter for the cult statue—a similar scenario is sometimes imagined for the sanctuary of Poseidon at Sounion.[91] Some Attic sanctuaries, however, may never have been restored: Pausanias (10.35.3) says that the sanctuary of Hera on the road to Phaleron and that of Demeter at Phaleron itself were left as half-burnt memorials to Persian sacrilege even down to his own day.

:::      90. Camp 2001: 306–8.

91. Boersma 1970: 51; Camp 2001: 301.

There are only two apparent exceptions to this general trend of not immediately repairing damaged temples, and both derive from literary sources rather than archaeological evidence. According to Plutarch (*Life of Themistokles* 1.3), Themistokles restored and decorated with paintings the Telesterion at Phlya, which belonged to his clan (*genos*), the Lykomidai, and which "had been burnt by the barbarians"; he cites as his source the early-fifth-century poet Simonides. Since Themistokles was exiled in 471 BCE and never returned to Athens, this restoration of a desecrated sanctuary would seem to defy the terms of any oath to leave the ruins as an eternal testament to barbarian impiety.[92] It has been suggested that Themistokles considered the Telesterion to be the seat of a private, family cult and therefore not covered by the terms of an oath

sworn in the name of the Athenian state;[93] if true, such self-exemption could well have been a contributing factor to his banishment. The second case is also reported by Plutarch (*Life of Aristeides* 20.3), this time in connection with not an Attic sanctuary but the sanctuary of Athena at Plataia. This was, according to Plutarch, either built or rebuilt with eighty talents of silver that the Athenians and Spartans donated to the Plataians out of the spoils of the battle.[94] The difference is, of course, critical, but unfortunately there is a discrepancy in the manuscripts between *oikodomein* (to build) and *anoikodomein* (to rebuild). Here, however, there is a variant tradition: according to Pausanias (9.4.1), the temple of Athena at Plataia was financed out of the spoils from Marathon.[95]

## Conclusion

It is ultimately impossible to know whether the Greeks collectively swore an oath before the battle of Plataia not to repair their desecrated sanctuaries: of the thirty-one city-states whose participation in the battle was commemorated on the Serpent Column at Delphi (ML 27), only five had witnessed firsthand the destruction of their temples.[96] It is, however, not unreasonable to suppose that the Athenians had made some such pledge, which they added to a formulaic oath invoked eleven years earlier before the battle of Marathon. The idea was probably not new: as we have seen, Isokrates (document 4.5) claims that the Ionians of Asia Minor had made a similar promise, and Pausanias (7.5.4) says that the temples of Hera on Samos and of Athena in Phokaia had been burnt down by the Persians and

still remained in ruins in his own day.[97] And it is also possible that the Eretrians, who fought together with the Athenians at Plataia, also decided to leave their temples in ruins after the Persians destroyed them in 490 BCE (see chap. 3). Whether or not there is any historicity to Plutarch's account of the Congress Decree, Herodotos (8.144.2) makes it clear that the issue of desecrated temples was a concern to the Athenians in the fifth century and not simply a conceit of fourth-century orators.

As for the Peace of Kallias, there are good reasons for supposing that peace negotiations were conducted with the Persians on three occasions in the fifth century: in the late 460s BCE, after the Greek victory at Eurymedon; ca. 449, in the wake of Kimon's operations on Cyprus; and in 424/3 BCE,

92. Boersma 1970: 50; Siewert 1972: 104.

93. Meiggs 1972: 506; cf. Mark 1993: 101 n. 42.

94. Siewert 1972: 103. It is for this reason, and the Telesterion at Phlya, that Siewert considers the clause about the sanctuaries not to be part of the original oath. Plutarch does not, however, specify how soon after the battle the Plataians set to work on the temple of Athena.

95. Mark 1993: 101 n. 42.

96. Athens, Megara, Eretria, Plataia, and Thespiai: Siewert 1972: 104; cf. Hurwit 2004: 53.

97. This might mean that the Ionian oath attested by Isokrates was not just a literary model that shaped the fourth-century elaboration of the oath, as Siewert (1972: 105) supposes, but documents an actual pledge that was adopted by the Athenians in 479 BCE.

the date of the so-called Peace of Epilykos. Kallias, son of Hipponikos, was very probably associated with the first two treaties, while another Kallias may have been a signatory to the third. We cannot know if these earlier treaties stipulated precisely the terms that we find in fourth-century orators, though it is hard to believe that they invented wholesale the tradition of a fifth-century peace treaty. The rhetorical effect of invoking this treaty would have been severely compromised had there not been some consensus among assembly-goers and jurymen as to the historicity of the peace.[98]

When we turn to the archaeological evidence, there does seem to be a reluctance, in the couple of decades immediately subsequent to the Persian invasion, to restore sanctuaries that were damaged during those hostilities. It is for this reason that many classical archaeologists are generally inclined to believe in the authenticity of the Oath of Plataia.[99] Furthermore, reconstruction of those damaged temples at first sight does seem to cluster around three different phases of activity: the 460s, the 440s and the 420s (table 4.3). The pattern looks satisfyingly neat, but two notes of caution still need to be sounded.

Firstly, absolute chronological precision with regard to dating fifth-century monuments is, for the most part, impossible to achieve. In the absence of inscriptions which offer explicit indications, dating is normally based on pottery found in foundation trenches, but even where the pottery has been studied exhaustively—which is not the case with all the sites under discussion here—ceramics can seldom be dated more precisely than within a decade or two. Stylistic datings of mouldings and architectural features are generally even less precise and, in any case, bear less on the date of initial

**TABLE 4.3**  Dates of reconstruction of sacked Attic temples

460s:
  Temple of Athena at Sounion
  Telesterion III at Eleusis?
  Temple of Athena Nike (phase 3)?
  "Polygonal" Temple at Rhamnous?

440s:
  Telesterion IV at Eleusis
  Temple of Poseidon at Sounion
  Temple of Nemesis at Rhamnous
  Parthenon?

420s:
  Temple of Athena Nike (phase 4)
  Temple of Artemis at Brauron
  Temple of Zeus Eleutherios?

execution. This means that, once allowance is made for a "margin of error," the distinctions between the chronological clusters tabulated in table 4.3 could be somewhat illusory. Secondly, the attempt to use the archaeology of Attic sanctuaries to confirm the Oath of Plataia is predicated on the rather naive assumption that the Greeks never broke their oaths. That they did, and did so frequently, is documented by a host of examples, including the case of the allies who revolted from the Athenian alliance despite having sworn everlasting allegiance,[100] not to mention the incessant need to reconfirm earlier treaties. It is entirely likely that the dejected Athenians in 479 BCE uttered imprecations and promises in good faith and that protracted peace negotiations with the Great King offered them some opportunity to renege on their promises but the constant recourse to solemn oaths sworn in the presence of the gods only serves ultimately to underscore how hollow those promises were.

: : :    98. For similar arguments about the political uses of myth, see Hall 2007.

99. E.g., Boersma 1970: 51; Miles 1998: 42; Camp 2001: 72–73; Hurwit 1999: 141–42; 2004: 94;

100. Plutarch, *Life of Aristeides* 25.1.

**4.1**   When the Persians were routed by the Spartans at Plataia, they fled in disorder to their camp and to the wooden fortification they had constructed in the region of Thebes. It is a marvel to me that although they were fighting beside the grove of Demeter, not one Persian either entered the precinct or died inside it; rather, the majority fell around it on unsanctified ground. If one should speculate about divine matters, I think that the goddess did not receive them because they had set fire to her holy *anaktoron* at Eleusis. (Herodotos 9.65)

**4.2**   The[a]ios made the motion: To bridge the Rhetos on the side toward the city, using stone blocks from those at Eleusis that have been taken down from the Old Temple and which they left when they used them in the wall. (*IG* I³ 79, lines 4–9)

**4.3**   Taken down from the temple: 1750 pairs of roof tiles, 54 column drums; 16 column bases, 21 wooden epistyles (one glued together from two), 18 rafters taken down from the portico, 3 pairs of doors, 10 posts (?). (*IG* I³ 386, lines 103–10)

**4.4**   All the Greeks at Plataia gave this pledge when they were about to line up and fight against Xerxes' empire; they did not invent it for the purpose but imitated the oath that was customary among you [Athenians]. It is worth hearing it, for although the deeds that were done on that occasion took place long ago, it is nevertheless sufficient to see the courage of those men in the words they wrote. Read it out for me: "I will not value living over freedom, nor will I abandon our leaders, whether living or dead, but I will bury all of our allies who die in the battle. And once we have defeated the barbarians in war, I will destroy none of the cities that fought on behalf of Greece but I will dedicate a tenth of the spoils from all those cities that chose the side of the barbarian. And I will rebuild not a single one of the sanctuaries that were burnt and destroyed by the barbarians but will allow them to remain as a memorial for the generations to come of the im-

piety of the barbarian." (Lykourgos, *Against Leokrates* 80–81)

**4.5**   For this reason, the Ionians also deserve to be praised, because after their sanctuaries were burnt, they called down curses on anybody who might disturb [the ruins] or wish to restore them to their ancient condition, not because they lacked the resources to repair them but rather so that they should be a memorial for the generations to come of the impiety of the barbarians. (Isokrates, *Panegyrikos* 156)

**4.6**   The oath which the Athenians swore when they were about to fight against the barbarians: "I shall fight so long as I live, and I will not value living over freedom, and I will not abandon the *taxiarchos* or the *enomotarchēs*, whether living or dead, and I shall not retreat unless the leaders lead the way and I will do whatever the generals order, and shall bury on the spot those of the allies who have died and will leave nobody unburied. And having been victorious fighting against the barbarians, I shall tithe the city of Thebes and shall not destroy either Athens or Sparta or Plataia or any other of the allied cities. And I shall not overlook those who are oppressed by hunger or cut them off from running water, whether they be friends or enemies. And if I stay true to what has been written in this oath, may my city be free from disease, but if I do not, may it be disease ridden; and may my city be unravaged, but if not, ravaged; and may my land bear fruit, but if not, may it be barren; and may women bear children like their parents, but if not, monsters." (*GHI* 88)

**4.7**   There are many important reasons that would prevent us from doing this even if we wanted to. First and foremost there are the statues and temples of the gods which have been sacked and destroyed; it is necessary for us to avenge these with all our might rather than come to an agreement with the man who did it. (Herodotos 8.144.2)

**4.8**   The Greek oath, which the Athenians say the Greeks swore before the battle against the barbarians at Plataia, is spurious (*katapseudetai*), as is the treaty of the Athenians with king <Darius?>; furthermore, the battle of Marathon did not take place in the way that everybody hymns it, and how many other things that the city of the Athenians says are feigned [or bragged about] (*alazoneuetai*) and mislead (*parakrouetai*) the Greeks? (Theopompos 115 *FGrH* 153)

**4.9**   Although they [the barbarians] used to ply the seas with 1,200 ships, we brought them down to such a state of humility that they did not launch a warship beyond Phaselis but kept quiet and waited for a more auspicious time rather than trusting in the force that was then available to them. And that these things were on account of the virtue of our ancestors is clearly shown by the fortunes of our city. For just as we were deprived of our empire, so it was the beginning of misfortunes for the Greeks. When, after the misfortune on the Hellespont, others became our leaders, the barbarians scored a naval victory, ruled over the sea, subdued most of the islands, crossed over to Lakonia, took Kythera by force and sailed round the whole Peloponnese, inflicting damage. And one may best gauge the magnitude of this reversal if one reads side by side the treaty that was made when we were dominant and that inscribed now. (Isokrates, *Panegyrikos* 118–20)

**4.10**   But when King Artaxerxes learned of the defeat at Cyprus, he conferred with his friends about the war and deemed it advantageous to conclude a peace treaty with the Greeks, and so he wrote to the leaders in Cyprus and to the satraps concerning the terms on which they could conclude a treaty with the Greeks. For this reason, the advisors of Artabazos and Megabyzos sent ambassadors to Athens to discuss a resolution. And since the Athenians agreed, they also sent plenipotentiary ambassadors under Kallias, the son of Hipponikos, and so a peace treaty came about between the Athenians and their allies and the Persians, of which the principal terms were these: "that all the Greek cities in Asia Minor are to be self-governing; that the Persian satraps are not to come nearer to the sea than a three-day journey, and that no Persian ship is to sail inside Phaselis and the Kyanean rocks; that, if the Persian king and his generals observe this, the Athenians are not to march into the territory over which the king rules." (Diodoros 12.4.4–6)

**4.11**   They [our ancestors] ravaged Phoenicia and Cilicia, triumphed by land and sea at Eurymedon, took one hundred triremes of the barbarians captive and sailed around the whole of Asia Minor devastating it. And to crown their victory, not content with having erected the trophy at Salamis, they fixed for the barbarians the boundaries necessary for the freedom of Greece, preventing them from going beyond them, and they drew up a treaty that they should not sail in a ship inside the Kyanean Rocks and Phaselis, while the Greeks should be free—not only those in Europe, but also those who were living in Asia Minor. (Lykourgos, *Against Leokrates* 72–73)

**4.12**   This deed so humiliated the plans of the king that he concluded that well-known peace, by which he was to stay a horse's course away from the Hellenic sea and was not to sail with a warship inside the Kyanean Rocks and Chelidonian islands. Kallisthenes, however, denies (does not say) that the barbarians concluded these terms, but says that in fact, the king did this through fear of that defeat and stayed far away from Greece, so that Perikles with fifty ships and Ephialtes with thirty sailed beyond the Chelidonian islands and ran into no barbarian fleet. But in the decrees which Krateros collected, copies of the treaties as if they took place have been put in order. And they say that the Athenians built the altar of peace on this account and paid special honours to Kallias, who had served as ambassador. (Plutarch, *Life of Kimon* 13.4–6 = Kallisthenes 124 *FGrH* 16 = Krateros 342 *FGrH* 13)

**4.13**   And the peace agreement with the barbarians has been falsified, because it is inscribed not in Attic, but Ionic, letters. (Theopompos 115 *FGrH* 154)

**4.14**  When the Spartans began to be bothered by the increasing power of the Athenians, Perikles, so as to encourage the people to think yet more ambitiously and to deem it worthy of great things, proposed a decree to summon all the Greeks, wherever they lived in Europe or in Asia Minor, whether in a large or small city, to send representatives to a congress in Athens. This was so that they might deliberate about the Greek sanctuaries which the barbarians had burned and the sacrifices which were owed by the vows they had made on behalf of Greece when they were fighting the barbarians, and also about the sea, so that all might sail without fear and keep the peace. . . . But nothing was done, nor did the cities send representatives, owing—it is said— to the opposition of the Spartans, since the attempt was rejected first in the Peloponnese. (Plutarch, *Life of Perikles* 17.1–3)

# 5

# Sokrates in the Athenian Agora

Apart, perhaps, from Perikles, there are few figures from Athenian history as famous as Sokrates. While the personality that emerges from Plato's dialogues is undoubtedly fictionalized to some degree, Sokrates' historicity is assured not only because of his appearance in dialogues written by other authors but also because he was evidently a target of lampoons on the Athenian stage.[1] In the version that Plato gives of Sokrates' defence, in 399 BCE, on a capital charge of impiety and corrupting the Athenian youth, the philosopher complains that the harder accusations to counter are those that have been circulating for decades, "and the thing that is strangest of all is that it is impossible for me to know or speak all the names [of my accusers], unless one of them happens to be a comic poet" (*Apology* 18c–d). The "comic poet" is Aristophanes and Sokrates is here alluding to the *Clouds*, first produced in 423 BCE, which portrayed the philosopher as the headmaster of a "thinking workshop" (*phrontistērion*), established to teach students to make "the weaker argument the stronger" (*Apology* 18b).[2]

Much as with the "great man" approach to history, the actions of an

::: 1. Cf. Plato, Apology 19b–d. In addition to Plato, Xenophon collects Sokratic dialogues in the *Symposium* and the *Memorabilia*, while fragments also survive of Sokratic dialogues written by Aischines (not the orator). Comic poets known to have satirized Sokrates on stage include Eupolis, Ameipsias, Kallias, and Mnesilochos. For a "biography" of Sokrates, see Diogenes Laërtios 2.18–20.

2. For the portrayal of Sokrates in *Clouds*, see Konstan 2011.

individual typically capture the popular imagination more than those of an anonymous social collectivity. In 1978, the American School of Classical Studies in Athens devoted one of its Excavations of the Athenian Agora Picturebook volumes to the physical landscape in which the historical Sokrates lived and breathed. As the volume's author, Mabel L. Lang, put it: "Instead of putting Socrates in the context of 5th-century B.C. philosophy, politics, ethics or rhetoric, we shall look to find him in the material world and physical surroundings of his favorite stamping-ground, the Athenian Agora. . . . Since Socrates was most truly at home in Athens' agora, it should be possible to follow his career in the remains there and rebuild in ideal form the surroundings in which he practiced what he preached."[3] The booklet then proceeds to trace Sokrates' peregrinations: to the Stoa Basileios, where the *Euthyphro* is set; the Stoa of Zeus Eleutherios, scene of the probably spurious *Eryxias* and *Theages*; the shop of a leatherworker named Simon; the marbleworkers' quarters and the law courts; and finally, the state prison where he was forced to end his life by drinking hemlock. Similarly, in a recent popular treatment of the historical Sokrates, Bettany Hughes seeks "[t]o follow the clues in Plato, Xenophon and Aristophanes to the physical reality of fifth-century Athens and therefore the physical reality of the story of Socrates' life."[4] But how securely identified are these locations and how legitimate is it to expect physical structures to reflect the movements of a man who was already legendary in his own lifetime—let alone in the subsequent tradition from which much of our literary evidence is drawn? To answer these questions, we will consider just two examples: the House of Simon and the State Prison.

## The House of Simon

Not much is known about Diogenes Laërtios, other than that he wrote a compilation of the lives and doctrines of ancient philosophers, probably in the first half of the third century CE. Diogenes notes that Sokrates used to visit the workshop of a shoemaker (literally, "leather cutter") named Simon, who took notes of his conversations and eventually published a collection of them (document 5.1). After listing the titles of these dialogues, Diogenes goes on to state (2.123) that once, when Perikles had asked Simon for his support, the latter declined because he did not want to surrender his freedom of speech (*parrhēsia*). Plutarch also refers to Simon the shoemaker and again links him to Perikles (document 5.2).[5] Conversely, while Xenophon (document 5.3) notes that Sokrates used to frequent a saddler's shop near the agora, neither he nor Plato refers to Simon by name. It is primarily for this reason that more philosophically minded scholars have generally doubted the historical existence of Simon. Ulrich von Wilamowitz Moellendorff even suggested that he was the literary invention of another Sokratic philosopher, Phaidon of Elis.[6] Some of those doubts were, however, dispelled with excavations undertaken in the Athenian agora in 1953.[7]

Adjacent to, but just outside, the southwest boundary stone to the agora are the remains of a house, which occupies a terraced triangular area between two streets (fig. 5.1). The earliest walls are associated with a courtyard, in which a well was dug ca. 500 BCE. A deposit of dissolved mud brick seems to indicate an act of destruction that left the house unroofed—perhaps as a result of the Persian invasion of 480–479 BCE—while debris was thrown

:::     3. Lang 1978: 2, 4.
        4. Hughes 2010: xxv.
        5. Other references are similarly late: e.g., the early-fifth-century CE Neoplatonist Synesios (*Dion* 14); the fifth-century CE philosopher Ammonios (*Interpretation of the Books of Aristotle* 205); the tenth-century CE *Souda* (s.vv. *Sokrates*; *Phaidon*); and the

*Letters of the Sokratics* (9.4; 11; 12; 13; 18.2), of unknown date and authorship. See Hock 1976: 41.
        6. Wilamowitz-Moellendorff 1879: 187. Similarly sceptical: Zeller 1868: 210; Kahn 1996: 10 n. 18. See generally Sellars 2003: 207 with further bibliography.
        7. First published in Thompson 1954: 54–55.

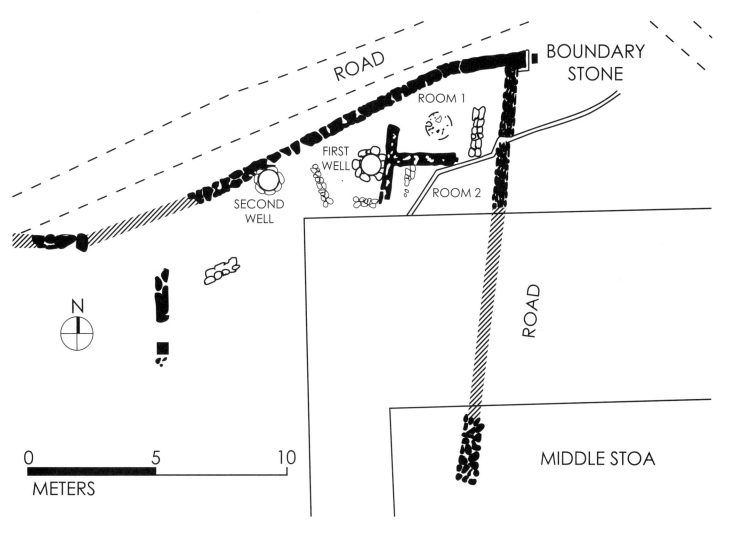

5.1   Plan of the House of Simon. (After Thompson 1960: 236.)

into the now-abandoned well; potsherds inscribed with the names of, among others, Aristeides and Themistokles are almost certainly ballots for one or several ostracisms and suggest that the house was abandoned for less than a decade. The new or former owners dug a new well and rebuilt the property with limestone polygonal blocks, extending some 13 metres to the west and roughly 15 metres to the south, and surrounding a courtyard, 5 by 6 metres. A posthole, on the north side of the courtyard, probably supported a lean-to roof, typical of domestic workshops. The floors, which consist of rolled yellow clay, were renewed no fewer than five times over the course of the fifth and early fourth centuries, down to the construction of a large stone drain in the adjoining street, which raised the level and increased the width of the street, necessitating the demolition of the house. Eventually, the western end of the Middle Stoa, which was built in the first half of the second century BCE, encroached on the site.[8]

It is the three floors that date to the fifth century that have yielded evidence thought to be crucial for identifying the function of the house. In

:::     8. Thompson 1960: 235–37; Thompson and Wycherley 1972: 173–74; Camp 2010: 53–54.

5.2 Base of a black-glaze *kylix* inscribed with the name Simon, Agora Museum, Athens. (Photo courtesy of the American School of Classical Studies: Agora Excavations.)

amongst broken pottery and lamps and coins were found quantities of short iron nails with large round heads; parallels—especially from the Roman period—would suggest that these were hobnails for boots or sturdy sandals. In addition, in the first two floors as well as outside the house, the nails were accompanied by bone rings, which have been interpreted as eyelets for lace-up boots. For this reason, the excavators believed that they had unearthed a shoemaker's residence and workshop, but an even more astounding find was made just outside the house, in a layer of gravel that is dated by pottery to the third quarter of the fifth century BCE (fig. 5.2). On the base of a black-glaze *kylix*, or two-handled cup, was inscribed the name SIMONOS (of Simon). In the words of Homer S. Thompson and Richard Wycherley: "It is hardly rash to assume that the cup belonged to the cobbler and that he was the philosophical cobbler Simon with whom Sokrates is said to have spent much time, and who recorded

their conversation in dialogues."[9] In a similar vein, Simon Hornblower notes that, although Simon "is never mentioned by Plato or Xenophon . . . his existence has now been confirmed by the discovery of a black-glazed cup on which is scratched ΣΙΜΩΝΟΣ ('Simon's'), together with hobnails and bone rings for laced boots, on a site just outside the *agora* . . .— evidently Simon's cobbler shop."[10] Much as with the Workshop of Pheidias at Olympia, a structure whose tentative identification—based, in part, on Pausanias—was seemingly confirmed by the discovery of a cup inscribed "I am of Pheidias," the retrieval of Simon's cup is almost "too good to be true."[11] While to cast doubt on the identification of the House of Simon might seem like a futile exercise in hypercriticism, it may nevertheless be instructive to examine in more detail the assumptions at work here. There are three issues: first, the belief that the house is the workshop of a shoemaker; second, the relationship between the occupant of the

: : :     9. Thompson and Wycherley 1972: 174; cf. Thompson 1960: 237–38.
    10. Hornblower, in *OCD*[3] (1996): 1409; cited in Sellars 2003: 208 n. 8. See also Brumbaugh 1991; Hughes 2010: 22–23.

    11. Mallwitz and Schiering 1964; Heilmeyer 1981: 447–48. See Snodgrass 1987: 24–27.

house and the Simon named on the cup; and, third, the identification of the owner of the cup with the Simon of the Sokratic tradition.

As appealing as the evidence of the short iron nails and bone rings is, one wonders to what extent their interpretation as hobnails and eyelets has been fashioned by contemporary understandings of shoemaking practices. Dorothy Burr Thompson states that nail-studded sandals have been found "in various places," but the only example that she illustrates dates to the Roman period.[12] She further hypothesizes that Simon's nails "were used in boots of the type called *crepides*," though a recent study of *crepides* describes them as "sandals with a complicated network of leather straps, sometimes covering the toes and sometimes leaving the toes exposed."[13] Whether or not they had hobnails in their soles, they do not seem to have required eyelets (for which, in any case, no parallels are adduced). Thompson also discusses representations of shoemaking on three Attic vases, but on none of these is the cobbler depicted as employing a hammer, let alone hobnails.[14] Indeed, on the most detailed example, a red-figure *kylix* now in the British Museum, the shoemaker works at a bench, surrounded by tools such as knives and saws, and appears to be cutting leather— a reminder that the Greek word we usually translate as "cobbler" or "shoemaker" has the more general meaning of somebody who cuts leather (*skutotomos*). If we are prepared to concede that shoemakers might also manufacture other leather products, then Xenophon's testimony (document 5.3) about Euthydemos's visits to a saddler's shop (*hēniopoieion*) could be brought into the discussion, but no evidence has been published from the so-called House of Simon of other accoutrements associated with the working of leather. That said, save in the direst of emergencies, it is unlikely that an artisan would have voluntarily abandoned the tools of his trade, so their absence need not be decisive.

While it is not unreasonable to assume that the cup bearing Simon's name was thrown out of the house and into the adjacent street, it is impossible to maintain with complete confidence that the cup has any connection with the building. The cup was found among pottery dated to the third quarter of the fifth century but that does not tell us when the name was scratched onto the base of the *kylix*. In fact, the spelling of Simon's name—with an omega representing the first "o"—might suggest a somewhat later date. While the Ionic alphabet distinguishes between long and short "o" grades (omega and omicron, respectively), the Attic alphabet generally renders both with omicron until the official adoption of the Ionic script towards the end of the fifth century. This is not to say that omega does not occasionally appear before this date on public inscriptions, but it is comparatively rare until the last decade of the fifth century: a case in point would be an inscription (*IG* I³ 84) regarding the sanctuary of Kodros, Neleus, and Basile, dated to 418/7 BCE, on which omega does appear but is vastly outnumbered by occurrences of omicron for long "o" grades. Orthographic conventions for private graffiti did not necessarily track exactly changes in public inscriptions. In fact, there are indications that the adoption of omega occurred a little earlier:[15] thus, while Kimon's name is spelled with an omicron on five *ostraka* from the Athenian agora that date to the mid-fifth century, six *ostraka* cast for Kleophon, son of Kleippides, in 417–415 BCE spell his name with an omega.[16] Still, it is not really until the last quarter of the fifth century that the Ionic script was regularly employed for private purposes.[17] The graffito could, of course, be earlier if it were written by a person accustomed to writing in the Ionic script, and, indeed, artisans were not infrequently "metics," or resident aliens, but such a supposition would directly contradict Diogenes Laërtios's explicit testimony (document 5.1) that Simon was an Athenian citizen.

12. Thompson 1960: 240.
13. Goldman 2001: 114.
14. Thompson 1960: 239–40.
15. Sickinger 2009: 79.

16. Lang 1990: 89 nos. 592–97 (Kimon), 90–91 nos. 600–605 (Kleophon).
17. Threatte 1980: 33.

Simon is not an uncommon name in Attica. No fewer than seventy-one attestations are known, including four resident aliens; of these, seven belong to the fifth century.[18] What, then, are the chances that the Simon whose name is scratched on the base of the cup is the Simon of the Sokratic tradition? As already noted, the earliest reference to the Sokratic Simon by name appears in Plutarch. There is no mention of him in either Plato or Xenophon, although Xenophon does refer to Sokrates' visits to a saddler's shop (document 5.3), while Aristotle's references (*On Interpretation* 20b 35–36; 21a 14–15) to a "leatherworker" (*skuteus*) are sometimes taken to be an oblique reference to Simon.[19] Thompson attempts to resolve the problem surrounding the silence of Sokrates' younger contemporaries by hypothesizing that Simon died around 420–415 BCE, when both Plato and Xenophon were children, and was thus unknown to them.[20] This, however, does not really explain how Plato and Xenophon could have been unaware of a tradition which was supposedly perpetuated down to the time of Plutarch—

and beyond—and in which Simon was a central character.

Indeed, "the traditional figure of Simon has been shaped less by historical reminiscence than by the philosophical issues and debates in which he played a not unimportant role, particularly in their Cynic form."[21] Promoted by the Cynics as the true heir of Sokrates for his exemplary self-sufficiency (*autarkeia*) and freedom of speech (*parrhēsia*), Simon became a central figure in debates as to whether the philosopher should associate with rulers—hence, the juxtaposition in Plutarch (document 5.2) of Simon with Perikles.[22] Whether or not the anonymous owner of Xenophon's saddle shop was really the prototype for the Sokratic Simon of the later Cynic tradition, it is clear that historical memory was largely irrelevant to the Cynics' purposes. In short, while it certainly remains possible that the workshop excavated just outside the agora is that of Sokrates' interlocutor Simon, the case is not as solid as is sometimes claimed.

## The State Prison

In the 1930s and late 1940s, the American School of Classical Studies excavated an industrial quarter southwest of the agora, including a large structure that was initially labelled the Poros Building on account of the fact that the footings for the walls included large white poros blocks (fig. 5.3). To judge from the presence of wells, the area was probably used for private housing from the Protogeometric period down to the early fifth century.[23] Located at the corner of what are conventionally called Piraeus Street and the Street of the Marble Workers, the Poros Building comprises three elements (fig. 5.4). The first, fronting Piraeus Street, is constituted by a corridor, running roughly north-south, off which

open five square rooms to the west and three to the east. It is assumed that the walls would have been of mud brick and the rooms—though not the corridor—were roofed. In the northwest corner of the room closest to Piraeus Street was a terracotta basin and, more to the centre, a *pithos* set into the clay floor. The second element, at the southern end of the corridor, is a large rectangular courtyard, which seems to have been unroofed. In the southwest corner of the courtyard was part of a light rubble construction, coated with red stucco made from marble dust, though it is unclear whether it is an altar, a bench, or simply a platform. Finally, at the northeastern corner of the building, and on a different

:::     18. *LGPN* 2: 398–99; Osborne and Byrne 1996.

19. Goulet 1997: 122–23; cited in Sellars 2003: 207 n. 3.

20. Thompson 1960: 239–40.

21. Hock 1976: 43.

22. Hock, 1976: 43–48; cf. Sellars 2003: 210–15.

23. The most detailed account of the excavations is to be found in Crosby 1951.

5.3    Aerial view of the Poros Building in the Athenian agora. (Photo courtesy of the American School of Classical Studies: Agora Excavations.)

orientation from it, is what is known as the Annex, tentatively subdivided into four rooms. It was not clear to the excavators whether the Annex was an integral part of the building.[24]

The building was dated largely on the basis of pottery. Ceramics found in the fill used to level the area of the courtyard date to the first half of the fifth century and include five *ostraka*—three bearing the name of Kimon and one each with the names of Themistokles and the elder Alcibiades. The rooms off the corridor and the Annex appear to be contemporary, and it is suggested that the Poros Building was constructed around the middle of the fifth century BCE. Evidence from the southern two rooms of the western wing, however, shows that a new floor was put down towards the end of the fifth century, and this also seems to be the approximate date at which a drain was laid along the length of the corridor. Masses of roof tiles found on the fifth-century floor indicate considerable damage to the walls and

roof of the Poros Building—but not the Annex—at the end of the fifth century, while, subsequent to this destructive event, a hard floor of marble dust and chips was deposited over the entire building, with a second marble-dust layer, including traces of emory, attested in the northern rooms and the Annex, probably in the course of the early fourth century. By the end of the first century BCE, the area had been overbuilt by private houses. There was then constant rebuilding during the Roman and Byzantine periods, followed by considerable robbing of the masonry in the tenth and eleventh centuries CE—thus accounting for the poor state of preservation of the Poros Building today.

Margaret Crosby, who first published the building, speculated on its function. Ruling out an apartment complex (*synoikia*) on account of its strategic location and the absence—at least in the fifth century—of an adequate water supply, she suggested that its size and location suggested a public build-

:::    24. Crosby 1951: 170: "Nowhere has any direct connection between the two been established. It is therefore uncertain whether the Annex was part of the main building or a separate structure."

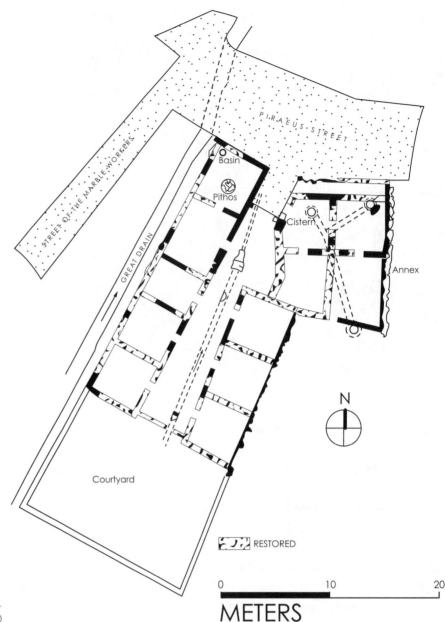

Basin

Pithos

Cistern

Annex

STREET OF THE MARBLE-WORKERS

PIRAEUS STREET

GREAT DRAIN

Courtyard

N

RESTORED

0            10            20

METERS

5.4   Plan of the Poros Building.
(After Camp 1990: 186, fig. 126.)

ing. There had been a conjecture that it might be a *dikastērion*, or law court,[25] but Crosby pointed out that the courtyard was not large enough to accommodate the five hundred jurors that are attested for some cases and could find no plausible explanation for the small rooms. Ultimately, she concluded that the building might originally have served as a civic office such as the *synedrion* or *archeion*, though, fol-

lowing its destruction towards the end of the fifth century, it had been occupied by marbleworkers.[26] Almost twenty-five years passed until, at a conference honouring Rodney S. Young, the archaeologist who oversaw the excavation of the industrial area, Eugene Vanderpool made the startling suggestion that the Poros Building was nothing other than the *desmōtērion*, or state prison, where Sokrates had

:::     25. Thompson 1948: 168.

26. Crosby 1951: 183–87; Thompson and Wycherley 1972: 74.

been executed in 399 BCE.[27] Vanderpool's reidentification was based on the location and layout of the building, as well as on what was found inside.

In terms of location, Plato (document 5.4) says that the prison in which Sokrates was held was "near" the law court. Elsewhere, in the *Laws* (908a), he talks of the existence of three prisons: one, for the majority of criminals, near the agora; one, named the *Sophronistērion*, near the place of assembly; and one in a deserted and wild spot in the middle of the countryside. Vanderpool pointed out that the Poros Building was situated about 100 metres southwest of the agora and that the closest public building to it is a large square enclosure that had tentatively been identified as the *Heliaia*—one of the principal law courts of Athens (fig. 5.5). Furthermore, he drew attention to a passage in Plutarch (*Phokion* 37), which describes how a mounted procession in honour of Zeus passed the doors of the prison just as the Athenian statesman and general Phokion was being executed in 318 BCE. This suggested that the prison was situated on a major thoroughfare such as Piraeus Street.

As for the layout of the Poros Building, Vanderpool proposed to identify the rooms opening off the corridor as cells—their surface area of roughly 20 square metres being sufficient in his mind to accommodate the some twenty to twenty-five people who are described as being present at any one time during the last day of Sokrates' life.[28] The northernmost room of the western wing, it will be remembered, was equipped with a terracotta basin and a sunken *pithos*, which, according to Vanderpool, served as bathing facilities: Plato (*Phaidon* 116b) recounts

how Sokrates "went to some room to bathe himself." The Annex, on the other hand, may have served as a guard tower, because its walls were thicker than those in the rest of the building, suggesting a two-storey structure. As for the courtyard, it could have served the purpose of confining larger numbers of prisoners, such as the forty malefactors who Andokides (1.48) says were incarcerated for having profaned the Eleusinian Mysteries in 415 BCE.

A cistern had been dug into the floor of the northwest room of the Annex, probably in the third quarter of the fourth century;[29] in it were found thirteen small vessels, each about 4 centimetres tall (fig. 5.6). Noting that they are "of a sort usually described as medicine pots," Vanderpool speculated that each was designed to contain a single dose of hemlock.[30] Finally, in the same room, among Late Hellenistic debris, there came to light part of a marble statuette of a bearded man with his cloak thrown back over one shoulder (fig. 5.7). On the basis of a similar statuette in the British Museum, Vanderpool identified the figure as Sokrates. Diogenes Laiërtios (2.43) tells us that the Athenians eventually repented of their action against Sokrates and erected a bronze statue of him at the Pompeion, and Vanderpool suggested that "[p]erhaps one of the prison officials thought it appropriate to have a small replica of the statue in the place where Socrates was executed."[31] He concluded his contribution by stating that the Poros Building "may be considered with some assurance to be the State Prison of ancient Athens,"[32] and the identification has since been enthusiastically adopted by several scholars.[33] Let us examine the proposition in a little more detail.

:::

27. Vanderpool 1980.

28. For the number of attendees, see Hunter 1997: 298.

29. The cistern seems to have been abandoned in the third century: Crosby 1951: 182.

30. Vanderpool (1980: 20) compares them to four small late-fifth- or early-fourth-century pots, found in the agora, which bear some resemblance to labelled medicine pots of the Hellenistic period; see Sparkes and Talcott 1970: 230, 376, and plate 96, nos. 2000–2004.

31. Vanderpool 1980: 21.

32. Vanderpool 1980: 21.

33. E.g., Wycherley 1978: 46–47, Hughes 2010: 344, 349 and, more cautiously, Allen 1997: 131 n. 35; 2000: 395 n. 112. In the 4th edition of the guide to the Athenian agora (Camp 1990: 185), the Poros Building is simply designated the State Prison: "a building . . . which has been identified with some probability as the public prison of Athens." In the 5th edition, however (Camp 2010: 176), a question mark has been added to the designation: "Many features of the building are appropriate to a commercial/industrial complex, though its identification as the state prison (*desmōtērion*) has also been proposed."

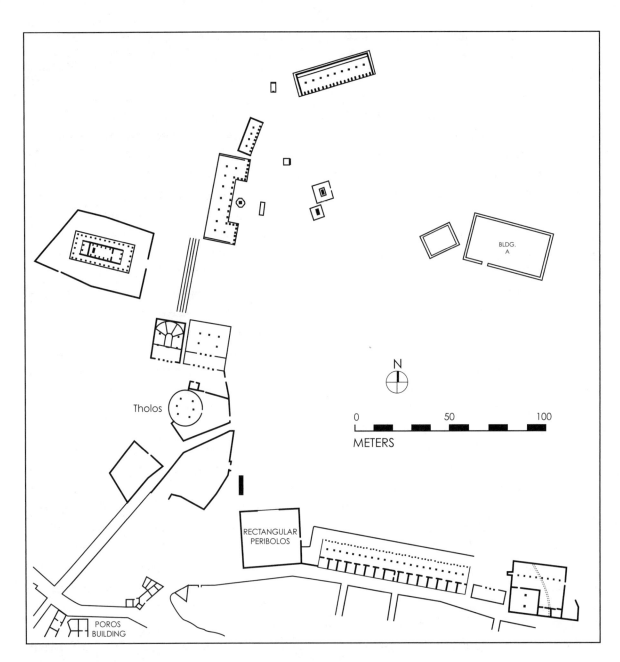

5.5  Plan of the Athenian agora at the end of the fifth century, with the locations of the Poros Building, the Rectangular Peribolos, the Tholos and Building A. (After Camp 1990: 25, fig. 4.)

## Sokrates on Death Row

Although there are several scattered references to a prison in Athens, none offers explicit geographical indications.[34] Plato's notice (*Laws* 908a) of a prison situated "near the agora" is of dubious historical

34. E.g., Antiphon, *On the Murder of Herodes* 17–18; Demosthenes, *Against Androtion* 34, 56, 68. See Wycherley 1957: 149–50; Hunter 1997: 297. Hesychios (s.v. *Thēseion*) says that the "prison among the Athenians" was known as the Theseion and suggests that the prison was in the Theseion district, which he places north of the agora. It is not, however, certain that "Theseion" denotes a district as opposed to being a "nickname" for the prison. See Koumanoudis 1984: 74–75.

5.6  "Medicine bottles" from the Poros Building, Agora Museum, Athens. (Photo courtesy of the American School of Classical Studies: Agora Excavations.)

value because the *Laws* prescribes arrangements in the ideal state of Magnesia. Even if the suggestion is put into the mouth of the Athenian stranger, it is difficult to gauge the extent to which actual Athenian topography of the late fifth century serves as a model for a philosophical reflection written roughly half a century after Sokrates' death.[35] In any case, simply describing the prison as being "near" the agora hardly offers the precision necessary to determine whether the Poros Building is a viable candidate. Of potentially more use is the comment Phaidon makes (document 5.4) that the prison was near the law court (*dikastērion*) in which Sokrates was condemned—especially since Demosthenes provides similar information (document 5.5). If we could only identify the law court in question,

we would be in a better situation to assess Vanderpool's reidentification of the Poros Building as the state prison. Unfortunately, the search for Sokrates' law court is as chimerical as that for the prison.

For law courts in the later fifth century, our most important testimony is Aristophanes' *Wasps*, performed in 422 BCE. In describing their daily activities, the chorus of waspish jurymen recounts how some of them attend the Archon's Court, others the Court of the Eleven, and others the Odeion Court (1108–10);[36] elsewhere in the play, we hear also of the New Court and the Court at Lykos (120, 389). We cannot necessarily assume that these were the only courts operating in the 420s: aside from courts for homicide, of which the most famous was the Areopagos, we know the names of several other courts

::: 35. Though see Lysias, *On the Property of Aristophanes* 55, where the speaker notes that, while he lives near the agora, he has never attended the law court or the *bouleutērion* (council chamber). Wycherley (1957: 148) assumes from this that the law court must have been situated close to—or even in—the agora. Xenophon's account (*Hellenika* 2.3.56) of Theramenes' execution also implies that the prison was situated near the agora.

36. Jacoby (1954b: 151) argues, on the basis of Photios (s.v.

*Odeion*), that only two courts are mentioned in this passage: the Odeion, presided over by the Archon, and the Parabuston, presided over by the Eleven; cf. Boegehold 1995: 6. However, MacDowell (1971: 274) has demonstrated convincingly that Aristophanes' text, as it stands, cannot support such a conclusion and that—in Aristophanes' day, at least—the Archon's Court and the Odeion must have been separate law courts.

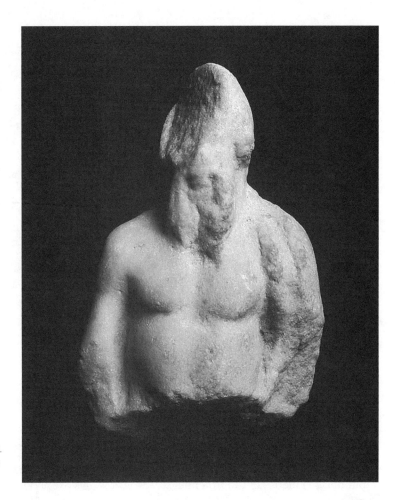

5.7 Statuette of a man, possibly Sokrates, Agora Museum, Athens. (Photo courtesy of the American School of Classical Studies: Agora Excavations.)

in the period prior to the middle of the fourth century, though some of these may be alternative names for the same court or names for different judicial bodies that sat in the same building.[37] For example, the New Court might be a court that held another official name but was simply "new" at the time when *Wasps* was performed,[38] while it is widely accepted that the Court of the Eleven was the same court named by later sources as the Parabuston.[39] Other courts attested before the end of the fourth century are the Heliaia—perhaps identical with the

"Heliaia of the Thesmothetai" as well as with the Metiocheion; the Greater Court; the Painted Stoa; the Kallion; and the Triangular Court.[40]

We are not told in which court Sokrates was tried and condemned. Athenian juries, which were drawn from an annually elected pool of 6,000 "heliasts," for which every citizen over the age of thirty was eligible, ranged in size from 201 up to as many as 2,501.[41] The fact that Sokrates observes that, but for a mere 30 votes, he would have been acquitted seems to imply a jury panel of 501, where 221

: : :    37. Wycherley 1957: 147.

38. Jacoby 1954b: 151.

39. MacDowell 1971: 274, based on Harpokration, s.v. *Parabuston*, and Pollux 8.121.

40. Heliaia of the Thesmothetai: *IG* I³ 1453,B.6–7 (?449 BCE); Andokides, *On the Mysteries* 28; Antiphon, *On the Choral Dancer* 21. Metiocheion: *Rhetorical Lexicon* 310.29–30; Photios, s.v. *Metichos*. Greater Court: Pollux 8.121 (citing Lysias). Painted Stoa: *IG* II²

1641.28–30 (ca. 330 BCE). Kallion: Androtion 324 *FGrH* 59. Triangular Court: Harpokration, s.v. *Trigōnon* (citing Lykourgos). See generally Jacoby 1954a: 164–67; 1954b: 146–53; MacDowell 1971: 273–75. Boegehold (1995: 6–7) suggests that the Parabuston was later known as the Triangular Court.

41. Hansen 1991: 187. On one occasion, the full panel of 6,000 sat in session (Andokides, *On the Mysteries* 17), but this seems to have been rare.

would have voted for, and 280 against, acquittal.[42] Two candidates have often been proposed for Sokrates' law court. The first is the Heliaia.[43] In the sixth century, the Heliaia seems to have been primarily a court of appeal and its name designated the constituents of the jury rather than the building in which cases were heard. By the fifth century, however, it had become a court of the first instance, and, by the fourth, the name of a structure identified with its judging body, which often numbered more than 1,000 jurors.[44] The second is the Parabuston. Pausanias (1.28.8) says that the Parabuston was located "in an obscure part of the city" for "insignificant cases," but that may have been true only in his day (the mid-second century CE), since an inscription (*IG* II² 1646), dating to the second half of the fourth century, has sometimes been taken to indicate a tally of 443 votes to acquit, suggesting a jury of at least 501.[45]

In the absence of clear literary indications for the location of any of these courts, attention has focused on archaeological evidence. The author of the Aristotelian *Constitution of the Athenians* (65–68) describes much of the equipment used in the law courts of his own day—ballots to vote for condemnation or acquittal; tokens, to prove the identity of the jurors; and water clocks to impose strict time limitations on the prosecution and defence speeches—and examples of these have been identified in the excavations of the Athenian agora. A particular concentration of such "dikastic" equipment came to light beneath the northern part of the Stoa of Attalos, constructed in the mid-second century BCE.[46] In the decades either side of 300 BCE,

a large square peristyle building was constructed, though its southern colonnade was never fully completed before being dismantled (fig. 5.8). Its sheer size, covering 3,429 square metres, together with the associated finds argues strongly for its identification as a law court. Indeed, in its configuration it bears striking similarities to literary descriptions of a "court complex," although it postdates these accounts by a few decades.[47] However, the fourth-century sources may be referring to an earlier, less "organic" complex of courts, since beneath the Square Peristyle (as it is termed) were discovered four smaller buildings (Buildings A–D), constructed between the late fifth and late fourth century, and clustered around a courtyard.[48] In the debris of Building C were found fragments of two Lakonian tiles—one bearing the painted letters PA, the other the letters ΤΟΠ. If these can be correctly reconstructed as [πα]ρά[βυστον] and τὸ π[αράβυστον], respectively, then we may have some secure evidence for the location of the Parabuston Court in the northeastern quadrant of the agora.[49] Building A, a rectangular enclosure to which a peristyle was later added, has in turn been tentatively identified as the Heliaia.[50]

There is, however, another candidate that has sometimes been put forward as the Heliaia. On the south side of the agora, immediately to the east of the Southwest Fountain House, are the remains of a rectangular enclosure, 31 by 26.5 metres, commonly designated the Rectangular Peribolos (fig. 5.5). Pottery from the foundations and stylistic features of the cornice molding indicate an initial construction date in the second half of the sixth century, with ex-

:::     42. Plato, *Apology* 35e.

43. Lang 1978: 23 fig. 22.

44. [Aristotle], *Constitution of the Athenians* 68.1; Scholiast to Demosthenes, *Against Timokrates* 21; *Etymologicum Magnum*, s.v. *Heliaia*; Harpokration, s.v. *Heliaia*; Photios, s.v. *Heliaia*; Pollux 8.123. See Wycherley 1957: 145; Boegehold 1995: 3–4.

45. Boegehold 1995: 8, though see the more cautious assessment in Boegehold and Crosby 1995: 182 no. 159. The inscription is very fragmentary, making a straightforward reading problematic.

46. Thompson and Wycherley 1972: 56. On p. 61, the authors note a second concentration just south of the Tholos but admit that this equipment may have been used in the nearby *bouleutērion*, rather than a law court.

47. [Aristotle], *Constitution of the Athenians* 63–69; Demosthenes, *Against Phainippos* 11; Deinarchos, *Against Aristogeiton* 14. See Townsend 1995a: 50–106; 1995b: 108–13. The term used for "court complex" is *dikastēria* (in the plural).

48. Townsend 1995a: 24–49; 1995b: 104–8. A fifth building (Building E) seems to have been an "intermediary" building, constructed while Buildings A–D were being dismantled.

49. Townsend 1995a: 47; 1995b: 112–13. See also Boegehold and Crosby 1995: 179.

50. Boegehold 1995: 12.

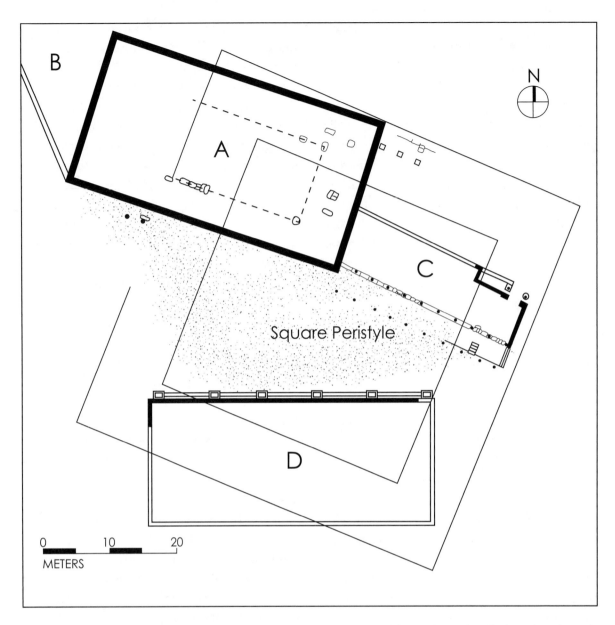

5.8 Structures beneath the northern end of the Stoa of Attalos in the Athenian agora. (After the drawing by J. Travlos in the archives of the American School of Classical Studies at Athens, accession number 82–283.)

tensive rebuilding in the early decades of the fifth century—perhaps as a result of the Persian invasion of 480–479 BCE. The approach to the enclosure was from the north, by a flight of five steps. The discovery of one of the blocks of the superstructure in situ reveals that the foundations of irregular chunks of limestone supported large squared blocks of hard grey limestone and that the walls were capped by a double cornice, although, since no parts of the cornice were found in their original position, it is impossible to know how high the walls were. Since there are no indications in this first phase for internal walls or supports and no trace of roof tiles, it is assumed that the building was unroofed. In the third quarter of the fourth century, the west wall was extensively rebuilt and a series of rooms was inserted along the west side of the enclosure, while a peristyle court was constructed inside at a later date—perhaps the middle of the second century BCE.[51]

The suggestion that the Rectangular Peribolos was the Heliaia was first made by Homer Thompson in 1954.[52] The enclosure was clearly public in nature and could provide capacity for the large juries that are attested as sitting in the Heliaia. Furthermore, an ancient etymological explanation for the name of the court—from *hēlios*, the word for sun—might suggest that the court was unroofed.[53] Alan Boegehold, who tentatively suggests that Building A in the northeast agora should be identified as the Heliaia, nevertheless believes that the Rectangular Peribolos was a law court—perhaps the Metiocheion.[54] The proximity of the Rectangular Peribolos to the Poros Building is, of course, one of the arguments that Vanderpool adduced for the identification of the latter as the state prison. It should, however, be pointed out that no trace of dikastic equipment was discovered within the enclosure.[55] Although a mechanical water clock was installed at the northwest corner of the building, it seems to date to the third quarter of the fourth century and may not, in any case, have been visible from within the enclosure.[56]

Ronald Stroud has proposed an entirely different identification of the Rectangular Peribolos.[57] An inscription, built into a repair wall of the Great Drain and discovered by John Camp in 1986, carries a law regulating a grain tax, which was proposed by a certain Agyrrhios in 374/3 BCE. Among the provisions is the requirement for a tax in kind to be conveyed from the Peiraieus to Athens and to be stored in the Aiakeion (document 5.6). Herodotos (document 5.7) describes how the Athenians established a precinct to Aiakos, an Aiginetan hero, in order to secure an advantage in their war against the island of Aigina and implicitly dates the episode to the period between the reforms of Kleisthenes in 508 BCE and the outbreak of the Ionian revolt in 499 BCE. Although he notes that it still stood in the agora in his own day, a more precise location is indicated by another inscription (document 5.8), dated to 414 BCE, which records property confiscated by those found guilty of profaning the Eleusinian Mysteries and mutilating the statues of the god Hermes throughout the city.[58] Among the confiscated property was land belonging to a certain Diodoros in the deme district of Kollytos, bordering the agora on one side and what is probably the Aiakeion on the other.[59] This seemed to confirm earlier suggestions that the deme of Kollytos was located immediately to the southwest of the agora[60] and is further corroborated by a lexicon of the second century CE, preserved on a papyrus fragment (*POxy* 2087), which mentions the Aiakeion in association with the Tholos, which lies about 50 metres northwest of the Rectangular Peribolos.[61]

The dating of the first phase of the Rectangular Peribolos is not inconsistent with the late-sixth-century date that Herodotos assigns to the Aiakeion. Although we have no descriptions of the sanctuary, Herodotos's use of the term *temenos* nearly always indicates an open precinct and Pausanias's description (2.29.6) of the Aiakeion on Aigina—where the hero was believed to be buried—as a quadrangular precinct (*peribolos*) made of white stone bears some similarities to the Rectangular Peribolos; indeed, the preliminary reports of the excavation of

::: 51. Thompson and Wycherley 1972: 63–65; Camp 1995.

52. Thompson 1954: 38; see also Wycherley 1957: 145; Thompson and Wycherley 1972: 63.

53. Scholiast to Aristophanes, *Wasps* 772b, e. The etymology could, however, be false. Several commentators note that an alternative explanation would derive the word from the verb *hali[a]zesthai* (to gather together): e.g., Bekker, *Anecdota Graeca* 1.310.28–311.2; Scholiast to Demosthenes, *Against Timokrates* 21; *Etymologicum Magnum*, s.v. *Heliaia*.

54. Boegehold 1995: 14; cf. Camp 1995: 103.

55. Thompson and Wycherley 1972: 62.

56. Thompson and Wycherley 1972: 63.

57. Stroud 1998: 85–108.

58. Thucydides 6.27–28, 53.2.

59. Only the first two letters of Aiakeion can be read on the inscription but, of the forty different gods and heroes known to have received cult in the agora, Aiakos's name is the only one to begin Ai-. See Stroud 1998: 90.

60. Young 1951: 140–43; Pritchett 1953: 275–76. See Stroud 1998: 89.

61. Stroud 1998: 90–91.

the Rectangular Peribolos even described it as made of Aiginetan limestone.[62] In Stroud's view, the Aiakeion, constructed towards the end of the sixth century to house the hero cult of Aiakos, was "repurposed" as a result of the grain-tax law of 374/3 BCE, when doors and a roof were added to suit its new purpose as a grain warehouse, and these modifications are reflected in the fourth-century repairs and additions that are attested for the Rectangular Peribolos.[63]

Whether or not Stroud's identification is correct, there is not a shred of positive evidence to maintain that the Rectangular Peribolos was a law court and hence no justification for identifying the Poros Building as the state prison on the grounds of proximity. The only solid physical evidence for the presence of juridical activity in the late fifth century comes from the opposite, northeastern side of the agora. If the Parabuston court has been correctly identified here, and if the Parabuston was the court in which Sokrates was tried and condemned, then it can hardly be considered to have been near to the Poros Building. It is, however, equally likely that Sokrates was tried in another court whose location is currently impossible to determine.[64]

As Virginia Hunter has pointed out, Vanderpool's characterization of the layout of the Poros Building, with its cells, guard tower, and exercise yard, is heavily influenced by modern notions of the penitentiary, as envisioned by Jeremy Bentham in his plan for the Pantopticon and realized, in 1842, in the model prison at Pentonville.[65] The penal system that emerged in the course of the nineteenth century viewed imprisonment as a punishment in its own right and incarceration as a project of correction and reform. By contrast, it is often argued that, in Classical Athens, a lengthy prison term

was not the default penalty and that prisons were principally populated by those awaiting trial or execution, violent criminals, traitors, and public debtors.[66] For Hunter, a more appropriate model for the ancient Athenian prison is the English prison in the period prior to 1775, which was "more a place of confinement for debtors and those passing through the mills of justice than a place of punishment."[67] English prisons in this period were typically temporary lodgings for inmates: the liberal use of fetters dispensed with the need for large numbers of custodians but also permitted relatively free traffic within the confines of the prison and allowed for unlimited visits.[68] While prisons were sometimes housed within castle keeps, their function could just as easily be discharged by cottages or lodging houses. As a consequence, the ancient Athenian prison may have resembled less the modern penitentiary and more a "large lodging house for inmates whose stay was temporary and usually very brief."[69]

Without any way of knowing how large Athens's prison population was at any one time, it is impossible to determine whether the Poros Building would have satisfied the city's incarceration needs. It is, however, difficult to believe that Sokrates' supposed twenty to twenty-five visitors could have been comfortably accommodated in a room measuring 4.5 by 4.5 metres, especially since Plato (*Phaidon* 60b, 89b) also refers to a couch and a stool in the cell. Nor is it likely that the forty-two conspirators thrown into prison in 415 BCE could have been kept in the courtyard, where exposure to the elements would surely have been too high a risk.[70] Vanderpool conceded that the 292 Lakedaimonians, captured on the island of Sphakteria in 425 and incarcerated at Athens for three and a half years, "were probably

:::      62. Stroud 1998: 86, 92, 101.
        63. Camp (2010: 120–21) now accepts the identification of the structure as the Aiakeion.
        64. Koumanoudis 1984: 72.
        65. Hunter 1997: 313–16, 323.
        66. The case has been fully stated in Hunter 1997. By contrast, Danielle Allen (1997; 2000: 224–32) argues that imprisonment was employed as a primary penalty more often than has previously been recognized.

        67. Ignatieff 1978: 28; cited in Hunter 1997: 309.
        68. Hunter 1997: 309–10. That chains were extensively used in ancient prisons is indicated by the word *desmōtērion*, which derives from the verb *deō* (I bind). See Allen 1997: 121–22.
        69. Hunter 1997: 314–16.
        70. Andokides, *On the Mysteries* 46–48; cf. Thucydides 6.60.

held elsewhere and not in the State Prison."[71] But Thucydides (4.41.1) specifies that they were kept in fetters and if they were distributed among various lodging houses, it is not in principal unreasonable to suppose that this was the common practice employed for incarceration.

Another objection to identifying the Poros Building as the state prison is its lack of a water supply—at least in its first phase.[72] Vanderpool referred to what he termed "simple arrangements for bathing" in the northwestern room of the structure, but Hunter argues that the hip baths that he cites as parallels at Eretria, Delphi, and Eleusis are all furnished with a water supply and a drainage system, neither of which is attested in the Poros Building.[73] Furthermore, in her original study of the building, Crosby noted that marble chips were found in the footing trench for the *pithos*, implying that it was not installed until after marbleworkers occupied the northern rooms of the Poros Building.[74] It is, therefore, difficult to avoid the conclusion that the so-called bathing facilities were in reality associated with the subsequent marble workshop.[75]

Whether or not the thirteen vessels found discarded in a cistern in the Annex are truly medicine pots, it is extremely unlikely that their function was to store single doses of hemlock.[76] The plant was ground in a pestle and mortar on the spot, not stored, and must have been administered in some

sort of cup rather than from a flask—indeed, Plato (*Phaidon* 117a–b) specifies that Sokrates drank the hemlock out of a *kylix*. Finally, it is worth noting that the vessels were found in a secondary (third-century) context in the Annex, not the main building. Although further clearing and study of the building has suggested that the building and Annex were *architecturally* related, it is impossible to know whether they were *functionally* related or whether they were separate units constructed by the same builder.[77] Certainly, the different orientation of the Annex might suggest the latter possibility.[78]

In short, none of the evidence that Vanderpool adduced in favour of his identification of the Poros Building as the state prison stands up to closer scrutiny. Quite what function the building served in its initial phase is difficult to determine: there have been suggestions that it was originally a medical centre or even a brothel,[79] but the likeliest explanation—on the basis of the buildings that surround it—is that it served some sort of industrial or commercial function. Susan Rotroff suspects that it was built by the Athenian state and "may be a forerunner of the Stoa of Attalos, bringing in income for the state in the form of rents."[80] Either way, it was taken over by marbleworkers at the end of the fifth century—perhaps even before the trial of Sokrates and certainly well in advance of Phokion's execution in 318 BCE.

## Conclusion

Nobody doubts that there was a historical Sokrates. The problem is that there is less certainty concerning the historicity of the figure that is represented by Aristophanes, Plato, Xenophon, Aristotle, and

later philosophical writers. In the early twentieth century, scholars such as A. E. Taylor and John Burnet upheld the view that whatever words Plato put into the mouth of Sokrates were generally faithful

::: 
71. Vanderpool 1980: 19. See Thucydides 4.38.5; 5.18.7.

72. Hunter 1997: 322.

73. Vanderpool 1980: 18; Hunter 1997: 321. The baths are illustrated in Ginouvès 1962, plates 7, 20–21, 30, 49, and 98.

74. Crosby 1951: 180–81.

75. Along similar lines, Hunter 1997: 321–22.

76. Hunter (1997: 320–21) is sceptical; cf. Koumanoudis 1984: 79. Rotroff (1997: 198 n. 4) suggests that they were used to store "a remedy of habitual use"; cf. Rotroff 2006: 164.

77. See Rotroff 2009: 44.

78. Koumanoudis 1984: 77.

79. Koumanoudis 1984: 77. The Poros Building does, in fact, exhibit some superficial similarities with the Asklepieion at Troizen, but the failure to provide it with a water supply at the outset probably argues against its identification as a medical centre.

80. Rotroff 2009: 45.

renditions of what Sokrates had actually preached, but such an optimistic view commands little support today.[81]

A case in point would be Plato's description, in the *Phaidon*, of Sokrates' death as the hemlock began to take effect. Although Enid Bloch has argued that the description does conform to medical accounts of hemlock poisoning, Christopher Gill and others have suggested that Plato has given a more anodyne, and less gruesome, account—perhaps to emphasize his master's stoicism in the most extreme of adversities.[82] If that is the case, it "should alert us to the possibility that many of what seem to be authentic glimpses into the life, and death, of the historical Socrates may in fact be illustrative pictures, attached or inset, like the myths of the dialogues, into Plato's arguments."[83] Indeed, there is now a general feeling among scholars that Sokratic literature is largely fictional in terms of characters, setting and content.[84] Offering a historically authentic picture of late-fifth-century Athens was almost certainly not high on the list of Plato's priorities, and we should therefore be extremely cautious about proposing topographical identifications based on the Sokratic dialogues.

There is, however, a broader point. In a city in which a democratic ideology constrained the ambitions of the wealthy and the educated to set themselves above their peers, where everybody was expected to at least feign to be no better than the rest,[85] one wonders whether archaeology is especially well equipped to identify individuals.[86] Perhaps it is no accident that attempts should have been made to trace the footsteps of an individual who was—at least in the perception of many—no friend of the people,[87] but even in more autocratic regimes, the search for the individual is not always straightforward, as the next chapter will discuss.

**DOCUMENTS FOR CHAPTER 5**

**5.1**   Simon the Athenian, a shoemaker. When Sokrates used to come to his workshop and discuss something, he used to take notes of what he remembered; this is why they call them the "Shoemaker Dialogues," and thirty-three of them are contained in a single volume. (Diogenes Laërtios, *Lives of the Philosophers* 2.122)

**5.2**   Should I, then, have been born Simon the shoemaker or Dionysios the schoolmaster, rather than Perikles or Cato, so that he would converse with—and sit down in front of—me, as Sokrates did with [Simon]? (Plutarch, *Moralia* 776b)

**5.3**   At first, Sokrates observed that he [Euthydemos] did not yet enter the agora because of his youth, but if he wanted to conduct some business, he would sit down in one of the saddler's shops near the agora, and so that is where Sokrates went with some of his companions. (Xenophon, *Memorabilia* 4.2.1)

**5.4**   I will try to take you through everything from the beginning. For the others and I had always made it our custom, even in the days before, to visit Sokrates; we would gather at dawn in the law court in which the trial took place, because it is close to the prison. On each occasion we used to wait until the

:::     81. Taylor 1911; Burnet 1911. See Guthrie 1971: 13; Dorion 2011: 6–7.

    82. Bloch 2002; Gill 1973; cf. Ober 1977; Graves et al. 1991.

    83. Gill 1973: 28.

    84. Dorion 2011: 7, 16.

    85. See especially Ober 1989.

    86. For the individual in the archaeological record: Johnson 2010: 224.

    87. In this vein, it is interesting to note the tentative identification of a bronze cauldron in the sun-dried brick tomb in the Kerameikos as the cinerary urn of Alcibiades, another enemy of the Athenian democracy. See Knigge 1991: 109–10.

prison opened, conversing with one another since it did not open early. (Plato, *Phaidon* 59c–d)

**5.5**   Suppose that shortly you were to hear an outcry right outside the law court and someone were to say that the prison had been opened and the prisoners were escaping; there is nobody, however old or contemptuous, who would not come to assist to the best of his ability. (Demosthenes, *Against Timokrates* 208)

**5.6**   The buyer of the tax will convey the grain to the Peiraieus at his own risk and he will transport the grain up to the city at his own expense and he will heap up the grain in the Aiakeion. The *polis* will make available the Aiakeion in watertight condition and provided with a door. (Agora Inv. No. I 7557, lines 10–16 [translated in Stroud 1998: 9])

**5.7**   When the Athenians heard these [words] that were brought back [from Delphi], they assigned a precinct (*temenos*) to Aiakos—the one that currently stands in the agora. (Herodotos 5.89.3)

**5.8**   Of Diodoros of Eiteia, a house in Kollytos, which is bounded, on one side, by the Ai[akeion] and, on the other, by the agora. (*IG* I³ 426, lines 5–8)

# 6

# The Tombs at Vergina

## *The Discovery of the Tombs*

On November 8, 1977, in the presence of a number of dignitaries, Mano-
lis Andronikos, professor of archaeology at the Aristotle University of
Thessaloniki, descended via the roof into a vaulted chamber tomb that
he had located a few days earlier. What he would find would prove to be
one of the most sensational discoveries ever made on Greek soil, comparable to Schliemann's excavation of Grave Circle A at Mycenae. They
were to guarantee Andronikos's status not only as a leading archaeological authority but also as one of the most significant public figures in
postwar Greece: shortly before his death in March 1992, he was awarded
the Grand Cross of the Order of the Phoenix, Greece's highest civilian
honour, and—unusually for an archaeology professor—the privilege of
a state funeral in the church of Agia Sofia in Thessaloniki.[1] But his discoveries also sparked a long and controversial debate that is still far from
being resolved.

By the 1970s, the modern village of Vergina, approximately 75 kilometres southwest of Thessaloniki (fig. 6.1), was identified by most scholars as the ancient site of Aigeai (see "Aigeai and Vergina" below). Aigeai
had been the original royal capital of Macedonia and continued to serve
as a ritual centre and burial ground for the Macedonian monarchs, the
Argeadai, after the capital was moved to Pella—probably under the late-

:::     1. Danforth 1995: 169; Hamilakis 2007: 125–27, 142–44.

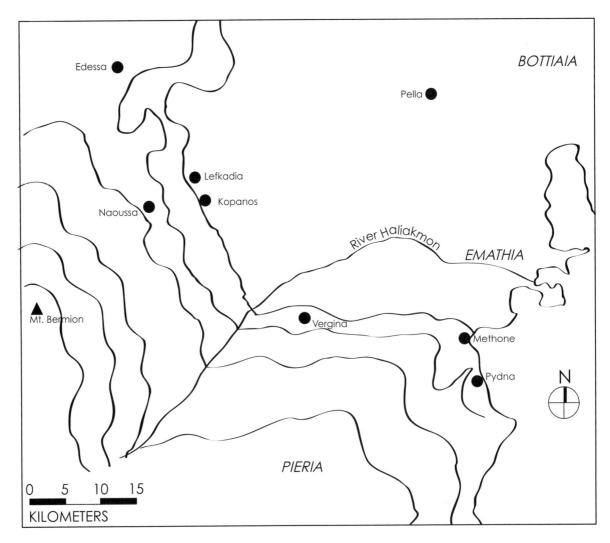

6.1 Map of Macedonia. (After Faklaris 1994: p. 610, fig. 1.)

fifth-century king Archelaos.[2] It was here that, in June 336 BCE, Philip II was assassinated and buried.[3] The earliest explorations in the area took place in the 1850s, when the French archaeologist Léon Heuzey identified the remains of a large palace on a hill to the south of the village; it was originally dated to the Hellenistic period, but recent excavations have suggested that it was first modelled in the middle of the fourth century.[4] Heuzey also located a large, artificial mound, 110 metres in diameter and 12 metres high and now generally known as the Great Tumulus (Megáli Toúmba), on the western periphery of the village. Andronikos had conducted limited excavations here in 1952 and, again, in 1962–63 but without significant results. The breakthrough came in 1976, when he started finding broken marble tombstones. These reminded him of Plutarch's description of the desecration of the royal tombs at Aigeai by Galatian mercenaries in 274/3 BCE (document 6.1).[5] The following year, he came across a rectangu-

:::     2. The date for the transfer of the capital is not given in any of our sources, though Pella was certainly the capital by 382 BCE (Xenophon, *Hellenika* 5.2.13): see Greenwalt 1999: 162–65; Kottaridi 2011b: 161–62; Akamatis 2011: 394.

3. Justin, *Epitome* 9.7.8.

4. Drougou 2006: 98–125; Saatsoglou-Paliadeli 2011a; Kottaridi 2011c; 2011d. For Heuzey: Galanakis 2011: 49.

5. Andronikos 1984: 55–62.

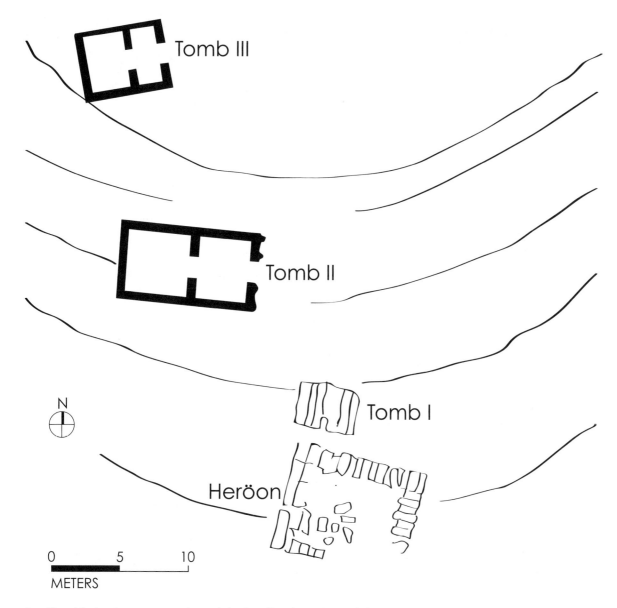

Tomb III

Tomb II

N

Tomb I

Heröon

0     5     10
METERS

6.2  Plan of the fourth-century graves beneath the Great Tumulus at Vergina. (After Drougou and Saatsoglou-Paliadeli, eds. 2008: 43, fig. 52.)

lar cist tomb (Tomb I), whose walls were decorated with paintings, including a particularly fine scene depicting Hades' rape of Persephone. Unfortunately, the grave had been robbed, though remains of uncremated bones—apparently belonging to a male, a female, and a newborn baby—were recovered. The construction aboveground of an enclosure immedi-ately to the south of the tomb suggested the prac-tice of some sort of postmortem tomb cult (fig. 6.2).[6]

Further digging to the northwest of Tomb I re-vealed the spectacular subterranean barrel-vaulted chamber tomb mentioned earlier (fig. 6.3). Tomb II had an impressive façade consisting of a double-leaved door flanked by two Doric columns; above

: : :     6. Andronikos 1984: 86–95; 1994a; Drougou 2006: 178–80. The tomb belongs to a tradition of built cist tombs in Macedonia that can be traced back to the early sixth century at the "royal" ceme-tery at Aiani, near Kozani: Karamitrou-Mentessidi 2008: 50–67; 2011: 100–106. I am grateful to Margaret Miles for drawing my attention to this.

6.3 The façade of Tomb II at Vergina. (Photo courtesy of Photostock/Studio Kontos.)

a Doric triglyph and metope frieze, on which the red and blue paint was still well preserved, was a painted frieze depicting a multiple-quarry hunt. Inside, the main chamber was square, 4.46 by 4.46 metres. In its southwest corner were two tripods, one of iron and the other of bronze, bronze vessels, three sets of bronze greaves, an iron helmet, a silver-gilt diadem, spears, an ivory-hilted sword and scabbard, an iron cuirass with gold decoration, and a heavy gilded wooden shield; by the north wall were a number of silver and clay vessels. Close to the west wall of the chamber was a square marble chest, inside which was a gold *larnax* (a cinerary container) weighing almost 11 kilograms and decorated with bands of lotus flowers and palmettes and, on its lid, a large radiate starburst motif (fig. 6.4). Inside the *larnax* was a carefully arranged heap of burnt bones that appeared to belong to a man, while in front of the marble chest were fragments of decomposed wood, gold, glass, and ivory—including

6.4   The gold *larnax* from the main chamber of Tomb II at Vergina. (Photo courtesy of Photostock/Studio Kontos.)

two miniature figures that may be depictions of Philip II and his son, Alexander the Great—which have been identified as the remains of a ceremonial couch. Andronikos then turned his attention to the antechamber, where he discovered another marble chest containing a gold *larnax*, smaller than that in the main chamber but similarly decorated; the *larnax* contained the burnt bones of a woman, though this time they had been wrapped in a purple and gold cloth. Among the grave goods in the antechamber were a variety of jars, a gold wreath, a gilded pectoral, the gold sheath of a *gorytos* (a case to store the short Scythian bow and arrows), and a pair of

gilded greaves. There were also traces of another couch.[7]

At the end of the 1977 season, Andronikos was relatively cautious in his interpretation of the tomb, stating that his "theory that this is possibly the site of the royal graves of Macedonia has received strong confirmation if not unshakable proof."[8] He believed that there were good reasons for assuming that this was the royal cemetery damaged by the Galatian mercenaries, whose desecration of Tomb I may have distracted them from searching for further treasures in Tomb II, and he conjectured that the Great Tumulus may have been constructed by

:::   7. Andronikos 1984: 97–197; Drougou 2006: 154–67.

8. Andronikos 1978: 47.

the Macedonian ruler, Antigonos Gonatas, soon afterwards in order to protect the burials from further depredations.[9] If that was the case, then the burials must have been considered significant enough to protect—a hypothesis seemingly confirmed by the wealth of grave goods in Tomb II and the quality of the wall paintings in Tomb I and on the exterior frieze of Tomb II. The presence of the diadem seemed to signal a royal burial, and since Andronikos dated Tomb II to the third quarter of the fourth century, he suggested that the occupant of the principal chamber was Philip II and that the cremation burial in the antechamber might be that of his last wife, Kleopatra, who had been murdered, shortly after Philip's burial, on the orders of Olympias, Philip's former wife and the mother of Alexander the Great (document 6.7).[10] He was, however, anxious to add a caveat: "Once again I feel impelled to reiterate that I have no intention of insisting on such a sensational point of view."[11] Such circumspection had all but disappeared by 1984, when Andronikos issued his lavishly illustrated report of the excavations. In this publication, Tomb II is identified as that of Philip II—albeit in quotation marks.[12]

In part, this increased confidence was the result of the discovery, in 1978, of a third unrobbed chamber tomb (Tomb III), often named the Tomb of the Prince on account of the cremated remains of an adolescent male found inside. Immediately to the north of Tomb II, Tomb III was similar to—if smaller and somewhat simpler than—its neighbour. The cremated bones had been placed in a silver *hydria*, crowned by a golden wreath, which had been placed on a marble table by the west wall of the principal chamber. Traces of yet another couch were found,

together with silver and bronze vessels and an iron lampstand as well as armour and items of clothing. Around the top of the walls in the antechamber ran a well-preserved frieze depicting a chariot race.[13] Since Tomb III seemed to postdate Tomb II, Andronikos tentatively accepted the opinion of Nicholas Hammond that the human remains were those of Alexander IV, the posthumous son of Alexander the Great who was murdered, along with his mother, Roxane, by Alexander's former general Cassander in 311/10 BCE (document 6.2).[14] The discovery, in 1982, of a theatre immediately below the palace at Vergina only served to strengthen Andronikos's suspicions, since it was in the theatre at Aigeai that Philip II was assassinated while conducting wedding festivities for his daughter Kleopatra.[15]

Since Andronikos's death, his identification of Tomb II as the resting-place of Philip II has been vigorously endorsed by his former colleagues and assistants, who continue to excavate at Vergina. But his views were challenged almost as soon as he had brought Tomb II to light. W. Lindsay Adams and Phyllis Lehmann were among the first of a long line of historians and archaeologists who argued that the occupants of Tomb II were not Philip II and Kleopatra but Philip III Arrhidaios, son of Philip II and half brother of Alexander the Great, and his wife, Adea-Eurydice.[16] Arrhidaios, who had been proclaimed joint ruler of Macedon—with Alexander IV—after Alexander's death in 323 BCE, had been executed on Olympias's orders at Pydna in the autumn of 317 BCE, while Eurydice had been persuaded to take her own life at around the same time.[17] Cassander had reburied the couple with full regal honours at Aigeai the following spring (docu-

---

:::    9. Cf. Adams 1991: 28. Hammond (1991: 78), by contrast, attributed the construction of the Great Tumulus to Lysimachos, the ruler of Macedon, in ca. 285 BCE.

10. Pausanias 8.7.7; Justin, *Epitome* 9.7.8. More recently, it has been suggested that the female burial is that of Philip's Thracian wife, Meda. See Kottaridi 2011a: 147; Lane Fox 2011b: 32.

11. Andronikos 1978: 51.

12. Andronikos 1984: 97.

13. Andronikos 1984: 198–217; Drougou 2006: 168–77.

14. Cf. Diodoros 19.52.4; Pausanias 9.7.2; Justin 15.2.3–4. See Andronikos 1984: 232; cf. Hammond 1982: 116; 1991: 74; Green 1982: 146–47; Borza 1987: 105; Musgrave 1991: 7–8. It should be noted that

Andronikos (1984: 224) originally dated Tomb III to ca. 325 BCE, while, on the basis of the identification with Alexander IV, Hammond (1991: 72) dated it to ca. 309 BCE.

15. Diodoros 16.93.1–2. For the theatre, tentatively dated to the third quarter of the fourth century, see Drougou 2006: 126–33. For the circumstances surrounding Philip's death: Hammond 1978: 339–43.

16. Adams 1980; Lehmann 1980: 1982. The idea had already been floated by E. Zachos in a letter to the Greek newspaper *Eletherotypia*, published February 13, 1978: see Hatzopoulos 2008: 94.

17. Arrian 156 *FGrH* 1; Diodoros 18.2; 19.11.5–7; Justin 13.2.8; Curtius Rufus 10.7; Aelian, *Miscellany* 13.36.

ments 6.3; 6.4). The disagreement that has ensued has, at times, been as bitter as it has been protracted, and the reasons for this are due in no small measure to political considerations.[18]

## The Political Dimension

The northern Greek region of Macedonia did not become part of the modern Greek state until it was formally ceded by the Ottoman Empire under the terms of the Treaty of London in May 1913.[19] Ten years later, the crushing defeat of the Greek army in Turkey resulted in a forcible exchange of populations and the arrival in Greece of well over one million refugees, many of whom settled in Macedonia and Thrace.[20] Indeed, the modern village of Vergina was created by the fusion of the hamlets of Koutles and Barbes, partly to accommodate the newcomers.[21] As a result, the historical attachment between people and place was less securely rooted in this part of Greece than it was further to the south.[22] To complicate matters further, this was the time when the Slavic-speaking populations of the upper Vardar valley to the north were starting to lay claim to their own distinctively Macedonian ethnicity. The origins of this movement seem to have arisen in intellectual circles in the late nineteenth century, as literary scholars attempted to establish a new literary language that was distinct from the spoken dialects. Even so, most inhabitants of the region apparently identified themselves as Bulgarians. In the early decades of the twentieth century, however, ethnic segregation was actively encouraged by the Serbs, who saw the promotion of an independent Macedonian identity as a way of detaching the populations of the Vardar valley from Bulgaria, and in 1944, the Communist Party of Yugoslavia laid claim to this part of the Balkans by creating the Socijalistička Republika Makedonija.[23]

All new nations have an urgent need to equip themselves with national histories and it was not long before Slavic Macedonia was "constructing distinctive myths of collective origin and claims of descent from Alexander the Great."[24] The fact that their language identified them as the descendants of Slavic speakers who first entered the Balkans about a millennium after the death of Alexander was obviously an obstacle but could largely be sidestepped by arguing that the Slavic immigrants had merely imprinted their language on an ancient Macedonian people, from whom the modern Macedonians claimed an ethnic continuity. That claim, however, required the Macedonians to deny that their ancient namesakes had any ethnic affiliation with the Greeks.

Such a denial ran directly counter to the Greek national narrative and especially the arguments of continuity that were developed and popularized by the Greek historian Konstantinos Paparrigopoulos in his five-volume *History of the Hellenic Nation*, published between 1860 and 1877.[25] In this narrative, Philip II plays a crucial role as the first ruler to unite the warring Greek city-states under his hegemony, while his son Alexander was responsible for exporting Greek culture and the Greek language as far east as the Indus valley.[26] Cultural resistance to the annexation of Greece and Asia Minor

::: 18. Romm 2011.

19. The treaty put an end to the First Balkan War of 1912–13, wherein Greece, Serbia, Bulgaria, and Montenegro combined forces to attack the crumbling Ottoman Empire. See Clogg 2002: 79–81.

20. Gallant 2001: 141–50; Clogg 2002: 91–106. According to the census of 1928, almost half the inhabitants of Macedonia and 60 percent of the Thracian population were of refugee origin.

21. Andronikos 1984: 17; Galanakis 2011: 50.

22. Hamilakis 2007: 162–67.

23. Danforth 1995: 56–69; 2010: 574–76.

24. Karakasidou 1997: 16; cf. Danforth 2010: 581.

25. Koliopoulos and Veremis 2002: 233–35, 245–46; Hamilakis 2007: 115–17.

26. For Paparrigopoulos's treatment of Alexander, see Demetriou 2001. In truth, ancient authors were far from unanimous as to whether the ancient Macedonians were Greek (which does not, of course, prove that they were not): see Badian 1982; Borza 1996; 1999: 27–43; Hall 2001. The insistence otherwise by Sourvinou-Inwood (2002) is not very convincing.

by Rome preserved the flame of Hellenism through the Byzantine Empire, while the Orthodox Church safeguarded the Hellenic legacy down to Greece's liberation from Ottoman rule during the War of Independence, which broke out in 1821. From this viewpoint, the claim on the part of the Slavic republic to the name Macedonia and to its inhabitants' descent from the ancient Macedonians represented, at best, a "theft of national 'property,' heritage, and identity"[27] and, at worst, a thinly veiled irredentist aspiration to the territory the Slavs termed Aegean Macedonia.

The underlying tensions erupted with the breakup of Yugoslavia and the declaration of independence, on September 8, 1991, by the self-styled Republic of Macedonia.[28] Conferences, books, lectures, and publicity campaigns, indignantly appealing to the propagation of the historical "truth," exploded on both sides of the border. In August 1992, the new republic adopted a national flag, on which was emblazoned the same radiate starburst motif that Andronikos had discovered on the gold funerary *larnax* in Tomb II—an evident attempt to lay claim to the heritage of the ancient Macedonians.[29] The Greek government responded by issuing a new hundred-drachma Greek coin with the "Star of Vergina" on the reverse and the head of Alexander on

the obverse and by renaming the airport of Thessaloniki the Macedonia International Airport.

Technically, of course, the identification of the mortal remains in Tomb II as those of Philip II did not, in itself, invalidate the arguments of the Slavic Macedonians. Of more potential significance was the fact that the material culture of the graves had clear Greek parallels and that names written in Greek appeared on grave *stēlai* recovered from the site.[30] But there can be no denying the talismanic properties that the corpse of a celebrity possesses or the awed fervour that it can inspire. As Yannis Hamilakis puts it, "[A] body that was identified with certainty as that of Philip II of Macedonia inspires piety and religious respect; in fact, it becomes elevated to the status of the holy relics of a new saint, a national, not strictly religious, saint."[31] Arrhidaios, on the other hand, is regarded as a rather more embarrassing torchbearer for Hellenism. The literary source tradition on him is almost overwhelmingly negative: Diodoros (18.2.2) says that he was "afflicted by an incurable mental condition" while an anonymous chronicler of Alexander's successors describes him as "slow-minded" and an "epileptic" (*Heidelberg Epitome* 155 FGrH 1).[32] He is, in other words, hardly a figure to command "religious piety and respectful fear."[33]

## Aigeai and Vergina

The first issue to address is whether Vergina has been correctly identified as the site of ancient Aigeai. If it has not, the graves that Andronikos found are not royal, and any discussion as to whether the cremated remains in Tomb II are those of Philip II or not becomes moot. When Heuzey first explored the area of Vergina, he identified it as the

relatively insignificant site of Balla—largely because a passage from Justin's *Epitome* of Pompeius Trogus's *Philippic Histories* (document 6.5) seemed to equate Aigeai with the city of Edessa, some 40 kilometres northwest of Vergina. By the late 1950s, however, that identification began to weaken as it became clear that Aigeai and Edessa were two sepa-

:::     27. Hamilakis 2007: 130.

28. The republic was admitted to the United Nations in 1993 but, at Greek insistence, under the title The Former Yugoslav Republic of Macedonia (FYROM). In the Greek media, the republic was more commonly referred to as Skopje, after its capital city.

29. See Brown 1994; Danforth 2010: 587–89.

30. Andronikos 1984: 56.

31. Hamilakis 2007: 144.

32. According to Plutarch (*Life of Alexander* 77.5), his illness was due to poison administered by Olympias.

33. Hamilakis 2007: 156; cf. Romm 2011.

rate, but coeval, cities,[34] and in 1968, Hammond argued that Aigeai was far more likely to be situated at Vergina.[35]

Hammond's case was argued largely on the basis of literary references. Firstly, both Justin (document 6.5) and the second-century CE geographer Claudius Ptolemy (3.13.39) situate Aigeai in the region of Emathia, which suggests that it faced the central plain of Lower Macedonia (fig. 6.1). Secondly, two texts imply that Aigeai should be situated further to the south of Edessa: the first is Theophrastos's observation (*On Winds* 27) that, in the area of Aigeai, the clouds were diverted northwards when the north wind blew because they could not pass over the twin mountains of Olympos and Ossa; the second is a restored inscription (*IG* IV 617) which lists sites in order from Thessaly northwards to Macedonia and in which Aigeai precedes Edessa. Thirdly, Diodoros (16.3.5–6) reports an incident in which Argaios, a pretender to the Macedonian throne, was sent to Aigeai from Methone, where the Athenian fleet was stationed—suggesting that the city was not far from the sea.

In 1994, however, an explicit challenge to the Aigeai-Vergina equation was launched by Panayiotis Faklaris, a former assistant to Andronikos. Faklaris criticized Hammond's original identification by complaining that neither Theophrastos nor Claudius Ptolemy provide the sort of specificity required to locate Aigeai at Vergina; he also noted that Diodoros offers no precise details concerning the distance between Aigeai and Methone. Furthermore, Aigeai was, according to an oracle cited by Diodoros (7.16), located in Bottiaia, the region north of the Haliakmon River, while Vergina is situated to the south of the river.[36] In describing the origins of the Argead monarchy, Herodotos (8.138.2–3) tells us that Perdikkas, the dynasty's founder, together with his two elder brothers settled in a part of Macedonia called the Gardens of Midas, on the slopes of Mount Bermion; from there, he set out to subdue the rest of Macedonia. As we have seen, Justin (document 6.5) also mentions a Midas in connection with Karanos's foundation of Aigeai.[37] For Faklaris, this was sufficient evidence to locate Aigeai on Mount Bermion (Vermion) and, more specifically, in the vicinity of the modern villages of Kopanos and Lefkadia, east of Naoussa (fig. 6.1), where graves from the Classical to Roman periods, along with remains of a theatre and of a large building dating to the last quarter of the fourth century, have been discovered.[38] As for Vergina, Faklaris suggested that Heuzey's original identification as Balla was correct all along.[39]

The problem is that Herodotos makes no reference to the city of Aigeai in connection with Mount Bermion. Nor does Justin equate Aigeai with the kingdom of Midas: what he actually says is that Karanos *subsequently* drove Midas from the lands he was occupying in Macedonia. If anything, the passage distinguishes between Aigeai and the Gardens of Midas.[40] Nor is it true that Claudius Ptolemy "refers to the cities of Emathia . . . without designating the precise location of each city":[41] in fact, he rather precisely reports the coordinates for Aigeai as being 48° 40′ longitude and 39° 40′ latitude (3.13.39). Admittedly, historians have long been wary about the utility of Ptolemy's measurements, and, if we were simply to input these coordinates into a modern GPS, we would end up in southeast Azerbaijan, though that is because

:::  34. Papazoglou 1957: 110–11, 343; cited in Faklaris 1994: 610 n. 12.

35. Published in Hammond 1970; 1972: 157–58. Hammond gained firsthand experience of northern Greece and the Pindos range during the 1930s. During the Second World War, he was parachuted into Thessaly, where he served as a British Military Intelligence liaison officer, training the resistance fighters of ELAS (the National People's Liberation Army): see Hammond 1983.

36. Faklaris 1994. Note, however, that his argument (pp. 612–14) that a lack of archaeological material at Vergina from ca. 650–

550 BCE was incompatible with the story of Aigeai's foundation in the first half of the seventh century has since been invalidated by further excavation: see Kottaridi 2004: 527.

37. For the substitution of Karanos for Perdikkas as the founder of the Argead monarchy, see Momigliano 1975; Hammond 1979: 5.

38. Faklaris 1994: 614–16.

39. Faklaris 1994: 614.

40. Greenwalt 1999: 178–80.

41. Faklaris 1994: 613.

Ptolemy's longitudinal coordinates took the Canary Islands—rather than Greenwich—as their baseline.[42] However, a recent study of Ptolemy's measurements, which corrects for this factor, suggests that, even allowing for a margin of error of approximately 10 kilometres, Aigeai is far more likely to be located at Vergina than at either Edessa or Kopanos-Lefkadia.[43] Finally, we should remember that it is modern scholarship, and not ancient authorities, that make the river Haliakmon the boundary between Bottiaia and Emathia. It is entirely possible that the boundary between these regions was permeable and shifted over time—not least because Justin and Ptolemy located Aigeai in Emathia.[44] The strong likelihood remains, then, that Vergina is ancient Aigeai.[45]

To avoid the charge of circularity, I have deliberately abstained in this section from using the "royal" character of the Vergina tombs as evidence for the equation of the site with ancient Aigeai. The fact of the matter is that adjudication of the burials as "royal" can only be a subjective judgement in the absence of any explicit epigraphic evidence that would alert us to the true identity of those buried at Vergina. One personality that is recorded on a silver strainer in Tomb II is that of Machatas—a name that is rarely attested before the second century BCE except in the case of the brother of one of Philip II's wives, Phila.[46] That is tantalizing evidence, but it is hardly conclusive. On the other hand, it remains the case, almost forty years after Andronikos's excavations, that no comparably wealthy complex of Macedonian tombs has come to light, and, while that remains a future possibility, there is—at least, for now—some justification in regarding the Vergina tombs as part of the royal burial ground of the Argead monarchs.

## The Occupants of Tomb II

The respective arguments for identifying the occupants of Tomb II as either Philip II and Kleopatra or Arrhidaios and Eurydice have focused on three aspects: the analysis of the cremated remains, the architecture and construction of the tomb, and the grave goods deposited inside. The second and third of these aspects will be considered in the following section.

The analysis of cremated bones for information about gender, age, and pathology is not impossible, but it is rendered difficult by the fact that identifiable skeletal material tends to be fragmentary and deformed, with the bones suffering from warping and differential shrinkage.[47] The first official report on the cremated bones found in Tomb II concluded that those in the main chamber "probably" belonged to a male between the ages of thirty-five and fifty-five—the caution is due to the fact that some female characteristics were also identified—and that he had been between 160 and 170 cm tall. The remains in the antechamber were assigned to a female around twenty-five years of age, and certainly no younger than twenty, who stood about 155 cm high. The two scientists who conducted the analysis were keeping their eyes open for any traumas that could be associated with three specific wounds that Philip II is said to have received: (i) a blinding arrow wound to the right eye, suffered during the siege of Methone ca. 354 BCE; (ii) a shattered right collar bone, received while attacking the Illyrians in 345 or 344; and (iii) a wound in the right thigh, inflicted during a campaign against the Triballoi in about 339, which left him lame.[48] Their findings were essentially negative: "An injury in the

:::       42. My thanks to Alain Bresson for explaining this to me.

43. Manoledakis and Livieratos 2007.

44. See Hatzopoulos and Paschides 2004.

45. Hatzopoulos 1996.

46. Green 1989: 164.

47. Xirotiris and Langenscheidt 1983: 143–44; Musgrave, Neave, and Prag 1984: 61; McKinley and Bond 2001.

48. Demosthenes, *On the Crown* 67; Theopompos 115 *FGrH* 52;

area of the right supraorbital margin could not be established. . . . On the bones of the lower extremities were no recognizable changes caused by injury."[49]

However, an independent examination, conducted by Jonathan Musgrave at the University of Bristol, came up with rather different conclusions. For Musgrave, the surviving fragments of the skull displayed several anatomical peculiarities and asymmetries that he felt could not simply be attributed—at least entirely—to the effects of cremation. In particular, he noticed what seemed to be a notch in the supraorbital margin and a fracture along the malar-maxillary suture, which he felt were entirely consistent with an eye wound.[50] On the basis of this anatomical report—as well as his own examination of the remains and consultation with facio-maxillary surgeons—Richard Neave, an expert in forensic facial reconstruction at the University of Manchester, made plaster casts of the better-preserved bone fragments, from which wax facsimiles were produced and set into a clay block; missing portions of the skull were built up with clay. Several plaster casts were taken of the reconstructed skull as well as one in wax, to which a makeup artist added skin colour and hair. A second, somewhat less gruesome model was constructed when it was realized that Philip's wound to the eye may have been treated (fig. 6.5).[51] Comparing this reconstructed face with the literary accounts concerning Philip as well as his representation in sculpture and on coins, Neave's Manchester colleague, the historian and archaeologist John Prag, noted numerous correlations, despite the fact that "the work of reconstruction was deliberately carried out without reference to the ancient portraits."[52] In his view, and that of his colleagues, there could no longer be

any doubt that the remains in Tomb II were those of Philip II.[53]

Yet Musgrave's examination also failed to find any obvious trauma to the clavicle or to either leg. In terms of the latter injury, the only piece of evidence that Andronikos could adduce was the mismatched pair of gilded greaves in the antechamber of Tomb II, in which the left greave is 3.5 centimetres shorter than its twin. Now, it has been pointed out that Didymos Chalkenteros, a first-century BCE Alexandrian scholar who wrote a commentary on Demosthenes' *On the Crown*, makes it clear that Philip's leg wound was to the thigh of the right, not the shin of the left, leg.[54] Other authors are, however, less specific, and Plutarch (*Moralia* 739b) even poses the question: "[I]n which leg was Philip lame?"[55] That does not, however, explain why the odd pair of greaves was deposited in the antechamber rather than the main chamber or why the three sets of greaves that were found in the main chamber were all of approximately equal length.[56]

In April 2000, Antonis Bartsiokas, a palaeoanthropologist at the Demokritos University of Thrace, challenged Musgrave's findings in the journal *Science*. Employing a technique called macrophotography, Bartsiokas argued that the supposed abnormalities identified by Musgrave were normal anatomical irregularities that had been accentuated by the effects of cremation and by the reassembly of the skeletal material for deposition in the *larnax*. He also confirmed that the rest of the skeleton bore no traces of the wounds to the collarbone and leg that are documented for Philip by the literary sources. Even more importantly, Bartsiokas concluded that the bones had been subject to "dry cremation," which is why they were preserved so well. In other words, the bones were unfleshed when they were

: : :   Marsyas 135–36 *FGrH* 16; Diodoros 16.34.5; Strabo 7 fr 22; 8.6.15; Justin 7.6.14; Plutarch, *Moralia* 331b. For further sources and discussion, see Riginos 1994.

49. Xirotiris and Langenscheidt 1983: 158.

50. Musgrave, Neave, and Prag 1984: 61–65; Musgrave 1991.

51. According to Pliny (*Natural History* 7.124), Philip's wound was treated by the doctor Kritoboulos. See Prag 1990.

52. Musgrave, Neave, and Prag 1984: 77.

53. See also Prag 1990; Prag and Neave 1997: 53–84.

54. Green 1982: 135–36.

55. Riginos 1994: 116–17.

56. Prag and Neave 1997: 70–71. Eugene Borza (pers. comm.) has pointed out to me that his analysis of greaves in the collection of the British Museum has revealed that no pair of greaves is exactly identical in terms of length.

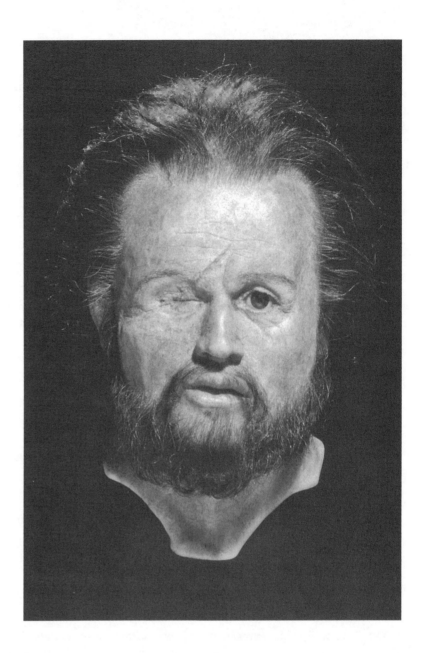

6.5 Reconstruction in wax of the head of Philip II. (Photo courtesy of Manchester Museum, University of Manchester. Reconstruction by Richard Neave, Unit of Art in Medicine.)

cremated, indicating that they had initially been buried and then exhumed prior to cremation.[57] If right, then the circumstances fit much better the facts of Arrhidaios's funeral, conducted with full honours at Aigeai some time after his death, than they do that of Philip II.[58]

In response, Musgrave and his colleagues have reasserted that the abnormalities of the skull can-not simply be the consequence of the cremation process.[59] Furthermore, they question Bartsiokas's claim for "minimal warping" of the skeleton— especially for the long bones (the femora, tibiae, right humerus, and left ulna) and the left side of the cranial vault. Their conclusion is that the male buried in the main chamber of Tomb II was a fleshed cadaver at the time of his cremation and could not,

:::   57. Bartsiokas 2000; 2008. This observation ran directly counter to Prag and Neave's claim (1997: 60) that "these bones had been burnt with flesh on them, not 'macerated' after a period of burial in the ground"; cf. Musgrave 1991: 5.

58. Borza and Palagia 2007: 107. Hatzopoulos (2008: 109–10) argues that Bartsiokas's "findings" were biased by his prior incli-nation towards Borza's views.

59. Musgrave et al. 2010: 3–4.

therefore, have been Arrhidaios.[60] They also offer three additional observations that, in their view, must exclude Arrhidaios and Eurydice as the occupants of Tomb II. The first is that any Greek would have baulked at exhuming rotting corpses for subsequent cremation: "Their rehandling would have been seriously polluting for participants and grotesquely contrary to Greek beliefs about contact with deposed corpses."[61] The second is that both Diodoros (document 6.3) and Diyllos (document 6.4) report that Eurydice's mother, Kynna, was buried alongside the royal couple, while only two corpses were discovered in Tomb II. And the third is that Eurydice would have been between the ages of eighteen and nineteen at the time of her forced suicide, whereas the female deposited in Tomb II cannot have been any younger than the age of twenty.[62] Let us consider these objections in reverse order.

Firstly, one is entitled to wonder whether physical anthropological analysis of a cremated body more than two thousand years old can really distinguish between a nineteen- and twenty-year-old female.[63] Secondly, an attentive reading of Diodoros and Diyllos reveals that neither claims Kynna was placed *in the same tomb* as Arrhidaios and Eurydice:

in fact, Diodoros's use of a *men . . . de* construction seems to distinguish between the royal couple and Kynna. Thirdly, while there is sufficient evidence to show that the Greeks thought that *miasma*, or pollution, emanated from dead bodies, we cannot recast this belief as a permanently or religiously enforced taboo. In any case, it was presumably not the rotting carcasses of Arrhidaios and Eurydice that were transported to Aigeai but rather the wooden coffins containing their remains. Finally, even if the male skeleton was fleshed when it was cremated, that hardly rules out Arrhidaios as a candidate. As even Musgrave and his colleagues admit: "Arrhidaios' body would still have had putrefying skin and muscle attached to his limb bones, and rotting viscera filling his thoracic, abdominal and pelvic cavities after even seventeen months in the ground."[64] Needless to say, it is next to impossible for a nonspecialist to decide between these conflicting scientific interpretations, but it is worth pointing out that, of the three teams of scientists that have examined the male skeleton, two have failed to find any signs of the traumas that Philip II is supposed to have suffered.

## The Tomb and Its Contents

One of the earliest objections to identifying Tomb II as the grave of Philip II was the barrel-vaulted roof employed in its construction. This, it has been argued, was a technique that was unknown in Greece until it was imported after Alexander's conquests in the east.[65] Although both Sophokles (fr. 367 Pearson) and Plato (*Laws*. 947d), who died in 348/7 BC, refer to vaults (*psalides*), Lehmann argued that

these referred to the corbelled variety, long known in Greece, rather than to barrel vaults.[66] Andronikos, however, was unconvinced that the technique could not have appeared earlier and sought a parallel in a barrel-vaulted tomb, the so-called Tomb of Eurydice, located approximately midway between the Great Tumulus and the palace. The date he ascribed to the tomb was ca. 340 BCE, on the basis of

---

:::

60. Musgrave et al. 2010: 5–9; Musgrave and Prag 2011.

61. Musgrave et al. 2010: 12; Musgrave and Prag 2011: 130; cf. Hatzopoulos 2008: 116; Lane Fox 2011b: 28–29.

62. Musgrave et al. 2010: 11: "There are no features on the bones from the antechamber that would permit an estimate as low as this." Cf. Hammond 1991: 79–80; Musgrave 1991: 5.

63. Romm 2011. In fact, Green (1982: 139, 145) maintains that Eurydice could have been twenty-one at the time of her death, while Kleopatra may have been as young as seventeen. Lane Fox's

claim (2011a: 35) that the female in Tomb II was "in her mid- to late twenties" is not what the first analysis of the remains demonstrated.

64. Musgrave et al. 2010: 9.

65. Lehmann 1980: 528–29. Cf. Boyd 1978; Borza 1987: 107–9.

66. Lehmann 1982: 338–40. For discussion: Fredricksmeyer 1981: 333–34; Hammond 1982: 115; 1991: 73; Tomlinson 1987: 308–9; Borza and Palagia 2007: 86 n. 23.

sherds from three Panathenaic amphorae inscribed with the first letters of the name Lykiskos, eponymous Archon at Athens in 344/3 BCE.[67] However, as Eugene Borza and Olga Palagia have pointed out, Panathenaic amphorae—awarded for victories in the Panathenaic games at Athens—were highly prized possessions that might enjoy a longer life cycle than is typical for ceramics, so the best that the archon date provides is a *terminus post quem*.[68] Richard Tomlinson also offered support for the idea that the barrel-vaulted tomb might be a spontaneous Macedonian invention in the years immediately preceding Philip's assassination but confessed that this was largely based on Neave's reconstruction of the skull, which persuaded him that the male in Tomb II was Philip II.[69]

Andronikos adduced two further peculiarities in the construction and execution of Tomb II that seemed to argue in favour of Philip II.[70] The first was his belief that the antechamber had been attached to the primary chamber, almost as an afterthought, at a second, slightly later stage. This seemed hard to reconcile with the literary accounts concerning the double burial of Arrhidaios and Eurydice but suited the circumstances of Kleopatra's murder shortly after that of her husband. The second was the apparent haste of execution and the unfinished state of the tomb. Imprints in the stucco that was applied to the exterior of the vault suggested that the plaster had not had time to dry before the funeral pyre was erected above the tomb. Furthermore, the stucco inside the primary chamber had been crudely applied and was, in some parts, only one layer thick; nor were there the frescoes that one might normally expect inside a wealthy Macedonian barrel-vaulted tomb. Again, the seemingly rushed nature of execution appeared to fit the unexpected circumstances of Philip II's assassination better than the funeral

that Cassander planned for Arrhidaios and Eurydice some six months after their death. Doubts concerning the first observation have been expressed by a civil engineer, who is unconvinced that differences in construction technique between the main chamber and the antechamber necessarily imply two different building phases.[71] The second observation, on the other hand, has never satisfactorily been addressed by those who believe that the occupants of the tomb are Arrhidaios and Eurydice.

One of the most distinctive features of Tomb II is the painted frieze which stands above the entrance to the antechamber and depicts a multiple-quarry mounted hunt, though its uniqueness makes it extraordinarily difficult to interpret, let alone date with any precision. While most scholars are inclined to see the frieze as representing historical Macedonian actors, controversy has focused on whether multiple-quarry hunts—especially hunts involving bears and lions—were a theme of Macedonian art prior to Alexander's conquests in the east or whether the iconography was borrowed from Near Eastern artistic traditions after 330 BCE.[72] Pierre Briant has argued forcefully that the Vergina frieze owes little or nothing to Achaemenid prototypes, and Chrysoula Saatsoglou-Paliadeli has pointed to a silver *statēr*, minted under Amyntas III, which displays a mounted hunter on the obverse and a lion on the reverse, suggesting the existence of lion hunts in Macedon as early as the 380s BC.[73] On the other hand, William Greenwalt has questioned whether the hunter on the *statēr* is actually meant to represent Amyntas III—as opposed to a mythological figure—while Olga Palagia notes that earlier depictions of multiple-quarry hunts in Greek art are found only in contexts associated with the Achaemenid empire. In her view, the first Greek representation of such a scene occurred on the funerary

67. Andronikos 1987: 5–7; 1994b: 154–61; Kottaridi 1999: 633. There are also fragments of two Attic red-figure *lekythoi*, attributed to the "Eleusis Painter" and dated ca. 350 BCE: see Kottaridi 2002: 80; 2006: 157; Lane Fox 2011b: 8.

68. Borza and Palagia 2007: 86.

69. Tomlinson 1987: 308.

70. Andronikos 1984: 97–100, 115–17, 226–31.

71. Zampas 2001: 562.

72. Tripodi (1991; 1998) and Borza and Palagia (2007: 96–97) argue in favour of the latter alternative.

73. Briant 1991; Saatsoglou-Paliadeli 2004: 108, 160. Cf. Hatzopoulos 2008: 108; Lane Fox 2011b: 11–13.

pyre that Alexander constructed for Hephaistion at Babylon in 324 BC, described in detail by Diodoros (17.115.4).[74]

Of the ten human figures that appear on the frieze, nine are beardless. Palagia suggests that this marks them out as hunters belonging to the court of Alexander the Great, during whose reign the fashion for shaving facial hair is supposed to have become standard,[75] though it could simply be an indication of their youth.[76] Two figures in particular command the attention of the viewer. The first, who occupies the centre of the frieze, framed by a pair of leafless trees, is a young rider who takes aim at the lion to his left; he is dressed in a short-sleeved purple *chitōn* and wears a crown of laurel on his head (fig. 6.6). Due, in part, to the iconographic parallels with the Alexander Sarcophagus in the Istanbul Archaeological Museum, most scholars have followed Andronikos in identifying him as Alexander the Great.[77] The second figure, towards the right edge of the frieze, is a bearded man on horseback who is about to spear the same lion. Naturally enough, those who attribute the tomb to Philip II are inclined to view him as Alexander's father,[78] while those who favour Arrhidaios identify him as his half brother.[79] To the modern viewer, this is somewhat perplexing. If the bearded figure—who is, it should be noted, the victor of the hunt—represents the occupant of the tomb, be it Philip II or Arrhidaios, why is he so off centre? And why would Alexander the Great—if it is him—take centre stage, when "[u]nder normal circumstances, the central position in the frieze would be reserved for the owner of the tomb"?[80]

Unfortunately, the artifacts deposited inside Tomb II offer little in the way of chronological precision in determining between two possible burial dates a couple of decades apart (336 and 316 BCE). The best they can offer is a *terminus post quem*. This is especially true of metal objects, which typically circulate for longer periods of time before being deposited in sanctuary or burial contexts. Among the contents of Tomb II, for example, is a bronze tripod awarded as a prize at the Hekatombaia games celebrated at the Argive Heraion; the letter forms of the inscription date it to shortly after 410 BCE.[81] The same is also true, albeit to a lesser degree, of ceramic objects. The fact, then, that the most recent study of the pottery from Tomb II dates the bulk of it to the middle of the fourth century cannot necessarily rule out the later of the two dates.[82] It is, rather, the objects that can be demonstrated to be chronologically later that are critical, and here there does seem to be a drift towards a date of 316.

So, for example, four Attic black-gloss saltcellars find their closest parallel to three examples from closed deposits in the Athenian agora which can be dated to between 325 and 295. The Vergina examples show little to no wear, indicating that they were brand new at the time of their deposition.[83] Another Athenian parallel for a pseudo-Cypriot amphora dates to around 310–250, while a black-gloss lamp could be as early as ca. 345 or as late as 275 BCE.[84] Furthermore, David Gill has argued that five pieces of silver plate in Tomb II carry alphabetic and acrophonic weight inscriptions which conform to a weight standard that was not adopted until the reign of Alexander the Great.[85] If the date of Tomb II

⋮⋮⋮    74. Greenwalt 1994: 125–31; Palagia 2000, 2008; Borza and Palagia 2007: 90–103.

75. Athenaios 13.565a–b. See Palagia 2000: 195–96; 2005: 291–93; Borza and Palagia 2007: 101.

76. Andronikos 1984: 115–17; Saatsoglou-Paliadeli 2004: 144–56.

77. Andronikos 1984: 116; Hammond 1991: 75; Saatsoglou-Paliadeli 2004: 153–56; Borza and Palagia 2007: 101; Hatzopoulos 2008: 114; Lane Fox 2011a: 37–38; Brecoulaki 2011: 213. Tripodi (1991: 147; 1998: 56–62), on the other hand, considers him to be Alexander IV.

78. Andronikos 1984: 116; Saatsoglou-Paliadeli 2004: 144–56; Hatzopoulos 2008: 114.

79. Tripodi 1998: 56–62; Palagia 2000: 195–96; Borza and Palagia 2007: 102–3.

80. Palagia 2000: 195.

81. Amandry 1980: 251.

82. Drougou 2005.

83. Rotroff 1984; Barr-Sharrar 1991: 11, though Hammond (1991: 80–81) and Hatzopoulos (2008: 111–12) are sceptical.

84. Rotroff 1997: 434, 442, 494; 2008; cf. Borza 1987: 106–7; Gill 2008: 345–47. Drougou (2005; 2011: 244–45) remains unconvinced by the lower dating.

85. Gill 2008. Hatzopoulos (2008: 117) argues that the Attic weight standard had already been adopted during the reign of

6.6 The figure at the centre of the frieze on Tomb II at Vergina. (Photo courtesy of Photostock/ Studio Kontos.)

is brought down closer to the date of Tomb III, that would certainly explain why similar types of a silver wine-strainer and silver stemless cups were found in both burials.[86]

Attention has also focused, however, on the character of the items deposited in the tomb. Andronikos considered the martial character of the objects and the subject matter of the frieze to be incompatible with the sickly Arrhidaios,[87] but presumably any Macedonian king could expect to be honoured with martial grave goods, regardless of his constitution. Borza, on the other hand, has observed that some of the more spectacular items—especially the iron helmet, bronze cuirass, and gilded shield—

::: Philip II, but this can only be verified for gold, not silver, coinage; cf. Kremydi 2011: 206; Lane Fox 2011b: 19.
86. Gill 2008: 348–49.

87. Andronikos 1984: 226–31; cf. Hammond 1991: 76; Lane Fox 2011a: 37.

bear an uncanny resemblance to literary descriptions of Alexander's military equipment.[88] Diodoros (18.61.1) narrates how, after Alexander's death, his secretary, Eumenes of Kardia, set up a tent that he furnished with the dead king's diadem, sceptre, and arms,[89] and Borza has argued that these personal items remained in Eumenes' possession, ultimately to be transported back to Aigeai and deposited in Tomb II.[90] Similarly, the martial character of the artifacts in the antechamber is thought by some to be more appropriate to the feisty Eurydice than to Philip's young wife.[91]

## A Third Possibility

According to Triantafyllos Papazoïs, a retired major general of the Greek army, the remains in Tomb II are not those of Philip II and Kleopatra, or even of Arrhidaios and Eurydice, but of Alexander the Great himself and his Baktrian wife Roxane.[92] This will, no doubt, come as a surprise to most classical scholars, since our sources make it perfectly clear that, a little over two years after Alexander's unexpected death in Babylon in 323 BCE, one of his generals, Ptolemy, conveyed the dead king's body to Egypt. Diodoros (18.26–28) recounts how Arrhidaios took charge of the funerary arrangements and began the journey home from Babylon in 321; when the cortege arrived in Syria, Ptolemy diverted Alexander's body to Alexandria.[93] According to Quintus Curtius Rufus (10.10.20) and Pausanias (1.6.3; 1.7.1), however, Ptolemy originally buried Alexander's body in Memphis before moving it to Alexandria, where it would subsequently be visited by Julius Caesar, Octavian/Augustus, Gaius (Caligula), perhaps Vespasian, and almost certainly Hadrian, among many others.[94]

Papazois's starting point is the Galatian desecration of the royal cemetery of Aigeai in 274 BCE (document 6.1). Since he finds it scarcely credible that Tomb II would have escaped the attention of the marauding mercenaries, he assumes that the human remains and the grave goods were de-

posited in the tomb after this event, although he does agree that Tomb II was originally designated for Arrhidaios rather than Philip II. For Papazois, what Ptolemy buried at Alexandria was merely a funerary effigy of Alexander; the king's actual remains were conveyed from Memphis to Aigeai and placed by Antigonos Gonatas—along with Alexander's personal effects—in the now-empty Tomb II. Meanwhile the remains of Roxane were exhumed at Amphipolis and carried back to Aigeai to be deposited in the antechamber of Tomb II, next to her royal husband.

Papazois's thesis certainly accords with the revised dating many scholars prefer for Tomb II, and it does have the advantage of explaining the central positioning on the frieze above the door of the tomb of what looks to be a representation of Alexander, but it is, of course, based on absolutely no literary authority; indeed, it is explicitly contradicted by every surviving text. It does, however, suggest an alternative possibility. What if Tomb II was originally built as the intended tomb for Alexander and was only used later by Cassander for the burial of Arrhidaios and Eurydice when it became clear that the dead king's body would not be returning to Macedonia?[95]

As Diodoros (18.28.2) notes, almost two years passed from when Alexander died to when his fu-

:::      88. The shield seems to portray Penthesilea and Achilles, from whom Alexander claimed descent on his mother's side: Palagia 2000: 192; Borza and Palagia 2007: 116–17.

     89. Cf. Quintus Curtius Rufus 10.6.4.

     90. Borza 1987: 110–18; 2008; Borza and Palagia 2007: 107–13. The thesis has been challenged in Lane Fox 2011b: 22–27.

     91. Borza 1987: 107; Carney 1991; 2008. Palagia (2000: 189–90) argues that the *gorytos* deposited in the antechamber invokes the

insignia of the Achaemenid monarchs whose authority Alexander usurped in 330 BCE.

     92. Papazois 2002.

     93. Cf. Strabo 17.1.8.

     94. See generally Saunders 2006.

     95. This possibility was suggested to me by Daniel S. Richter during a visit to Vergina in June 2000.

nerary cortege left Babylon. The delay was due, in part, to the lengthy period of time it took to construct a funeral carriage worthy of the Macedonian monarch (18.26-27), but it may also have been a consequence of the need to prepare a suitable tomb. Alexander apparently expressed a dying wish to be buried in the sanctuary of Ammon in the Siwah Oasis, and Perdikkas, who supervised affairs after the king's death, gave the order that Arrhidaios should accompany the body to Siwah.[96] At this time, Perdikkas and Ptolemy were still close allies, and it is highly probable that the latter was expected to assist with the transfer of Alexander's remains to Egypt.[97] By the spring of 321, however, Perdikkas had distanced himself from Ptolemy and contracted a marriage alliance with Antipater, the appointed ruler of Macedon.[98] As a result, a decision seems to have been taken to convey the dead king's body to the ancestral royal burial ground at Aigeai: Pausanias (1.6.3) says explicitly that the Macedonians had been charged with escorting Alexander's cortege back to Aigeai. In the end, of course, Arrhidaios handed the body over to Ptolemy, against Perdikkas's will,[99] though plans had presumably already been put in place to receive Alexander's remains at Aigeai. Indeed, it may hardly be coincidental that the frieze which decorates the exterior of Tomb II at Vergina exhibits certain similarities to literary descriptions of Alexander's funeral carriage.[100]

This alternative possibility conforms to the somewhat lower date for Tomb II that recent study of the artifacts suggests. It also, however, has several advantages over the thesis that Tomb II was initially designed with Arrhidaios and Eurydice in mind. Firstly, it explains the central position of the young horseman on the frieze. If this is, as many suspect, a depiction of Alexander the Great,

it makes sense that it would stand over the door of the tomb originally constructed for him. Secondly, it explains why the otherwise embarrassing Arrhidaios was granted the honour of the largest and most elaborate tomb covered by the Great Tumulus: it was not designed with him in mind. Thirdly, it explains why the interior of Tomb II was left unfinished—with only one coat of plaster in places and no wall paintings—as well as the apparent haste with which the work was executed. The haste would have been due to the need to prepare a suitable tomb once the decision was taken to repatriate the king's remains to Aigeai, while the incomplete state probably resulted from the eventual realization that Alexander's body would not, after all, be returning to Macedonia. The tomb would have been a more than sufficient resting-place for Arrhidaios, at least for Cassander's purposes, but perhaps it was felt that Arrhidaios's status hardly warranted the costly completion of interior decoration.

As Peter Green has stressed, any attempt to identify the occupants of Tomb II at Vergina must take account of the burials in the neighbouring tombs.[101] Virtually every scholar has accepted that the adolescent male buried in Tomb III is Alexander IV, since he is the only (legitimate) royal personage known to have been killed at the age of twelve or thereabouts.[102] For as long as the burials in Tomb II were thought to be those of Philip II and Kleopatra, the male occupant of the adjacent Tomb I was tentatively identified as Philip's father, Amyntas.[103] If, however, the occupants of Tomb II are Arrhidaios and Eurydice, then the adult male, young female, and newborn baby whose bones were found in Tomb I could well be Philip II, his young wife Kleopatra, and their newborn baby Karanos.[104] This identification would explain the construction of a

96. Curtius Rufus 10.5.4; Diodoros 18.3.5; Justin, *Epitome* 13.4.6. For the credibility of the account, see Badian 1968: 186.

97. Curtius Rufus 10.7.16.

98. Diodoros 18.3.2, 23.1; Justin, *Epitome* 13.4.5.

99. Arrian, *History of the Successors* 1.25.

100. Miller 1986: 410.

101. Green 1982: 137.

102. See, most recently, Borza and Palagia 2007: 83-84.

103. Hammond 1978: 333.

104. Prestiani Giallombardo and Tripodi 1980; Borza and Palagia 2007: 82-83. Tarn (1948: 260-61) and Bosworth (1988: 27 n. 10) both argue that Philip and Kleopatra had only one child, a daughter named Europa, who was born about a year before Philip's assassination. However, Pausanias (8.7.7) clearly marks the murdered infant as male, while Diodoros (17.2.3) explicitly says that the child had been born just a few days before his father's death. See Green 1991: 141-42; Lane Fox 2011b: 5-6.

*heroon* beside Tomb I, since we know that Philip was worshipped "as a god" at Amphipolis.[105] Furthermore, parallels with cist tombs at Derveni suggest that Tomb I may not be as old as Andronikos originally assumed.[106] There are, however, three potential objections that need to be addressed.

First of all, Diodoros (document 6.2) says that the guard charged with killing Roxane and Alexander IV was ordered by Cassander "to hide their bodies but not communicate the fact to any of the others." This hardly seems compatible with the conjecture that Alexander IV received a lavish burial right next to the tomb where Cassander had interred the remains of Arrhidaios and Eurydice just six or so years earlier. There are two possibilities that might explain this apparent contradiction. The first is that Diodoros is here drawing on the fourth-century historian Hieronymos of Kardia, who was transmitting anti-Cassander propaganda by implying that the would-be successor was not only responsible for exterminating the vestiges of Alexander's line but also guilty of impiety in not providing adequate funerary honours.[107] The other is that Diodoros might have misunderstood—if he did not misrepresent—what Hieronymos wrote. Justin (document 6.6), who is probably following the same source, says that the bodies of Hercules (Herakles), Alexander's other (illegitimate) son, and his mother Barsine were secretly hidden, but he does not specify similar treatment for the corpses of Alexander IV and Roxane.[108] This makes it a distinct possibility that it was Diodoros, not Hieronymos, who attributed the same act of impiety towards both of Alexander's sons.

Secondly, the human bones found in Tomb I do not appear to have been burned, whereas it is often assumed that cremation was the favoured rite at the funerals of Macedonian kings.[109] In fact, the literary sources are far from explicit as to what method of disposal was practised for Philip's funeral. Diodoros (17.2.1) mentions only that Alexander took care of the *taphē* of his father—a word that can mean either "burial place" (i.e., tomb) or the "act of burial," be it inhumation or cremation. Attention has therefore focused on Justin's description (document 6.7) of how Olympias cremated the remains of Philip's assassin, Pausanias, "above the remains of her husband." The self-consciously "Homeric" lifestyle of the Macedonian aristocracy might tempt us into thinking that Pausanias was being sacrificed on the pyre of Philip much as Achilles had put to death twelve Trojan youths on the pyre of Patroklos.[110]

That is not, however, what Justin says. First of all, the cremation of Pausanias took place "a few days after" the funeral of Philip, not on its occasion. Secondly, while the Trojan youths were slaughtered and then burned on Patroklos's pyre, Pausanias seems to have been cremated in his own right—a mark of respect that forms part of Justin's argument here that Olympias's actions created the suspicion that it was she who had ultimately been behind the assassination of Philip. Thirdly, Justin says merely that the cremation took place "above" the remains of Philip, which could easily mean that the pyre was set up above an already-sealed tomb or even above a tumulus constructed above it. The passage offers no conclusive evidence that Philip himself was cremated. Indeed, there is some evidence that, at the time of Philip's death, both inhumation and cremation were being practised in Macedonia.[111]

Thirdly, it has been suggested that Tomb I is, in fact, the burial of the young woman and her

:::     105. Hammond 1978: 333.

106. Tomb B at Derveni is dated by coin evidence to the 330s BCE. See Borza 1987: 118–19; Adams 1991: 32; Gill 2008: 354. The paintings in Tomb I at Vergina are dated by Paspalas (2011: 194) to "the mid fourth century or very slightly later" and by Brecoulaki (2006: 77) to the second half of the fourth century.

107. Borza 1987: 120.

108. Saatsoglou-Paliadeli (2011b: 201) suggests that Herakles is to be identified with the late-fourth-century cremation burial of an adolescent in the agora of Aigeai.

109. Hammond 1978: 332; Musgrave 1991: 7.

110. Homer, *Iliad* 23.175–77.

111. Themelis and Touratsoglou 1997: 202; Guimier-Sorbets and Morizot 2006: 121; Borza and Palagia 2007: 84. See, however, Kottaridi (1999: 637–38), who argues that cremation had been practised for Macedonian royal burials since at least the later sixth century.

baby and that the male skeleton belongs to one of the grave robbers who plundered the tomb.[112] The explanation is based on the fact that the deceased male's remains were found among the debris rather than on the floor of the tomb.[113] It is difficult to know how to assess this interpretation ahead of full publication of the archaeology of the tomb, other than to comment on what must be a virtually unparalleled stroke of misfortune. It is, however, worth returning to the passage of Plutarch (document 6.1)

that initially persuaded Andronikos of the royal character of the tombs beneath the Great Tumulus. Plutarch explicitly says that the Galatian mercenaries "impiously scattered the bones" of the "kings buried there." It may not be impossible, then, that Tomb I was a casualty of this impiety and that the remains of Philip II, presumably suitably regaled, were dragged out of the tomb, despoiled, and then tossed back in.

## Conclusion

The suggestion that Tomb II was initially planned and executed with Alexander in mind and then only later reused for Arrhidaios and Eurydice solves many of the problems involved in accepting either of the two alternatives normally suggested for the identification of the individuals whose remains were found buried within. But it also raises further questions. If the tomb was commissioned for Alexander, why would the conqueror of the east be depicted as a youth engaged in a lion hunt in which it is not he, but perhaps his father, who ultimately dispatches the prey? Was the tomb perhaps commissioned earlier, prior to Alexander's departure to the east? If so, why are there signs of hasty and unfinished execution? And why is the antechamber unusually deep for a Macedonian tomb? Was its size dictated by the need to accommodate a second couch and, if so, for whom?

We can, I think, be sure of one thing. The evidence of Diyllos (document 6.4), who was probably active towards the latter part of the fourth century, gives us no reason to doubt that Arrhidaios and

Eurydice were buried in Aigeai. So, the only way to exclude them from being the occupants of Tomb II would be to identify their remains in another burial site. Indeed, Angeliki Kottaridi has done precisely that, suggesting that the royal couple was interred in a tomb with an Ionic façade, discovered in 1985 next to the *dimarkhio* (town hall) of Vergina, some 200 metres from the Great Tumulus.[114] The ultimate adjudication of this claim will have to await full publication and the scrutiny of international scholarship but it does beg two final, and interrelated, questions. Firstly, just how large was the "royal cemetery" and how many tombs have we yet to find? Secondly, what exactly motivated the construction of the Great Tumulus? If its purpose was, as Andronikos suggested, to protect the tombs of the Argead monarchs, why is it not centred on what we currently regard as the wealthiest and grandest of the Macedonian royal burials (fig. 6.2)? Until these questions are answered, speculation about the identity of the couple interred in Tomb II is still, perhaps, a little premature.

:::  112. Kottaridi (2011a: 142) suggests that this is the tomb of Nikesipolis of Pherai, one of Philip II's mistresses; Green (1982: 147–48) attributed it instead to Phila, an earlier wife of Philip—an identification cautiously accepted in Lane Fox 2011b: 7.

113. See Lane Fox 2011b: 4.

114. Kottaridi 2011a: 142. According to the most recent ar-

chaeological guide to Vergina (Drougou and Saatsoglou-Paliadeli, eds. 2008: 64), the tomb, which had been destroyed and looted, shares with Tomb II the characteristic of a deep antechamber but is dated to the early third century—too late, in other words, to be associated with Arrhidaios. Elsewhere, Drougou (2011: 253) dates it to ca. 300 BCE.

**6.1** After the battle, he [Pyrrhos] immediately captured the cities. He conquered Aigeai and generally mistreated its inhabitants, and he left behind in the city a garrison of Gauls who were campaigning with him. But the Gauls, a people who are insatiable for money, set upon digging up the graves of the kings buried there, and they plundered the treasures and impiously scattered the bones. (Plutarch, *Life of Pyrrhos* 26.11–12)

**6.2** Afraid for himself, he [Cassander] ordered Glaukias, who had been charged with the custody of the child [Alexander IV], to murder Roxane and the king and to hide their bodies but not communicate the fact to any of the others. (Diodoros 19.105.2)

**6.3** After this, [Cassander], already conducting matters concerning the realm in a kingly manner, buried in Aigeai Queen Eurydice and King Philip [Arrhidaios], as well as Kynna (whom Alketas had taken up), according to the custom practised for royalty. And having honoured the dead with funerary games, he decided to march to the Peloponnese and summoned the fittest of the Macedonians. (Diodoros 19.52.5)

**6.4** Diyllos the Athenian, in the ninth book of his *Histories*, says that Cassander returned from Boiotia after burying at Aigeai the king and the queen, and in conjunction with them Kynna, the mother of Eurydice, and bestowing on them the appropriate honours, and he instituted a single-combat competition. (Diyllos 73 *FGrH* 1 = Athenaios 4.41)

**6.5** But Karanos, with a great crowd of Greeks, was ordered by an oracle to seek a new habitation in Macedonia. When he arrived in Emathia, he followed a herd of goats who were fleeing from a storm and seized the city of Edessa, whose inhabitants did not hear him coming on account of the greatness of

the rain and fog. And he recalled to mind the oracle by which he had been ordered to "seek a kingdom where goats are leaders" and established this city as the seat of his rule. Later, wherever he directed his troops, he religiously took care to have goats march in front of his standards so that he would have as leaders of his undertakings those goats that he had as founders of his kingdom. He named the city of Edessa Aigeai and its inhabitants Aigiadai, in commemoration of the gift [the Greek word for "goat" is *aix/aigos*]. Then, he expelled Midas, who also held a part of Macedonia, as well as other kings and established himself as sole king in place of all. By uniting the tribes of various peoples, he was the first to make a single body, as it were, of Macedonia, and he laid firm foundations for the expansion of his growing kingdom. (Justin 7.1.5–7)

**6.6** Then, so that Hercules, the fourteen-year son of Alexander, should not be acclaimed to the throne of Macedonia through the influence of his father's name, he [Cassander] ordered him to be killed secretly, along with his mother Barsine, with their bodies buried under earth, lest the murder be betrayed by formal burial. Then, as if he admitted only a modicum of guilt, first with regard to the king himself and then towards his mother Olympias and her son, he killed, with equal deceit, Alexander's other son along with his mother Roxane. It was as if he could not accede to the Macedonian throne to which he aspired except by wickedness. (Justin 15.2.2–4)

**6.7** A few days after, she [Olympias] cremated the body of the assassin, after it had been taken down, above the remains of her husband and made him a tomb in the same place. . . . After this, she forced Kleopatra, for whom she had been divorced from Philip, to end her life by hanging herself, having first killed her daughter in her lap. (Justin 9.7.8)

# 7

# The City of Romulus

In an article on the credibility of early Spartan history, Chester Starr exclaimed, with some incredulity: "Moses has become virtually a historical character; Lycurgus has been resuscitated; soon, no doubt, Romulus will again stride across pages of Roman history."[1] Sure enough, forty years later, the Italian newspaper *Il Messaggero* of February 14, 2005, carried the headline: "ROME: IT'S ALL TRUE." The author of the piece, Claudio Marincola, went on to explain that "excavations in the Forum are bringing to light the house of the king of the city and the hut where the sacred fire of the priestesses burned. And they confirm the birth of the city in 753 BCE." The revelation, widely disseminated in the national and international press at the time, was but the latest of a series of claims arising from excavations in the Roman forum conducted by Andrea Carandini, former professor of archaeology at the University of Rome "La Sapienza" and one of the most prominent archaeologists in Italy.

Twenty years earlier, just west of the Arch of Titus, where the northern slopes of the Palatine hill meet the forum (figs. 7.1, 7.2), Carandini had discovered the remains of Late Republican houses—one of which has been identified as the house of Marcus Aemilius Scaurus, consul for 115 BCE.[2] Beneath these were four sixth-century *atrium* houses, but further exca-

:::

1. Starr 1965: 272.
2. Carandini 2010: 100–101.

7.1 View of the Roman forum from the northwest. The area of Sector 9 is indicated by *A*; that of the Domus Regia by *B*. (Photo by author.)

vations from 1986 to 1993 revealed that the Archaic houses had been built on an artificial platform, under which was preserved a stretch of wall, apparently including a bastion and a gate and dating back to the middle years of the eighth century.[3] Caran-

dini identified the gate as the Porta Mugonia and the wall as the circuit that, according to several literary sources, was erected around the Palatine hill by Romulus, founder and first king of Rome.[4] The new findings became the centrepiece of an exhibition,

:::     3. Carandini 1992; Carandini and Carafa, eds. 1995.
4. See, however, Coarelli 2007: 81–82, who locates the Porta

Mugonia more to the northwest, near the medieval portico that stands in front of the Basilica of Maxentius.

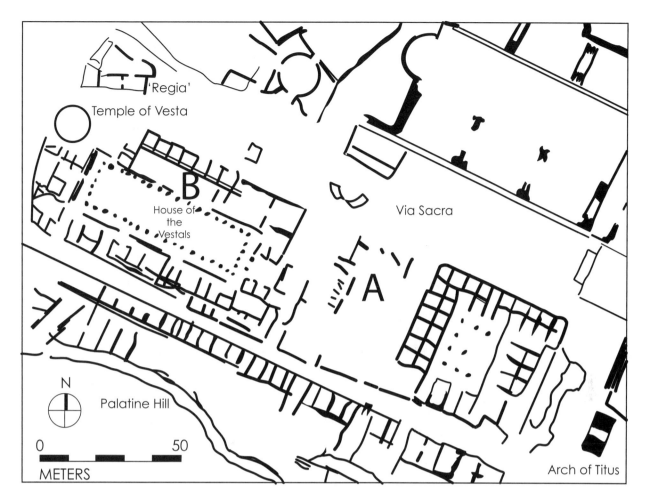

7.2 Plan of the southeastern part of the Roman forum. The area of Sector 9 is indicated by *A*; that of the Domus Regia by *B*.

entitled "Rome, Romulus, Remus and the Foundation of the City," held in the Baths of Diocletian in 2000.[5]

Then, in 2001, the excavations shifted westwards to the area of what had hitherto been identified as the Domus Publica, the official residence of the Pontifex Maximus. Twelve phases were identified in total, running from the middle of the eighth century—thus contemporary with the Palatine wall—down to the building's destruction, possibly in the great fire of 64 CE. During the second half of the eighth century, an imposing courtyard building was constructed, which, in the opinion of Caran-

dini, could only have been the royal residence if not of Romulus, then at least of his successor, Numa Pompilius.[6] Now, most recently, a grotto has been discovered 7 metres beneath the House of Augustus on the Palatine that Carandini has tentatively identified as the Lupercal—the cave where the twins Romulus and Remus were thought to have been suckled by a she-wolf after being washed up on the banks of the Tiber. As Francesco Rutelli, then the minister of cultural heritage, put it: "It is incredible to think that one can finally find a mythological place that today has finally become real."[7]

::: 5. Carandini and Cappelli 2000.
6. Carandini 2004; Filippi 2004.
7. Cited in C. A. Bucci, "Trovato il Lupercale, la grotta di Ro-

molo e Remo," *La Repubblica*, November 21, 2007. Ahead of full publication of the cave, Carandini and Bruno (2008: 4–29) offer preliminary thoughts. It is worth noting that both Adriano La Regina,

In his article in *Il Messaggero*, Marincola describes the discovery of the so-called Domus Regia, the first royal residence at Rome, as a *svolta vera* (a true turning point) and so it is—though not perhaps for the reasons that he attributes. Ever since Giacomo Boni's excavations in the Roman forum at the end of the nineteenth century, archaeologists have disagreed as to when Rome first became a proper city and whether this was the result of a gradual expansion of a single inhabited nucleus or a conscious and deliberate unification of various formerly independent village settlements.[8] But most agreed that archaeology offered an independent and more reliable approach to Rome's past than the mythical traditions, which were generally discounted as being historically worthless. It is, then, not a little ironic that Carandini, who has often championed the value of material evidence over literary testimony (see chap. 9), should appear to threaten archaeology's autonomous status as a historical discipline by appealing precisely to those mythical traditions.[9] Yet, as anybody who studies myth knows only too well, traditions normally exist in a plurality of variants, some of which are mutually incompatible. The question then arises as to whether it is methodologically legitimate to distinguish between "more" and "less" authentic myths and whether archaeology is the appropriate tool with which to do this.

## Untangling the Foundation Myths of Rome

It will probably come as no surprise that all our sources for the origins of Rome are late, with very few predating the emperor Augustus's foundation of the Principate in 27 BCE. The version of the foundation myth that we find in Livy, Dionysios of Halikarnassos, and Plutarch's *Life of Romulus* is, by now, familiar. After the Greek sack of Troy, Aeneas led Trojan refugees to the shores of Latium, where he engineered a treaty with Latinus, ruler of a mixed group of Greek Aborigines, Pelasgians from Thessaly, Arkadians under the leadership of Evander, and Greeks who had accompanied Hercules to Italy. He married Latinus's daughter, Lavinia, and founded the city of Lavinium (fig. 7.3). Thirty years later, his son Ascanius/Iulus founded a new city at Alba. His descendants continued to rule over Alba down to the reign of Amulius, who deposed his brother Numitor and compelled the latter's daughter, Ilia or Rhea Silvia, to become a Vestal Virgin so that there should be no rival heirs to claim the throne. Rhea Silvia became pregnant—perhaps by Mars, though some of our authors are sceptical about this—and gave birth to twin sons. She was either executed or imprisoned, and Amulius issued orders that the sons should be cast into the River Tiber, but the men charged with carrying out these orders were reluctant to approach too closely the floodwaters of the Tiber and left the twins in a coracle on the banks of the Tiber, at the foot of the Palatine hill. They were saved by a she-wolf, who nursed them, and then rescued and reared by a herdsman named Faustulus, who named them Romulus and Remus. Upon reaching adulthood, the twins killed Amulius, restored their grandfather, Numitor, to the throne of Alba, and decided to found a new city at the place where they had been rescued by the wolf, but faction arose between the two brothers and their followers, during which Remus was killed—in some accounts, at the hands of Romulus himself.[10]

former archaeological superintendent for Rome, and Fausto Zevi, professor of archaeology at the University of Rome "La Sapienza," have expressed doubts concerning the identification, noting that the literary sources seem to place the Lupercal further to the west, near the temple of Magna Mater. See "E´ uno splendido ninfeo, ma il Lupercale non era lì," *La Repubblica*, November 23, 2007. As Carandini and Bruno (2008: 10) note, however, the information of Dionysios of Halikarnassos (*Roman Antiquities* 1.32.5) on the placement of the Lupercal is far from specific.

8. See Cornell 1995: 97–103; Forsythe 2005: 91–93.

9. See Fentress and Guidi 1999: 464: "By concerning himself with the texts Carandini has handed the sceptical historians the opportunity to reject archaeology *en bloc*."

10. Livy 1.1–7; Dionysios of Halikarnassos, *Roman Antiquities*

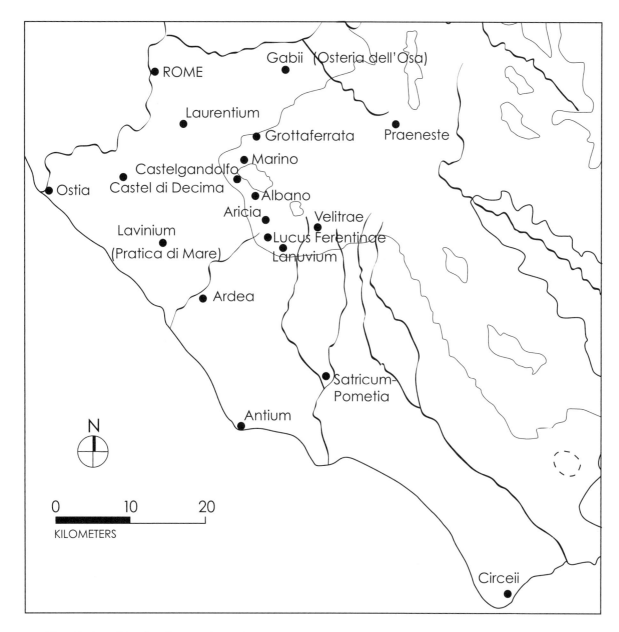

7.3  Map of Latium. (After Cornell 1995: 296 map 5.)

This almost seamless narrative probably owes much to Rome's first historian, Quintus Fabius Pictor, writing—in Greek—towards the end of the third century BCE.[11] But authors such as Livy or Dionysios were all too aware that their accounts were a *bricolage* of multiple, often mutually inconsistent, traditions that originated in the oral domain and were transmitted by a vast array of *literati*, initially Greeks and then Romans also. Dionysios (*Roman Antiquities* 1.72–73), for example, notes eleven alternative accounts for the foundation of Rome, while Plutarch (*Life of Romulus* 1–2) discusses—only then

::: 1.9–90; Plutarch, *Life of Romulus* 3–10; cf. Vergil, *Aeneid* 1.254–79, 6.756–87.

11. Fabius Pictor's account was probably little modified in

Cato's *Origines*, published in the mid-second century. See Gruen 1992: 32–34.

to discount—ten different traditions for the origin of the city. In Sextus Pompeius Festus's second-century CE abridgement of Verrius Flaccus's *De Verborum Significatu* (On the Meaning of Words), no fewer than fifteen versions of Rome's foundation story are recounted, involving five different named founders (s.v. *Roma*).[12]

As table 7.1 shows, many of these variants attribute the city's origins to eponymous founders such as Rhomos/Romus, Rhome/Roma/Rhomis, or Romanus—indeed, the last is doubly implausible in the sense that it is not a noun but an ethnic or adjective derived from the toponym *Roma*. The habit of inventing eponymous founders whose only function is to explain the name of the city to which they are supposed to have given their own name is something of a pathological obsession among Greek ethnographers and antiquarians, and, although it was common practice in the Hellenistic period for kings and queens to give their names to settlements, there is little credible evidence that this was also true for older settlements. That Greek authors should have attributed Greek origins to the populations of Italy is not so surprising. The Greeks sought to accommodate the numerous and various populations with whom they came into contact within their conceptual schema of the world by forging genealogical connections between non-Greek eponymous ancestors and Greek heroes, and the retrieval of Corinthian pottery from the Archaic sanctuary beneath the current church of Sant'Omobono may well suggest a Greek commercial presence in the area of the Forum Boarium at Rome from the later eighth century.[13] What has been more surprising to scholars is the assumption that the Romans placidly accepted the foundation stories that Greek writers invented for them. In the view of Elias Bickerman, this was because the Greeks were almost unique in delineating a boundary between history and fable

and in developing "a scientific prehistory which no other people of the ancient world possessed."[14] Put another way, if non-Greek peoples wanted to find their voice and place in the broader world, they had little option but to resort to the interlocking system of origin myths that Greek ethnographers had developed. "Under the double impact of Greek power and of Greek science, the barbarians, mostly ignorant of their own primitive history, as soon as they had become a bit hellenized, accepted the Greek schema of *archaiologia*."[15]

As we have seen, in the version of Rome's foundation story that is most familiar to us through Livy and Virgil, Aeneas and his son Ascanius are responsible for the foundation not of Rome but of Lavinium and Alba, respectively, while Romulus and Remus found Rome many generations later. It is, however, clear that this is an attempt to reconcile two fundamentally different narratives about the origins of Rome—one (almost certainly Greek in origin) involving Aeneas and one involving Romulus. Attempts to link the two traditions can be detected from at least the later fourth century: the Sicilian antiquarian Alkimos (560 *FGrH* 4) attributed the foundation of Rome to a great-grandson of Aeneas, while the Roman poets Gnaeus Naevius and Quintus Ennius, both writing shortly after the appearance of Fabius Pictor's supposedly "authoritative" history of Rome, declared that Romulus was the son of Aeneas's daughter.[16] The chronographical researches of Timaios of Tauromenion and Eratosthenes of Cyrene, however, exposed a fatal flaw in this conjunction: the foundation of Rome was dated to a period some four centuries later than the date that was calculated for the Trojan War and, hence, for Aeneas's departure for the west. The solution, perhaps "discovered" by Diokles of Peparethos and then followed by Fabius Pictor, was to invent some fifteen generations of Alban kings to plug the

:::
12. For the sources on early Rome: Cornell 1995: 1–30; Wiseman 1995: 160–68; Forsythe 2005: 59–77; Carandini, ed. 2006.

13. Bayet 1920; La Rocca 1974–75; 1977; Holloway 1994: 69; Cornell 1995: 69; Smith 1996: 80; Coarelli 2007: 308.

14. Bickerman 1952: 70. See also Malkin 1998: 29, 176.

15. Bickerman 1952: 73. For a criticism of this admittedly influential hypothesis: Hall 2005.

16. Servius, *Commentary on Aeneid* 1.273.

| Founder | Further details | Festus | Plutarch | Dionysios | Source of attribution |
|---|---|---|---|---|---|
| Rhomos/Romus | Son of Aeneas | √ | | √ | Apollodoros, Kephalon of Gergis, Demagoras, Agathyllos |
| | Son of Ascanius | | | √ | Dionysios of Khalkis |
| | Son of Romulus | √ | | | Agathokles |
| | Son of Jupiter | √ | | | Antigonos |
| | Descendant of Aeneas | √ | | | Agathokles |
| | Follower of Aeneas | √ | | | Kephalon of Gergis |
| | Son of Emathion | | √ | √ | |
| | Son of Italus | | | √ | |
| | Son of Odysseus and Kirke | | | √ | Xenagoras |
| Rhome/Roma | Wife of Latinus | √ | | √ | Kallias |
| | Wife of Aeneas | | √ | | |
| | Wife of Ascanius | | √ | | |
| Aborigines/Pelasgians | | √ | √ | | Cumaean Chronicle |
| Aeneas/Trojans | | | √ | √ | Hellanikos, Damastes of Sigeion |
| Achaeans/Arkadians | | √ | | √ | Herakleides Lembos, Aristotle |
| Rhomis | King of Latins | | √ | | |
| Romanus | Son of Odysseus and Kirke | | √ | | |
| Romulus | Son of Latinus | √ | √ | | |
| | Son of Telemakhos and Kirke | √ | | | Kleinias |
| | Grandson of Numitor | √ | | | Diokles of Peparethos |
| | Son of a Vestal Virgin and an unknown father | √ | | | |
| | Son of Aeneas | | √ | √ | |
| | Grandson of Aeneas | | | √ | |
| | Son of Mars | | √ | | |
| | Son of a slave woman | | √ | | |

gap between Aeneas and Romulus.[17] Is it possible, though, to determine just how far back the respective traditions on Aeneas and Romulus stretch?

The figure of Aeneas appears on imported Greek pottery and on objects of local manufacture in Etruria from the later sixth century.[18] More than half of these depict Aeneas rescuing his father, Anchises, from the burning ruins of Troy, though other episodes—notably Aeneas's combat with Diomedes—are also attested. Nevertheless, all that this demonstrates is that the figure of Aeneas and the exploits associated with him were popular in Late Archaic Etruria. There is, in this material, no explicit connection made between Aeneas and settlement in Italy, nor is there even any reference to Aeneas's deliverance and conveyance of Troy's ancestral gods, to which later traditions referred in order to account for the origins of the *Penates* (the household gods of the Romans).[19] An even earlier representation of Aeneas has been claimed on a late-eighth-century bronze from Castel di Decima near Rome, which depicts a naked ithyphallic male figure being blinded by two birds and a naked female figure nursing an infant. According to Carandini, the female and infant are Aphrodite/Venus and Aeneas, the male being blinded is Anchises, punished for his sexual union with Venus, and the aggressive birds are woodpeckers—*pici* in Latin, and therefore associated with the mythical king Picus, whom Latin myth associated with Zeus/Jupiter.[20] If true, this would constitute an astonishingly early association of Aeneas with Latium, but the identification of the figures is far from secure, and most accounts of Anchises' punishment have him blasted with Zeus's thunderbolt; only Theokritos apparently had him blinded but mentions no birds.[21]

Another piece of evidence commonly cited is a panel from the *Tabula Iliaca Capitolina*, a carved relief of ca. 15 BCE that depicts episodes from the Homeric epics and the epic cycle. The panel shows Aeneas departing from Troy under the guidance of Hermes with Anchises, who holds the household gods, and Ascanius. An inscription informs us that the scene shows "Aeneas departing for Hesperia with his family" and claims that it is taken from the *Ilioupersis* of Stesichoros (840 *FGrH* 6b), a Sicilian poet of the first half of the sixth century. The problem is that the name "Hesperia" (literally "of the evening," hence "of the west") is not otherwise employed to designate Italy before Apollonios of Rhodes in the third century BCE, and Dionysios of Halikarnassos, who was certainly familiar with Stesichoros's *Ilioupersis*, nowhere cites it in his account of the various versions of Aeneas's wanderings.[22] It is therefore supposed that the depiction is only very loosely based on Stesichoros—if it is not an outright invention.

At first sight, a notice in Dionysios looks a little more promising (document 7.1). The "compiler of the priestesses of Hera in Argos" can hardly be anyone else than the fifth-century historian Hellanikos of Lesbos.[23] Whether Hellanikos imagined Aeneas accompanying or following Odysseus to Rome, he indisputably links him to the city's foundation. Some scepticism has been voiced on the grounds that no explicit mention is made of Aeneas's journey to the west in Hellanikos's *Troika* (4 *FGrH* 31), also cited in Dionysios (*Roman Antiquities* 1.46–48),[24] though arguments from silence should always be treated cautiously and it is difficult to believe that Dionysios wilfully fabricated or so completely misinterpreted the evidence to hand. Nevertheless, even if this information was genuinely recorded by Hellanikos, it is far from certain that it was derived from local

: : :   17. Finley 1985: 9; Gruen 1992: 20, 38; Cornell 1995: 70–71; Forsythe 2005: 94; Feeney 2007: 88–89. For Fabius Pictor's debt to Diokles, see Plutarch, *Life of Romulus* 3.1.

18. Schauenberg 1960; Galinsky 1969: 103–40; Horsfall 1979: 386–87.

19. Horsfall 1979: 383–88; Gruen 1992: 22; Cornell 1995: 66.

20. Carandini and Capelli 2000: 101; Carandini 2003: 45.

21. Anchises' punishment: *Homeric Hymn to Aphrodite* 286–88.

For Theokritos: Servius, *Commentary on Aeneid* 2.35, 687. See Wiseman 2001: 183.

22. Perret 1940: 84–89; Horsfall 1979: 375–76.

23. Damastes of Sigeion is said to have been a contemporary, and pupil, of Hellanikos: Dionysios of Halikarnassos, *On Thucydides* 5.330.

24. Horsfall 1979: 376–83; Gruen 1992: 17–18.

7.4   The sanctuary of the thirteen altars at Pratica di Mare. (Photo by author.)

Italian traditions or that it was enthusiastically and immediately accommodated within those same traditions. The earliest unambiguous literary evidence that connects Aeneas and the sacred objects that he brought with him from Troy to Italy is to be found in the brief description of the shrine of the Penates at Lavinium, written by the Sicilian historian Timaios (566 *FGrH* 59) in the late fourth or early third centuries BCE and cited by Dionysios of Halikarnassos (*Roman Antiquities* 1.67.4).

A little earlier (1.64.4–5), Dionysios notes that, after Aeneas's miraculous disappearance during a battle against hostile neighbours, the Latins built a hero shrine to him, with the inscription "To Father Indiges, who presides over the river Numicus." He describes it as a small mound, surrounded by rows of trees. Similarly, Livy (1.2.6) says that Aeneas was worshipped by the river Numicus under the title Jupiter Indiges.[25] Interesting in this respect are the two complexes that were excavated in the 1950s and 1960s near the village of Pratica di Mare. The first is a sanctuary with thirteen altars (fig. 7.4) that may be a shrine to the Penates, although a sixth-century dedication (*ILLRP* 1271a) refers to the Dioskouroi, Castor and Pollux.[26] The second, almost 100 metres to the east of the altars, is a tumulus, identified by

::: 25. Cf. Festus 94 Lindsay.
26. Castagnoli 1975. A fourteenth altar was later found at a short distance from the complex. Interestingly, Macrobius (*Satur-*

*nalia* 3.4.7–9) seems to imply a syncretism between the Dioskouroi, the Great Gods of Samothrace, and the Penates. I owe this reference to Erika Jeck.

7.5   The fourth-century hero shrine at Pratica di Mare from the south, with the seventh-century tomb partially underlying the nearest corner. (Photo by author.)

its excavators as the mound which Dionysios describes (figs. 7.5, 7.6).[27] The tumulus covers a burial that dates to ca. 670–660 BCE, but two vases were inserted in the tomb, possibly signifying a cultic observance, about a century later—contemporaneously with the construction of the first of the thirteen altars in the sanctuary opposite. Towards the end of the fourth century BCE, the tumulus was furnished with a small stone shrine. If the tumulus has been correctly identified, then this fourth-century shrine is almost certainly that described by Timaios

at about the same time. But since it is more likely that a cult of Aeneas was "grafted on" to an earlier cult of Pater Indiges, rather than vice versa, there is no guarantee that Aeneas's connection with the site stretches back any earlier than the later fourth century.

This is also the period in which Alba is first attested as claiming an association with Aeneas—documenting, perhaps, a struggle with Lavinium for the credit of being Rome's metropolis.[28] The confluence of evidence that can be securely dated

: : :   27. Sommella 1971–72; 1974. See discussion in Holloway 1994: 128–38; Cornell 1995: 66–68; Carandini 2003: 539–42. Cornell (1977) and Gruen (1992: 25), on the other hand, object that the tumulus corresponds with Dionysios's mound in neither size nor location.

28. Alkimos 560 *FGrH* 4.

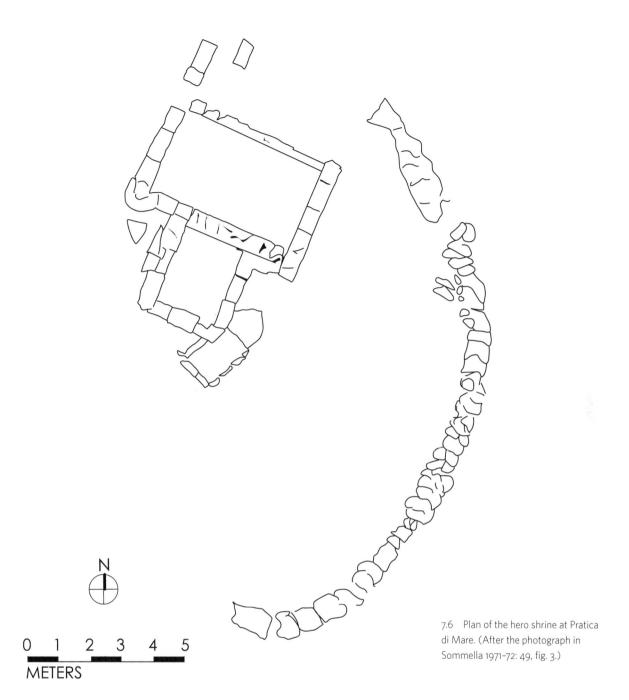

7.6 Plan of the hero shrine at Pratica di Mare. (After the photograph in Sommella 1971–72: 49, fig. 3.)

0 1 2 3 4 5
METERS

to the end of the fourth century is, at the very least, striking, and Erich Gruen has suggested a plausible historical context in which the Romans might have adopted and adapted the Trojan myth—namely, shortly after 338 BCE, when Rome had dissolved the Latin League and was beginning to extend its influence into Campania.[29] By involving the ancient Latin cities of Alba and Lavinium in the tradition of Rome's origins, the victors allowed their subjugated Latin neighbours to salvage their prestige and priority. The adoption of Aeneas, a Trojan prince but also a figure of Greek myth and even cult, served a double purpose: on the one hand, it validated Rome's associations with the Greek world at a time when Rome was entering into intensive diplomacy with the Greek cities of southern Italy and Sicily; on

::: 29. Gruen 1992: 28–31.

the other, it served to distinguish the Romans from the Greeks and to safeguard their distinct identity within the unifying mythical narratives that Greek authors had created for themselves and others.

## Romulus and Remus

The first literary source that explicitly links *both* Romulus *and* Remus by name to the foundation of Rome is astonishingly late. It is an inscription (*SEG* 16 486) from the Greek island of Chios, dated to either the late third or early second century, which refers to a commemorative monument to the twin founders of the city. The Romans, however, were clearly familiar with the story of the twins by at least the early third century: Livy (10.23.12) describes how, in 296 BCE, the aediles Gnaeus and Quintus Ogulnius prosecuted several moneylenders and, from the fines levied, set up near the Ficus Ruminalis on the Palatine hill a statue group of "the founders of the city as infants being suckled by the she-wolf." The monument evidently made an impression, because it was reproduced on the reverse of silver didrachms minted between 269 and 266 BCE.[30] A bronze mirror, dated to ca. 340 BCE, and found at Bolsena but probably manufactured at Praeneste (modern Palestrina), may allow us to push this date back by about half a century. The mirror is fussily decorated with a pastoral scene that depicts, at its centre, an animal suckling two infants.[31] It might seem perverse not to recognize the two infants as Romulus and Remus, but there are some doubts. Firstly, the animal that is nursing the infants may be a lioness rather than a she-wolf—certainly there are parallels for this in Etruscan art.[32] Secondly, the presence on the mirror of what most recognize as the god Mercury causes some difficulty, since he is not part of the Romulus and Remus myth—at least in the versions that we have.[33]

One further piece of evidence that has sometimes been taken into account is the famous bronze statue of a she-wolf, now prominently displayed in the Palazzo dei Conservatori on the Campidoglio (Capitoline hill) at Rome. It was long recognized that the twins suckling beneath her were additions made during the Renaissance,[34] but the wolf's distended teats implied lactation, and the work itself was thought by many to be an Etruscan work of the late sixth or early fifth centuries, which would plausibly allow us to retroject the Romulus and Remus myth to the Late Archaic period.[35] That assumption has now, however, been questioned. Apart from doubts that the casting technique used to manufacture the statue was known in antiquity, a series of radiocarbon analyses carried out between 1996 and 2011 by the University of Salento on fragments of straw used to bind the clay core in the casting process suggests that the wolf is a product of the eleventh or twelfth centuries CE.[36]

The legend of Romulus and Remus is decidedly strange. Apart from its unedifying tales of illegitimacy, an ignominious upbringing, an appeal for support from runaway slaves, debtors, and murderers, deceit on the part of Romulus in selecting a site for the new city, and the rape of the Sabine women, not to mention fratricide, it is oddly lopsided.[37] Why have twin founders if one of them is to be killed off at the very moment of foundation?

:::     30. Cornell 1995: 61; Wiseman 1995: 72–76.

31. Carandini (2003: 180–81; cf. 2011: 37–40) identifies the figures as Mercury, Lara, the woodpecker of Picus, Faunus, Latinus, and Romulus and Remus.

32. Cornell 1995: 63; Forsythe 2005: 95.

33. Wiseman (1995: 65–71; 2001: 184–85) notes that, according to Ovid (*Fasti* 607–16), Mercury was the father of the Lares, agricultural deities associated both with the dead and with the protection of the household, and therefore suggests that it is they who are represented on the mirror. This identification has been endorsed and developed further in Coarelli 2003: 50–53.

34. Wiseman 1995: 63–65.

35. Cornell 1995: 61.

36. Carruba 2007.

37. For the myth: Promathion 817 *FGrH* 1; Cicero, *On Duties* 3.41; Livy 1.8–9; Dionysios of Halikarnassos, *Roman Antiquities* 1.86.3–4; Horace, *Epodes* 7.17–20; Lucan, *Civil War* 1.95; Plutarch, *Moralia* 270f–271a; *Life of Romulus* 2, 9, 14–15; Augustine *City of God* 18.21;

It is for this reason that Herman Strasburger argued that the Romulus and Remus legend was the product of anti-Roman propaganda, produced perhaps among the cities of southern Italy in the later fourth century.[38] Tim Cornell, on the other hand, finds it hard to believe that the Romans would have willingly adopted a pejorative tradition foisted on them by the Greeks. In his view, the dysfunctionality of the story actually argues for its antiquity, in that the Romans are unlikely to have embraced and perpetuated it unless it was sanctioned by long-hallowed tradition.[39]

Like Strasburger, Peter Wiseman also thinks that the Romulus and Remus legend was coined in the later fourth century, but he attributes it not to Greek but to Roman invention, propagated through the *ludi scaenici*—theatrical shows instituted in the third century BCE.[40] Recognizing the duality implicit in the story of the twins, he believes that the myth was coined to provide a charter for the twin consulate—an institution whose establishment he dates to 367 BCE (see chap. 8). Noting that it was not until 342 BCE that the consulship was formally opened up to nonpatrician plebeians and that an ancient source entitled *The Origins of the Roman People* (21.5) connects the name Remus with the Latin verb *remorari* (to delay), Wiseman speculates that "Remus stands for the plebeians, whose share in the power was long delayed."[41] Furthermore, he suggests that the motif of Remus's murder entered the story soon after the Romans resorted to human sacrifice ahead of the Battle of Sentinum in 295 BCE; the unlucky twin thus commemorates the sacrifice that was made to guarantee Rome's invulnerability.[42] On this reading, the tradition of Romu-

lus's and Remus's foundation of Rome would have coalesced in the late fourth and early third centuries—contemporary with, if not even a little later than, the tradition that ascribed Roman origins to Aeneas and his descendants.[43]

There is, however, another possibility. When Romulus is first attested in literary sources, it is alone, without Remus.[44] That this may be more than simply accidental is suggested by the fact that the younger twin is something of a pale spectre compared with his sibling. Firstly, our sources tell us that, in deciding where to situate their new city, Remus chose a locality named variously as Remoria, Remuria, or Remora. The fact that the toponym is so obviously derived from Remus's name hardly commands confidence and neither does the fact that authors disagreed as to exactly where this locality was: some placed it around 7.5 kilometres from Rome, others near the river Tiber, about 5.5 kilometres from the city, and yet others on the Aventine hill.[45] By contrast, the vast majority of our sources state that Romulus chose the Palatine hill for his settlement and that it was here that his city first arose (documents 7.2-4, 6-8, 10).[46] Such unanimity is surprising and may suggest that the tradition that associated Romulus with the Palatine was more entrenched than that which credited both twins with the foundation of the city.

Secondly, as several scholars have suspected, the name Remus is probably a Latinized form of the eponymous Rhomos, credited by several Greek authors with the foundation of Rome (table 7.1).[47] The name Romulus has also often been treated similarly: Cornell, for example, states that it "is an eponym formed from the name of the city, and perhaps

::: Tertullian, *Against the Pagans* 2.9.39; Servius, *Commentary on Aeneid* 1.273; Justin, *Epitome* 28.2.8-10.

38. Strasburger 1968.

39. Cornell 1977: 8-11; 1995: 60-61.

40. Wiseman 1995.

41. Wiseman 1995: 110. See Livy 6.42.9-10 for the admission of plebeians to the consulship.

42. For sceptical reactions: Gabba 1997; Carandini 2006: xlix; Purcell 1997. Conversely, Forsythe (2005: 96) thinks that the "thesis makes perfectly good sense."

43. Cf. Ampolo (1988b: xxxix–xl), who believes the foundation story was invented after 338 BCE, when the Romans began

to penetrate into Campania and came into increased contact with Greek foundation stories.

44. Alkimos 560 FGrH 4. See Wiseman 1995: 61.

45. Five miles (ca. 7.5 kilometres): *Origins of the Roman People* 23.1. Thirty stades (ca. 5.5 kilometres) from Rome: Dionysios of Halikarnassos, *Roman Antiquities* 1.85.6. Aventine: Plutarch, *Life of Romulus* 9.4. It is this geographical indeterminacy which makes it difficult to accept Coarelli's identification (2003) of Remoria with Colle delle Piche.

46. One notable exception is Ennius, *Annals* 75-76 Skutsch, where Romulus is associated with the Aventine.

47. Cornell 1977: 28; Forsythe 2005: 94.

means simply 'the Roman' (cf. Siculus = Sicilian); we may take it as certain that no such person as 'Romulus' ever existed."[48] This is not, however, entirely accurate. "The Roman" would, in Latin, be *Romanus* and the parallel adduced with "Siculus" is misleading because it is a Latinization of the Greek *Sikelos*.[49] Furthermore, we now have evidence that Romulus was a genuine proper name rather than an eponymous construction. In the cemetery of Crocifisso del Tufo, on the slopes of the Etruscan city of Orvieto, one of the tombs has an architrave inscribed with the Etruscan proper name Rumele. Linguistic parallels from other Etruscan inscriptions indicate that Etruscan Rumele would become Romulus in Latin. By contrast, had the Etruscans borrowed the personal name from Latin, it would have been rendered *Rumule*, not Rumele.[50] It is also clear that the name Rumele cannot be an Etruscan form of *Romanus*, which we know was *Rumate* in the Etruscan language. This suggests strongly that the name Romulus was Etruscan in origin and that its adoption into Latin probably occurred at an early, though unspecifiable, date.[51]

This does not, of course, argue for the historicity of the Romulean foundation of Rome. While it is intrinsically unlikely that the Romans waited more than four centuries before speculating on the circumstances of their city's origins, the initial settlement of Rome, like other settlements in antiquity, must have been an experiment whose outcome was unknowable, and it is quite likely that the desire to preserve an accurate memory of what must have been an uncertain and risk-laden endeavour was not foremost among the concerns of the original settlers. All that it suggests is that at some point, perhaps quite early in Rome's history, there existed a tradition that attributed the beginnings of Rome to a figure named Romulus, who founded a settlement on the Palatine hill. That this was far, however, from being *the* official foundation myth of Rome is demonstrated by the multiple variants that existed even as late as the third century BCE, when Fabius Pictor sought to reconcile these often mutually incompatible stories within a single narrative.[52] He could have chosen to ignore the legends concerning Aeneas. That he did not may imply that he regarded them as no less authoritative than those concerning Romulus.

## The Early Kings Materialized?

Beneath an Archaic atrium house (*Domus* 4), Carandini found the evidence that convinced him he had unearthed part of Romulus's Rome. Here, a settlement of huts, dating to between the Latial IIB and IIIA phases, was destroyed before the end of Latial IIB and buried beneath a uniform stratum of earth designed to provide a firm bedding for the foundations of a wall (fig. 7.7).[53] The stretch of wall that has been excavated in Sector 9 runs approximately 12 metres from northwest to southeast; four building phases have been identified, commencing in Latial IIIB and ending in the second third of the sixth century, when this part of the wall was buried beneath the atrium house.[54] In its first phase, the stone foundations of the wall were punctuated by large masses of red tufa, placed at points where the wall changed directions, with a superstructure of clay reinforced by wooden posts. Carandini—though not, it should be noted, all of his collaborators—interprets an apparent gap in the wall as a gate and even reconstructs a bastion and a wooden square "guardroom" structure in association with it.[55] The construction

:::     48. Cornell 1995: 70.

49. Cf. Grandazzi 1997: 170.

50. Contra Grandazzi 1997: 170.

51. De Simone 2006. I am grateful to Gabriël Bakkum for explaining and verifying the phonological issues involved.

52. See Wiseman 1995: 160–68.

53. Brocato 1995.

54. See generally Carandini and Carafa, eds. 1995.

55. Ricci, Brocato, and Terrenato 1992: 112–13; 1995: 139–40.

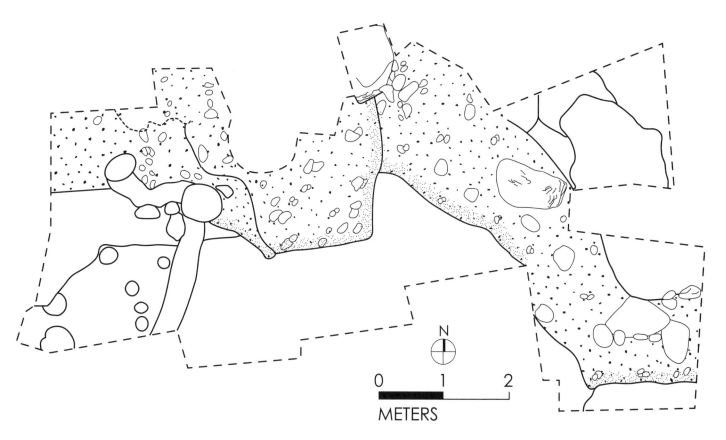

7.7 Plan of the wall excavated in Sector 9, phase 2. (After Carandini and Carafa, eds. 1995: 139, fig. 95.)

of the wall is dated by a rectangular trench beneath the so-called gate, which contained two fibulae, a pierced bone disk, a brown impasto cup, an Italo-Geometric cup, and an Italo-Geometric piriform rattle, all dating to Latial IIIB.[56] It is not unusual to find what are called "foundation deposits," made to propitiate the gods, beneath early Roman structures, but the rattle is an artifact that is typically found in female burials. For this reason, although no skeletal evidence was recovered, the excavators wondered if the trench was a tomb or a cenotaph, marking a propitiatory human sacrifice, whether real or symbolic.[57] In the course of Latial IVA, the wall was destroyed and its ruins carefully buried in a large circular pit just outside where the gate had stood. A second wall was constructed, and beneath it was deposited this time what was undeniably an infant burial in a *dolium*, accompanied by a cup, an impasto bowl, some beads, and a necklace bead made of blue glass paste. This too has been tentatively interpreted as a human sacrifice—perhaps a rite of expiation for the destruction of the previous wall.[58]

A number of authors note that Romulus's first city arose on the Palatine hill. Walls are specifically mentioned by Varro (document 7.11), Tibullus (document 7.6), and Dionysios of Halikarnassos (documents 7.4–5), who also informs us that Romulus later strengthened the Palatine fortifications and extended them to include the Capitoline and Aventine hills.[59] Diodoros (document 7.2), Tacitus (document 7.8), and Aulus Gellius (document 7.10),

∴∴∴    56. Ricci, Brocato, and Terrenato 1992: 114, 117; Carafa and Brocato 1992: 129; Carafa 1995: 194.

57. Ricci, Brocato, and Terrenato 1992: 116–17; 1995: 154–57; Carandini 2003: 503; 2011: 59.

58. Ricci, Brocato, and Terrenato 1992: 117; 1995: 146, 159–60; Carafa and Brocato 1992: 130; Carandini 2003: 505–6; 2011: 61–63.

59. Dionysios of Halikarnassos, *Roman Antiquities* 2.37.1.

TABLE 7.2 The various dates given for the foundation of Rome

| | |
|---|---|
| 814 | Timaios of Tauromenion (566 *FGrH* 60) |
| 754/753 | Varro (in Censorinus, *On His Birthday* 21.6), Velleius Paterculus 1.8.4 |
| 752/751 | Cato (*Origines* fr. 17) |
| 751/750 | Diodoros of Sicily (7.5.1) |
| 748/747 | Fabius Pictor (809 *FGrH* 3a) |
| 729/728 | Cincius Alimentus (810 *FGrH* 1) |

on the other hand, talk about a trench, designed to mark out the *pomerium*, or "sacred boundary," of the Romulean city; Tacitus notes that this was marked by "stones . . . placed at certain intervals" (*interiecti lapides*). The wall in Sector 9 is, then, approximately in the right location, but what about its date? As we have seen, the first phase of the wall is dated to Latial IIIB. On the standard chronology, largely elaborated on the basis of associations between Italian material and imported Greek pottery in the Latial IV phase, this would be ca. 750–725 BCE.[60] Ancient authors gave various dates for Romulus's foundation of Rome, ranging from 814 BCE down to 729/8 BCE at the extremes, but most cluster within a few years of Varro's date of 754/3 BCE (table 7.2). This seemingly happy match, together with the location of the wall, was enough to convince Carandini: "The coincidence between the monument that we have brought to light and that which is described by the literary sources is, for a person of Western culture, quite natural, not to say inescapable. Only a masochist, a pervert [*sic*], or a hypocrite could fail to see it."[61]

Matters may not, however, be so simple. Even if the standard chronology is correct, we need to ask ourselves one very basic question: how did ancient authors arrive at their dates for the foundation of the city? It is extremely improbable that the Romans kept a year-by-year account of events dating back to the foundation of the city, and it is unlikely—to judge from the example of the first Greek chronographers—that they showed much interest in keeping annual records until the later fifth, or even fourth, century. This means that dates prior to that period must have been calculated by some other method—probably generational. By the time of the Late Republic, tradition held that Rome had been ruled by seven kings, from Romulus down to Tarquinius Superbus, whose forced departure from the city ushered in the Republic, dated by Varro to 509 BCE (see chap. 8). Now, when one computes that the 245 years that intervene between 754 and 509 BCE are equivalent to seven thirty-five year generations, it becomes clear that the Varronian foundation date is merely an estimated calculation (the slight variations to be found in other authors are probably the result of employing different generational lengths and chronological baselines).[62] But, quite apart from the inherently legendary characteristics of many of the early kings (see chap. 8), a reign is not the same thing as a generation. In fact, there are no historical parallels for a 245-year period in which only seven kings reigned.[63] Whether there were more than seven rulers, whether their collective rule was shorter than 245 years, or whether the entire regal period is utter fiction, the literary date for the foundation of Rome is essentially meaningless, and there is no justification in claiming that it is "confirmed" by archaeology if it ultimately rests on no solid basis.[64]

::::

60. Bietti Sestieri 1980; Holloway 1994: 42–46. Radiocarbon dates from sites in Latium may now suggest a slightly higher chronology for the earlier Latial phases: see Bietti Sestieri and De Santis 2008; Bietti Sestieri 2009. Marco Bettelli (1997: 191–98) has proposed even earlier dates for Latial I–IIIA on the basis of dendrochronological dates from Switzerland and Austria; cf. Sperber 1987. The "High Chronology" is, however, disputed in Fantalkin, Finkelstein, and Piasetzky 2011: 185–88.

61. Carandini 2003: 492. The "coincidence" is certainly accepted by Grandazzi (1997: 143–76).

62. Cornell 1995: 72–73. See, however, Feeney (2007: 90–96), who suggests that the regal period was dated by counting *forward* from the Trojan War, not *backward* from the foundation of the Republic, and that the responsibility for this should be credited to Timaios, Diokles, and Fabius Pictor.

63. Finley 1985: 9–10; Cornell 1995: 121.

64. See also Feeney 2007: 91–92.

Another problem regards the precise function of the wall in Sector 9. Some possibilities can be ruled out: it is not part of a building, because there are no abutting walls; it is not a terrace wall, because there is no redeposited fill on the interior; and were it a drainage channel, it should be running north-south rather than northwest-southeast.[65] Nor can we be absolutely positive that it was part of a continuous wall that encircled the Palatine, though the fact that further short stretches of both the first and second phases of the wall have been excavated some 30–40 metres to the west, near the House of the Vestals, makes this a distinct possibility.[66] But the excavated portion of the wall hardly squares with those literary sources that talk about fortifications. For one thing, at barely 1 metre across, it is not very sturdy. For another, we would expect fortification walls to stand at a higher elevation to be truly effective.[67] Furthermore, although the wall was swiftly rebuilt after its destruction in Latial IVA, its successor was less substantial, lacking even a foundation trench. It is difficult to avoid the suspicion that what mattered most was the symbolism of the wall itself rather than any defensive function it may have served.[68]

By the Late Republican period, the Romans celebrated two festivals on December 11. The first was the *Agonalia* in honour of Indiges, in which the whole population participated; the second was the *Septimontium* which, according to Festus (474 Lindsay [citing the Augustan jurist Antistius Labeo]), was a festival celebrated by the hills (*montes*) of Rome.[69] On the basis of Varro's comment (*On the Latin Language* 5.41) that "where Rome now is, there used to be the Septimontium, named from the same number of hills which the city later included within its walls," scholars have generally inferred that the festival of the Septimontium was celebrated by the inhabitants of Rome's seven hills.

TABLE 7.3 The members of the Septimontium according to Antistius Labeo (in Festus), Varro, and Servius

|  | Antistius Labeo | Varro | Servius |
|---|---|---|---|
| Palatine | √ | √ | √ |
| Velian | √ | [√] |  |
| Fagutal | √ |  |  |
| Subura | √ |  |  |
| Cermalus | √ | [√] |  |
| Oppian | √ | [√] |  |
| Cispian | √ | [√] |  |
| Caelian | √ | √ | √ |
| Capitoline |  | √ |  |
| Aventine |  | √ | √ |
| Viminal |  | √ | √ |
| Quirinal |  | √ | √ |
| Esquiline |  |  | √ |
| Janiculum |  |  | √ |

The long-lived literary topos of Rome and its seven hills goes back to Vergil (*Georgics* 2.543–45), who tells how "Rome became the most beautiful city of the world and surrounded her seven citadels with one wall."[70] Yet Servius (*Commentary on the Aeneid* 6.783), the great fourth-century CE commentator on Vergil, notes that great doubt (*grandis . . . dubitatio*) arose as to exactly which, of Rome's various prominences, were enumerated among the seven. Indeed, his now seemingly canonical list of the seven (table 7.3) includes the Janiculum, which originally lay on the western, Etruscan bank of the Tiber, and the Aventine, which tradition held was still outside the

65. Ricci, Brocato, and Terrenato 1995.

66. Interestingly, at this latter location too there are burials similar to that associated with the destruction of the first phase of the wall. See Carandini 2003: 505.

67. Harris 2001: 543; Carandini 2003: 496; Smith 2005: 94.

68. Terrenato 1995: 138; 1996: 317.

69. Sextus Pompeius Festus produced, in the late second century CE, an abridgement of a dictionary entitled *De Verborum*

*Significatu* (On the Meaning of Words), written by the Augustan scholar Marcus Verrius Flaccus. Approximately half of the only surviving manuscript of Festus's abridgement was destroyed by fire but can be partially reconstructed using an epitome of the work that was written by Paul the Deacon in the ninth century CE.

70. Cf. *Aeneid* 6.783; Horace, *Carmen Saeculare* 7; Tibullus, *Elegies* 2.5.55–56. For Vergil's responsibility in propagating the topos of Rome and its seven hills, see Gelsomino 1975: 57–58.

*pomerium* in the reign of Servius Tullius. Varro's list actually enumerates ten hills, though he clearly regarded the Velian and Cermalus as components of the Palatine and the Cispian and the Oppian as part of the Esquiline.

The problem is that Festus's list contains eight, not seven, names—including the Subura, which is not properly speaking a hill at all—and diverges considerably from Varro's list. Furthermore, in enumerating the hills included in the Septimontium, Festus specifies that sacrifices were offered only on behalf of the Palatine and the Velia. It could be that Festus's catalogue represents an earlier constituency of participants in the Septimontium,[71] but since—as far as we can tell—he offers no specific number with regard to the participants in the festival, it is equally possible that Varro's derivation of *septimontium* from *septes* (seven) and *montes* (hills) is a false etymology. In fact, it has been suggested that the name of the festival derives not from *septem* but from *saepti* (enclosed), perhaps with reference to only the Palatine and Velian hills.[72] The verb *saepire* is often employed for enclosing altars and sacred areas, and, although this etymological derivation is not accepted by all scholars,[73] it is an explanation that accords well with the seemingly symbolic character of the wall in Sector 9.

About 75 metres northwest of Sector 9, adjacent to the sanctuary of Vesta and beneath what Gianfilippo Carettoni had identified as the Domus Publica,[74] Carandini's next series of excavations revealed a large structure, of which twelve building phases have been identified, stretching from the middle of the eighth century BCE down to the first century CE (fig. 7.2).[75] To the first phase, which dates to Latial IIIB and is therefore contemporary with the first Palatine wall, belongs a rectangular building,

approximately 8 by 4.5 metres, constructed from pisé (rammed earth) and reinforced on the interior by wooden posts. Shortly afterwards, the structure was rebuilt on a grander and more complex scale (phase 2) and comprised a large room flanked by a chamber on either side, of which one contained a hearth (fig. 7.8). Although the remains are poorly preserved, it appears that a bench ran around the inside of the large hall, perhaps suggesting that it served as a venue for feasting. On the southern side of the building, a portico opened out on a large paved courtyard, bringing the total area of the compound to approximately 22 by 5 metres. The date of this second phase is provided by an infant burial, deposited after the walls were founded but before the pavement was laid, in which were found two fibulae, two bracelets, a pendant, some glass jewellery, and an impasto cup dating to the later Latial IIIB period. This building was also destroyed in Latial IVA.[76]

In describing the destruction wreaked by the great fire of Rome in 64 CE, Tacitus mentions the royal residence (*regia*) of Rome's second king, Numa Pompilius, which he seems to associate with the Sanctuary of Vesta (document 7.12)—a location confirmed by Plutarch (document 7.13). For this reason, and on account of its size and apparent importance, Carandini has argued that the second phase of this building should be the Domus Regia of Numa, leaving open the possibility that the first phase was built by Romulus himself, and that an apsidal building originally excavated to the west in 1879 is the Aedes Larum (the shrine of the Lares).[77] The building would have maintained this function until the time of Tarquinius Priscus, who established a new royal residence further to the east, near the Porta Mugonia;[78] at this point, the Domus Regia became the official residence of the Rex Sacrorum.[79] This is,

: : :   71. This is the argument of Carandini 2003: 267–380; cf. 2011: 18–22.

72. This is the suggestion of Holland (1953), who documents other instances of orthographic variation between -ae- and -e-.

73. E.g., Carandini 2003: 270–71. Fridh (1987: 123) notes that, while Holland's suggestion explains why eight names are included in Festus's list, it does not account for why the Subura could be considered a *mons*.

74. Carettoni 1978–80.

75. See generally Filippi 2004.

76. Filippi 2004: 107–9, 113–14; Carandini 2004: 54; 2011: 70–74.

77. Carandini 2011: 70.

78. Solinus 1.24.

79. Carandini 2004: 52–54; 2011: 75–80; cf. Filippi 2004: 103, 121. See, however, Cornell (1995: 241), who speculates that the Rex Sacrorum was evicted from the Domus Regia at the beginning of the Republic and his place taken by the Pontifex Maximus.

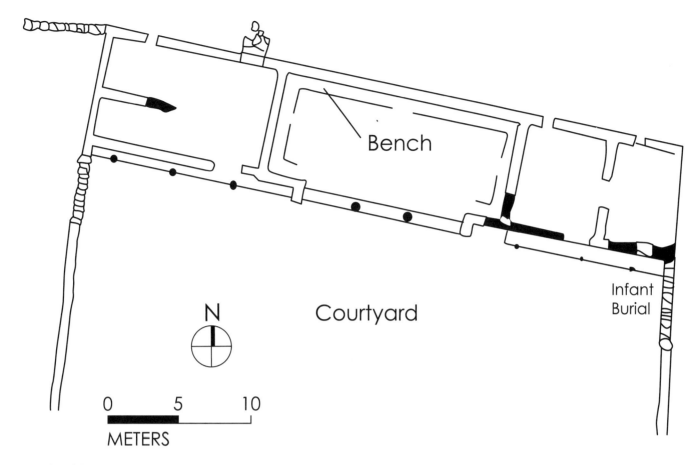

Bench

Courtyard

Infant
Burial

METERS

7.8  Plan of the Domus Regia, phase 2. (After Carandini 2011: 72, fig. 35.)

of course, a bold hypothesis, and it requires us to accept the historical existence of Numa (see p. 152). What is undeniable about this building is that it is currently unparalleled at Rome in terms of its size and construction technique.[80] At the same time, it is precisely this scarcity of parallels that makes it difficult to determine the exact function that the building served.

There is, however, a far more fundamental question of method here. We cannot simply raid, in an undisciplined way, the literary testimony and the material record for elements that initially seem to match with one another and ignore every other piece of evidence that fails to fit so satisfyingly, or even threatens to compromise, the general picture we want to construct. In our analysis of the literary evidence, we examined the Romulean tradition against other versions in order to emphasize that it was just one of a variety of tales that had been recited over many centuries. In the case of the material evidence, it is similarly indispensable to situate the wall in Sector 9 and the large building by the sanctuary of Vesta within the general context of the urban transformations that are revealed by archaeology to have taken place in the eighth and seventh centuries BCE.

:::  80. The closest parallel comes from a late-eighth-century building at Tarquinia: Filippi 2004: 108.

Determining an archaeological foundation date for a city such as Rome, where more or less continuous settlement stretches back to the Middle Bronze Age (ca. 1600–1300 BCE), is far from straightforward.[81] To complicate matters further, three millennia of habitation and overbuilding, together with natural occurrences such as floods and earthquakes that have deposited up to 6 metres of debris in the area of the Roman forum, have made it extremely difficult to reconstruct the urban fabric of the city in its entirety at any one stage of its development.[82]

The first secure indications of intensive settlement in the centre of Rome come from the cemetery of forty-one cremation and inhumation graves excavated by Giacomo Boni between 1902 and 1905 on the northern side of the forum, by the church of San Lorenzo in Miranda (incorporating the temple of Antoninus and Faustina). At first, it was thought that the juxtaposition of inhumation and cremation rites reflected the ethnically specific practices of two different populations—Latins, based on the Palatine, and Sabines on the Quirinal.[83] This theory was largely abandoned due to the typological classification of Roman burials drawn up by Hermann Müller-Karpe, which seemed to suggest that the cremation burials should be dated to the Latial I phase while none of the inhumations predated Latial II.[84] In other words, the difference was to be explained in chronological rather than cultural terms.[85] Even this interpretation, however, has been challenged. On the basis of her excavation of the Iron Age site of Osteria dell'Osa, some 20 kilometres to the east of Rome, Anna Maria Bietti Sestieri has argued that

Müller-Karpe's analysis, which was based on the associations of bronze artifacts, did not account for family groupings and that the earliest cremation and inhumation burials in the forum are probably contemporary and date to the very end of Latial I.[86] At Osteria dell'Osa, and in the Quattro Fontanili cemetery at Veii, there are indications that the rite of cremation was reserved for elite males, so it is likely that status distinctions may also explain the diversity of mortuary disposal in the forum.[87] An early cremation burial beneath the House of Livia on the Palatine and reports of cremation graves from the slopes of the Quirinal suggest scattered settlements occupying the hills around what would later be the forum.[88]

Down to the end of the Latial IIA phase, the burial practices at Rome are similar to those found at other sites in Latium—most notably Osteria dell'Osa but also Lavinium and, in the Alban hills, Grottaferrata, Marino, and Castel Gandolfo. Indeed, the Alban hills seem to be at the centre of a network of trade routes and communications that connected Latium to both Etruria to the north (bypassing Rome) and Campania to the south. With the transition to Latial IIB, however, the quantity of tombs and material from the Alban sites seems to decline, while Rome now emerges as the nodal point of transregional routes.[89] Significant in this regard is the appearance of a new necropolis on the Esquiline hill. Unfortunately, the material from the Esquiline was collected haphazardly and hastily in the course of the urban planning that accompanied the designation of Rome as Italy's capital in 1870, but it is clear that

∴  81. Carandini 2003: 114, 126, 218, 238–39.

82. Terrenato 2003; Heiken, Funiciello, and De Rita 2005: 87–95.

83. An original division between Latins and Sabines was also invoked to explain why, in Republican Rome, citizens were variously called *Romani* and *Quirites*. Livy (1.13) says that the name Quirites was derived from Cures, the capital of the Sabines, while Varro (*On the Latin Language* 5.51) notes that, shortly after Romulus's inauguration of the Palatine, the Sabine king Titus Tatius occupied the Quirinal. Similarly, the priestly college of the Salii was divided between the Salii Palatini, who served Mars, and the

Salii Collini, who served Quirinus. See Carandini 2003: 114–15, 335–36, 341, and—more sceptically—Momigliano 1989: 26–27.

84. Müller-Karpe 1962.

85. For a general discussion: Holloway 1994: 27–36; Smith 1996: 51; Forsythe 2005: 83.

86. Bietti Sestieri 1980: 67–69.

87. Bietti Sestieri 1982: 126–29; Cornell 1995: 51–53; Smith 1996: 51.

88. Carettoni 1954–55: 299; Cornell 1995: 54, 72; Forsythe 2005: 82, 85.

89. Bietti Sestieri 1982: 70–75; Cornell 1995: 48–55.

the necropolis was large and that its origins date to Latial IIB.[90] That, together with its location at some distance from the earlier nuclei of settlement on the Palatine and Capitoline, indicates an expanding settlement, although there is some disagreement as to whether this represents an expansion of the Palatine nucleus or the physical unification of formerly separate communities on the Palatine, Capitoline, and Quirinal hills.[91] Furthermore, in the subsequent Latial III phase, costlier funerary equipment begins to appear in some of the graves at Rome. Although we should be careful about assuming a direct relationship between the wealth of grave goods and the status of the deceased person whom they accompany, this does at the very least suggest that there was more wealth available to be disposed in funerary contexts and this, in turn, should indicate the emergence of social stratification and a basic division of labour—both inevitable consequences of an expanding population.[92]

The settlement traces on the Palatine, together with the "extraurban" Esquiline cemetery and the division of labour that seems to be attested for Latial III, persuaded Müller-Karpe that the origins of Rome should be dated to the eighth century and that the city gradually expanded outwards as part of a process he terms *Stadtwerdung* (urban evolution).[93] By contrast, the Swedish archaeologist Einar Gjerstad argued that mere evidence of expanding settlement nuclei was insufficient and that other criteria should be sought to determine when Rome first became a city.[94] In the 1950s, Gjerstad had excavated a grid measuring 5 by 3.5 metres in the Roman forum, where he identified no fewer than twenty-nine distinct layers. Dating the lowest six to a "pre-urban" phase, characterized by a hut settlement lasting into Latial IV, Gjerstad focused

attention on a gravel layer in stratum 22, which he dated to 575 BCE. For Gjerstad, this represented the first pavement of the forum and therefore served to mark Rome's transition to urban status in the first quarter of the sixth century: "The Forum Romanum is the birth-place of Rome."[95]

Gjerstad's chronology, which was based on his study of impasto pottery, is now generally regarded as too low, and many scholars prefer to raise the date of the first pavement of the forum to ca. 625 BCE, but his belief that the laying out of the forum marked a significant stage in Rome's development has won many supporters.[96] So, for example, Carmine Ampolo notes that concrete signs of political and religious life at Rome rarely predate the later seventh century. Among these, Ampolo includes the first dedications on the Capitoline hill (which he dates to Latial IVB), contemporary domestic and cultic material from a well near the Regia, constructed around the end of the seventh century, and the establishment in the area of the *comitium* (the meeting place for the citizen assembly) of a shrine to Vulcan (the Volcanal).[97] Similarly, Cornell considers the construction of monumental buildings and the establishment of public cults to be a significant indication that Rome's urban origins belong to the decades either side of 625 BCE.[98]

Terms such as "urbanization" and "state formation" are fraught with definitional difficulties: what the ancients classified as a "city" would, in many parts of the world today, barely classify as a medium-sized town, while "state organization" can assume different degrees of complexity in different contexts. At this point, there might be some value in considering the comparative example of Greece.[99] We do, of course, need to be sensitive to

::: 90. Holloway 1994: 21–27; Forsythe 2005: 82.

91. Ampolo 1988a: 160–61; Grandazzi 1997: 144–45; Gusberti 2005b: 169.

92. Gjerstad 1965: 20; Smith 1996: 50–53; Fentress and Guidi 1999: 465. For the risks in establishing direct correlations between grave goods and status, see Ucko 1969; Leach 1977.

93. Müller-Karpe 1962: 61–62.

94. Gjerstad 1965: 21–22.

95. Gjerstad 1965: 24. See also Gjerstad 1953: 43–52; 1966: 358–63; 1973: 83–89.

96. It is also becoming clearer that Gjerstad's "hut settlement" in the forum basin may be phantomatic. See Ammerman 1990; Filippi 2005: 103–5.

97. Ampolo 1988a: 156–58.

98. Cornell 1995: 102–3.

99. For the value of the comparative approach: Raaflaub 1986a: 29–30; Momigliano 1989: 6.

regional differences—indeed, it would be inaccurate to say that, even in Greece, processes of urbanization and state formation proceeded everywhere at the same pace—but recent decades of collaborative work have revealed certain commonalities among Greek, Etruscan, and Phoenician polities, and some scholars have even posited direct influence.[100] There is, however, one further advantage of looking at the phenomenon in the Greek world: no modern scholar takes seriously traditions such as the foundation of Argos by Phoroneus, the son of the River Inachos, or of Sparta by Lakedaimon, son of the mountain nymph Taÿgetos.[101] For this reason, studies of the development of the Greek polis have been conducted largely on archaeological grounds, without the distraction of literary sources.

Sites such as Athens, Argos, and Corinth were occupied throughout the Early Iron Age by small communities clustered in village-like settlements. In the course of the eighth century, these separate settlements expanded to form a single settlement nucleus at Athens and Argos, though the process may have taken a little longer at Corinth. By about 700 BCE, in both Athens and Argos, burial grounds scattered throughout the new urban habitat were abandoned, with the dead now being buried in outlying "extramural" cemeteries. In the last half of the eighth century, there is also greater variation between burials in terms of grave goods, which is probably symptomatic of increasing socioeconomic differentiation. Evidence for fortifications is rare—at least on the Greek mainland—until the sixth century.[102] Although there is now increasing evidence for cultic observance in the tenth and ninth centuries, it is also the eighth century that witnesses the commencement of archaeologically visible cult in what are evidently civic contexts. The earliest public buildings, on the other hand, do not appear

to predate the seventh and sixth centuries: inscriptions documenting the appearance of "ascribed" named magistracies and literary references to a self-conscious aristocratic class—both sure evidence for a "state" apparatus—are features of the same period. Finally, while open spaces in conjunction with cult buildings at Zagora (Andros), Emborio (Chios), Koukounaries (Paros), and Dreros (Crete) may have served as a civic meeting place or agora, a formal agora does not seem to have been laid out at Argos until the sixth century, when the marshy area at the foot of the Larisa acropolis was drained. At Athens, the Classical agora cannot have been laid out until the Eridanos valley was filled and levelled in the later sixth, or even early fifth, century.[103]

The picture that we have of Rome in the same period is not radically different. In the Latial II phase (ninth and early eighth centuries on the conventional chronology), small, isolated settlements, indicated by hut foundations and burials, occupied the Palatine and Capitoline and perhaps also the Quirinal and some of the other hills; in the case of the Capitoline, where there is also evidence for metalworking, the settlement may stretch back into the Late Bronze Age.[104] In Latial IIIA (mid-eighth century), the shift to a larger and more distant cemetery on the Esquiline and the more evident status distinctions in the mortuary record almost certainly testify to a larger, more unified but socioeconomically stratified population. This is also precisely the time at which Rome begins to eclipse its Alban neighbours. There is, as yet, no clear evidence for fortifications or public buildings, but further research has now identified cultic deposits that stretch back to the Latial IIIA phase—most notably on the Capitoline, perhaps in association with the cult of Jupiter Feretrius, but also in what would be the sanctuary of Vesta and the Volcanal.[105] Accord-

:::     100. For a comparative study of city-states, see Hansen, ed. 2000. For the influence of the Greek polis on Italian city-states: Momigliano 1989: 6. Smith (2005:102–4) wonders whether the influence might be in the opposite direction.

101. Pausanias 2.15.5, 4.1.2.

102. Frederiksen 2011.

103. See generally Hall 2014: 72–90, 127–144, 200–214. Morris (1991) argues that "state formation" precedes "urbanization" in

Greece, but this depends on how each is defined. For the Athenian agora: Ammerman 1996b; Papadopoulos 1996. An earlier agora may have existed to the east of the Athenian acropolis, but its origins are, as yet, undated: Miller 1995.

104. Carandini 2003: 491–92; Mazzei 2007: 153; Cifani 2008: 99; Albertoni and Damiani 2008: 51.

105. Carandini 2003: 500–501; 2011: 91; Filippi 2005: 103; Gusberti 2005a; Mazzei 2007: 153; Cifani 2008: 79; Albertoni and Da-

ing to recent geophysical investigations, what Gjerstad originally identified as layers of hut settlements belong instead to a massive public works project, by which about 20,000 cubic metres of earth was deliberately deposited to fill the Velabrum gully and raise the ground level—much as in the case of Athens.[106] The most recent investigations suggest that the first landfill and pavement of the forum dates to around the beginning of the seventh century while the second should be assigned to the period ca. 650–625 BCE.[107]

Against this exclusively archaeological background, the construction of the wall on the Palatine hardly seems to mark a "foundational" moment within the spatial or organizational development of the city. If anything, it serves to *separate* the Palatine from its surrounding habitat.[108] But that is not what we find in the literary sources, which recount the progressive expansion of an original Palatine nucleus. And why, after all, should the royal residence of Rome's first kings be situated *outside*, rather than *inside*, this circuit (cf. document 7.5)?

## Conclusion

Carandini's eagerness to harness excavated material to literary traditions in order to construct a "mental cinema" in the minds of his public runs the risk of undermining the true significance of his findings.[109] Two facts, however, stand above the perfunctory dismissal of the discoveries by his academic critics. Firstly, the building that he has identified as the Domus Regia is, at present, unparalleled in central Italy in terms of its size and construction. Secondly, whatever the Palatine wall is, it was evidently considered significant enough to rebuild three more times after its initial construction. The possibility cannot be entirely discounted that both were indeed projects realized by Rome's earliest kings, but the lack of clear correspondences between the material evidence and the literary testimonia, together with the variegated and amorphous nature of the traditions concerning the origins of Rome, make this an unlikely proposition. It is not, I would suggest, that there is necessarily no connection between the material remains and the literary

traditions of Rome but, rather, that the relationship between the two needs to be reconceptualized.

The so-called Domus Regia survived, in various incarnations, down to the first century CE. It is not, then, impossible that this was indeed the building that Tacitus (document 7.13) and Plutarch (document 7.14) believed, rightly or wrongly, to be the royal residence of Numa Pompilius. The case of the wall—especially its first phase—is even more suggestive. The stretch that was excavated in Sector 9 had long disappeared from view by Tacitus's day, but the red tufa blocks that punctuate its foundations do remind us of Tacitus's description of "stones . . . placed at certain intervals" (document 7.9), which might imply that, by the first century CE, isolated stretches of this wall were in fact believed to mark the earlier *pomeria*, although the tone of the Tacitean passage suggests that there was no universal agreement as to exactly which *pomerium* was that of Romulus.[110] Rather than assuming that the material record of Rome can confirm or re-

:::    miani 2008: 52. The earlier failure to identify material older than the late seventh century from the area of the *comitium* could be due to the fact that the ground level to the east was cut away at that time to further emphasize an outcrop of volcanic rock that formed an important and now more prominent natural feature of the site: see Ammerman 1996a; Carafa 2005.

106. Ammerman 1990: 641–44. See Wiseman 2008: 2, 13.

107. Filippi 2005: 105–15; Carandini 2011: 89.

108. As admitted by Carandini (2003: 496–97), though to draw

a distinction between the nebulous "Septimontium" and a properly urban, Romulean phase of the city.

109. For the image of the "mental cinema": Carandini 2000: 155. See Wiseman 2008: 272–73.

110. Cf. Varro (*On the Latin Language* 5.143), who refers to *cippi*, or boundary stones, which marked the *pomerium* of Rome, although he seems to imagine a circular—rather than quadrilateral—formation.

fute the literary traditions surrounding its foundation, it might be more fruitful to regard those literary traditions as themselves aetiological attempts to make sense of the palimpsest of ruined antiquities that later Romans saw all around them.

DOCUMENTS FOR CHAPTER 7

**7.1** The compiler of the priestesses of Hera in Argos and the events that occurred during each of their periods of office says that Aeneas came from the Molossians to Italy with [or after] Odysseus and became the founder of the city [Rome] but that he named it after a Trojan woman named Rhome. He says that this woman encouraged the other Trojan women to set fire to their boats together, because she was weary of wandering. And Damastes of Sigeion and some others agree with him. (Dionysios of Halikarnassos, *Roman Antiquities* 1.72.2 = Hellanikos 4 *FGrH* 84 = Damastes of Sigeion 5 *FGrH* 3)

**7.2** Romulus, founding Rome, drew a trench around the Palatine with haste, lest some of the people who dwelled around should try to prevent his choice. (Diodoros 8.6.1)

**7.3** And so Romulus gained sole power; the city that he founded was called by the name of its founder. And he fortified first the Palatine, where he had been raised. (Livy 1.7.3)

**7.4** Having called everybody to the designated place, he drew a tetragonal pattern around the hill, having yoked a bull and a cow to a plough, and he sketched a continuous furrow, destined to receive the wall. From this time, this habit of ploughing around places in the settlement of cities remains among the Romans. (Dionysios of Halikarnassos, *Roman Antiquities* 1.88.2)

**7.5** In fact, it was not Romulus who dedicated to the goddess [Vesta] the place in which the sacred fire is guarded—the best proof for this is that it lies outside the so-called Roma Quadrata that he en-

walled. (Dionysios of Halikarnassos, *Roman Antiquities* 2.65.3)

**7.6** Romulus had not yet fashioned the walls of the eternal city, which was not to be inhabited by his co-ruler Remus, but at that time cows were grazing on the grassy Palatine and low huts stood on Jupiter's peak. (Tibullus 2.5.23–26)

**7.7** For the custom of the Lupercalia was initiated by Romulus and Remus, rejoicing in the fact that their grandfather Numitor, king of the Albani, had permitted them to found a city in the place where they were brought up, under the Palatine hill, which the Arkadian Evander has consecrated. (Valerius Maximus 2.2.9)

**7.8** In this regard [the right to extend the *pomerium* of the city], the ambition or glory of the kings is narrated variously. But I do not think that it is absurd to know the beginning of the foundation and which *pomerium* was established by Romulus. The furrow for the marking out of the *oppidum* began from the Forum Boarium, where we now see the bronze statue of a bull—the type of animal that was placed under the plough—so that it should embrace the Ara Maxima of Hercules; from there, stones were placed at certain intervals at the feet of the Palatine up to the Altar of Consus, then to the Curiae Veteres, and then to the shrine of Larunda. And they believed that the Forum Romanum and the Capitoline hill were added to the city not by Romulus but by Titus Tatius. (Tacitus, *Annals* 12.24)

**7.9** And they [Romulus and Remus] founded the city on the river, beside which they had been exposed and reared, and then once reared had practiced brigandage, and they called it Rome, though it was then called "tetragonon" because its perimeter was sixteen stades, with each side having four stades. (Appian, *Basilike* fr. Ia 9)

**7.10**  But the most ancient *pomerium*, which was instituted by Romulus, was delineated at the roots of the Palatine hill. (Aulus Gellius, *Attic Nights* 13.14.2)

**7.11**  For as Varro, a very precise author, affirms, Rome was founded by Romulus, born of Mars and Rhea Silvia, or as some say, Mars and Ilia. And first of all Rome was called "Quadrata" because it was designed symmetrically (?). It begins from the grove that is in the area of Apollo and has its end at the top of the steps of Cacus, where there was the hut of Faustulus. This is where Romulus lived, who, after taking auspices, laid the foundations of the walls eleven days before the calends of May. (Solinus 1.17–18)

**7.12**  It would be difficult to calculate the number of houses, tenement blocks, and temples that were lost; but some of the ancient religious structures were completely burnt, including the temple Servius Tullius dedicated to the moon, the great altar and shrine which the Arkadian Evander dedicated in the presences of Hercules, the temple of Jupiter Stator, vowed by Romulus, and the royal residence of Numa and the sanctuary of Vesta which housed the Penates of the Roman people. (Tacitus, *Annals* 15.41)

**7.13**  When he [Numa] had organized the priesthoods, he built, near the sanctuary of Vesta, what is known as the Regia, or royal residence. (Plutarch, *Life of Numa* 14.1).

# 8

# The Birth of the Roman Republic

## The Temple of Jupiter Capitolinus

The latest addition to the Capitoline Museums is a glass pavilion, designed by the Italian architect Carlo Aymonino and built over part of what was the Roman Garden of the Palazzo dei Conservatori. Officially opened to the public in December 2005, the Exedra of Marcus Aurelius—named after the gilded bronze equestrian statue of the emperor that dominates the sunlit space—also encloses part of the imposing foundations of the temple of Jupiter Capitolinus (fig. 8.1).[1] The preserved stretch, in squared *cappellaccio* blocks, belongs to the eastern side of the podium. Though plundered since antiquity for building stone, its remains were still visible in the twelfth century CE and largely dictated the perimeter and internal division of space within the Palazzo Caffarelli that was built over it in the last decades of the sixteenth century.[2]

Cicero, Livy, Dionysios of Halikarnassos, and Tacitus (document 8.1) all say that the temple was originally inaugurated by Rome's fifth king, Tarquinius Priscus, in return for victory over the neighbouring Sabines but was still under construction during the reign of his son, Tarquinius Superbus, the last king of Rome.[3] Several sources specify, how-

:::     1. The temple of Jupiter Capitolinus, also often referred to as the temple of Jupiter Optimus Maximus, was more accurately dedicated to the Capitoline triad of Jupiter, Juno, and Minerva.

    2. Albertoni and Damiani 2008: 32–34.

    3. Cicero, *On the Republic* 2.36; Livy 1.38.7, 55.2; Dionysios of Halikarnassos, *Roman Antiquities* 3.69.1, 4.59.1; cf. Pliny, *Natural History* 3.5.70.

8.1    The foundations of the temple of Jupiter Capitolinus, Rome. (Photo by author.)

ever, that the temple was finally dedicated only after the expulsion of Tarquinius Superbus by Marcus Horatius Pulvillus, a member of the first-ever college of consuls (documents 8.2–5). Polybios dates Horatius's consulship and the dedication of the temple to 509 BCE, though Tacitus assigns it to 498. Dionysios even suggests that Horatius's name was inscribed on the façade of the temple, perhaps on the pediment.[4] So, do the archaeological remains of the temple of Jupiter Capitolinus vindicate the widespread belief that its origins coincide with the birth of the Roman Republic?

The date given by the literary sources has been defended on the basis of architectural terracottas retrieved from the zone and a votive deposit— found in association with a temple that is unidentified but whose foundations resemble those of the Jupiter temple—which was sealed towards the end of the sixth century.[5] We cannot, however, be absolutely certain that the terracottas belong to the Jupiter temple as opposed to one of the other cult sites mentioned by the sources,[6] while the relationship between the votive deposit and the temple of Jupiter Capitolinus is difficult to assess. The style of the foundations themselves offers little assistance: the Romans continued to use *cappellaccio* tufa down to as late as 396 BCE, when the capture of Veii gave them access to the harder-wearing *Grotta Oscura*

:::        4. See also Cicero, *On His household* 139; Seneca, *Dialogues* 6.13.1; Plutarch, *Life of Publicola* 14.2.

5. Gjerstad 1960: 168–201.
6. Livy 1.55.2–4.

8.2 Reconstructed plan of the temple of Jupiter Capitolinus at Rome. Existing stretches of foundations are shown in black. (After Claridge 2010: 237, fig. 109.)

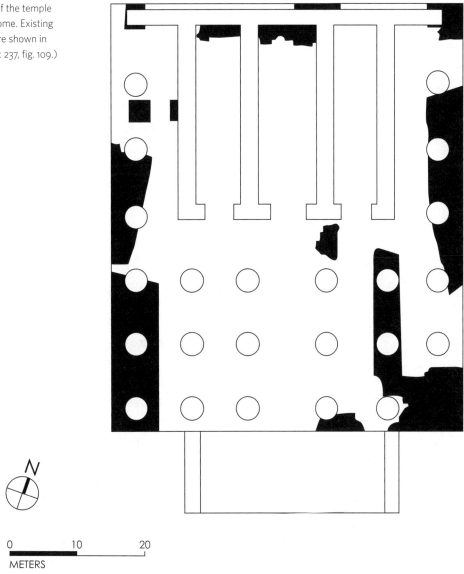

0    10    20
METERS

quarries.[7] Indeed, some scholars have suspected that the temple of Jupiter Capitolinus is really a construction of the fourth century.[8] At issue here is Dionysios's description of the temple (document 8.6). Although it is clear that Dionysios is describing the temple that was restored by Sulla in the first century BCE, he explicitly states that it stood on the same foundations—and had the same dimensions—as its predecessor, and the dimensions that he gives certainly match those of the excavated foundations,

estimated at about 62 by 54 metres (fig. 8.2). Furthermore, the disposition of the foundations indicates that they were designed to support a façade of six columns. This would result in intercolumniations (the distance between adjacent columns) ranging from 8 to 12.5 metres, necessitating the employment of wooden—rather than stone—architraves, which seems to accord with Vitruvius's statement (*On Architecture* 3.3.5) that the Capitoline temple was of the "aerostyle" type, where wooden architraves support

::: 7. Holloway 1994: 18–19; Forsythe 2005: 107. The dating criteria are those of Frank (1924).

8. E.g., Kaschnitz-Weinberg 1962: 58; Alföldi 1965: 323–28; Castagnoli 1974: 434–36; Kölb 1995: 92–96.

pedimental sculpture in terracotta. This seemingly happy coincidence has, however, troubled scholars precisely because there are no other parallels for a temple of this plan or even approaching these dimensions until the fourth century.[9]

New evidence for the origins of the Jupiter temple has emerged from excavations undertaken between 1998 and 2002 in the Roman Garden in preparation for the construction of the Exedra of Marcus Aurelius. Among material found in the fill of one of the foundation trenches were part of the foot of a *bucchero* cup and the edge of an ovoid jar, both dated to the late sixth or very early fifth century. A nearby well, in which votives dating back to the eighth century were found, also belongs to the end of the sixth century.[10] We can, then, be fairly certain that construction of the foundations began in the years around 500 BCE, though estimating when the temple was completed is more difficult. It has, for example, been observed that the height of the *cappellaccio* blocks changes from the twelfth course of the foundations upwards, leading to the suggestion that, while the temple may have been initiated at the end of the sixth century, work was interrupted until much later—perhaps 378 or 376 BCE, when another Marcus Horatius was military tribune with consular power.[11] On the other hand, it is odd that the hypothesized late completion of so important a monument evokes no comment in our literary sources. The change in the size of tufa blocks in the temple foundations could well indicate the resumption, after a break, of building activity, but that hiatus need not have lasted for as long as two centuries.[12]

Either way, we can be fairly confident that work on the construction of the temple of Jupiter Capitolinus commenced around the end of the sixth or beginning of the fifth century. Furthermore, there are some hints that the project was conceived a little earlier than that. In the Latial II and III phases (roughly the ninth and eighth centuries on the conventional chronology), the area that was to be occupied by the Jupiter temple was used for burial—eight graves, mainly of infants and adolescents, were discovered in the course of the most recent excavations—and there is also evidence for iron-working. Burials and metallurgy continue to be attested for the seventh and early sixth centuries—a period during which traces of dry-walled huts and roof tiles indicate the existence of a modest settlement. This settlement, however, seems to have been destroyed—whether accidentally or by design—around the middle of the sixth century, a few decades before the laying of the temple foundations.[13] In broad outlines, then, the archaeological evidence is not inconsistent with the literary accounts that tell of the establishment of the temple of Jupiter Capitolinus.[14] But what is the link between this and the origins of the Republic, and what exactly do we mean by the "birth of the Roman Republic"? To answer that, we need to examine, firstly, the evidence for the Roman monarchy and, secondly, that for the establishment of one of the most characteristic features of the Roman Republic—namely, the twin consulship. Before that, however, some source criticism is in order.

:::     9. See generally Ridley 2005.

10. Cassatella 2005; Mazzei 2007; Cifani 2008: 79, 99; Albertoni and Damiani 2008: 60–61.

11. Livy 6.31.1. See Alföldi (1965) 323–28; Holloway 1994: 8–10; contra Cornell 1995: 420 n. 48. Holloway (1994: 177 n. 42) draws a parallel with the temple of Olympian Zeus at Athens, initiated under the Peisistratids in the sixth century BCE but then interrupted until work was resumed by Antiochos IV Epiphanes (ruled 175–163 BCE) and only finally completed under the emperor Hadrian in 131/2 CE. However, the Peisistratid temple had reached

a far more final state of completion than what Holloway proposes for the Capitoline temple. Interestingly, in his reconstruction of the temple, Sulla reused some of the pentelic marble columns of the Athenian Olympieion: Pliny, *Natural History* 36.45.

12. Alternatively, as Gjerstad (1960: 167) supposed, the bottom eleven courses may have belonged to the substructure of the temple, which was not intended to be visible aboveground.

13. Albertoni and Damiani 2008: 51–57; Cifani 2008: 99.

14. For a discussion, ultimately defending the date and reconstruction of the temple, see Hopkins 2012.

## The Fall of a Tyrant

The end of the monarchy and the establishment of the Republic have been immortalized in the account of Livy (1.48–2.21). Lucius Tarquinius Superbus (the epithet means "proud" or "arrogant") is supposed to have seized the throne at Rome in 534 BCE, claiming that he was the son and rightful heir of Tarquinius Priscus while his father's successor, Servius Tullius, whose assassination he engineered, was a mere usurper. His reign is marked by some notable successes in foreign affairs, such as the capture of Gabii and Suessa Pometia, and Tarquin's Rome was soon playing a dominant role within the League of Latin cities. At home, however, he is endowed with all the characteristic vices of the worst Greek tyrants: he refuses to allow Servius's corpse to be buried; he surrounds himself with a bodyguard; he holds private trials of his enemies; he puts the poor to work on civic projects—including the construction of the Cloaca Maxima, the principal drainage sewer of the city; and he acts without consultation of either the senate or the people. As with several of the Greek tyrants, he is regarded as an ethnic outsider. And, like many Greek tyrants, his regime is associated with sexual violence against women. In this case, the perpetrator is his son, Sextus, whose rape of Lucretia provokes the unfortunate woman's suicide. Swearing vengeance for the outrage, Tarquinius's own nephew, Lucius Junius Brutus, enters into a pact with Lucretia's husband, Lucius Tarquinius Collatinus, and her father, Spurius Lucretius, as well as with Publius Valerius Publicola. The conspirators successfully win over the Roman army during a siege of the Latin town of Ardea, and Tarquinius and his immediate family are banished from Rome, from where they make their way to Etruscan Caere. Brutus and Collatinus are elected consuls for a one-year term, but the latter's family connections with the Tarquins provoke suspicion, and he goes into voluntary exile, replaced as consul by Valerius. Brutus induces the Romans to swear an oath that they will never again accept a king and establishes the priesthood of the Rex Sacrorum.

Tarquinius, however, is anxious to avenge the humiliation inflicted upon him. Supported by the Etruscan cities of Veii and Tarquinii, he fails to capture Rome, although Brutus is killed in battle and replaced as consul by the aging Lucretius, whose death after just a few days in office results in the election of Marcus Horatius Pulvillus as Valerius's consular colleague. Next, Tarquinius seeks the support of Lars Porsenna, king of Cluvium, who marches to Rome and proceeds to lay siege to the city. Impressed, however, by Roman acts of heroism, including Horatius Cocles' suicidal defence of the Sublician bridge across the Tiber, Porsenna admits failure and sues for peace; a subsequent attack on the Latin town of Aricia is repulsed by the Latins in alliance with Aristodemos, the Greek tyrant of Cumae. Tarquinius now seeks help from the Latin cities but endures yet another defeat at Lake Regillus in either 499 or 496 BCE. With no prospect of regaining his throne, he retires to the court of Aristodemos, where he dies in 495 BCE.[15]

That the account of Livy—like that of Dionysios—is suffused with romantic elements concerning intrigue, acts of heroism, and larger-than-life protagonists is undeniable. Attilio Mastrocinque has argued that Livy's account of Tarquinius Superbus is influenced in part by a drama entitled *Brutus* by Lucius Accius, two fragments of which are preserved by Cicero (*On Divination* 1.22, 44–45).[16] The play was probably performed in 133 BCE for Accius's patron, Decimus Junius Brutus Callaicus, who—as his name testifies—claimed to belong to the family of the Republic's founder.[17] This, in itself, raises the strong possibility that the play rehearsed a politi-

---

:::     15. Dionysios of Halikarnassos's account (*Roman Antiquities* 4.38–6.21), though more detailed than Livy's, does not diverge significantly from it.

    16. Mastrocinque 1983, surmising that Livy may have become familiar with the play through the *Annales* of Lucius Calpurnius Piso Frugi.

    17. The legend of "Brutus the Liberator" would also, of course, be resurrected ahead of Julius Caesar's assassination in 44 BCE.

cal agenda but Mastrocinque also demonstrates that the little that can be reconstructed of the *Brutus* reveals themes which have been borrowed from Greek tragedy and especially Euripides' *Elektra*. That would certainly account for some of the more romanticized elements in Livy's account, but it offers little help in assessing whether some fundamental veracity underlies the embellishments.

Here, we are at the mercy of our sources—or, more precisely, the lack of them. Roman historiography began in the late third century BCE with Quintus Fabius Pictor's and Lucius Cincius Alimentus's histories of Rome, but, as Arnaldo Momigliano pointed out, "[I]n the third century BC no one had any clear idea of what Roman society had been like in the first half of the fifth century."[18] In fact, the profile of historical writing across the centuries before the Common Era resembles the "hourglass" model that Jan Vansina proposes for oral cultures generally: there is a tremendous amount of (largely legendary) detail about the early kings of Rome and a wealth of more reliable documentation for the late fourth century onwards, but comparatively little in between.[19] For example, of the seven volumes that Calpurnius Piso devoted to Roman history, the first two dealt with the regal period, while the third volume already treats the aedileship of Gnaeus Flavius in 304 BCE; Ennius's *Annales* seem to follow a similar pattern.[20]

Cicero (*On the Orator* 2.52–53) says that the Pontifex Maximus used to write down the events that occurred each year and post a copy on a whitened board that was placed outside his house for the public to consult; he adds that the *Annales Maximi*, as they were called, ran "from the beginning of Roman affairs down to the Pontificate of Publius Mucius Scaevola" (130–115 BCE). The elder Cato, however, who wrote his *Origines* around the middle of the second century BCE, remarks that the *tabula* (panel) displayed at the Pontifex's house contained little that was of use for his purpose, save for the price of grain or lunar events.[21] This is one of the reasons for doubting that the *Annales Maximi* contained any accurate historical information dating back to the beginning of the Republic.[22] What the third-century annalists had at their disposal, then, was not so much a continuous lineal narrative of events as a mishmash of elite family traditions, popular lore, monuments, inscribed documents such as calendars and laws, paintings and sculptures, possibly lists of magistrates (though see below), and—no less significantly—accounts written by Greek, and perhaps Etruscan, historians.[23] Indeed, there is a strong emphasis in our literary testimonia on the Corinthian origins of the Tarquin family: Tarquinius Priscus was said to be the son of the Corinthian aristocrat Demaratos, who fled to Tarquinii to escape the tyranny of Kypselos. This Corinthian dimension, together with Tarquinius Superbus's associations with Aristodemos of Cumae, has suggested to some that the accounts we possess concerning the end of the Roman monarchy derive from a Greek historian based at Cumae.[24] If that is the case, then any analysis of Roman conceptions of monarchy must consider how the topic was treated by Greek writers.

:::     18. Momigliano 1986: 177; cf. Finley 1985: 9–10.

19. Vansina 1985: 168–69.

20. Raaflaub 1986a: 2; Gabba 2000: 25–26.

21. Aulus Gellius, *Attic Nights* 2.28.6.

22. Fraccaro 1957: 60–62. See the discussion in Forsythe 2005: 69–72. Frier (1999: 179–200) argues that the *Annales Maximi* were a product of the Augustan period. Rüpke (2008: 34–38), instead, believes that accurate pontifical commentaries, from which the information on the *tabula* was displayed, were kept from ca. 249 BCE and that Scaevola was responsible for the publication of the *Annales Maximi*, including the insertion of considerable amounts of historically dubious—and even invented—material for the earlier periods.

23. Momigliano 1963: 96.

24. Alföldi 1965: 70–71; Zevi 1995; Gabba 2000: 30–33; Wiseman 2008: 293. Gallia (2007) is more sceptical.

## The Nature of the Kingship

Aristotle (*Politics* 4.10.10 1297b) took it for granted that, at an early date and throughout the Greek world, monarchies had yielded to aristocracies. At Corinth, according to Diodoros (fr. 7.9.2-6), a hereditary monarchy had ruled until around the middle of the eighth century, when the elite Bakchiadai family seized the chief magistracy. At Argos, the last monarch, Meltas, was supposedly overthrown perhaps as late as the sixth century, although Pausanias (2.19.2) believed that the king's powers had been strictly limited nine generations earlier.[25] A similar situation is recounted for Athens, where the hereditary kingship is supposed to have been replaced by a lifetime magistracy—that of the Archon—in either the reign of Medon, son of Kodros, or that of his son, Akastos.[26] The word that these authors employ for "king" is *basileus*, and that is precisely the term that Dionysios uses to describe the Roman kings. However, an examination of how the term *basileus* is used in Late Bronze Age Linear B tablets and the poems of Homer and Hesiod, together with the archaeological evidence of Iron Age settlements and burials, makes it clear that the word "king," at least in the sense in which it is generally understood today, is not a very accurate translation of the Greek *basileus*.[27] Early Greek *basileis* presided over small and relatively unranked communities; they owed their position less to heredity and more to the status and charismatic authority they derived from martial prowess, provision of feasts, display of wealth, and acts of calculated generosity, and their leadership was dependent upon maintaining a delicately balanced contract both with their followers and with their peers. In short, they resembled chieftains or warlords rather than what we would call mon-

archs. For this reason, it is highly likely that—with the exception of Sparta, which had two concurrent hereditary monarchs down to the Hellenistic period—the literary traditions concerning the early royal houses of Greek poleis are ultimately untrustworthy. Does this offer any cautionary lessons for the study of regal Rome?

There is, unfortunately, no evidence, independent of our extant literary sources, that documents the existence of kings at Rome. Some initial excitement was caused in 1899, when Giacomo Boni excavated the Lapis Niger. This was an area of the Comitium, or assembly place in the forum, marked by a black stone pavement and identified variously in antiquity as the grave of Romulus, Faustulus or Hostilius, grandfather of Tullus Hostilius.[28] Partially covered by the black pavement, Boni discovered a U-shaped altar, a truncated column and part of a *cippus*, or stone pillar, of *Grotta Oscura* tufa, on which was inscribed an Archaic Latin inscription which includes the word *recei*. The word is normally believed to be an archaic form of the dative for *rex* or "king,"[29] though it has also been suggested that it is the passive infinitive of the verb *regere*, which simply means "to lead."[30] A variety of dates throughout the sixth century has been proposed for the inscription, though it need not be earlier than ca. 500 BCE—that is, after the regal period, according to the literary tradition.[31] But even if the inscription dates earlier, the title *rex* could designate a priestly magistrate rather than a king: at Athens, for example, the second most important magistrate with religious functions was named the Basileus (see below, p. 153). The graffito *rex* appears elsewhere in the forum on the foot of a *bucchero* cup, dating to the last quarter of

---

25. For a sixth-century date for Meltas, see Robinson 1997: 92-94. The dating of Meltas depends in part on the date assigned to the shadowy tyrant of Argos, Pheidon. For the competing views, see Huxley 1958; Tomlinson 1972: 82-83; Kelly 1976: 94-11; Koiv 2000; 2003: 239-97; Hall 2014: 154-64.

26. [Aristotle], *Constitution of the Athenians* 3.3; Pausanias 4.5.10. There was also an alternative tradition, no doubt coined during the early democracy, that it had been Theseus who had renounced the monarchy: Plutarch, *Life of Theseus* 25; Pausanias 1.3.3.

27. Drews 1993. See generally Hall 2014: 127-34.

28. Romulus: Scholiast to Horace, *Epodes* 16.13-14. Faustulus: Festus 194 Lindsay. Hostilius: Dionysios of Halikarnassos, *Roman Antiquities* 3.1.2.

29. Holloway 1994: 81-86; Cornell 1995: 94.

30. Momigliano 1989: 132.

31. Coarelli 1983: 178-88; Forsythe 2005: 73; Holloway 1994: 83-86.

the sixth century and discovered during the excavation of the Regia. Here, it is normally taken as referring to the Rex Sacrorum, the priest who is often assumed to have exercised his functions in the Regia until he was displaced by the Pontifex Maximus.[32] Since the Rex Sacrorum was responsible for performing the ceremony of the Regifugium, or "King's Flight," at the Comitium on February 24 each year, it is entirely possible that it is to him that the *rex* on the *Lapis Niger* inscription refers.[33]

One thing is certain: much of the literary tradition concerning the seven kings of Rome is inherently untrustworthy. We have already seen (p. 134) that it is impossible for only seven kings to have ruled over a period of 245 years. Further suspicion arises from the evident symmetry of the traditional account. So, for example, the first (Romulus) and third (Tullus Hostilius) kings were Latin, while the second (Numa Pompilius) and fourth (Ancus Marcius) were of Sabine origins and the fifth (Tarquinius Priscus) and seventh (Tarquinius Superbus) from Etruria. In addition, Numa and Tullus Hostilius are presented as antitypes of one another: Numa is pacific and pious, the reputed founder of a good number of Rome's festivals, priestly colleges, and the religious calendar, while Tullus Hostilius was fierce and belligerent—characterizations, no doubt, that arose from the perceived association of Numa's name with the Latin word *numen* (divine power) and of Tullus Hostilius's name with the Latin *hostilis* (warlike).[34]

It might have been supposed that our information for the last three kings of Rome, traditionally dated to the late seventh and sixth centuries, would be more reliable, but here too there are problems—

especially with regard to the two Tarquins. The tradition, followed by Livy, that Tarquinius Superbus was the son of Tarquinius Priscus was supposedly already recounted in Fabius Pictor's history, but Dionysios of Halikarnassos (*Roman Antiquities* 4.6-7) points out the impossibility of this: if the elder Tarquin came to Rome in 634 BCE at the age of around twenty-five, then even his youngest son cannot have been born much later than 603; this means that Tarquinius Superbus must have been around seventy when he usurped power after the forty-four year reign of Servius Tullius and over one hundred when he fought at Lake Regillus. It was for this reason that Calpurnius Piso made the younger Tarquin the grandson, rather than son, of Tarquinius Priscus.[35] Suspicion has also arisen, however, from the fact that the same acts are attributed to both Tarquins—for example, the construction of sewers, viewing-stands in the circus and, as we have seen, the temple of Jupiter Capitolinus. This might suggest that monuments originally assigned by tradition to "a" king Tarquinius were credited to one or the other of the Tarquins by the first generation of annalists and then to both by their successors.[36] As for the "interloper" Servius Tullius, the tradition that Livy (1.39-41) follows is entirely at variance with an Etruscan tradition that was known to the emperor Claudius.[37] According to this, Servius was originally an Etruscan warrior named Mastarna, who is depicted on the painted walls of the François Tomb at Vulci, dated to the second half of the fourth century.[38]

There are two respects in which the traditions on Roman kings display some similarities to what we think we know of the *basileis* of early Greece.

32. Holloway 1994: 62; Cornell 1995: 234.

33. Forsythe 2005: 74. For the Regifugium: Festus 346 Lindsay.

34. Forsythe 2005: 97. See Wiseman 2008: 314-16 for the possibility that Tullus Hostilius and Ancus Marcius were later creations.

35. See Cornell 1995: 122-27. The difficulty probably arose from the synchronism between Tarquinius Priscus's father, Demaratos, and the Kypselid tyranny at Corinth, which Eusebius dated to 657 BCE. The problem is obviated to some extent if we accept the "low" chronology of ca. 620 for the Kypselids that was proposed by Will (1955: 383-440), but this has not met with much acceptance among

Greek historians. The fragmentary archon list found in the Athenian agora (ML 6) would seem to support the higher dating. See Servais 1969; Oost 1972: 16 n. 26; Mosshammer 1979: 234-45.

36. Cornell 1995: 128-30.

37. According to Livy (1.39-41), Servius Tullius was born a slave but was raised in the palace of Tarquinius Priscus, where he married Tarquinius's daughter and secured the assistance of his wife, Tanaquil, in succeeding to his throne.

38. Holloway 1994: 5-7; Cornell 1995: 133-41; Forsythe 2005: 103-5.

Firstly, with the exception of Ancus Marcius, who is said to have been the grandson of Numa Pompilius,[39] and Tarquinius Superbus, son or grandson of Tarquinius Priscus, the kingship at Rome does not seem to have been hereditary: Numa, Tullius Hostilius, Tarquinius Priscus, and Servius Tullius did not succeed their fathers. Secondly, if we are to give any credence to Livy's observation (1.49.3) that Tarquinius Superbus differed from his successors in not ruling "at the bidding of the people nor with the authority of the senate," then this suggests that the authority of the early "kings" was only maintained through a reciprocal contract with their followers and peers. Livy also claims that it was in the regal period that the office of *interrex* was established, whereby, on the death of a king, the heads of the leading "patrician" families would each govern for five days, up to the period of a year.[40] Again, the procedure implies a reciprocal arrangement between the "king" and his elite peers. It is not, however, easy to determine whether the apparent parallels between Greek *basileis* and Roman *reges* are historical or historiographical in nature.

The Rex Sacrorum has often been compared to the Archon Basileus at Athens.[41] In both cases, the magistracy is assumed to have been instituted to guarantee the continued performance of ritual duties that had formerly been discharged by the king. According to Livy (2.2.1), the first Rex Sacrorum was appointed in the first year of the Republic, but the priesthood was immediately placed under the authority of the Pontifex Maximus. Clearly, this makes little sense, and Cornell hypothesizes that the office of Rex Sacrorum must have existed prior to the Republic. Basing his argument on a notice of Festus (198 Lindsay), according to which an unspecified *rex* is ranked above the Pontifex Maximus,

he suggests that at some point, possibly at the time of Servius Tullius, the former king "was not abolished so much as kicked upstairs" and left with only circumscribed ceremonial duties.[42] On this reading, the prohibition against the Rex Sacrorum holding political office or being a member of the senate would have been an attempt to prevent an erstwhile monarch from ever again aspiring to political dominance.[43]

The proposed parallel with the Archon Basileus at Athens, however, should urge caution. As we have seen, the tradition that hereditary kings originally ruled at Athens is almost certainly unreliable. The Archon Basileus, together with the chief Archon and the Archon Polemarchos, exercised religious, executive, and military authority, respectively, and later authors assumed that all these duties had formerly been discharged by the king. But if there was no institutional monarchy at Athens, then any assumed continuity between the king and the Archon Basileus is illusory. The Athenian magistracies were probably introduced in the seventh century, with the Archon Basileus taking his name from a term that had earlier designated a rather vague achieved authority rather than an ascribed office: *basileis* are also attested as magistrates on Chios and at Argos.[44] We cannot exclude the possibility that the same scenario holds for Rome and that the association between the Rex Sacrorum and the early "kings" was an invention of later authors. One possible context in which this belief might have been elaborated was the festival of the Regifugium. Presided over by the Rex Sacrorum, the Regifugium dramatized, in ritual form, the waning of the old Roman year, but Roman antiquarians were to interpret it as commemorating the expulsion of Tarquinius Superbus.[45] In short, the office of the Rex Sacrorum offers no in-

: : :    39. Livy 1.32.1.

40. Livy 1.17.5–11; 1.22.1; 1.32.1; 1.35.1–6; 1.41.6; 1.46.1; 1.47.10. See Forsythe 2005: 110. In later Republican times, an *interrex* was appointed in situations where both consuls were unable to complete their term of office. It is impossible to know whether the position really predates the Republic.

41. E.g., De Sanctis 1956: 389; Momigliano 1989: 145.

42. Cornell 1995: 233–36. The date of the *rex* graffito in the Regia would certainly support this idea. For a detailed—but ulti-

mately inconclusive—discussion of the Rex Sacrorum, see Beard, North, and Price 1998: 54–59.

43. Livy 40.42.8.

44. ML 8, 42. See Hall 2014: 127–38. In Homer and Hesiod, *basileis* do not seem to be institutionalized offices. For the view that Homer provides valuable evidence of eighth-century society, see Morris 1986; Raaflaub 1998.

45. Forsythe 2005: 136–37.

disputable proof that an institutionalized monarchy had ever ruled Rome.

Our literary sources make a clear distinction between the reign of the "good" king Servius Tullius and the "bad" tyrant Tarquinius Superbus.[46] As Cornell points out, however, Servius was no less a "usurper" than the younger Tarquinius.[47] Indeed, it has been suggested that Servius's "other" name, Mastarna (*Macstrna* in Etruscan) is the Etruscan equivalent to the Latin *magister* (master) and that this is shorthand for an office that the Romans called the Magister Populi (Master of the People).[48] Since both Varro (*On the Latin Language* 5.82) and Festus (216 Lindsay) say that the Magister Populi was an alternative title for the Dictator—a temporary office of supreme authority, supposedly instituted early on in the Republic to deal with emergencies— it has been supposed that Servius Tullius held a lifetime magistracy or dictatorship that was different in nature from his presumed royal predecessors.[49] The difficulty here is that the Republican office of Dictator was not a life-term magistracy and could only be held for a period not to exceed six months. Furthermore, even if *Macstrna* is the Etruscan form for *magister*, it is far from certain that it refers specifically to the Magister Populi.

Evidence from Etruria may offer some sort of glimpse into the nature of authority in Late Archaic central Italy. A gold plaque found in 1964 at Pyrgi, the port of Caere, and inscribed with a Phoenician text, dated to ca. 500 BCE, records a dedication to the Phoenician goddess Astarte by a certain Thefarie Velianas, in his third year as *melek* (the Phoenician word commonly used for "king"). Two further gold plaques carry Etruscan inscriptions, usually thought to be translations of the Phoenician, which describe Velianas's position as *Zilaθ*, an Etruscan title that was later equated with the Roman magis-

tracy of Praetor.[50] Nothing further is known of the position, though the reference to Velianas's "third year" might indicate that no term limits applied. If Servius Tullius and Tarquinius Superbus are truly historical figures, they are perhaps better viewed as powerful military leaders in the mould of Velianas rather than successors to any constitutionally defined monarchic office. Nor would they have been alone: in Livy's account of the foundation of the Republic, the Etruscan Lars Porsenna of Cluvium marches on Rome in order to restore Tarquinius Superbus, only to then sue for peace and withdraw. But Tacitus (document 8.1) believed that the city had surrendered to Porsenna, and Pliny (*Natural History* 34.139) adds that, after expelling Tarquinius, Porsenna imposed a settlement on the Romans that forbade them to use iron except for agricultural purposes—in other words, a humiliating disarmament.[51]

The impression one gets, then, of later-sixth-century Rome is one in which powerful warlords battled against one another for supreme control over the city, and that is a picture that is reinforced by an inscription from Satricum, dated to ca. 500 BCE. The inscription records a dedication to Mars by the *sodales* of Poplios Valesios—perhaps the Publius Valerius Publicola who, according to tradition, is supposed to have replaced Tarquinius Collatinus as consul. *Sodales* is a term that literally means "companions" but is here interpreted as meaning an "armed band"— which is presumably why a dedication to the Roman god of war would have been especially appropriate.[52] The inscription testifies to an unstable world of armed militias and competing warlords that hardly squares with the traditional account of a strong monarchy yielding almost instantaneously to a fully fledged Republic.

---

46. This is not the place for a full discussion of Servius's political and military reforms, for which see Cornell 1995: 173–97. For the centuriate organization, however, see below (p. 157).

47. Cornell 1995: 127, 235.

48. Mazzarino 1945: 177; Ogilvie 1976: 63, 88. See Forsythe 2005: 105.

49. Cornell 1995: 235. For the institution of the Dictatorship: Livy 2.18.4.

50. Fitzmyer 1966; Heurgon 1966; Cornell 1995: 197, 232; Forsythe 2005: 45–46.

51. Alföldi 1965: 72–84; Cornell 1995: 217; Forsythe 2005: 149; Wiseman 2008: 317–18.

52. Cristofani 1990.

## The Origins of the Consulship

Traditionally, the origins of the Republic were marked by the institution of the twin consulship (document 8.2).[53] In theory, if we could determine exactly when the consuls were first established as the annual rulers of Rome, we would be closer to understanding the origins of a political system that was said to have lasted for almost five hundred years. Modern scholars have sought to construct consular lists from the testimony of authors such as Livy, Dionysios of Halikarnassos, and Diodoros of Sicily as well as the surviving portions of the *fasti consulares*. One set of these, inscribed in the first century BCE, was found at Antium (the *fasti Anatiates maiores*) while the other most important set was inscribed under Augustus ca. 19 BCE and probably fixed to an arch in the forum that had been erected to celebrate the emperor's victory over the Parthians.[54] Livy (2.21.4) admitted that it was difficult to know "which consuls succeeded which, and in which year an event happened," but, while there are inevitably some variations in the lists that are preserved by each source, the differences are no more than might have been anticipated. Furthermore, the order in which the names of consuls are recorded within any single year is largely uniform, which might suggest that they are all dependent on a single protosource.[55] Dating or assessing the reliability of that protosource is another matter. It is not, in principle, unthinkable that annual records were kept from the times of the first consuls,[56] though there is at present no extant evidence to suggest that the idea of consular lists predates ca. 173 BCE, when Marcus Fulvius Nobilior—perhaps

with the help of the poet Quintus Ennius—dedicated a temple to Hercules and the Muses and published a calendar, to which he added a list of consuls and censors.[57] Certainly, Livy (document 8.4) thought that, in the earliest times, a series of nails stood in lieu of written records. In the absence of independent evidence, arguments about the authenticity and accuracy of the consular lists have been made on the basis of the names that they contain.

We do not get off to a very promising start. According to Livy (see above, p. 149), in the first year that the Romans decided to institute the twin consulship, no fewer than five individuals occupied the position: (i) Lucius Junius Brutus, killed in the battle of Silva Arsia against forces from Veii and Tarquinii; (ii) Lucius Tarquinius Collatinus, forced into exile because of his family connections to the Tarquins; (iii) Publius Valerius Publicola; (iv) Spurius Lucretius, dead after just a few days in office; and (v) Marcus Horatius Pulvillus. In Peter Wiseman's view, "The canonical story of the first year of the Republic, as it appears in Livy, Dionysius and Plutarch, is patently an artificial combination of rival claims to have inaugurated the Republic."[58] Wiseman notes further that Servius Auctus (*Commentary on the Aeneid* 3.96) and Dionysios (*Roman Antiquities* 4.69.3) both talk about a seizure of power by Brutus alone. In his view, the twin consulship was not actually instituted until as late as 367 BCE.[59]

The internal politics of Rome in the later Republican period are dominated by the so-called struggle of the orders—a class warfare between the elite patricians and their social inferiors, the plebeians.

: : :    53. Polybios offers this information in the context of the first treaty between Rome and Carthage, which he then proceeds to cite. Mommsen (1859: 320–25) doubted the authenticity of the document on the basis of Diodoros's statement (16.69.1) that the first treaty between Rome and Carthage was drawn up in 348 BCE, but Cornell (1995: 210–14) defends Polybios's date on the basis of late-sixth-century Carthaginian interests in the Tyrrhenian, as documented by the Phoenician shrine at Pyrgi. The treaty testifies to Roman influence over Latium as far south as Terracina, though, as Gabba (2000: 243) points out, it is hardly balanced in Rome's favour.

54. Nedergaard 2001; Rüpke 1995: 191–96. Discovered in the forum in the 1540s, these inscriptions are known as the *fasti capitolini* because they were transferred to the Capitoline hill in 1586.

55. Drummond 1978: 80–81; Frier 1999: 146–47.

56. Momigliano 1963: 96.

57. Rüpke 1995.

58. Wiseman 2008: 298; cf. Forsythe 2005: 153–54.

59. Wiseman 1995: 103–10; 2008: 298. Contra Cornell 1995: 228.

Our literary authorities assume that the struggle must have gone back to the earliest years of the Republic, and so it is that debates concerning issues that were more properly of concern to annalists of the late third century—for example, the distribution of public land, the abolition of debt bondage, integration of the popular assembly (the *comitium plebis*) within the governance of the city, and access to magistracies—were all retrojected back to the early decades of the fifth century.[60] Of particular relevance to the present discussion is the supposed prohibition on plebeians' holding the consulship, which is said to have been in effect from the establishment of the Republic down to 367 BCE, when, after almost eighty years of government by panels of military tribunes with consular power, Lucius Sextius was elected as the first plebeian consul.[61] Yet the consular lists, especially in the period running from 509 to 483 BCE, include many names that are deemed to be plebeian—or, to be more accurate, names indicating an affiliation to a *gens*, or "clan," which is known to have been of plebeian status in the later Republic.[62] Among them are Spurius Cassius Vicellinus (named as consul for 502, 493, and 486), Marcus and Publius Minucius Augurinus (497 and 491, and 492, respectively), and—most notably—one of the first consuls, Lucius Junius Brutus.[63]

For some, the appearance of these "plebeian" names proves that the earlier parts of the consular lists are a forgery, interpolated at some point later than the mid-fourth century to furnish plebeian consular families with a more distinguished pedigree.[64] Indeed, Cicero (*Brutus* 16) makes a point of saying that the lists were full of "false triumphs, duplicated consulships and false genealogies," though his rhetorical agenda in making this claim should make us wary about accepting it too uncritically, and there are, in fact, other possibilities.[65] One is that a *gens* included both patrician and plebeian families and that the patrician branch had died out by the later Republic.[66] A variant of this explanation is that, at some point, an originally patrician family had voluntary converted to plebeian status—a poorly understood process known as *transitio ad plebem*.[67] Another possibility is that the nonpatrician names in the consular lists are not necessarily those of plebeians. By the time of the Late Republic, senators were often called *patres conscripti*, but Livy (2.1.11) seems to distinguish between the two terms in the formula *qui patres quique conscripti* and adds that the *conscripti* were those who were enrolled in the senate to make up numbers.[68] Cornell compares the situation to the distinction between hereditary and life peers in the British House of Lords.[69] It is, then, possible that the "plebeian" names in the consular lists are actually those of *conscripti*, whose descendants did not automatically inherit patrician status, and that these initially formed an intermediary class between patricians and plebeians.[70] A final possibility, of course, is that our sources are simply wrong to assume that the consulship was always restricted to the patricians. Gaetano De Sanctis suggested that there was originally no sharp distinction between patricians and plebeians and that this only emerged a little later with what he calls the "closure" of the patriciate.[71] Ultimately, the range of possible interpretations for the appearance of

---

:::

60. Raaflaub 1986a: 19; Cornell 1995: 242; Gabba 2000: 27.

61. Livy 6.42.9. The consular lists do not, however, regularly record plebeian consuls until 342 BCE. It is possible that legislation of 367 opened up the consulship to plebeians while in 342 a law—perhaps the plebiscite of Lucius Genucius (Livy 7.42)—made it obligatory to elect at least one plebeian consul. See Cornell 1995: 338–40.

62. For Roman "clans," see Smith 2006.

63. See generally Cornell 1995: 252–56; Forsythe 2005: 156–57.

64. Most notably, Beloch 1926: 9–22, 43–52. He did, however, accept the historicity of Marcus Horatius as consul for 509: see Ridley 1980: 279.

65. Ridley 1980: 272; Smith 2006: 268–73.

66. See Forsythe (2005: 161–62), who adduces the example of the Papirii, the Claudii, and the Veturii, though Cornell (1995: 254) points out the rarity of known cases where a patrician and plebeian branch of the same *gens* are attested.

67. Cicero, *Brutus* 62; Livy 4.16.3.

68. Cf. Festus 304 Lindsay.

69. Cornell 1995: 247.

70. Momigliano 1986: 182, 187–88; 1989: 153–54; Richard 1986: 122–23.

71. De Sanctis 1956: 228–30. See, however, Raaflaub (1986b: 228–34), who believes that De Sanctis's patrician "closure" was in reality a reaction to plebeian militancy. For a recent survey of the various interpretations of the consular *fasti*: Smith 2011.

**TABLE 8.1** The centuriate organization attributed to Servius Tullius

| Property class | | Number of centuries | |
| --- | --- | --- | --- |
| | | *Iuniores* | *Seniores* |
| I | Heavily armed | 40 | 40 |
| II | Heavily armed | 10 | 10 |
| III | Heavily armed | 10 | 10 |
| IV | Lightly armed | 10 | 10 |
| V | Lightly armed | 15 | 15 |

seemingly plebeian names in the early consular lists means that no conclusive adjudication of their authenticity is possible.

Plinio Fraccaro pursued a different direction by connecting the institution of the consulship with a military reform.[72] According to Livy (1.43) and Dionysios (*Roman Antiquities* 4.16–18), Servius Tullius divided the Roman citizenry into five property classes, each of which was split into two age groups that were then subdivided into centuries (table 8.1). Of these five classes, the top three were heavily armed while the remaining two were only lightly armed. Limiting himself to the *iuniores*, the younger men of military age between the ages of seventeen and forty-six, Fraccaro noted that the number of centuries in the heavily armed classes I–III equalled sixty, which was the standard complement of a Roman legion. And if, as etymology suggests, a century had originally been constituted by one hundred men, then the Servian legion would have been six thousand strong. But at the time of Polybios (6.21.9) in the second century, a Roman legion comprised three thousand heavily armed infantrymen, although it still had sixty centuries. At some point,

an original legion of six thousand must have been split into two legions of three thousand, and Fraccaro suggested that this was due to the institution of the twin consulship, which must, therefore, postdate the reign of Servius Tullius.[73]

The problem is that the five-class system attributed to Servius cannot possibly have been designed originally with military considerations in mind. The equal distribution of centuries between *iuniores* and *seniores* cannot have matched the demographic profile of the citizenry, because the centuries of *seniores* would have been much smaller than those of the *iuniores*. Similarly, given that wealth was restricted to a relatively small percentage of the population, the centuries of the wealthier classes would have numbered fewer than those of the more numerous poorer classes. The system as described was probably introduced in the late fourth or early third centuries for the purposes of the *comitia centuriata*, the political assembly that elected senior magistrates, declared war and peace, and imposed the death penalty for political offences, in which older citizens and the wealthy had a disproportionate electoral advantage.[74] One solution that has been suggested to the problem draws on a statement by Aulus Gellius (*Attic Night* 6.13) that the men of Class I belonged to the *classis* while all the rest were *infra classem* (below the *classis*).[75] Since the word *classis* originally seems to have denoted a "levy," thereby implying the entire military force, many modern scholars have concluded that an original heavily armed legion of sixty centuries was, at some point, subdivided into the three so-called Servian classes (with forty centuries assigned to Class I, and ten each to Classes II and III). If this happened after the hypothesized duplication of the legion, perhaps for the purposes of the *comitia centuriata*, then Fraccaro's theory can be largely salvaged.[76]

The theory is ingenious and has won widespread

:::      72. Fraccaro 1931.

73. For a summary, see Cornell 1995: 181–83; Forsythe 2007: 31–32.

74. For the date: Raaflaub 1986b: 209; Cornell 1995: 180; Forsythe 2005: 113.

75. Cf. Festus 110 Lindsay.

76. Cornell 1995: 183–90; Forsythe 2005: 112–13. Momigliano (1963: 120) accepts an original Servian army of sixty centuries but believes that, early in the Republican period, the *classis* was reduced, for the purposes of the *comitia centuriata*, to the forty centuries of class I, while the remaining twenty centuries, equally distributed between classes II and III, were henceforth *infra classem*.

acceptance, but if we accept Kurt Raaflaub's calculations that the adult male citizen population of Rome ca. 500 BCE was 6,600–9,900, then a Servian army of 6,000 heavily armed infantrymen is simply impossible.[77] This brings us to the crux of the problem. The supposition that an original legion was subdivided into two under consular command at the start of the Republic is based on the belief that there is some truth to the tradition concerning Servius Tullius's military reforms. Yet, quite apart from the fact that a standing army of 6,000 men in the mid-sixth century is unlikely on demographic grounds, it runs counter to the picture already sketched of a city in which *sodales* and private armies jostled for control. If instead, as seems likely, the organization of a standing army of sixty centuries is later, then its subdivision into two legions must be later still. It could well have been the consequence of the twin consulship, but it offers no precise chronological indication for the date of the consulship's origins.

A final complication concerning the institution of the consulship is presented by Livy's statement (document 8.4) that the Praetor Maximus (Greatest Praetor) was charged with marking the beginning of each year by driving a nail into the wall of the temple of Jupiter Capitolinus. The practice had fallen into abeyance before Livy's day, but his description of an inscription "written in archaic letters and language" implies that the ceremony was of ancient date even though it offers no concrete chronological indications.[78] This has suggested to some that there had originally been only one magistrate who governed Rome prior to the introduction of the twin consulship.[79]

Andreas Alföldi thought that "Praetor Maximus" was an alternative title for the Magister Populus, or Dictator. who, in his view, had first ruled over Republican Rome.[80] If this is true, it was clearly misunderstood by Livy, who believes that the consuls had ruled the city from the beginning of the Republic. But Livy (3.55.12) also later notes that the consuls had originally been called praetors, and, in fact, Greek authors regularly translated praetor as *stratēgos* (general) and consul as *stratēgos hupatos* (highest general).[81] It is, then, possible that the term Praetor Maximus, retranslated back from a Greek author, simply refers to the consul who, at the start of the new year, was in possession of the *fasces*—the bundle of rods that symbolized the supreme authority of the consul and was held by each consul on an alternate basis. The objection that the superlative *maximus* implies a comparison with more than one colleague is not compelling, since Terence (*Adelphoe* 881) uses the term to describe the elder of two brothers. Alternatively, the term Praetor Maximus might designate the person who held ultimate authority at any one time, be it the consul who held the *fasces*, an *interrex* or a Dictator.[82] In short, there is no scholarly consensus on the reliability of the consular lists and the belief that they serve to date the origins of the Republic to 509 BCE is ultimately a matter of faith.

## *"Etruscan" Rome*

Krister Hanell attempted to dissociate the early consular lists from the establishment of the Republic. Although he was inclined to trust the chronological accuracy of the *fasti*, he believed that they sig-

:::   77. Raaflaub 1986a: 44. The calculations are based on the population estimates of Ampolo (1980) and the size of Roman territory that was conjectured for this period by Beloch (1926: 178 n. 217).

78. Oakley (1998: 73–76) suggests that the practice of driving a nail into the wall of the temple originated as an apotropaic ritual and that it was only at some later, unspecified, date that the possibility of counting years by this method suggested itself.

79. E.g., Wiseman 2008: 299. Festus 152 Lindsay also refers to the Praetor Maximus.

80. Alföldi 1965: 43–44, 81; cf. De Martino (1972: 191–92), who believes that the two names recorded in the early consular lists are those not of the consuls but of the Dictator/Magister Populi and his assistant, the Magister Equitum (Master of Cavalry).

81. Cf. Festus 249 Lindsay. See Stavely 1956: 98; Momigliano 1989: 149; Brennan 2000: 20–23; Forsythe 2005: 152. Oakley (1998: 77–80) thinks that "praetor" was the official term for "consul" in the period ca. 509–451 BCE.

82. Momigliano 1989: 149.

nified the adoption of a new calendar at the time of the dedication of the temple of Jupiter Capitolinus and a new practice of recording years, borrowed from Greece, according to eponymous magistrates—in this case, the Praetor Maximus. But he also believed that these annual magistrates initially exercised their functions under the kings—just as archons had continued to be annually appointed under the Peisistratids in Athens. Initially, he argued, the *fasti* had recorded only the Praetor Maximus; additional names were then interpolated later, after the establishment of the twin consulship. This he dated to ca. 449 BCE, when fluctuations in the numbers of magistrates recorded in the consular lists suggest that the original system was starting to break down.[83] Hanell's thesis was enthusiastically adopted by Einar Gjerstad, who, as we have seen (p. 139), wanted to date the foundation of Rome to ca. 575 BCE. Gjerstad was reluctant, however, to dispense with the traditions concerning the kings: if the city had been founded in the sixth—rather than eighth—century, then either the kings had to be downdated, or their reigns shortened, or both. To justify this recalculation, he appealed to the archaeological evidence of two constructions that tradition attributed to Servius Tullius.

During the siege of Veii in 396 BCE, according to Livy (5.19.6) and Plutarch (*Life of Camillus* 5.1), the Roman general Marcus Furius Camillus swore that "if Veii were captured and the senate agreed, he would hold great games and would restore and dedicate the temple of Mater Matuta, which had already been dedicated earlier by king Servius Tullius." The temple was situated in the Forum Boarium by the river Tiber and was often mentioned in conjunction with the temple of Fortuna.[84] In 1937, excavations in Piazza della Bocca della Verità revealed a podium that supported twin temples—the more northerly of which lay under the fifteenth-century church of Sant'Omobono—which were swiftly identified by

their excavator as the temples of Mater Matuta and Fortuna (fig. 8.3).[85] The structures themselves were originally dated to the fourth century BCE, but beneath the southeast corner of the platform was the podium of an earlier temple, with which were associated numerous fragments of a terracotta pediment depicting panthers, a frieze with a procession of chariots, and a statue group that represented Hercules and Minerva—all now displayed in the Exedra of Marcus Aurelius.[86] Adopting the "low" chronology that he had elaborated from his work on the forum burials, Gjerstad dated this earlier temple to the early years of the fifth century, and, since he trusted the tradition that credited Servius Tullius with the dedication of the temple to Mater Matuta, the inevitable consequence was that Servius's reign would need to be downdated to ca. 500 BCE.[87]

The second construction that is attributed to Servius Tullius by Livy (1.44) and Dionysios of Halikarnassos (*Roman Antiquities* 4.13) is the Republican fortification circuit of Rome, of which one of the best preserved stretches still stands outside Termini railway station (fig. 8.4). Due to the use of blocks of *Grotta Oscura* tufa, this section of the walls may be a fourth-century repair to earlier defences, which can be traced at various points by the use of *cappellaccio* tufa.[88] The section that runs from the Quirinal to the Esquiline hill is reinforced by a massive earth mound (*agger*) and ditch, and in this mound was found an Attic red-figure sherd, dating to the first quarter of the fifth century. It was this that led Gjerstad to conclude that the *agger* was part of the Servian circuit, thus confirming the lower date for Servius's reign.[89]

Convinced that the monarchy had lasted well into the fifth century, Gjerstad argued that its demise could be archaeologically identified by a decline in the volume of imported artifacts, which seems to occur around the middle of the fifth century—that is, at about the time when Hanell dated

::: 83. Hanell 1946; cf. Rüpke 1995: 190. Smith (2011: 23–24) is sceptical.
84. Ovid, *Fasti* 6.477–79; Livy 25.7.6; 33.27.4.
85. Colini 1938.
86. For a summary: Holloway 1994: 68–80.

87. Gjerstad 1960: 458–63; 1967: 19–20.
88. Barbera and Magnani Cianetti 2008; see also Cifani 2008: 51–58; 2010.
89. Gjerstad 1954; 1966: 349–57.

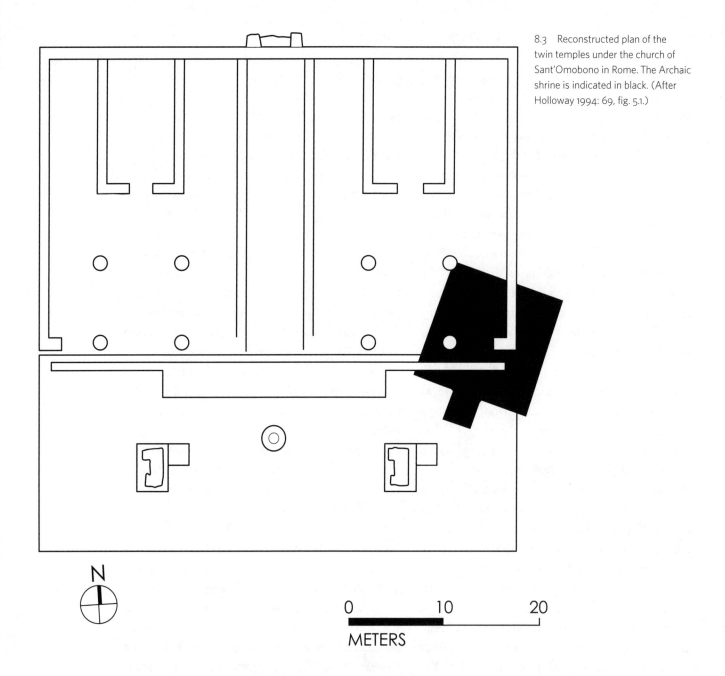

8.3 Reconstructed plan of the twin temples under the church of Sant'Omobono in Rome. The Archaic shrine is indicated in black. (After Holloway 1994: 69, fig. 5.1.)

0        10        20

METERS

the institution of the twin consulship. Since the vast quantities of imported Greek materials in Etruria during the Archaic period suggested that it was the Etruscans who were primarily responsible for the imports in central Italy more generally, Gjerstad believed that the tailing-off of these imports at Rome was due to weakening Etruscan influence, which

he attributed to the departure of the last Etruscan king of Rome.[90] The view was accepted by, among others, Robert Werner, who sought to trace the collapse of Etruscan power in central Italy to the defeat its fleet met, at the hands of Hieron of Syracuse, off Cumae in 474 BCE.[91] The underlying assumption in all these treatments is that the reigns of the "Etrus-

:::        90. Gjerstad 1973: 198–200. For the tailing-off of Attic imports to Rome and the major cities of southern Etruria in the fifth century, see Meyer 1980.

91. Werner 1963: 482; cf. Heurgon 1973: 137–55. The view that Rome was an Etruscan city under the Tarquins is advanced most energetically in Alföldi 1965: 176–233.

8.4    The "Servian" walls outside Termini railway station, Rome. (Photo by author.)

can" kings—Tarquinius Priscus, Servius Tullius (by adoption), and Tarquinius Superbus—are archaeologically traceable.[92]

That Rome was the beneficiary of cultural exchanges with its neighbours on the opposite bank of the Tiber is undeniable. The Romans themselves believed that the insignia of the Roman kings—the *fasces*, the *toga praetexta* (a white robe with a purple hem), and the *sella curulis* (a folding chair of ivory)—as well as the chariot, gold crown, and ivory sceptre of triumphant generals, were of Etruscan origin. The introduction of haruspicy (divination through the examination of a sacrificial victim's liver), certain musical instruments, and a particular style of architecture were also credited to the Etruscans, and Etruscan craftsmen are even said to have been responsible for the construction of the temple of Jupiter Capitolinus.[93] Some of these cultural influ-

:::    92. For the historiographical inclination to treat the Rome of the Tarquins as an Etruscan city, see Cornell 1995: 151–53.
   93. Livy 1.56.1. See Cornell 1995: 165–66, though he also notes (p. 169) that sometimes the adjective "Etruscan" was employed simply to indicate something that was deemed archaic.

ences, however, go back well before the period in which the Tarquins are supposed to have ruled—including the practice of inurned cremation, sometimes in "hut urns," which is characteristic of the Protovillanovan culture of northern Italy and is represented at Rome during the Latial I phase.[94] All this ultimately proves is that Rome was an "open city" that was receptive to outsiders, be they Latins, Sabines, Etruscans, Greeks, or perhaps even Phoenicians.[95] Such a supposition is supported by the handful of Etruscan inscriptions known from Archaic Rome as well as a smattering of seemingly Etruscan names in the early consular lists, including Avile Acvinlnas (Gaius Aquillius), consul for 487 BCE, who made three dedications at Vulci and in the Portonaccio sanctuary at Veii.[96]

There is not, however, a shred of evidence to suggest that Archaic Rome was politically dependent upon the cities of southern Etruria.[97] This marks a strong contrast with the situation in Campania. Velleius Paterculus (1.7.2), himself a Campanian, believed that the cities of Capua and Nola were established by the Etruscans as early as the eighth century,[98] and Dionysios of Halikarnassos (*Roman Antiquities* 7.3.1) notes that the Etruscans, in alliance with other Italic peoples, attacked the Campanian Greek city of Cumae in 524 BCE. Furthermore, unlike at Rome, more than one hundred Etruscan inscriptions are known from a number of sites in Campania.[99] Counterintuitively, then, Latium constituted an enclave between Etruria to the north and the Etruscan-dominated cities of Campania to the south. As for the Tarquins, there is no hint in the sources that they ruled Rome as agents of Etruscan cities rather than as private

individuals who had made their home in Rome.[100] The inference to be drawn from all this should be obvious: if there are no positive archaeological indications for an Etruscan political domination of Rome, then an apparent decline in foreign imports and Etruscan influence in the fifth century need not have anything to do with a hypothesized collapse of Etruscan power in Latium or with the departure of the Tarquins. In fact, internal factors such as a debt crisis, together with Rome's external wars, are more likely to be the causes for the apparent disruption in commercial activity.[101]

Nor have the arguments that Gjerstad advanced for downdating the reign of Servius Tullius stood the test of time. First of all, the "low" chronology that he adopted has failed to convince most archaeologists. Further investigations of the Archaic sanctuary at Sant'Omobono have suggested that there were actually two phases; the first, probably associated with the "panther pediment," dates to ca. 580 BCE, while the second—to which the terracotta frieze and the statues of Hercules and Minerva belonged—is now assigned to the last quarter of the sixth century.[102] To complicate matters further, however, the most recent excavations of the site, conducted by the Sovraintendenza Comunale di Roma in association with the Universities of Calabria and Michigan, have determined that the podium and twin temples, originally assigned to the fourth century, should in fact date to the second half of the fifth century—in which case, their identification with the shrines of Mater Matuta and Fortuna is far less secure.[103] As for the "Servian" wall, the presence of a single imported pottery sherd is hardly sufficient proof to offer a secure dating for the fortification.[104]

::: 94. Holloway (1994) 44.

95. See Rebuffat 1966.

96. Cornell 1995: 157–59, 222. For Aquillius: Ampolo 1975.

97. Momigliano 1989: 141–43; Musti 1990: 12.

98. Although Velleius also says that the Elder Cato (*Origines* 3.1) dated the capture of Capua to 471 BCE. Modern scholars have assumed an error and change the date to either 683 or 600: see Cornell 1995: 154–55.

99. Frederiksen 1984: 124.

100. Cornell 1995: 156. Cornell perhaps goes too far, however,

in emphasizing the Tarquins's Greek origins over their Etruscan affiliations (cf. p. 224). In Livy, at any rate, Tarquinius Superbus appeals for help from the Etruscan cities on the basis of his compatriotism: 2.6.2, 4; 2.9.1, 4.

101. Momigliano 1989: 137; Cornell 1995: 225.

102. Pisani Sartorio 1995.

103. Doubts on the identification had already been voiced by Holloway 1994: 10–11. I am grateful to Nicola Terrenato for guiding me around the current excavations at Sant'Omobono in July 2012.

104. Cornell 1995: 199.

## Conclusion

Departing just slightly from the Varronian chronology, Dionysios (*Roman Antiquities* 5.1.1) dates the origins of the Republic to the beginning of the 68th Olympiad (508/7 BCE), "when Isagoras was Archon at Athens." The synchronism is not without significance, because it was during Isagoras's archonship that, according to Herodotos (6.131.1), Kleisthenes "instituted the tribes and the democracy for the Athenians." A new political regime for the Athenians, then, but only because, two years earlier, the last Peisistratid tyrant, Hippias, had been expelled from Athens. Indeed, Pliny (*Natural History* 34.17) also points to the parallel by noting that the Athenians had erected statues to the tyrannicides Harmodios and Aristogeiton "in the same year in which the kings were expelled at Rome." The apparent coincidence of the two events should, at the very least, be regarded as highly suspicious.[105]

Once again, the parallel with Athens may prove instructive. Herodotos (5.63–65; 6.123.2) and Thucydides (1.20.2; 6.54–55) were both adamant that the tyranny had been ended by the Spartans, but popular tradition held that the establishment of *isonomia* (equal rights) had been the action of Harmodios and Aristogeiton, who assassinated Hippias's younger brother, Hipparchos, in 514 BCE. Within a few years of the event, a drinking song celebrating the tyrannicides' heroism was circulating and the statue group, created by Antenor and described by Pliny, was set up in the *agora*; at some point, certainly before the fourth century, cultic honours were offered annually at the tomb of the couple and their descendants were granted exemption from taxes and the right to free meals in the *prytaneion*.[106] At both Rome and Athens, then, tradition assumed a swift and violent transition from tyranny to democracy. In reality, however, true democracy—that is, the rule by the *dēmos*, or the "ordinary" (nonelite) people—

had to wait until the late 460s and the reforms of Ephialtes, by which the aristocratic council of the Areopagos was stripped of most of its powers. It is no accident that a paraphrase of the word *dēmokratia* makes its first appearance precisely at this time or that this is the decade in which the Athenian proper name Demokrates is first attested.[107] It is extremely likely that the birth of the Roman Republic was a similarly messy and drawn-out experiment in design rather than the short revolutionary transition from monarchy to Republic that is sketched by the literary sources. And, if true, this would suggest that the synchronism between the foundation of the Republic and the dedication of the temple of Jupiter Capitolinus was "discovered" at a later date.

In 304 BCE, Gnaeus Flavius, son of a freedman and scribe to Appius Claudius Caecus, dedicated a shrine to the goddess Concordia at the foot of the Capitoline (document 8.7). On a bronze inscription, he recorded that the shrine was dedicated 204 years after the temple of Jupiter Capitolinus, yielding a date of 508/7 BCE. The figure 204 can hardly be derived from generational dating. It speaks, rather, to an ability to resort to a more or less precise calibration of time at just about the same time as Fabius Pictor was compiling his history of Rome. Nor is it without interest that Flavius is said to have been the first to publish a calendar of *dies fasti*—days on which public business could be conducted. This surely represents the *terminus post quem* for the "adjustments of Roman memory" by which "the dedication of the Capitoline Temple was tied to the political narrative, and linked in an epochal synchronism to the *metabolē*, or constitutional revolution, by which the regal state gave way to its successor."[108] If that is right, then, as with the case of the "wall of Romulus" or the "palace of Numa" (chap. 7), it is tempting to wonder whether it is not so much the

---

:::     105. Feeney 2007: 21; Wiseman 2008: 136–39. This is not, however, to say that such synchronisms must necessarily be late inventions: see Purcell 2003: 24–26.

     106. *PMG* 474–75, 893–96; *IG* I³ 131; [Aristotle], *Constitution of the Athenians* 58.1; Andokides 1.98; Isaios 5.47.

107. Aischylos, *Suppliant Maidens* 604. See Hansen 1991: 70.
108. Purcell 2003: 32; cf. Feeney 2007: 141–42.

case that the material evidence confirms the literary sources as that the literary traditions have themselves been shaped by, and around, the visible presence of earlier monuments.

## DOCUMENTS FOR CHAPTER 8

**8.1** This was the most grievous and repugnant event that befell the Republic of the Roman people since the foundation of the city. For although there was no external enemy and the gods were propitious (allowance made for our morals), the seat of Jupiter Optimus Maximus, founded auspiciously by our ancestors to be the guarantee of empire, which neither Porsenna, when the city had surrendered, nor the Gauls, when it was captured, were able to profane, was destroyed by the madness of the emperors. The Capitol had burned before during civil war, but as a result of the crime of individuals. Now it was openly besieged and openly set alight, and what were the causes of these hostilities? What was the reward for so great a disaster? Was it for the fatherland that we were fighting? It was vowed by King Tarquinius Priscus during the Sabine war, and he laid its foundations more in the hope of future greatness than in accordance with the meager resources that were then available to the Roman people. Next, Servius Tullius, with the commitment of the allies, and Tarquinius Superbus, from enemy spoils once Suessa Pometia was captured, raised the superstructure. But the glory of the project was reserved for freedom: after the expulsion of the kings, Horatius Pulvillus, in his second consulship [498 BCE], dedicated it—a building so magnificent that in later times the immense resources of the Roman people would embellish rather than increase it. It was rebuilt on the same site after it had been destroyed by fire during the consulship of Lucius Scipio and Caius Norbanus [83 BCE], after a period of 415 years. After his victory, Sulla took charge of the restoration but did not dedicate it—the only thing denied to his good fortune. The name of Lutatius Catulus remained among all the great works of the emperors down to the reign of Vitellius. It was this temple that was now burning. (Tacitus, *Histories* 3.72)

**8.2** The first treaty between the Romans and the Carthaginians was made in the year when Lucius Junius Brutus and Marcus Horatius were the first consuls, after the expulsion of the kings; and it was they who also dedicated the temple of Jupiter Capitolinus. This was twenty-eight years before Xerxes crossed into Greece [509/8 BCE]. (Polybios 3.22)

**8.3** The temple of Jupiter on the Capitol had not yet been dedicated: Valerius and Horatius drew lots as to who should dedicate it, and it fell by lot to Horatius, while Valerius set out to wage war against Veii. (Livy 2.8.6)

**8.4** There is an ancient law, written in archaic letters and language, to the effect that whoever is Praetor Maximus should drive in a nail on the Ides of September. It was affixed on the right side of the temple of Jupiter Optimus Maximus, where the shrine of Minerva is. Since writing was rare in that period, this nail is said to have marked the number of years, and the law was dedicated on that shrine of Minerva because numbers are the invention of Minerva. Cincius, a diligent author concerning monuments of this kind, affirms that nails were also affixed to mark the number of years at the temple of Nortia, an Etruscan goddess. According to this law, the consul Marcus Horatius dedicated the temple of Jupiter Optimus Maximus in the year after the kings were expelled. Later, the ceremony of driving in the nail was transferred from the consuls to the dictators, since their power was greater. Later, since the custom had been suspended, it was deemed worthy enough for the creation of a dictator. (Livy 7.3.5–8).

**8.5** In this year the temple of Jupiter Capitolinus was brought to completion, as I described in the book preceding this one. Marcus Horatius, one of the two consuls, dedicated and inscribed his name on it before the arrival of his colleague; for at that time it chanced that Valerius had set out with a force to aid the country districts. (Dionysios of Halikarnassos, *Roman Antiquities* 5.35.3).

**8.6** When he heard these things from the ambassadors, Tarquinius set the artisans to work and built much of the temple, though he did not manage to complete the whole work, since he was soon driven from power; but the Roman people brought it to completion in the third consulship. It stood on a high podium and was eight hundred feet in perimeter, with each side measuring almost two hundred feet; indeed, one would find the excess of the length over the width to be little, not even fifteen feet in all. For the temple that was built on the same foundations in the time of our fathers, after the conflagration, was found to be little different from the an- cient structure with regard to the costliness of its materials, and comprised three rows of columns on the south-facing façade and a single row on each side. Inside are three parallel shrines that share the same dividing walls; the central one is of Jupiter, while on one side is that of Juno and on the other that of Minerva, all three covered by one pediment and one roof. (Dionysios of Halikarnassos, *Roman Antiquities* 4.61.3–4).

**8.7** This was done in the consulship of Publius Sempronius and Publius Sulpicius (304 BCE): Flavius vowed a temple to Concordia, if he should reconcile the upper classes with the people, and, since this could not be decreed with public money, he made a bronze shrine in the area of the Graeco- stasis, which was then situated above the *comitium*, from the fines that had been exacted from those condemned for usury. And, on a bronze panel, he inscribed that this shrine was dedicated 204 years after the Capitoline temple. (Pliny, *Natural History* 33.19)

# 9

# Imperial Austerity:

# The House of Augustus

In early August 30 BCE, Caius Julius Caesar Octavianus emerged triumphant from the civil wars that had devastated Rome and its imperial possessions for decades. Mark Antony and Cleopatra, whose fleet had been routed the previous autumn off Actium in western Greece, had taken their own lives in Alexandria. Octavian, who adopted the name Augustus in 27 BCE, would rule without interruption for the next forty-four years, establishing what is known as the Principate—the succession of emperors who governed the Roman Empire down to the deposition of Romulus Augustulus in 476 CE.[1] Yet, despite the immense wealth that accompanied his monopoly of power, Augustus earned a reputation for simplicity in his private life. The biographer Suetonius (*Augustus* 73, 79.1), who held positions in the imperial administration under Trajan (ruled 98–117 CE) and Hadrian (117–38 CE), recounts how the first emperor wore simple clothes, woven and sewn by his wife, sister, and daughter, and was generally negligent of his personal appearance.[2] Abstemious in his drinking and dining habits, he hosted restrained dinner parties (74, 76–77). And such was his disdain of lavish villas that he demolished a property belonging to his granddaughter Julia because he deemed it too excessive

:::       1. Following what has become a convention, C. Julius Caesar Octavianus will be referred to as Octavian for the period prior to 27 BCE and as Augustus for the period after that date.

      2. Suetonius's career is known from an inscription to him, found at Hippo Regius in Numidia: see Marec and Pflaum 1952.

(72.3). In the record of his own accomplishments, published on two bronze tablets affixed to his great Mausoleum in the Campus Martius, Augustus claims that he "handed down exemplary practices in many things for posterity to imitate" (*Res Gestae* 8).[3] To judge from Suetonius (document 9.1), those examples included the emperor's own house on the Palatine hill.

Just how modest was Augustus's house? In March 2008, after a programme of restoration that cost almost two million euros, the Soprintendenza of Rome opened to the public four rooms belonging to a complex excavated in the 1950s and early 1960s by Gianfilippo Carettoni and identified by him as belonging to Augustus's Palatine residence. For Carettoni, "the restrained elegance of the decoration and the limited dimensions of the rooms" accorded well with Suetonius's description of the house.[4] But renewed investigations in the first decade of this century suggest that the rooms excavated by Carettoni were only part of a much larger building,[5] prompting Andrea Carandini to cast doubt on the value of Suetonius's testimony.[6] By contrast, Peter Wiseman—who also considers the Carettoni House to be "luxurious"—presents Suetonius's description as a reason for doubting the identification of the house as that of Augustus.[7]

The disgreement that surrounds the so-called House of Augustus raises a series of questions. Is the building that Carettoni excavated really the residence of Rome's first emperor? Did Suetonius mean that the house was modest by comparison with other Late Republican residences—for instance, the adjacent House of Livia—or was his point of comparison rather with the sumptuous Palatine residences of later emperors?[8] Just how reliable in any case was Suetonius's information about a structure that was, by his day, almost certainly damaged by at least two conflagrations?[9] And, finally, is it even a valid exercise to seek archaeological confirmation—or refutation—of a term that is as subjective and relative as "modest"?

## The House Unearthed

The modern visitor to the Palatine is confronted by a confused jumble of ruins which presents challenges even to the trained eyes of archaeologists. Centuries of construction—and especially the vast palaces built by Nero in the 60s CE and by Domitian a generation later and subsequently modified by Trajan and Hadrian in the early second century and the Severan emperors in the third century—have greatly disturbed the stratigraphy of the site. In addition, the earliest excavations, conducted in the 1720s for the Farnese family and then again in the 1860s for Napoleon III, fell far short of the standards we would expect today.

In 1869, as part of the campaign of exploration commissioned by Napoleon III, Pietro Rosa excavated a well-appointed Late Republican house to the northwest of Domitian's palace, the Domus Augustana (fig. 9.1). The house, constructed from concrete faced with tufa *opus reticulatum*, dates to about 75–50 BCE, but its decoration with paintings, assigned to an advanced phase of what is called the "second style," shows that it was modified ca. 30 BCE. The house almost certainly had two stories, of which only the lower, subterranean level is preserved today. In its first phase, the principal entry was from the east into an atrium court, while a courtyard or garden with a portico occupied the western part of the property; it is possible that, in a

:::      3. The *Res Gestae Divi Augusti* is known today from a copy set up at Ankara in Turkey.
4. Carettoni 1967: 67. Cf. Zanker 1988: 51: "The house itself was relatively modest."
5. Iacopi and Tedone 2006.
6. Carandini and Bruno 2008: 50, 61–62, 83–84.

7. Wiseman 2009: 528.
8. Degrassi 1967: 80. Carettoni (1967: 56) notes that the House of Livia is less modest than the House of Augustus.
9. Tacitus, *Annals* 15.38.2; Cassius Dio 62.18.2. See Wiseman 2009: 535.

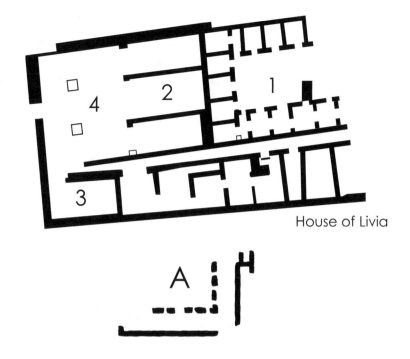

House of Livia

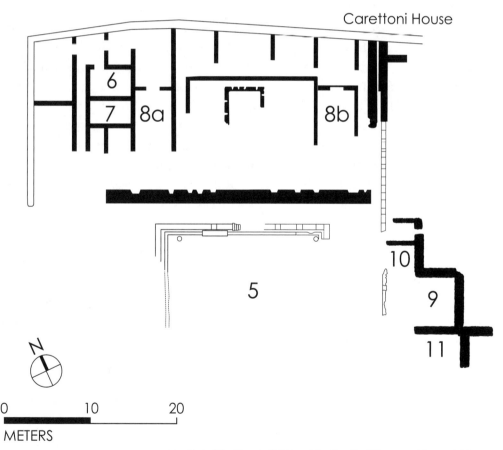

Carettoni House

N

0　　　　10　　　　20
METERS

9.1 Plan of the House of Livia and the Carettoni House. 1: *atrium*; 2: *tablinum*; 3: *triclinium*; 4: courtyard; 5: peristyle; 6: room of the masks; 7: room of the pine garlands; 8a and 8b: libraries; 9: tetrastyle room; 10: small room with upper storey; 11: ramp; A: peristyle of the House of Augustus. (After Iacopi and Tedone 2006: table 6.)

second phase, the orientation of the house was reversed, with a new atrium constructed to the west and a peristyle courtyard over the former atrium. At the centre of the eastern side of the courtyard was what was probably the *tablinum*, or principal reception room, its walls decorated with mythological scenes such as Polyphemos and Galatea and Zeus's seduction of Io, framed by architectural vistas. Either side of this are rooms whose walls display painted colonnades beneath a frieze portraying Egyptianizing landscapes. On the southern side of the courtyard, what was probably the *triclinium*, or dining room, was richly decorated with painted colonnades against backgrounds depicting rural sanctuaries.[10] Three lead water pipes, found in underground passageways, were stamped respectively with the names Domitian, L. Pescennius Eros, and Julia Augusta—the latter a title held by several imperial consorts, including Augustus's third wife, Livia. It is for this reason, along with the date assigned to the paintings, that the residence is generally termed the House of Livia, although the identification is far from secure.[11]

Rosa undertook some superficial investigation of the area south of the House of Livia in 1865, and some fragments of collapsed vaulting and squared tufa blocks were discovered by Alfonso Bartoli in 1937, but it was not until 1956 that excavations began in earnest.[12] The structure which Carettoni brought to light had been buried beneath several metres of earth and rubble and comprised a series of rooms, constructed from squared blocks of tufa (*opus quadratum*), which bordered a peristyle court. Six rooms to the north, which are relatively small and decorated with simple geometric mosaic pavements and wall paintings in the "second style," were identified as belonging to the private quarters of the residence.

One room was decorated with paintings inspired by theatrical scenographies, with masks portrayed on the cornices; another depicts wooden columns strewn with pine garlands. The remaining rooms, which adjoin the northern and eastern sides of the peristyle, are larger and furnished with stucco ceilings, marble floors, and more luxurious wall paintings; for this reason, they are deemed to have served a more public function. Two rooms on the northern side of the peristyle have niches in their lateral walls and were interpreted as libraries, while in the centre of the eastern side of the peristyle is a large tetrastyle reception room, with an inlaid marble floor and wall paintings of figures, masks, and vegetal decoration on a black background. Immediately to the north is a small, richly decorated room whose upper storey is remarkably well preserved with figured friezes and panels that evoke Alexandrian themes. Finally, to the south of the tetrastyle room is a lavishly decorated ramp that Carettoni believed gave direct access to the imposing temple which stood on an upper terrace to the east (fig. 9.2).[13]

In the absence of epigraphic clues, it is the temple that offered Carettoni a possible identification for the complex. Little of it survives today, save for part of its concrete core supported by barrel vaults, but fragments of architectural elements and blocks allow us to reconstruct a temple built from blocks of tufa and travertine in *opus quadratum*, faced with marble from Luni, and standing on a tall podium that measured ca. 24 by ca. 45 metres; across its façade stood six tall Corinthian columns.[14] It was originally identified as the temple of Jupiter Victor, but Carettoni's discovery of a marble door jamb, decorated with acanthus leaves sprouting from a tripod, together with fragments of what might be a large statue of Apollo, suggest instead

::: 10. Coarelli 1980: 129–31; 2007: 138–40; Tomei 1998: 31–33; Iacopi 1995a; Carandini 2010: 120–25; Claridge 2010: 135–36.

11. Among recent scholars who accept the identification: Tomei 1998: 31, 33; Wiseman 2009: 533–34. Claridge (2010: 135) believes the attribution to be "purely conventional." Carandini and Bruno (2008) consistently refer to the "so-called House of Livia." Coarelli (1980: 131; 2007: 140) and Royo (1999: 79) are ambivalent. Pinza (1910), Richmond (1914), and Lugli (1946: 438) identified the house as the residence of Augustus.

12. Carettoni 1967: 61.

13. Carettoni 1967: 61–64; 1983; Iacopi 1995b; Tomei 1998: 34–36. For the paintings of the house: Iacopi 2008.

14. Coarelli 2007: 142–43; Carandini and Bruno 2008: 64; Claridge 2010: 142–44. See Servius's commentary on Vergil, *Aeneid* 8.720.

9.2 Carettoni House: ramp.
(Photo by author.)

that the foundations are those of the temple of Palatine Apollo.[15] The historian Velleius Paterculus, who lived through the reigns of Augustus and his successor, Tiberius, records that Octavian vowed the temple to Apollo after his defeat of Sextus Pompeius in 36 BCE (document 9.2); Cassius Dio (53.1.3), writing in the early third century CE, notes that the temple, together with its surrounding precinct and libraries, was finally dedicated in 28 BCE.[16] According to the elder Pliny (*Natural History* 36.5.24–32),

∷     15. Carettoni 1967: 71. The identification had already been proposed in Pinza 1910 and Lugli 1946: 468–75.

16. It is often stated that Octavian vowed the temple to Apollo in thanks for his victory over Pompeius (e.g., Zanker 1988: 50),

the cult statues of Apollo, Diana, and Letona were fourth-century originals by the Greek sculptors Skopas, Timotheos, and Kephisodotos, respectively, while in the pediment stood Archaic works by the sixth-century Greek sculptors Boupalos and Athenis of Chios (36.5.12).[17]

Velleius makes it clear that the properties Octavian was buying up were adjacent to his own, and, although he is not explicit, he seems to indicate a connection between these and the temple of Apollo. Other authors are more direct: Suetonius (document 9.3) says that the temple was built in a "part of his Palatine residence" that was struck by lightning—an event dated by Cassius Dio (document 9.4) to 36 BCE—and Ovid (document 9.5) describes a Palatine domicile shared equally by Apollo, Vesta, and Augustus. It is for this reason that Carettoni, who believed that the house on the lower terrace was "structurally connected" to the temple via the ramp, identified the former as the residence of Augustus that is described by Suetonius.[18] Admittedly, the marble inlays found in the eastern wing of the house are hard to reconcile with Suetonius's insistence that Augustus's residence lacked such decorative features, but Carettoni assumed that Suetonius was referring to the simpler, more "private" set of rooms in the northwest angle of the house. Further, he suggested that the richly decorated upper room might be identified with the "elevated" (in edito) little study to which Suetonius gives the sobriquet "Syracuse."[19] In Carettoni's opinion, the Alexandrian themes in the decor of the room suggest that this upper storey was completed a little later than the rest of the house—perhaps after Octavian's victory at Actium and his conquest of Egypt.[20]

That interpretation has, however, recently been challenged by renewed investigations of the zone.[21]

Far from being contemporary with the temple and its associated structures, the house excavated by Carettoni actually predates the temple terrace (fig. 9.3). Indeed, the western part of the terrace that stands in front of the temple and supported a large portico, whose columns were interspersed with statues representing the daughters of Danaos, cuts through a good part of the earlier house.[22] At the opposite, eastern end of the terrace is an apsidal structure, which Irene Iacopi and Giovanna Tedone identify as the Latin Library in which meetings of the senate were occasionally convened towards the end of Augustus's life (cf. document 9.3).[23] What Carettoni interpreted as a ramp connecting to the courtyard of the temple was instead designed to give access to the upper storey of the earlier house.[24] In addition, Iacopi and Tedone found some evidence for further construction to the east of the Carettoni House, which they interpreted as belonging to an extension of the house around a second peristyle, symmetrical to the first and connected to it by a vaulted corridor which was bisected by a monumental gateway.[25] The extension appears not to have been completed at the time when much of this complex was buried beneath a fill of about 7 metres in preparation for the construction of the temple of Apollo, its portico and library.[26]

In their wish to reconcile the material evidence with the literary notices, Iacopi and Tedone suggest the following reconstruction. In around 42 BCE, the young Octavian acquired, as Suetonius (document 9.1) tells us, the house of Q. Hortensius Hortalus. Two years earlier, Hortensius had sided with M. Junius Brutus, one of Julius Caesar's assassins.[27] It is, then, likely that Octavian came into possession of Hortensius's property as a result of the "pro-

::: but no ancient source explicitly says this: see Gurval 1995: 113–15, 119–23.

17. here See Zanker 1988: 240–42; Carandini and Bruno 2008: 64.

18. Carettoni 1967: 62; 1983: 9, 86; cf. Zanker 1988: 51.

19. Carettoni 1983: 11–16; cf. Iacopi 1995b: 48.

20. Carettoni 1983: 86–93.

21. Iacopi and Tedone 2006.

22. For the portico of the Danaidai, see Iacopi and Tedone 2006: 355–58; cf. Ovid, Amores 2.2.3–4; Propertius, Elegies 2.31.1–16.

23. Iacopi and Tedone 2006: 352–55; cf. Tomei 2000: 9–10. A papyrus (P.Oxy 25.2435), found at Oxyrhynkos in Egypt, records how, in 12/13 CE, Augustus received an Alexandrian delegation "in the Latin library in the sanctuary of Apollo"; cf. D. L. Thompson 1981; Corbier 1992: 898–901.

24. Iacopi and Tedone 2006: 363.

25. Iacopi and Tedone 2006: 366–67.

26. Iacopi and Tedone 2006: 370–71.

27. Antony had Hortensius executed after the battle of Philippi in 42 BCE because of his support for Brutus: Plutarch, Life

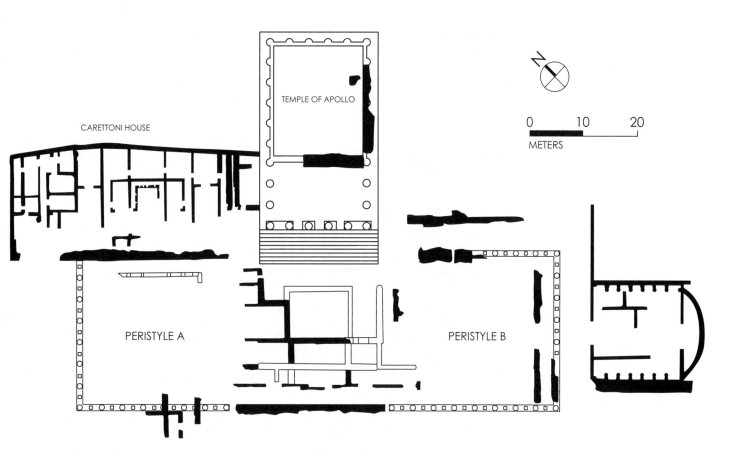

9.3   The Carettoni House and sanctuary of Apollo. (After Iacopi and Tedone 2006: table 6.)

scriptions" that were launched by Octavian, Mark Antony, and M. Aemilius Lepidus, by which political—and private—enemies were deprived of their property and often their lives.[28] Once in possession of Hortensius's house, Octavian reorganized it around a peristyle court (fig. 9.4). After his victory over Sextus Pompeius in 36 BCE, Velleius Paterculus (document 9.2) tells us that Octavian was planning to expand his house by buying neighbouring properties, and it is to this phase that the project to extend the house by adding a second peristyle should date.[29] According to Velleius, this was also when Octavian vowed to build a temple to Apollo, but the project was not finally completed until 28 BCE. Iacopi and Tedone therefore hypothesize that Octa-

vian took the decision to abandon work on his house and build instead a temple to Apollo ca. 31 BCE in the immediate aftermath of Actium—a battle that he believed he had won with Apollo's help. They further surmise that, in need of a new residence, Octavian constructed new private quarters immediately to the west of the temple of Apollo, overlying the northern rooms of the Carettoni House as well as a good part of the House of Livia. Due to continuous overbuilding, little remains of this residence, save for part of a tufa peristyle (see fig. 9.1, A), but literary sources suggest that it must have been rebuilt at least once, after a devastating fire of 3 CE which destroyed also the temple of Magna Mater some 20 metres to the west (document 9.6).[30]

:::   *of Antony* 22.4; *Life of Brutus* 29.1; Velleius Paterculus 2.71.2. See Carandini and Bruno 2008: 140; Wiseman 2009: 528.

28. For the proscriptions: Hinard 1985; Corbier 1992: 889–91.

29. This would imply that the painted decoration of room 15

should predate Actium. Iacopi and Tedone (2006: 374) postulate the presence in Rome of an Alexandrian artist before the battle—perhaps as early as Cleopatra's first visit to the city in 46–44 BCE.

30. Cf. Suetonius, *Augustus* 57.2; Valerius Maximus 1.8.2. The

9.4 Carettoni House: Peristyle A. (Photo by author.)

## *From* Dux *to* Princeps

This re-evaluation of the Carettoni House constitutes the starting point for a rather more conjectural reconstruction of the House of Augustus on
the part of Andrea Carandini and Daniela Bruno.

While Iacopi and Tedone assume that Octavian "reorganized" the house that had been confiscated
from Hortensius, Carandini and Bruno suggest that
he destroyed Hortensius's house to make way for a

:::    fact that the Carettoni House shows no signs of fire damage is
another indication that it had already been buried by 3 CE: Iacopi
and Tedone 2006: 371.

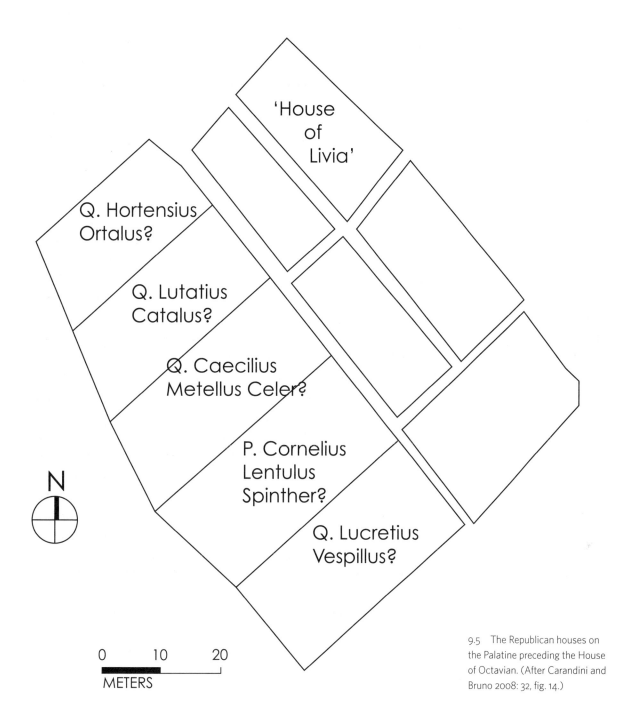

'House
of
Livia'

Q. Hortensius
Ortalus?

Q. Lutatius
Catalus?

Q. Caecilius
Metellus Celer?

P. Cornelius
Lentulus
Spinther?

Q. Lucretius
Vespillus?

N

0        10        20

METERS

9.5   The Republican houses on
the Palatine preceding the House
of Octavian. (After Carandini and
Bruno 2008: 32, fig. 14.)

new palace.[31] In fact, by calculating the area of land that would eventually be occupied by Octavian's extended residence and then dividing that by the average size of a Late Republican house (ca. 1,035 square metres in the case of the House of Livia), they estimate that five houses originally stood side by side on the site of what they call the House of Octavian (fig. 9.5). The first house, at the northwest end of the row, is assigned to Hortensius on the grounds that this constitutes the epicentre of the Carettoni House. Since Suetonius (document 9.7) tells us that the grammarian M. Verrius Flaccus was appointed

31. Carandini and Bruno 2008: 33, 141–42. Subsequently, Carandini (2010: 165) has accepted the view of Iacopi and Tedone

that the House of Hortensius was remodelled rather than destroyed.

the tutor of Augustus's grandsons and moved to the Palatine, where he taught in the atrium of the house of Q. Lutatius Catulus, and since Catulus's daughter was married to Hortensius, Carandini and Bruno then suggest that Catulus's house was adjacent to that of Hortensius.[32] The other three houses are tentatively assigned, in order, to Q. Caecilius Metellus, P. Cornelius Lentulus Spinther, and Q. Lucretius Vespillus.[33] For Metellus, we know at least that his house is supposed to have shared a wall with that of Catulus, but we have no clear indications for the houses of Lentulus or Lucretius, other than that they resided on the Palatine.[34] In fact, there are virtually no material traces for any of these houses, let alone firm identifications of their owners. Carandini and Bruno suggest that two tufa pilasters and two *peperino* bases found at a lower level of the Carettoni House were part of Catulus's house, but Iacopi and Tedone attributed them to the first phase of the House of Octavian.[35]

Like Iacopi and Tedone, Carandini and Bruno posit two phases to the House of Octavian: a first phase, dated to ca. 39 BCE, in which the houses of Hortensius and Catulus were demolished to make way for the peristyle building that Carettoni excavated (Peristyle A); and a second phase, dated to ca. 39–36 BCE, in which the final two houses in the row—those attributed to Lentulus and Lucretius—were bought and levelled for the construction of the symmetrical eastern wing posited by Iacopi and Tedone (Peristyle B). Peristyle A would, in their view, be the "private quarters" of the house, while Peristyle B was designed to serve more pub-

lic functions. But over the house of Metellus, and dating to the time of Peristyle A, they hypothesize the existence of a *vestibulum-atrium-tablinum* complex, lying on the exact axis of the later temple of Apollo.[36] Had this project been brought to fruition, Octavian's palace would have occupied an area of ca. 8,600 square metres—more than eight times larger than the House of Livia and hardly a modest dwelling on any reckoning (fig. 9.6).[37]

At a little under 25,000 square metres, the temple complex that replaced Octavian's proposed palace was even larger, but much of it was given over to the god. In fact, Carandini and Bruno follow Iacopi and Tedone in placing Octavian's new residence—what they term the House of Augustus to distinguish it from its predecessor—immediately to the west of the temple of Apollo (fig. 9.7). Using the House of Pansa at Pompeii as their model, they estimate an area of 2,126 square metres for the new residence—decidedly more restrained than what they imagine Octavian had intended for his earlier palace.[38] But, as in the earlier design, they also conjecture the existence of a similar, symmetrical complex to the east of the temple, which would have served more public functions; this would eventually have been transformed into the Domus Publica when Augustus became Pontifex Maximus in 12 BCE (document 9.8; cf. document 9.6).[39] Again, however, the archaeological indications for such a complex are almost nonexistent—namely, a short stretch of wall and a subterranean passage, leading eastwards from the House of Livia, whose termination is unknown.[40] This part of the Palatine has, it is true,

:::     32. Carandini and Bruno 2008: 30–31, 141–43; cf. Corbier 1992: 891. Pliny (*Natural History* 17.2) says that the house of Catulus was wealthier even than that of Crassus; for this reason, Carandini and Bruno hypothesize that both the Hortensius and Catulus houses originally belonged to Catulus and were then split upon the marriage of Hortensius to Catulus's daughter. Coarelli (2007: 140), however, suggests that the house of Catulus was a Late Republican house, part of which has been excavated between the Carettoni House and the House of Livia. More recently, Carandini (2010: 120–25, 182–83) has accepted a suggestion of Andrew Wallace-Hadrill that Catulus's house is to be identified with the House of Livia.

    33. Carandini and Bruno 2008: 32–33, 144–46.

    34. Royo 1999: 70–75. Metellus's house: Cicero, *For Caelius* 24.

    35. Carandini and Bruno 2008: 143; Iacopi and Tedone 2006: 366.

    36. This then allows them to suppose that the bolt of lightning which Apollo cast to mark the future site of his temple would have struck Octavian's house exactly between the *vestibulum* and *tablinum*, causing him to halt work on the expansion project: Carandini and Bruno 2008: 33–53, 146–79; Carandini 2010: 169–76.

    37. Carandini and Bruno 2008: 50.

    38. Carandini and Bruno 2008: 61–62.

    39. Carandini and Bruno 2008: 55, 192–94.

    40. Carandini and Bruno 2008: 102, 181 fig. 79, 182. Carandini and Bruno's reconstruction of a vast, six-storey terrace in front of the Portico of the Danaidai, which provided a vertical connection between the temple of Apollo and the Lupercal at the foot of the

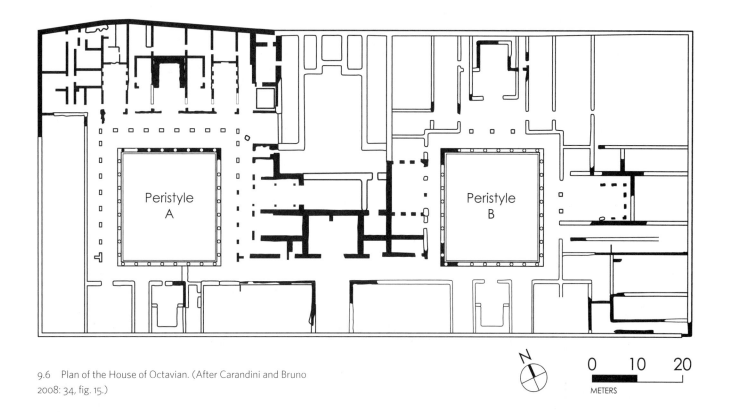

9.6   Plan of the House of Octavian. (After Carandini and Bruno 2008: 34, fig. 15.)

0   10   20

METERS

been heavily disturbed by the construction of the Flavian Domus Augustana, but that does not alter the fact that the supposed existence of the Domus Publica is largely predicated on a priori assumptions and imaginative speculation rather than any hard physical evidence.[41]

While Carandini and Bruno consider the House of Augustus to conform relatively closely to the typical layout of a Roman house, they note that the model for the earlier House of Octavian is rather that of a Hellenistic palace, such as the palace of Philip II at Aigeai/Vergina (see p. 98) or that of Demetrios Poliorketes at Pella.[42] As Carandini puts it: "[I]n the first nine or ten months of 37—down to the culmination of work on the first house—Octavian's power had been entirely illegal and thus of a despotic character. He is a young man who imitates the Greek heroes and the Hellenistic monarchs" and "now he

has at his disposal a Hellenistic palace."[43] In a similar vein, Ronald Syme describes Octavian in the late 30s BCE as a *dux*—a "term . . . familiar from its application to the great generals of the Republic; and the victor of Actium was the last and the greatest of them all." But in the years leading up to his adoption of the name Augustus in 27 BCE, he came to feel that "[t]he word had too military a flavour for all palates: it would be expedient to overlay the hard and astringent pill of supreme power with some harmless flavouring that smacked of tradition and custom."[44] A more magisterial and quasi-Republican appellation—that of *princeps* (leader)—came to be used instead.

This ideological shift from Hellenistic *dux* to faux-Republican *princeps* can also be registered in visual imagery. In January 43 BCE, the senate and people of Rome voted to erect a gilded equestrian

::: Palatine, is not of concern here. For a critique, see Wiseman 2009: 539–44.

41. Wiseman 2009: 539.

42. Carandini and Bruno 2008: 176–78, 190.

43. Carandini and Bruno 2008: 42–43.

44. Syme 1939: 311. For the patent influence that Mussolini's Italy exerted on Syme's view of Augustus, see Momigliano 1966b: 729–37 (translated by T. J. Cornell in Momigliano 1994: 72–79).

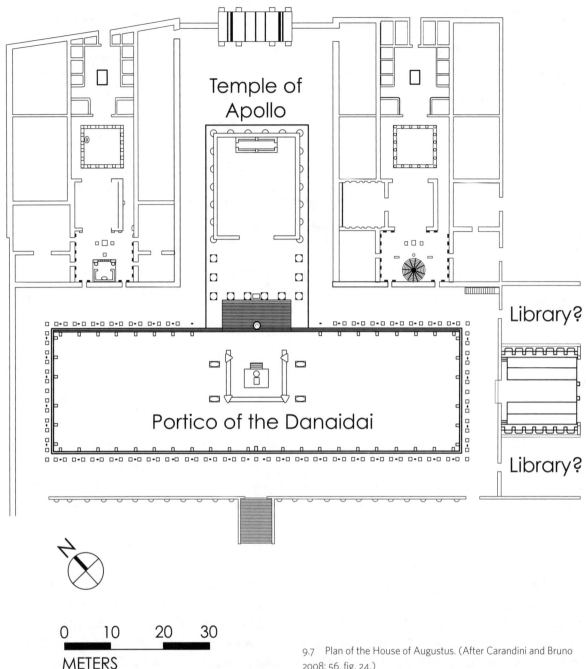

Temple of
Apollo

Portico of the Danaidai

Library?

Library?

N

0    10    20    30
METERS

9.7   Plan of the House of Augustus. (After Carandini and Bruno 2008: 56, fig. 24.)

statue of Octavian by the speakers' platform in the forum. To judge from representations of it on coins of the 40s and 30s, Octavian was portrayed *à la grecque* as the heroic scion of a god, with bared chest and a garment fluttering about his hips. And in coins minted to celebrate his victory over Sextus Pompeius in 36 BCE, Octavian is represented nude,

resting his right foot on a globe—a pose often used for statues of Hellenistic rulers.[45] In the immediate aftermath of Actium, Octavian even used the image of Alexander the Great on his personal seal. By the time of the dedication of the temple of Apollo on the Palatine, however, there were no representations of Octavian to be seen. Instead, the sanctuary was out-

:::   45. Zanker 1988: 38–39; Gurval 1995: 47–65; cf. Brendel 1931.

fitted with golden tripods, financed by the melting-down of eighty silver statues of the emperor, some on foot, some on horseback, and some in chariots.[46] The new imperial portraiture that emerges in this period looks not to Hellenistic models but to the styles of Classical Greece and of Polykleitos in particular.[47]

A similar picture may emerge from Wiseman's suggested reconstruction of the topographical development of the Palatine. His starting point is book 6 of the *Aeneid* (756–76), where Anchises introduces his son Aeneas to his future descendants. First to be mentioned is Romulus, then the Phrygian goddess Magna Mater, and finally Julius Caesar and his adopted heir, Augustus. In Wiseman's opinion, Vergil's audience would have felt itself transported from the Lupercal at the foot of the Palatine, where Romulus and Remus were said to have been raised by the she-wolf, up to the temple of Magna Mater, dedicated in 191 BCE, and finally to the house of Augustus himself.[48] This, according to Wiseman, was originally the principal approach to the Palatine, and he compares it with the entrance to a Greek acropolis. The poet Ovid, on the other hand, writing towards the end of Augustus's long reign, seems to have a different route in mind (document 9.9). Here, the approach to Augustus's house—albeit "a house worthy of a god"—is from the Roman forum to the north, past the temple of Vesta and the Regia, and then, after a right turn, past the temple of Jupiter Stator. As Wiseman points out, this route would have taken a visitor past a succession of Late Republican houses, marking out the emperor as primus inter pares rather than the Hellenistic dynast of the Actium period.[49]

Ovid twice notes that the door of Augustus's residence displayed a wreath of oak (documents 9.5; 9.9). The emperor himself tells us the senate decreed that the doorposts of his house should be festooned with laurel and that an oak wreath—the *corona civica*—should be fixed over his door in 27 BCE, when he adopted the name Augustus.[50] This entrance is very probably portrayed on a statue base, normally dated to the late Augustan period and now in the Museo Correale of Sorrento.[51] Though fragmentary, enough of it survives to identify its subject matter. On one of the longer sides is Magna Mater and a Corybant; on the other, a ceremony involving a seated Vesta and the Vestal Virgins in front of what has been identified as the temple of Vesta on account of the Palladium inside it. One of the shorter sides depicts the divine triad Apollo, Diana, and Latona, while on the other are figures who have been identified as Mars Ultor and the Genius of the Romans, together with a door crowned with an oak wreath (fig. 9.8).[52] All four sides, then, seem to refer to the aspect of the Palatine in the period after 12 BCE when, as newly appointed Pontifex Maximus, Augustus welcomed the cult of Vesta to the public part of his residence—an event celebrated by Ovid (document 9.5) and recorded in the Praenestine calendar (document 9.10).[53] The imperial residence may also be depicted on eastern provincial coins, minted between 29 and 27 BCE, which show a monumental entrance with the words IMP[ERATOR] CAESAR inscribed on the architrave; on some coins, trophies and arms have been added to the doors.[54]

A prominent feature on the Sorrento base is what appears to be a continuous Ionic colonnade. In book 7 of the *Aeneid*, Vergil describes Latinus's palace as "raised high on a hundred columns," perched on

::: 

46. Augustus, *Res Gestae* 24; Suetonius, *Augustus* 52.

47. Zanker 1988: 79, 85–86, 98–99.

48. Wiseman 1987: 402–3.

49. Wiseman 1987: 403–6, dating the reorientation to after the fire of 3 CE. Cf. Ovid, *Metamorphoses* 1.168–76, which describes the houses of distinguished gods that line the road to Jupiter's palace—a situation that Ovid explicitly compares to the Palatine. See also Carandini 2010: 162–65.

50. Augustus, *Res Gestae* 34.2; cf. Valerius Maximus 2.8.7.

51. Hölscher 1988: 375–78.

52. Rizzo 1932; Degrassi 1967; Roccos 1989: 573–76; Wiseman 2009: 533.

53. Cecamore 1996: 25, 28. See, however, Stucchi (1958: 7–24), who thinks that the Sorrento Base represents buildings on the southern side of the Roman forum. Degrassi (1967: 104–7) suggests that the temple of Vesta in the forum was close enough to Augustus's Palatine residence to be symbolically associated with it; cf. Tomei 2000: 29–31.

54. Castagnoli 1964: 193–95; Degrassi 1967: 96; Royo 1999: 160.

9.8 Statue base from the area of Sorrento, side D, first third of the first century CE, Museo Correale, Sorrento. To the right is Mars, flanked by the young Eros; to the left is part of a figure holding a cornucopia, perhaps the Genius of the Palatine. The oak wreath attached to the central doorway can be seen at top left. (Photo courtesy of the Deutsches Archäologisches Institut; negative number D-DAI-ROM-65.1251.)

the highest part of the city, serving as both a senate house and a temple and with weapons mounted on its columns (document 9.11). Vergil refers to it as a "building to be revered" (*tectum augustum*) and he earlier (152–54) describes how Aeneas ordered one hundred ambassadors "to go to the revered battlements of the king" (*augusta ad moenia regis*). Since these are the only two occurrences of the adjective *augustus* in the entire *Aeneid*, it is difficult to believe

that Vergil did not want his audience to think of Augustus's own Palatine residence, and that is exactly what Servius, the fourth-century commentator on Vergil, tells us (Commentary on *Aeneid* 7.170). Latinus's palace bears a striking resemblance to Ovid's "house worthy of a god" (document 9.9), but how can we reconcile these descriptions with Suetonius's "modest" House of Hortensius (document 9.1)?

## Reconciling the Evidence

There are two respects in which the house excavated by Carettoni does not accord well with Suetonius's description of the House of Hortensius (document 9.1). The first concerns the supposed modesty of the imperial domicile. While the discovery of the bases of two *peperino* columns in Peristyle A might match the "short porticoes with columns of Alban stone," the Carettoni House has floors with mosaics and inlaid marble, which flatly contradicts what Suetonius says.[55] To argue, as Carettoni does, that Suetonius is referring only to the private quarters of the house is hardly convincing.[56] Furthermore, if Iacopi and Tedone are right in arguing that the peristyle house excavated by Carettoni was really just part of a much larger complex, with a further peristyle projected to the east, then the residence is hardly modest in terms of space. The second concerns the history of the structure. Although Suetonius does not say explicitly that Augustus remained in the House of Hortensius until his death in 14 CE, the fact that he provides us with the emperor's former address, before moving to the Palatine, but mentions no subsequent move would seem to imply just that.[57] Yet, as we have seen, the Carettoni complex was partly demolished and buried to make way for the temple complex ca. 30 BCE.

We could, of course, salvage Suetonius's reputation by arguing that the Carettoni House has been wrongly identified as the House of Hortensius. After all, there is no explicit epigraphic support for the identification. Nor need we assume that the small, richly decorated room on the second storey (room 15) is the "Syracuse" mentioned by Suetonius, because Suetonius does not specify that the Syracuse was actually part of Augustus's house: indeed, the fact that he would retreat either there or to the suburban house of one of his freedmen probably suggests that it was not.[58] Wiseman notes that, while Suetonius (document 9.3) relates how the lightning bolt that marked out the future site of the temple of Apollo fell on part of the *domus*, Velleius Paterculus (document 9.2), a writer who certainly had firsthand knowledge of the Palatine in the Augustan era, and Cassius Dio (document 9.4) seem to imply that the Apollo temple stood on land *adjacent* to the house.[59] This might suggest that the term *domus* is not being used to denote what we would call a house, but rather to indicate a villa or estate—a hypothesis for which there is some literary support.[60]

Firstly, Suetonius elsewhere (document 9.7) tells us that M. Verrius Flaccus "taught in the atrium of the house of Catulus, which in those days was part of the Palatine." Carandini and Bruno attempt to argue that Flaccus taught in a part of their House of Octavian that overlay the now-destroyed Republican house of Catulus,[61] but a far more natural reading would suggest that Catulus's former house, perhaps like that of Hortensius, remained intact on the newly acquired estate of Octavian.[62] Secondly, in describing the assassination of the emperor Gaius (Caligula) in 41 CE, Josephus (*Jewish Antiquities* 19.102–4) narrates how the emperor exited the palace (*basileion*) and took an "empty alleyway" (*stenōpon ēremēkota*), which was a shortcut to the baths. A little later (19.116–17), Josephus tells us that the assassins went by other streets (*hodous . . . heteras*) to

:::     55. For the *peperino* column bases: Iacopi and Tedone 2006: 366. Other architectural elements that have been assigned to the house are columns, inlaid with precious coloured stones, and highest-quality Luni marble: see Pensabene 1997.

56. Carettoni 1967: 63–64.

57. Wiseman (2009: 528) points out that the specification that Augustus "remained in the same bedroom both in summer and in winter" need not literally mean that he slept in the same room for more than forty years but rather that he did not follow the common Roman practice of using separate bedrooms for the summer and winter seasons.

58. Degrassi 1967: 80; Wiseman 2009: 528.

59. Wiseman 2009: 529; cf. Carettoni 1967: 56.

60. Degrassi 1967: 80; Wiseman 2009: 529. For the latter definition: Wardle 2000.

61. Carandini and Bruno 2008: 143.

62. Wiseman 2009: 533. The existence of three subterranean galleries leading from the peristyle of the House of Livia also suggests intercommunication between detached residences: see Tomei 2000: 17–20.

the house of Germanicus and explains that, while the *basileion* was a single site, it was "constituted by buildings belonging to each of those who had been born into the imperial line and taking their name from those who had built them or had even begun to build parts of them."[63]

On this view, the picture that emerges is one of a large imperial estate that comprised older, individual houses, separated by streets and passageways.[64] It was almost certainly approached via a monumental entrance and one of the most conspicuous features of the zone would have been the temple of Apollo and, in front of it, the portico of the Danaidai—perhaps the "one hundred columns" that Vergil (document 9.11) describes in connection with Latinus's palace. To the east of the portico was the Greek and Latin library, in which meetings of the senate were occasionally convened (documents 9.3; 9.11). Within this complex would have been the House of Hortensius, whose precise location, according to Wiseman, has not yet been established.[65] In his view, the large palatial structure identified by Iacopi and Tedone has nothing to do with Hortensius or Octavian and was, instead, "part of some Roman grandee's palatial property," later "redeveloped by the young Caesar after 36 BC to house the Apollo temple and its porticos and library."[66] Yet one wonders precisely who, in the 40s BCE, would have had the overweening confidence to begin work on such a prodigious residence in so exalted a location.[67] In light of the representations of the younger Octavian, as presented by both literary sources and iconographic evidence, it is indeed tempting to believe that it was he who started work on the double-peristyle complex before abandoning the project in the late 30s. This is suggested further by the proximity of the house to the slightly later temple of Apollo and to the stamp IULIA AUG[USTA], found on one of the water pipes in the House of Livia,

which would seem to mark out the property as belonging to the imperial family.

If, on the other hand, the Carettoni House has been correctly identified, Suetonius's implication that Augustus lived out his life in the House of Hortensius is relatively easy to address. He may simply have been unaware that the House of Hortensius had been remodelled after 36 BCE and rebuilt twice—once around 30 BCE, and again after the fire of 3 CE. In any case, it is by no means impossible that this part of the imperial estate continued to be known by the name of its erstwhile owner. The description, on the other hand, of the house's modest dimensions and decor cannot be dismissed so easily and begs the question as to whether we should really give so much credence to a single literary source—especially when it seems somewhat at odds with the information provided by Ovid (document 9.9) and Vergil (document 9.11).

As an imperial secretary and librarian, Suetonius seems to have had unfettered access to archival material, including much of the personal correspondence of Augustus himself. Indeed, despite the chronological distance, Suetonius has much more information for Julius Caesar and Augustus than he does for subsequent emperors—though, as we have seen repeatedly, the quantity of available literary information need not say anything about its quality. Furthermore, unlike many historians of his age, Suetonius frequently cites documents and evidently prides himself on a style aimed at precision rather than literary merit.[68] Yet, in spite of all this, he seems to be unaware—or simply uninterested—that Augustus's house was severely damaged by fire in 3 CE (document 9.6).

Ultimately, Suetonius was a biographer, not a historian, and his subject matter is ordered accordingly. The description of the House of Hortensius comes in a section of the *Life of Augustus* where

::: 63. Castagnoli 1964: 188–90; Degrassi 1967: 92; Wiseman 2009: 534–35.

64. See Corbier (1992: 876), who notes that the complex is often termed *domus Palatinae* (in the plural) in the funerary inscriptions of imperial freedmen; cf. Tomei 2000. Contra Carandini 2010: 177–79.

65. Wiseman 2009: 530.

66. Wiseman 2009: 545. Royo (1999: 123) observes that our sources attest only fourteen Palatine properties in this period—half the number that is documented for the Late Republic.

67. Carandini 2010: 176.

68. Wallace-Hadrill 1983: 19–21, 61, 91.

Suetonius discusses Augustus's private life and, in particular, his penchant for simplicity; in other words, it is cited primarily to corroborate Augustus's character. It could well be that Suetonius uses the word "modest" in a relative sense, meaning that Augustus's domicile was modest compared with the vast Flavian palace of his own day. But the important point to remember is that Suetonius's verdict is not based on autopsy: the Carettoni House was no longer visible at the dawn of the second century CE.

The information derives, then, either from a third-party eyewitness account or—perhaps more plausibly—Augustus's own correspondence. If so, perhaps Augustus described the condition of the house when he first took possession of it. But we are also entitled to wonder whether Augustus's professions of simplicity were no less disingenuous than his claim to have restored the Republic to the senate and people of Rome.[69]

## Conclusion

In retrospect, it is truly remarkable that so much controversy could have been sparked by a single literary notice, written approximately a century after the events it records. For Carandini and Bruno, the whole episode vindicates the primacy of the role that archaeology can play in reconstructions of the past: "[O]ne can here observe how the archaeological data offer an essential check for interpreting critically the literary sources, which often describe complex events in a vague and simplified manner that we can ultimately misunderstand."[70] In truth, that is perhaps a somewhat exaggerated claim. After all, while archaeology has identified various successive phases in the construction of the Carettoni House, there is nothing in the archaeological data that ties these phases to specific years such as 42, 36, 28, 12, and 3 BCE. All those dates are supplied by literary sources. Still, it remains surprising that Suetonius's description of Augustus's modest resi-

dence could have been so programmatic within the archaeological exploration of the Palatine.

There is, however, another observation that arises from this case study which is equally surprising. In chapter 5, I suggested that the self-consciously democratic ideology of Athens makes it especially difficult to track individuals in the material cultural record, but chapter 6 revealed that even powerful rulers such as Philip II are also hard to pin down. The effects of Augustan power and ideology are registered everywhere in the archaeological record—in art, in architecture, in inscriptions, and in coinage—as they are in the prodigious literary production of the period. Augustus's final resting-place, on the east bank of the Tiber, is assured, yet the archaeological footprint of the living emperor is far more ethereal, despite his lengthy reign.

**DOCUMENTS FOR CHAPTER 9**

**9.1** He lived first near the Roman forum, above the *Scalae Anulariae*, in what had been the house of the orator Calvus, and afterwards on the Palatine, but in the no-less-modest house (*nihilo minus aedibus modicis*) of Hortensius, which was conspicu-

ous neither for space (*laxitate*) nor for refinement (*cultu*), since it had short porticoes with columns of Alban stone and rooms without any marble or special paving. And for more than forty years, he remained in the same bedroom both in summer and in

:::     69. Augustus, *Res Gestae* 34.

70. Carandini and Bruno 2008: 83.

winter, although he found the city not at all healthy for his constitution in winter even as he continually spent winter in the city. And if ever he intended to do something privately or without interruption, he had a particular elevated place, which he used to call "Syracuse" or "the little workshop"; he used to move there or into the suburban properties of one of his freedmen; but when he was sick, he used to sleep in the house of Maecenas. (Suetonius, *Augustus* 72.1–2)

**9.2** After his victory, Caesar [Octavian] returned to the city and announced that he was designating for public use several houses that he had purchased together through agents so that his own should have more space, and he promised to build a temple of Apollo with porticos around it—something that he carried out with extraordinary munificence. (Velleius Paterculus 2.81.3).

**9.3** He raised the temple of Apollo in that part of his Palatine residence (*Palatinae domus*) which, after a lightning strike, the soothsayers pronounced was desired by the god; he added porticos along with a Latin and Greek library, and it was here that, in his old age, he often held meetings of the senate or revised the list of jurors. (Suetonius, *Augustus* 29.3)

**9.4** [*Describing events of the year 36 BCE*] Then they resolved that a house should be given to him at public expense; for he made public the place on the Palatine that he had bought for building on and dedicated it to Apollo, when a lightning bolt struck it. (Cassius Dio 49.15.5)

**9.5** Carry off the day, Vesta. Vesta has been received on the threshold of her kinsman, for thus ordered the just senators. Phoebus [Apollo] has one part, the other part gives place to Vesta; and he himself [Augustus] holds as a third partner what remains. Stand, you Palatine laurels! May the house, wreathed with oak, stand: one house holds three eternal gods. (Ovid, *Fasti* 4.949–54).

**9.6** Once, when a conflagration destroyed the palace, and many people were offering him great sums of money, he took nothing other than a gold piece from communities and a single drachma from individuals. . . . But Augustus built his house and turned all of it over to the public, either because of the contributions made by the people or because he was the high priest (*Pontifex Maximus*) and wanted to dwell in a property that was simultaneously private and public. (Cassius Dio 55.12.4–5)

**9.7** For this reason, he [M. Verrius Flaccus] was also selected by Augustus to be the tutor of his grandsons, and he transferred to the Palatine together with his whole school. . . . And he taught in the atrium of the house of Catulus, which in those days was part of the Palatine, and he received one hundred thousand sesterces a year. (Suetonius, *On Grammarians* 17.2)

**9.8** He [Augustus] departed from the chamber; those things [measures to vote honours to Augustus] were not passed, and he did not receive a house at public expense. But, because the Pontifex Maximus must always live in public, he made public part of his own house. (Cassius Dio 54.27.3)

**9.9** He obeyed and, leading the way, said, "These are the Fora of Caesar; this is the road that takes its name from the rites; this is Vesta's locale, which preserves the Palladium and the fire, and this was the small palace of ancient Numa." Then, turning right, he said, "This is the Palatine gate and this the temple of [Jupiter] Stator; it was in this place that Rome was first founded." While I was admiring each and every thing, I saw prominent doorposts hung with gleaming weapons and a house worthy of a god. "And is this," I said, "the house of Jupiter?" This was a thought that came to my mind on account of the wreath of oak. When I learnt who its master was, I said, "Then it is true that this is the house of great Jupiter." But why are the doors veiled with affixed laurels, and why does the dark tree encircle the revered leaves? Is it because this house earned everlasting triumph or because it is loved forever by the God of Leukas? (Ovid, *Tristia* 3.1.27–42)

**9.10**  Holiday by decree of the senate; because on that day the statue (?) and altar (or shrine?) of Vesta was dedicated in the house of the emperor Caesar Augustus, Pontifex Maximus, during the consulship of Quirinius and Valgius. (*Inscr.It.* 13.2, 132–33)

**9.11**  The palace of Laurentine Picus was a building to be revered (*augustum*), raised high on a hundred columns and standing in the highest part of the city; it was a place of awe, with groves and ancestral piety. Here it was a solemn custom for kings to receive their scepter and to raise the rods of office; this was their senate house and their temple, this was the venue for their sacred feasts; here, the elders were accustomed to sacrifice a ram and to take their seat at the long tables. Here too, in the entrance hall (*vestibulo*) stood effigies made from ancient cedar wood of the ancestors of old, set in sequence—Italus and Father Sabinus, planter of the vine, guarding the curved sickle under his image; and aged Saturn and the two-headed image of Janus, and other kings from the earliest times and those who had suffered war wounds in fighting for their fatherland. Furthermore, on the sacred pillars were hung many weapons, captured chariots, curved axes, crests from helmets, massive bars from gates, spearheads, shields, and rams torn from ships. (Vergil, *Aeneid* 7.170–86)

# 10

# The Bones of St. Peter

*The Discovery of the Tomb*

On June 28, 2009, in a ceremony held at the Basilica of St. Paul outside the Walls on the Via Ostiense in Rome, Pope Benedict XVI announced the results of a recent investigation of the sarcophagus beneath the high altar, long identified by a slab inscribed PAULO APOSTOLO MART(YRI) as that of St. Paul:

> On the sarcophagus, which has never been opened in so many centuries, a very small perforation was made to introduce a special probe, through which we noticed traces of a precious material of dyed purple linen, a laminated gold sequin, and a fabric that was blue with linen filaments. We also noticed the presence of grains of red incense and of proteins and calcareous substances. Furthermore, very small fragments of bone, subjected to a carbon 14 test by experts who were unaware of their provenance, appear to belong to a person who lived between the first and second century. This seems to confirm the unanimous and undisputed tradition that they are the mortal remains of the apostle Paul.[1]

Regrettably, the pontiff did not go on to explain how the finding that the physical evidence does not contradict ecclesiastical tradition neces-

: : :    1. Cited in E. Pinna, "Sonda nella tomba di S. Paolo: trovati i resti dell'apostolo," *Corriere della Sera*, June 29, 2009.

sarily translates into a positive identification of the apostle, nor why physical confirmation was necessary in the first place if the tradition was so "unanimous and undisputed." Shortly afterwards, in an interview with the official Vatican newspaper, *L'Osservatore Romano*, Cardinal Andrea Cordero Lanza di Montezemolo, the priest-in-charge of St. Paul's, explained that the investigation had actually been carried out a year earlier but that an official announcement had been delayed, because "we did not want to repeat the errors committed in the past, on the occasion of the discovery of the tomb of St. Peter and his bones."[2]

One of the "errors" to which the cardinal was referring was the fallout from a Christmas radio broadcast of 1950, in which Pope Pius XII proclaimed that the tomb of St. Peter had been found. Since 1939, when work to lower the crypt of St. Peter's to accommodate the coffin of Pius XI had exposed an ancient necropolis under the basilica, the pope had charged a team of archaeologists, under the general direction of Monsignor Ludwig Kaas, the canon of St. Peter's, to investigate the site in the utmost secrecy.[3] Beneath the high altar, constructed under Clement VIII (1592–1605), the archaeologists found a niched shrine, or *aedicula*, which stood above what appeared to be a grave apparently dating to the first century CE. A large number of coins, dating from the first through to the fifteenth century, indicated that the shrine had been a destination for pilgrims from all over Europe, while Christian graffiti, including an explicit reference to Peter, were discovered scratched on walls and surrounding tombs in the vicinity.

Pius XII stopped short of saying that the actual remains of St. Peter had been identified. A pile of bones, found at one end of the grave, had provisionally been identified by the pope's personal physician as belonging to a well-built man, aged sixty-five to seventy; furthermore, the apparent absence

of a skull seemed to accord with the belief that the apostle's head had been transferred to the church of St. John Lateran in the ninth century CE.[4] The pope decided, however, that he should seek a second opinion and therefore entrusted the remains to Venerando Correnti, professor of medical anthropology at the University of Palermo. The results—which arrived a few years after the Christmas broadcast—were hardly encouraging: Correnti discovered that the bones actually belonged to three individuals, two men in their fifties and a woman aged between seventy and seventy-five, and that they were also mixed with animal bones, including pieces of cockerel, pig, and horse.[5]

The discovery prompted, however, a long-running and polemical exchange of views between Antonio Ferrua, a Jesuit archaeologist who had been part of the original excavation team, and Margherita Guarducci, a noted epigraphist from the University of Rome "La Sapienza." The disagreement centred not on the supposed grave itself but on a marble-lined niche, or *loculus*, found in a small buttress-wall next to the shrine. Ferrua always maintained that the *loculus* "was empty, with only insignificant remains of bone chips, a piece of lead, a pair of silver threads and a coin of the counts of Limoges."[6] Guarducci, however, claimed that, according to the foreman of the basilica's workmen, Kaas had secretly removed human remains from the *loculus* before the rest of the team had had the opportunity to examine it.[7] In 1963, Guarducci alerted the newly elected pope, Paul VI, who was an old family friend, to the existence of the remains. They were analyzed by Professor Correnti, who concluded that they belonged to a "robust" man of between sixty and seventy years of age.[8]

Traces of earth found on the bone matched soil samples taken from the area of the shrine, indicating that the body had originally been buried in the immediate vicinity and then transferred to the

: : :   2. M. Ponzi, "La tomba di San Paolo fra storia e fede," *L'Osservatore Romano*, July 3, 2009.

3. Apollonj Ghetti et al. 1951: vii–viii.

4. Curran 1996: 31–32.

5. Curran 1996: 35–36.

6. Cited in O. Petrosillo, "Quelle ossa? Per l'archeologo gesuita non sono state ritrovate," *Il Messagero*, February 1, 2001. See Toynbee 1953: 24.

7. Guarducci 1965: 21.

8. Correnti 1965.

*loculus*, while minute scraps of material showed that the remains had been wrapped in a purple garment with fine gold threads.[9] Furthermore, although almost all areas of the skeleton—including the skull—were identified from the remains, the feet were missing. Guarducci, who had also in the meantime claimed to "decipher" many cryptic Christian graffiti on the wall next to the shrine, was convinced that the bones were those of the apostle: the absence of feet accorded with the tradition that Peter had been crucified upside down, meaning that

the executioner would simply have hacked off the feet to remove the corpse from the cross. At some point, probably under the emperor Constantine, the skeleton had been removed from its original burial place, wrapped in a costly robe, and placed in the *loculus*. Pope Paul was convinced by the conclusions of his friend and announced, during an audience held in St. Peter's on June 26, 1968, that the mortal remains of the apostle had finally been found beneath the high altar of the basilica.[10]

## Beneath St. Peter's

The Vatican, situated on the right (west) bank of the Tiber, defined in antiquity an unhealthy, malaria-infested plain that rose from the river to meet an arc of hills extending from Monte Mario in the north to the Gianicolo (Janiculum hill) in the south. In around 60 CE, the emperor Nero consolidated the estates of his maternal grandmother, Agrippina, and his paternal aunt, Domitia Lepida, and completed a circus that had been initiated by the emperor Gaius (Caligula).[11] The Circus Gai et Neronis was probably situated just to the south of the present-day basilica of St. Peter.[12] A few tombs dating to the first century are known from the area, but from around 130 CE wealthier mausolea begin to appear, decorated with mosaics and wall paintings. Their disposition in two rows suggests that they were part of a necropolis that lined a road running east-west, a little south of the modern Via della Conciliazione, which connects the Castel Sant'Angelo (Hadrian's Mausoleum) to Piazza San Pietro (fig. 10.1).[13] On the basis of the juxtaposition of Greek cognomina with Latin family names (e.g., Gaius Popilius Heracla; Marcus Aurelius Hieron), many of the tombs belonged to

wealthy *liberti* (freed slaves) and their families.[14] Pictorial representations of Cupid and Psyche or scenes such as Pluto's abduction of Proserpina suggest that many of the deceased followed traditional Roman beliefs, though the so-called Tomb of the Julii was certainly being used by Christians in the third century, to judge from a golden mosaic that depicts Christ as the sun-god Helios/Sol.[15]

The area of the necropolis that concerns us is an enclosed courtyard (Campo P), directly below the current high altar of St. Peter's and situated at the western end of an alleyway running for about 300 metres. The courtyard belongs to a systematization of the area, which included the construction of a wall along the western boundary of Campo P, known as the Red Wall on account of the colour of the stucco with which it was faced, and, behind this to the west, a ramp (*clivus*) that rises to the north (fig. 10.2).[16] On its eastern face, looking out onto the courtyard, three superimposed niches were carved into the Red Wall, the lowest ($N^1$) into its foundations. A travertine slab, supported by two small columns, separated the remaining two niches ($N^2$

:::    9. Lauro and Negretti 1965; Stein and Malatesta 1965.
    10. Curran 1996: 41–43.
    11. Apollonj Ghetti et al. 1951: 8–9. In what follows, references will generally be made to the official Vatican report of the excavations. For descriptions in English, see Toynbee 1953; Toynbee and Ward-Perkins 1956; Kirschbaum 1957; Guarducci 1960; O'Connor 1969: 158–206; Walsh 1982; Curran 1996.

    12. Toynbee 1953: 9–10.
    13. Apollonj Ghetti et al. 1951: 23–27.
    14. Tonybee and Ward-Perkins 1956: 32, 105–7.
    15. Apollonj Ghetti et al. 1951: 38–42.
    16. Apollonj Ghetti et al. 1951: 107.

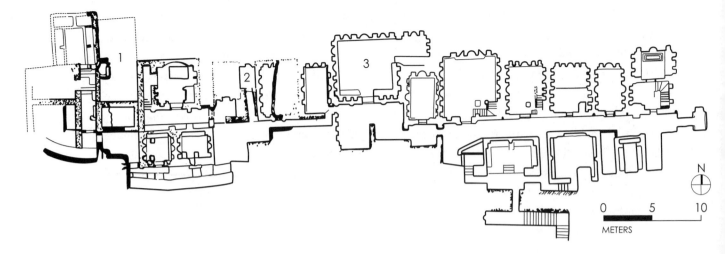

10.1   Plan of the Vatican necropolis. 1: Campo P; 2: Tomb of the Julii; 3: Tomb of the Valerii. (After Toynbee 1953: 5, fig. 1.)

and N³) to constitute what is called the *aedicula*.[17] The whole complex can be dated to the middle of the second century CE on the basis of five tile stamps found on a gutter beneath the *clivus*, which record their manufacture in a furnace owned by Aurelius Caesar and his wife, Faustina Augusta. Faustina received the title of Augusta in about 146, while Aurelius Caesar succeeded Antoninus Pius to become the emperor Marcus Aurelius in 161, thus providing a *terminus post quem* and a *terminus ante quem*, respectively, for the systematization of Campo P.[18]

Although the *aedicula* is, for all practical purposes, contemporary with the Red Wall, there are indications that it was not initially part of the same project. Firstly, there is a distinct rise in the foundations at the point where the Red Wall meets N¹. Secondly, the *aedicula* was constructed not entirely flush with the Red Wall but at a slight angle to it. The suspicion is that, during the construction of the foundations for the Red Wall, something unexpected was encountered that led to a slight reconfiguration of the foundations and the erection of a small monument.[19] Further digging beneath N¹ revealed a trench, and it was here that the excavators discovered the pile of human and animal bones

mentioned above as well as the numerous coins dating from the first to fifteenth centuries.[20] Most of these must have been dropped into the trench via a small rectangular hole that was cut into a marble slab that covered it at the base of the *aedicula*.

There are no means of assigning a precise date to the grave—if that is what this trench is—but an interesting pointer is provided by the fact that it is surrounded by inhumation graves that are oriented not on the axis of the Red Wall but on N¹, of which the two earliest are tombs gamma and theta.[21] Tomb gamma, lined with rough masonry and topped with a brick structure, contained a child's gabled terracotta sarcophagus. The roof was pierced by a small lead pipe that allowed libations of wine or milk to be poured onto the remains—an originally pagan practice, though one also practised by many Christians.[22] Tomb theta was less carefully constructed but is the only tomb that can be dated with some certainty: one of the brick tiles that had been used to cover the corpse carried a stamp indicating that it had been made in a workshop during the reign of the emperor Vespasian (69–79 CE). Although the tile could theoretically have been reused for the burial, a lamp found nearby, which bore the stamp of a

:::    17. Apollonj Ghetti et al. 1951: 122–28.
18. Apollonj Ghetti et al. 1951: 103–4, 140.
19. Toynbee and Ward-Perkins 1956: 158–59.

20. Apollonj Ghetti et al. 1951: 120–22, 229–44.
21. Toynbee and Ward-Perkins 1956: 153.
22. Apollonj Ghetti et al. 1951: 111–13.

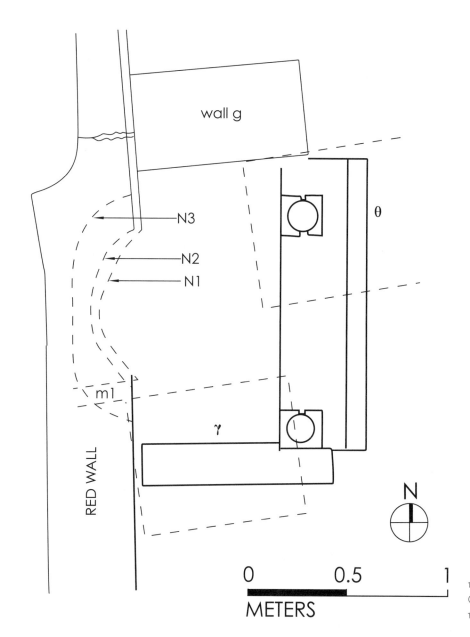

wall g

N3

N2

N1

θ

m1

γ

RED WALL

N

0          0.5          1

METERS

10.2   Plan of the western part of
Campo P. (After Toynbee 1953:
18, fig. 8; 23, fig. 12.)

workshop that was active ca. 70 CE, corroborates the presence of graves of this period in the area.[23] We cannot, however, be certain that these are Christian burials: although cremation rather than inhumation tended to be the norm for traditional Roman burials in the first century CE, it is not at all clear that there was a single, recognizably "Christian" style of burial at this date.[24] Nor is it possible to determine whether the trench beneath the *aedicula* predates or postdates tomb theta, though two additional features are of interest. The first is that the trench beneath N[1] never seems to have been encroached upon by other graves, which is not the case with some of the surrounding burials. The second is that a short stretch of wall immediately to the south of the trench (M[1]), which passes under—and therefore predates—the Red Wall, may have served to demarcate this spot from the graves that flanked it.[25]

: : :      23. Apollonj Ghetti et al. 1951: 114–15, 134; Guarducci 1960: 58–59.

24. O'Connor 1969: 188–89; Snyder 2003: 199. For the observation about traditional Roman burials: Toynbee and Ward-Perkins 1956: 148.

25. Apollonj Ghetti et al. 1951: 133–35.

The efforts taken by the builders of the Red Wall to respect the trench seem to have compromised its structural integrity. At some point in the third century, a large crack appeared immediately to the north of the *aedicula*, necessitating the construction of a small buttressing wall (wall g), perpendicular to the Red Wall (fig. 10.2). At this point, the south side of wall g and niche N² were faced with marble while a white mosaic pavement with a green border was laid on the surface of Campo P.[26] The north side of wall g was originally decorated with a pictorial motif in red and blue but was quickly invaded by a mass of graffiti, one of which refers to the Battle of the Milvian Bridge in 312 CE, when Constantine defeated Maxentius to become ruler of the Western Roman Empire.[27] Carved into this wall was the marble-lined quadrangular repository or *loculus*, from which—according to Guarducci—Kaas had removed the bones that Pope Paul VI would later identify as those of St. Peter.[28]

As noted, the north face of wall g was covered by a "palimpsest" of graffiti, most of them written in Latin and combining the personal names of what are conjectured to be pilgrims, together with the formula VV—standing for *vivas* or *vivate* (may you [singular or plural] live)—and the chi-rho monogram symbolizing the name of Christ.[29] For many observers, the absence of specific references to Peter was surprising, but Guarducci claimed to recognize a cryptographic system, known from other early Christian sites. Amongst this mass of symbols, many of them apparently visible only to Guarducci's trained eye, were the recurring letters *P, PE,* and *PET*, indicating the name of the apostle, as well as the formulae *AP, APE,* and *APET*, which she interpreted as *ad Petrum* (near Peter).[30]

There was, however, one patently visible graffito that did refer to Peter, scratched onto the part of the Red Wall that was subsequently covered by the construction of wall g (fig. 10.3). On the first line were the letters pi, epsilon, and tau, followed by what could be a rho; on the line below were traced the letters epsilon and nu. Ferrua, who initially discovered this graffito, restored it as "Petr[os] en[i]" (Peter is inside), although the reading "Petr[os] en[dei]" (Peter is missing) has also been suggested.[31] Another clear—albeit decidedly ungrammatical—reference to the apostle was found scratched onto the wall of the family tomb of the Valerii, to the east of Campo P: "Petrus roga Christus Iesus pro sanctis hominibus Chrestianis ad corpus tuum sepultis" (Peter, pray to Jesus Christ on behalf of the holy Christian men buried near your body). Above it was the chi-rho monogram and two crude representations of male heads, traced in charcoal, of which one is almost certainly Christ and the other possibly Peter.[32] No precise date can be given to this graffito, though it is often supposed that it was written by one of the labourers who worked on the construction of the monumental, five-aisled Constantinian building, probably completed in the 320s CE.[33] To create a level space on the Vatican hill to accommodate his new structure, Constantine's workers had to go to a considerable effort, demolishing the roofs of many of the mausolea and packing them with earth but also cutting back the steep slope of the hillside. The emperor could have chosen more level ground further to the south, and the fact that he did not suggests strongly that he regarded it as important that the monument which constituted the focal point of his new building should be situated directly above the *aedicula* of Campo P.[34]

To summarize, four distinct phases can be recognized in the archaeological development of Campo P. In the first phase, starting in the second quarter of the first century CE and extending pos-

:::     26. Apollonj Ghetti et al. 1951: 140–44.

27. Toynbee 1953: 24; Guarducci 1958: vol. 2, 444.

28. Toynbee and Ward-Perkins 1956: 166–67.

29. Toynbee 1953: 24; Toynbee and Ward-Perkins 1956: 165.

30. Guarducci 1958: vol. 1, 45–357.

31. E.g., Carcopino 1956: 284. See generally Toynbee and Ward-Perkins 1956: 186 n. 33, with references; Guarducci 1965: 37–42.

32. Toynbee and Ward-Perkins 1956: 14.

33. Apollonj Ghetti et al. 1951: 147–60. It is not entirely clear whether the Constantinian building was a basilica, a martyrium, or a covered cemetery; although it had five aisles and a transept, it lacked an altar until the time of Gregory I. See Armstrong 1974; Snyder 2003: 204; MacMullen 2010: 600–601.

34. Toynbee 1953: 6–7; Toynbee and Ward-Perkins 1956: 13.

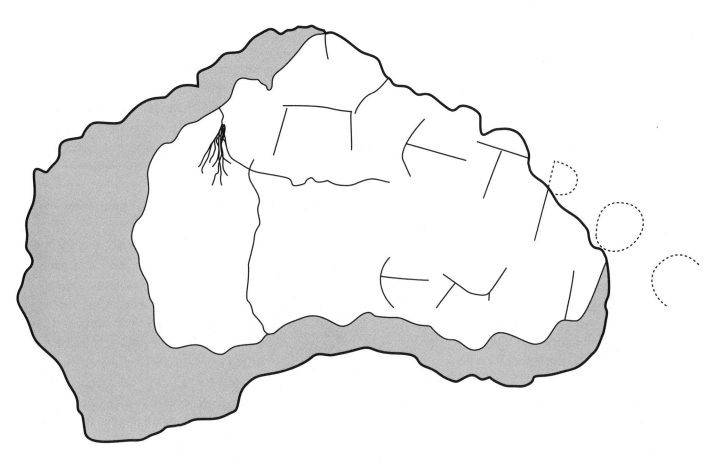

10.3    Graffito scratched onto the Red Wall. (After Guarducci 1960, fig. 39.)

sibly well into the second century, Campo P was the site for fairly modest inhumation burials. Four of these (tombs gamma, eta, theta, and iota) flank a trench, in which some skeletal material was found, and the trench itself may have been demarcated, at least in part, by a wall (m¹). Towards the end of this phase, wealthier (pagan) mausolea begin to appear to the east of Campo P. In the second phase, dating to the years around 150 CE, preparations were made to construct a ramp (the *clivus*) which would provide access to funerary areas further up the Vatican hill and which was bounded to the east by the Red Wall. In the course of constructing this wall, however, the builders became aware of something that caused them to drop shallower foundations at the point where the wall crossed the trench and to con-

struct the *aedicula* directly above the trench on an axis that respected not the Red Wall but the earlier graves. A graffito dating to this phase makes direct reference to Peter. In the third phase, sometime in the third century, the structural instability of the Red Wall occasioned the construction of a buttressing wall (wall g), on which pilgrims scratched prayers and invocations; at about the same time, the *aedicula* was slightly remodelled and the courtyard to its east paved with a marble floor. Finally, probably in the 320s, a large Christian building was constructed above Campo P, its apse symmetrically centred on the *aedicula* below, as if to give pride of place to a hallowed spot that still lies directly beneath the high altar of the present St. Peter's.[35]

: : :    35. The Constantinian church began to be demolished in the mid-fifteenth century, on the orders of Pope Nicholas V, to make

way for today's basilica, designed by Bramante and Raphael and eventually dedicated in 1626.

Numerous texts from the fourth century CE onwards recount that the apostle Peter was executed in Rome. The late fourth-century theologian Jerome (Eusebius Hieronymus) tells how Peter led the Christian community of Rome for twenty-five years until he was crucified—upside down—on the orders of the Emperor Nero in 68 CE (document 10.1). The sixth-century *Liber Pontificalis* (document 10.2) concurs on the date of Peter's crucifixion, which it synchronizes with the martyrdom of Paul, and notes that the apostle was buried in the Vatican near the "palace of Nero." The palace in question may in fact be the Circus Gai et Neronis (see above), since a fourth-century Latin text, conventionally but erroneously attributed to the first-century bishop Linus (*Martyrdom of the Blessed Apostle Peter* 10), specifies that Peter was crucified "at the place which is called Naumachia, near the obelisk of Nero on the hill" and Pliny (*Natural History* 36.74) tells us that an obelisk, made by the Egyptian Nencoreus, son of Sesosis, stood in the circus.[36] Certainly, the Via Aurelia and the Via Triumphalis, both mentioned in the *Liber Pontificalis*, were found in the area of the Vatican, although the whereabouts of the Naumachia, a venue for the staging of naval contests, has not been located up to now.[37]

As the tradition developed over the centuries, the crucifixion of Peter was considered to have taken place within the context of the pogrom that Nero launched against the Christian community of Rome, charged—probably without basis—with having started the great fire which devastated the city in 64 CE (document 10.3). Seneca (*Consolatio ad Marciam* 20) adds that he had personally seen criminals being crucified upside down. The great historian of the early church Eusebius of Caesarea (*Ecclesiastical History* 2.25) cites the early-third-century Christian apologist Tertullian to claim that Nero was the first emperor to persecute the Christians and goes on to associate Paul's beheading and Peter's crucifixion with these events. Lactantius (ca. 240–ca. 320 CE) also associates the apostles' demise with Nero's attacks on the Christians of Rome (*Of the Manner in Which the Persecutors Died* 2), but the connection is not made explicit by either Jerome or the *Liber Pontificalis*.

Nor is it found in the apocryphal *Acts of Peter*. This is the name conventionally given to a Latin text, dated to the fourth century, a sole manuscript of which was discovered in 1891 at Vercelli in northwest Italy. It has long been assumed that the text is a truncated translation of a Greek original, probably dating to the 180s CE, though this has recently been questioned by Matthew Baldwin, who argues that the Latin version derives not from a single text but from "a matrix of both oral and written discourse about Peter."[38] According to the Vercelli text, Peter is crucified on the orders of the otherwise unknown Roman official Agrippa, without the knowledge of Nero, and his corpse is taken care of by a senator named Marcellus—an outcome that was not the normal fate of executed Roman criminals, whose bodies were regularly thrown into the Tiber, and which reminds us of the tradition that Joseph of Arimathea buried Christ in the tomb that he had prepared for himself.[39] Two Greek manuscripts from Mount Athos and Patmos seem to belong to the same textual tradition as the Vercelli manuscript but provide a more detailed account of Peter's crucifixion, including the information that Marcellus buried the apostle in a marble coffin and that Nero was intending to punish Peter's followers but was warned against doing so by a vision.[40]

---

::: 36. For the date of the "Linus text": Thomas 2003: 42–43.

37. It is often believed that the obelisk to which Pliny refers is that which now stands in the Piazza San Pietro, though see Toynbee (1953: 12) for doubts.

38. Baldwin 2005: 18. For the argument that the Greek original predates 200 CE, see Schmidt 1930. Klauck (2008: 82–83) dates the first identifiable form of the *Acts* to ca. 200 CE.

39. *Gospel of Mark* 15.43–47; *Gospel of Luke* 23.50–53; *Gospel of John* 19.38–42. See Toynbee 1953: 13; Finegan 1981: 24.

40. For the *Acts of Peter*, see Elliott 1993: 397–426; Klauck 2008: 81–112.

Tertullian seems to have been the first author to state explicitly that Peter was executed on Nero's orders.[41] Indeed, Tertullian's younger contemporary Origen (in Eusebius, *Ecclesiastical History* 3.1.2) refers to the crucifixion of Peter but does not relate it to Paul's martyrdom under Nero. A little earlier, the *Ascension of Isaiah* (4.2–3), a composite text probably dating to the second half of the second century, talks about a lawless and matricidal king who "will persecute the plant which the Twelve Apostles of the Beloved have planted" and into whose hands "one of the Twelve will be delivered." The "matricidal king" is often assumed to be Nero, who murdered his mother, Agrippina, in 59 CE, while the "one" apostle who is delivered into the emperor's hands is more likely to be Peter than Paul, since the latter was not one of "the twelve," though absolute certainty is impossible.[42]

An especially valuable testimony, cited by Eusebius (document 10.4), is provided by the Roman priest Gaius, active during the episcopate of Zephyrinus (199–217 CE), who claimed to be able to point out the *tropaia* of Peter in the Vatican and of Paul on the Ostian Way, respectively. Originally, a *tropaion* was a trophy, erected on a battlefield to commemorate a military victory; here, it probably signifies a monument commemorating a victory achieved through martyrdom, and although the Vatican monument could have marked the place of Peter's execution, the context of Eusebius's citation seems to imply that he believed it stood over the apostle's tomb.[43] It is widely assumed that Gaius's Vatican *tropaion* is the *aedicula* that was excavated beneath the crypt of St. Peter's.[44] Certainly, the laying-out of the Constantinian structure seems to have been dictated by the location of the *aedicula*, which raises the distinct possibility that Constantine himself

sought to identify it with Gaius's *tropaion*. The *Liber Pontificalis* (5.2) may preserve a memory of the monument's construction when it states that Anacletus "built and systematized a memorial to the Blessed Peter" and was buried next to the body of the apostle. Anacletus lived towards the end of the first century CE, but if the compiler of the papal records has confused this bishop with Anicetus, whose episcopate ran from 155 to 165 CE, then this would accord with the archaeological dating of the *aedicula*.[45]

Predictably, as we move back into the second century, the details concerning Peter's martyrdom and fate become sketchier. In a letter addressed to the Romans, Dionysius, bishop of Corinth around 170 CE, recounts that Peter taught in Italy together with Paul and that the two were martyred at the same time (document 10.5). Almost concurrently, Irenaeus, bishop of Lyon, proclaimed Peter and Paul to be the founders of the church in Rome (*Against Heresies* 3.3.2). The two apostles are also associated with Rome in Ignatius of Antioch's *Epistle to the Romans* (4.3), perhaps written in the early second century, but the *First Epistle to the Corinthians* (5), later attributed to Clement, bishop of Rome in the late first century, refers to Peter's martyrdom without mentioning where or when it took place.[46] Chapter 6 of the same epistle describes the "unspeakable torments" that were suffered by the "multitude of the elect." The language is similar to that employed by Tacitus in his account of Nero's persecution of the Christians (document 10.3), though that does not necessarily mean that the author believed Peter's martyrdom to have taken place within this context.[47]

The absence of detailed references to Peter's end from the writings that would later constitute the ca-

41. Thomas 2003: 47, 52.

42. Cullmann 1962: 112; O'Connor 1969: 68–69.

43. Cullmann 1962: 118; Finegan 1981: 24. It should, however, be noted that Eusebius also uses the term *tropaion* to indicate monuments such as the church of the Holy Sepulchre (*Ecclesiastical History* 7.18.1) as well as the sign of the cross that is supposed to have appeared in the sky before the battle of the Milvian Bridge (*Life of Constantine* 3.1).

44. Toynbee 1953: 23; Chadwick 1957: 31; Cullmann 1962: 148; Guarducci 1965: 8; O'Connor 1969: 205; Finegan 1981: 28–29; Curran 1996: 30.

45. Toynbee and Ward-Perkins 1956: 155; O'Connor 1969: 190.

46. The epistle is attributed to Clement by Eusebius (*Ecclesiastical History* 4.23.11) and by the manuscript traditions.

47. Cullmann 1962: 91–110; O'Connor 1969: 85–86; Finegan 1981: 22–23.

nonical New Testament is particularly troubling.[48] According to a passage that is generally recognized as a secondary addition to the *Gospel of John* (21.18–19), Christ told Peter: "'When you are old, you will stretch out your hands and another will bind you and take you where you do not wish to go.' He said this to indicate by what manner of death he would glorify God." The phrase "to stretch out one's hands" was a relatively common euphemism at the time to mean crucifixion,[49] though the temporal progression here—where an apparent reference to crucifixion precedes the act of being bound and taken somewhere—is more than a little ambiguous.[50] Compared with the peregrinations of Paul, however, which are documented in detail in the *Acts of the Apostles*, very little is said of Peter's movements. In either 41 or 44 CE, he is said to have departed from Jerusalem and "went to another place,"[51] though later in that decade—that is, the time when, according to Jerome (document 10.1), Peter was in Rome—Paul found Peter first in Jerusalem and later in Antioch, where they argued.[52] But the passage from *Galatians* also makes it clear that while Paul regarded it as his mission to preach to Gentiles, Peter's ministry was to be among Jews.[53] No mention is made of Peter in Paul's *Epistle to the Romans*, thought to be written in the mid-50s CE, and when Paul says that it is his intention not to preach the gospel where Christ has already been named "so as not to build on another man's foundations" (*Romans* 15.20), a plausible interpretation would be that he is distinguishing his own ministry in the west from that of Peter in the east.[54]

The only possible allusion in the entire New Testament to Peter's presence in Rome is found in the closing salutation of Peter's first epistle (document 10.6). Even if the attribution is authentic, the pas-

sage is the subject of considerable scholarly controversy. The mention of a "son" has caused some to regard "she who is in Babylon, one of the chosen ones (or elect)" as Peter's wife, though it may in fact refer to the fledgling church. As for the mention of Babylon, there is a widespread opinion that it is not the Mesopotamian city that is meant. Josephus (*Jewish Antiquities* 18.9) tells us that the Jewish community in Babylon was all but annihilated by the emperor Gaius, while Pliny (*Natural History* 6.121-22) says that, save for the survival of the temple of Jupiter Belus, the city had returned to being a desert. It is, therefore, often suspected that "Babylon" here is a coded term for Rome—especially since the *Book of Revelation* (17.5, 9–10) seems to associate "great Babylon, mother of harlots and abominations of the earth" with seven hills and seven kings.[55] According to this reading, Peter was reluctant to reveal his precise whereabouts due to the antagonism shown towards Christians by Roman officials.[56] On the other hand, it is legitimate to wonder to what degree this metaphorical interpretation has been conditioned by the later tradition on Peter's ministry at Rome.

The literary testimonia that early Christian authors offer for the martyrdom of Peter are tabulated in table 10.1. Two observations are immediately apparent. The first is that the Vatican is not specifically named as the place of execution in our extant sources until around 200 CE—that is, *after* the construction of the *aedicula* beneath St. Peter's. The second is that our evidence tails off the closer we reach back to the assumed date of Peter's execution. One way of interpreting this pattern would be to infer that the tradition developed gradually over three centuries, reaching its final form in the course of the fourth century CE. That is certainly possible,

:::      48. For the Waldensians of the early thirteenth century, the biblical silence about Peter's presence in Rome was sufficient to disprove the tradition; Luther was also sceptical. See Cullmann 1962: 72–78; O'Connor 1969: 3–7; Zwierlein 2009.

49. Cf. Irenaeus, *Against Heresies* 5.17.3.

50. O'Connor 1969: 62.

51. *Acts of the Apostles* 11.17. For the date: Finegan 1981: 18–20.

52. *Epistle to the Galatians* 2.1-14. Finegan (1981: 21) argues, however, that the tradition of Peter's leadership of the Roman

church for twenty-five years does not necessitate that he was in Rome for the entirety of that period.

53. Cullmann 1962: 44–47.

54. O'Connor 1969: 10. Cullmann (1962: 80–81) argues, however, that Paul is here apologizing for encroaching on Peter's apostolic mission.

55. O'Connor 1969: 14–18; Finegan 1981: 21.

56. Cullmann 1962: 84–87.

TABLE 10.1  Literary accounts for the martyrdom of Peter

| | Manner of execution | Place of execution | Date of execution | Responsibility for execution |
|---|---|---|---|---|
| *Liber Pontificalis*, 6th century? | | Rome: Vatican, near Palace of Nero | AD 68; same time as Paul's execution | Nero |
| Jerome, ca. 348–420 | Crucified upside down | Rome | AD 68 | Nero |
| Eusebius, ca. 260–340 | Crucified | Rome: Vatican | Reign of Nero | Nero |
| Lactantius, ca. 260–340 | Crucified | Rome | Reign of Nero | Nero |
| Tertullian, ca. 160–240 | Crucified | Rome | Reign of Nero | Nero |
| Origen, ca. 185–255 | Crucified upside down | Rome | | |
| Gaius, ca. 200 | | Rome: Vatican | | |
| *Acts of Peter*, ca. 180? | Crucified upside down | Rome | Reign of Nero | Agrippa |
| Dionysius of Korinth, ca. 170 | | Rome | Same time as Paul's execution | |
| Ignatius of Antioch, early 2nd century? | | Rome | | |
| [Clement], late 1st century? | | Rome? | | |
| *Gospel of John*, ca. 90? | Crucifixion | | | |
| *First Epistle of Peter*, ca. 64? | | Rome? | | |

but it fails to take into account the arbitrary nature of textual survival as well as the possibility that there was no single tradition on the apostle's death but rather multiple and potentially contradictory traditions that were only reconciled in the fourth century. Support for this conjecture can be found in the traditions that located Peter's burial on the Appian Way.

## Peter on the Appian Way

In 1892, excavations began beneath the church of St. Sebastian, situated three miles south of Rome on the Via Appia. What came to light was a history that presents several parallels to that of St. Peter's. In Republican times, the area, known as Catacumbas, had been the site of pozzuolana quarries, into which tombs were cut.[57] In the first century CE, a double row of columbaria (sepulchral chambers with niches for inurned cremations) began to be constructed aboveground, several of which were richly adorned with stucco decoration and frescoes (fig. 10.4). To the southeast of the columbaria and dating to the same period belongs the so-called large villa, with rooms surrounding a courtyard paved with a white mosaic. Its proximity to the tombs suggests that it served as some sort of meeting place for funerary cult; it may have been the seat of one of the city's many *collegia*—voluntary associations which

57. The name Catacumbas probably derives from the Greek *kata kumbas* (near the cavities): Tolotti 1953: 84–85. It was not until the medieval period that the term was extended to designate subterranean cemeteries more generally.

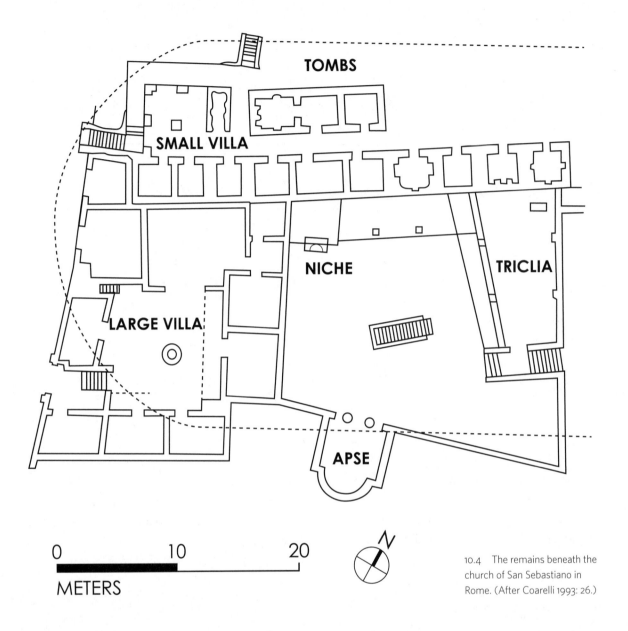

0   10   20

METERS

N

10.4   The remains beneath the church of San Sebastiano in Rome. (After Coarelli 1993: 26.)

often guaranteed a burial place for their members. At some point, probably in the early decades of the second century, the quarry to the south of the columbaria collapsed, creating an open hollow known as the "piazzuola." On the floor of this, carved into the rockface, were constructed three richly decorated pagan tombs, with niches for cremation and *loculi* for inhumations, dating to the second and third centuries. A fish and anchor, scratched onto the wall of the central of these three tombs (the Tomb of the Innocentiores) may indicate that, by the third century, some Christians were buried in the cemetery. In the first half of the third century, a smaller villa was built immediately to the north of the "large villa." Consisting of a paved courtyard and covered portico, under which was a large room with a bench running around the walls, the "small villa" probably served a similar function to its larger neighbour.[58]

58. Tolotti 1953: 54–114; O'Connor 1969: 140–47.

In the middle of the third century, the piazzuola was filled in with earth to accommodate a trapezoidal courtyard, 23 by 18 metres, paved with brick; on the eastern side of the courtyard was a covered portico known as the *triclia*. Its walls were covered with red plaster, and a bench ran across the back wall.[59] At a slightly later date, an apse fronted by two columns was built into the southern wall of the enclosure, designated perhaps as the tomb of a wealthy Christian family, while, facing it, a niched memorial was constructed, which may have served as a *mensa* (an offering table or altar).[60] In the early fourth century, very possibly on the orders of Constantine, a large basilica dedicated to the apostles was constructed above the ancient necropolis, centred almost exactly above the niched structure near the *triclia*. Drastically remodelled by Scipio Borghese in the early seventeenth century, the basilica still stands today, though at some point before the seventh century it was rededicated to St. Sebastian, the late-third-century soldier martyred under the Diocletianic persecutions whose body was interred in the crypt of the church.[61]

Scratched onto the back wall of the *triclia* are some six hundred graffiti dating to the second half of the third century; most are in Latin, though some are in Greek. In contrast, however, to the comparable graffiti beneath St. Peter's, there are numerous unencoded references to Peter and Paul, such as "Paule et Petre petite pro Victore" (Paul and Peter, pray for victory) or "Petre et Paule in mente nos habeatis" (Peter and Paul, keep us in mind).[62] For this reason, modern scholars generally call this complex the Memoria of the Apostles. There are also several references to a *refrigerium* (meal, refreshment) "near Peter and Paul."[63] In the later fourth century, Pope Damasus set up an inscription, recorded by a ninth-century pilgrim as well as in several medi-

eval manuscripts, that informed the passerby that Peter and Paul had once "dwelled" (*habitasse*) at the site (document 10.7). It is not clear whether Damasus intended his readers to understand that the apostles formerly dwelled there in life or in death— that is, were actually buried there—but a graffito, scratched onto a nearby fourth-century mausoleum, makes reference to the *domus Petri* (the house of Peter). The natural inference, then, would be that the two apostles were thought to have once lodged here on the Appian Way and that, from around the middle of the third century, the Christian community in Rome built the Memoria to house common meals in honour of both. Indeed, the *Chronograph of 354* (CIL 1.2), edited in the mid-fourth century by Furius Dionysius Philocalus, the future secretary of Pope Damasus, includes a section on the dates of martyrs' feast days: for June 29, there is the entry: "Of Peter *in Catacumbas* and of Paul on the Ostian Way," and the inauguration of the festival is assigned to the consulship of Tuscus and Bassus in 258 CE. The *Martyrology of Jerome*, a work of the mid-fifth century, details the same year as the inauguration of the June 29 feast day but says that Peter was celebrated in the Vatican, Paul on the Ostian Way, and both *in catacumbas*.[64]

The Latin word *refrigerium*, however, could also be employed in a more specialized sense to mean a funerary meal in honour of the dead.[65] If this is its meaning in the graffiti of the Memoria, then we would have yet another instance where the Christian community continued—and gave new meaning to—a formerly pagan practice, but this raises the question as to whether the Christian participants, like their pagan predecessors, also believed that the apostles whose memory they celebrated were buried in the vicinity.[66] In fact, the fifth-century *Acts of Sebastian* records that the body of Sebastian

---

::: 59. Tolotti 1953: 154–84. O'Connor 1969: 147–51.

60. Tolotti 1953: 185–221; O'Connor 1969: 152.

61. See, most recently, Nieddu 2009.

62. O'Connor 1969: 150–51.

63. Toynbee and Ward-Perkins 1956: 171–72.

64. See Lønstrup 2008: 41. Lietzmann (1927: 109) suggests that, at the time the *Chronograph of 354* was compiled (around 336 BCE), the new basilica to St. Paul on the Ostian Way had been

completed but that of St. Peter's in the Vatican may have still been under construction.

65. Finegan 1981: 31.

66. O'Connor 1969: 150. MacMullen (2010: 602–4) discusses the non-Christian origins of the *refrigerium* as part of a larger argument that the Christian cults of saints emerged from traditional ancestor worship.

was buried "near the vestiges of Peter and Paul," and the sixth-century pope Gregory the Great, in a letter to the empress Constantina (*Epistles* 4.30), remarks that Peter and Paul were temporarily buried at Catacumbas "at the time they were martyred." Pseudo-Marcellus's *Martyrdom of Peter and Paul* (66) narrates that the bodies of the apostles were buried on the Via Appia for one year and seven months before their removal to the Vatican and the Ostian Way, though the seventh-century *Salzburg Pilgrim's Itinerary* says that no fewer than forty years elapsed before their remains were transferred to their final resting-places.[67] The most surprising information, however, comes from the *Liber Pontificalis* (document 10.8), according to which Pope Cornelius, whose pontificate lasted from 251 to 253, removed the remains of both Peter and Paul from their burial place on the Appian Way.

The apparent synchronism between 258 CE, the date at which the commemoration of Peter and Paul on the Appian Way is supposed to have been inaugurated, and the archaeological dating of the Memoria of the Apostles is certainly striking. Furthermore, this is the year in which the emperor Valerian launched a persecution of the Christian community, which resulted in the execution of Pope Sixtus II, among many others. It has therefore been suggested that, against this background of violent instability, the remains of both Peter and Paul were transferred from the Vatican and the Via Ostiense, respectively, and housed at Catacumbas on the Appian Way to spare them from possible desecration. Only at the time of Constantine and the construction of the great basilicas of St. Peter's and St. Paul's outside the Walls were the bodies returned to their original resting-places.[68] In this case, could the human remains that Guarducci claimed were removed surreptitiously from the *loculus* in wall g under St. Peter's and which were identified by Correnti as belonging to a robust man in his sixties be those of the apostle, reinstalled at the Vatican shortly before the construction of the Constantinian basilica?

There are, in fact, numerous objections to the "transferral theory." In the first place, the *Acts of Sebastian*, the letter of Gregory I, the Marcelline *Martyrdom*, and the *Salzburg Pilgrim's Itinerary* all state that the remains of the apostles were initially buried on the Appian Way, not that they were conveyed there in the third century, while the *Liber Pontificalis* does talk about a third-century transferral of remains but in the *opposite* direction—that is, *from* the Appian Way *to* the Vatican and the Via Ostiense. Secondly, there is nothing in the archaeological evidence from the Memoria to indicate that it ever housed the tombs of the apostles.[69] Thirdly, it is far from clear that the site on the Appian Way would have offered any greater protection to the remains of the apostles from Valerian's depredations than the cemeteries in the Vatican or on the Ostian Way—not least because we know from two inscriptions (*ILS* 2216, 2222) that there was a station of the imperial guard only a few hundred metres away from the Memoria, near the first-century tomb of Caecilia Metella. Fourthly, the Roman law concerning *violatio sepulchri* (violation of a tomb) would have made a transferral of human remains to the Via Appia not only illegal but highly dangerous in such a charged atmosphere. Fifthly, if Constantine had reinterred the remains of Peter in his new basilica in the Vatican, it is unlikely that a simple cavity carved into an unassuming buttressing wall would have been deemed a fitting resting-place for the "prince of the apostles." Sixthly, the graffiti discovered on wall g and the Red Wall indicate that the Vatican necropolis continued to attract pilgrims during the third and early fourth centuries.[70] Finally, chemical analysis confirmed that the particles of soil adhering to the bones that were supposedly found in the *loculus* in wall g matched samples taken from the soil beneath the Red Wall. For these reasons, Guar-

:::    67. De Rossi 1864: 138–39. See generally Chadwick 1957: 38–39.
68. Duchesne 1886: civ–cvii; 1923. See O'Connor 1969: 126–34.
69. O'Connor 1969: 152–58.

70. For all these objections, see generally Toynbee 1953: 13–14; Cullmann 1962: 128–29; Snyder 1969: 9.

ducci was convinced that Peter's body had never left the Vatican but that at a certain point the remains had been transferred from the trench beneath N¹ to the *loculus* in wall g, perhaps to protect them from the effects of flooding.

Ultimately, the "transferral theory" is predicated on the belief that the literary sources and archaeological evidence can be reconciled to arrive at a single, "true" tradition concerning the fate of Peter's remains, but what if there was more than one tradition? It has been suggested that the Memoria of the Apostles belonged to a sect founded by Novatian in 251 CE, after he lost out to Cornelius in the election to the papacy, and that it was established as a cult centre in rivalry to those of the Vatican and the Via Ostiense. In time, this rival cult of the apostles would have been suppressed by the Vatican and replaced with that of St. Sebastian.[71] Be that as it may, it is hard to avoid the suspicion that the hypothesis of a transferral of remains is an aetiological myth, intended to reconcile "two originally rival and antithetical traditions."[72] On this interpretation, the story of Cornelius's conveyance of Peter's remains to the Vatican and Paul's to the Via Ostiense would have been designed to conserve for the cult centre on the Via Appia the memory that it had once housed the remains of the apostles while simultaneously sealing for the future the legitimacy of the claims made by the shrines in the Vatican and on the Ostian Way.

If Cornelius genuinely "staged" such a transferral, then it was evidently a failure, to judge from the numerous graffiti from the Memoria which postdate 251 CE. For this reason, it is more likely that the story of Cornelius's transferral of the remains was invented at a later date—perhaps by Damasus himself. If this is the case, then the true significance of the Latin verb *habitasse* (dwelled) in the inscription that Damasus set up in the basilica on the Appian Way (document 10.7) resides not in whether it refers to the apostles dwelling there in life or in death but in the fact that the perfect (past) tense is used.[73] In effect, Damasus is telling expectant pilgrims that their hopes of finding the bodily remains of the apostles on the Via Appia will be in vain.[74] At the same time, however, the reconciliation of rival claims also served to legitimate Rome's claim over cities such as Antioch or Constantinople to be the supreme apostolic see, which is surely what lies behind Damasus's assertion towards the end of the inscription that Rome is "more powerful" (*potius*). That superiority was confirmed by the Ecumenical Council of Constantinople in 381 CE, and this is almost certainly the historical context behind Damasus's proclamation.[75]

## Peter in Jerusalem

As we have seen, the New Testament offers, at best, only very ambiguous evidence for Peter's presence in Rome. Accordingly, it has sometimes been suggested that it was in Jerusalem, where the apostle practised his ministry among the Jewish community, that he died and was buried.[76] From 1953 to 1955, excavations beneath the Franciscan monastery of Dominus Flevit, on the western slope of the Mount of Olives at Jerusalem, revealed a cemetery that contained both simple pits and more elaborate chamber tombs. In the southeast corner of the site, a large complex known as the Sepulchre of the

⠇⠇⠇ 71. Mohlberg 1952; Cullmann 1962: 153. One of the arguments in favour of this hypothesis is the surprising absence of Cornelius's name from the *Depositio Martyrum* (in the *Chronograph of 354*), which established June 29 as the feast day for Peter in *Catacumbas*.

72. Chadwick 1957: 42; cf. Lietzmann 1927: 297.

73. It should be noted, however, that some of the manuscripts have *habitare* in the present tense: Lietzmann 1927: 107.

74. Chadwick 1957: 51.

75. Lønstrup 2008: 43–45.

76. E.g., Erbes 1901; Robinson 1945; Davis 1952.

Monogram consists of a central chamber, furnished with a bench, off which lead passages to seven funerary chambers. In one of the larger chambers (no. 79) were fourteen ossuaries (repositories for bones), of which one (no. 19) carried an inscription, traced in charcoal, apparently reading "Simon Bar Jona."[77] The tomb was dated by the excavators to the second half of the first century CE.[78] According to the *Gospel of John* (1.42), Simon Bar Jona (i.e., Simon, the son of Jonah) was one of the first disciples to follow Christ, who renamed him—perhaps to avoid confusion with other Simons—Kephas in Aramaic, or Petros (Peter) in Greek. The Greek word *petros* means "rock," and the *Gospel of Matthew* (16.18) explains that Christ gave Simon this name because he would be the "rock" on which he intended to build his church.[79]

The theory that Peter's tomb is, in fact, beneath the monastery of Dominus Flevit rather than St. Peter's basilica has been disseminated most energetically by an independent scholar from Indiana named F. Paul Peterson, both in print and on various websites.[80] Peterson's polemic, however, is driven by a decidedly anti-Catholic agenda, and the evidence for a Petrine tomb in Jerusalem is far from compelling, however probable it might be on other grounds. For a start, even the coauthor of the original excavation report conceded that the patronymic "Bar Jona" could be read differently.[81] Indeed, one scholar has recently argued that, when read according to the Seleucid Aramaic script that was widely used in the first century CE, the name that appears on the ossuary is actually Shimon Bar Zilla or Simon Barzillai.[82] But, even if the reading were secure, a comparison of the Dominus Flevit inscriptions with similar epitaphs from the sites of Silwan and Talpiot demonstrates that the name Simon was extremely common among Judaic communities.[83] Ultimately, however, the burial at Dominus Flevit, unlike that beneath St. Peter's, never seems to have been the object of a centuries-old veneration.[84] That, in itself, need not be decisive but it hardly aids the case for a Judaean tomb of Peter.

## Conclusion

The belief that Peter and Paul were martyred in Rome and that Peter entrusted the leadership of the church that he had founded to papal successors has long been central to the primacy claimed by the Roman Catholic Church within the broader, worldwide Christian community. To adopt any position on the issue, then, immediately ensnares the scholar in a web of political and ideological presuppositions and dispositions.[85] For all the caveats, however, a relatively dispassionate conclusion might look something like this:

In the first place, it is necessary to regard the identification of the apostle's tomb and the identifications of his human remains as two separate questions. This is, in fact, precisely what Pope Pius XII did when he announced the discovery of Peter's tomb in his Christmas broadcast of 1950; it was Paul VI who insisted on the identification of Peter's remains. We cannot automatically exclude that Peter's bones were among the mixed skeletal material that had been pushed to the far end of the trench beneath the Red Wall,[86] but such treatment of the remains of

:::

77. Bagatti and Milik 1958: 6–9, 52, 83.

78. Bagatti and Milik 1958: 44.

79. Cullmann 1962: 19–23.

80. Peterson 1960. Among numerous websites, see http://www.aloha.net/~mikesch/peters-jerusalem-tomb.htm (last accessed September 2012).

81. Bagatti and Milik 1958: 83.

82. Pfann 2007.

83. Bockmuehl 2004: 67–69; cf. Bagatti and Milik 1958: 77.

84. Margaret Mitchell (pers. comm.) has noted that when Egeria made a pilgrimage to the Holy Land in the fourth century, she visited what was known as the "house of Peter" at Capernaum in Galilee, not a tomb shrine in Jerusalem.

85. Cullmann 1962: 71–72.

86. This is the view of Curran (1996: 45–46), who thinks that, at some point, perhaps during a Saracen raid on Rome in the ninth century, somebody sought to protect the relics of Peter by hiding them under the Red Wall.

the founder of the Roman church hardly seems very reverential. As for the remains that were supposed to have been found in the *loculus* in wall g, no certain conclusion can be given, because the circumstances of the find were irreversibly compromised—if, as Guarducci maintained, Kaas had secretly removed skeletal material from the *loculus* without duly recording the fact. The declaration that the contents of the lead-lined box that were analysed by Correnti were those that Kaas had removed from the *loculus* more than twenty years earlier was, at best, based on hearsay evidence (Guarducci's discussion with Giovanni Segoni, the foreman of the Sampietrini workmen) and hardly unimpeachable. The results of chemical analysis conducted on the soil clinging to the bones makes it virtually certain that they had, at some point, been dug up in the immediate vicinity of the *aedicula*, but that could apply to any number of burials from the cemetery there; the absence of feet, while certainly suggestive, could equally well be the consequence of the original burial being disturbed by later funerary deposition or building activity. But, even if Guarducci was right and human remains were indeed removed from beneath the Red Wall and deposited in the *loculus*, surely a more decorous resting-place could have been found for a corpse that was believed to be that of Peter. In short, either set of remains *could* be those of the apostle but there is no positive proof in favour of the proposition. What about the tomb?

It can, I think, be accepted that the emperor Constantine intended to identify the *aedicula* with the tomb of Peter: the amount of effort and resources expended on ensuring that the fourth-century basilica should be centred on the *aedicula* when easier options were at hand can hardly be explained satisfactorily in any other way. It is also extremely probable that Constantine associated the *aedicula* with

the *tropaion* described by Gaius around 200 CE. What Gaius meant, however, by the term *tropaion* and whether or not the constructors of the *aedicula* thought that they were marking the grave of Peter are harder to ascertain. John Walsh argues that those responsible for setting up the *aedicula* were keenly aware of what lay beneath it, taking care to "disguise" it as a "pagan" monument in order to conceal from the authorities the final resting-place of the apostle.[87] Conversely, Henry Chadwick, while accepting that Eusebius took Gaius's *tropaion* to mark a grave, is reluctant to exclude the possibility that Gaius himself considered the monument to be a cenotaph, perhaps marking the approximate spot of Peter's crucifixion.[88] Given the lacuna in the material evidence between ca. 70 CE, when the trench beneath the Red Wall is thought to have been prepared for a burial, and ca. 160 CE, when the *aedicula* was built, archaeology offers little assistance on this question.[89]

What ultimately, however, tells against a continuous tradition concerning the burial of Peter in the Vatican is the funerary cult offered on the Via Appia from the mid-third century. As with the case of Romulus (chap. 7), any approach that seeks, firstly, to strip away extraneous accretions to lay bare a "true" tradition and, secondly, to test that single, unitary tradition against the archaeological record displays a fundamental misunderstanding of the nature and function of tradition. And again, as with the case of Romulus but also that of the foundation of the Roman Republic (chap. 8), it could very well be that the *aedicula*, while probably arising out of a tradition concerning Peter whose origins are now no longer discernible, was also co-opted as a "magnet" around which memorial traditions concerning the apostle's martyrdom coalesced.

∴∴∴    87. Walsh 1982. It should, however, be noted that there is now increasing scholarly doubt concerning the feasibility of distinguishing "Christian" from "pagan" material culture in the first and second centuries CE.

88. Chadwick 1957: 43–44; cf. Cullmann 1962: 152–53. Chadwick goes on to suggest that, prior to the third century CE, the legitimacy of a cult centre was not so heavily dependent on the existence of the physical remains of a saint, though this is not

what appears to be suggested by the second-century *Martyrdom of Polycarp* (17–18).

89. Heid (2007: 410) argues—on the basis of Ignatius (*Epistle to the Romans* 4.2–3)—that Peter's and Paul's bodily remains were visible as early as ca. 110 CE. The implication is possible, though far from explicit, and much depends on the date to be assigned to Ignatius.

## Postscript: The Tomb of St. Philip

On November 14, 2011, Bartholomew I, ecumenical patriarch of Constantinople, celebrated a eucharist in honour of St. Philip among the ruins of Hierapolis (modern Pammukale in Turkey). According to the apocryphal *Acts of Philip*, Philip, one of the twelve apostles, was crucified upside down and buried at Hierapolis. To confuse matters, however, Hierapolis was also said to be the burial place of another Philip, St. Philip the Deacon, who is mentioned in the *Acts of the Apostles* (21.8–9) and whose life and works were clearly confused at an early date with those of the apostle.

From the late 1950s, Paolo Verzone of the Turin Polytechnic identified and excavated an imposing late antique structure on the hill that rises to the east of Hierapolis—an area that seems to have been part of the east necropolis of the ancient city. The heart of the building is a domed octagonal hall, with rectangular rooms opening off each of the eight sides; the octagon itself was enclosed within a square structure composed of a single circuit of 28 rooms and four entrance halls, each of which was entered from the exterior of the complex.[90] Although it was initially identified as the "Martyrion" of St. Philip, excavations conducted in 2010 and 2011 under the direction of Francesco D'Andria of the University of Salento have revealed that it was but one element of a more extensive complex of buildings, probably to be dated to the early fifth century CE and associated with the worship of St. Philip.[91] At the foot of the hill, to the southwest of the Martyrion, was an octagonal-shaped bath building on a road leading from the city; after having performed their ablutions here, pilgrims would then have ascended the hill via a monumental staircase. At the top of the staircase, on the left, was the Martyrion, now interpreted as a place of "incubation"—a ritual well attested in ancient Greek and Roman "healing sanctuaries" such as those of Asklepios, whereby suppliants would spend a night in the sanctuary in the hope that the god (or saint) would appear to them in a dream and heal their ailment. On the right, was a three-aisled basilica.

The basilica itself seems to have been consciously constructed above a monumental tomb (C127), dated to the late first century or early second century CE and now empty, which was discovered beneath the floor of the northern aisle at its western end. At the time when the basilica was constructed, the tomb was faced with a metal frame, traceable today only by holes drilled into the façade, and a staircase was built to connect the narthex (entrance porch) with a platform constructed immediately above the tomb. In the central nave, next to the tomb, were two rectangular pools, lined with marble slabs, which were probably used for ritual healing through immersion and which seem to date to the fourth century. The altar of the basilica stood on a monolithic marble slab, beneath which was found a rectangular sepulchral chamber, connected to the floor of the church by a terracotta tube. To judge from other martyr shrines, pilgrims would lower strips of material (*brandea*) through the tube into the subterranean chamber so as to sanctify them as relics by means of contact with the vestiges of the saint. In this case, one would have to assume that pilgrims of the Middle Ages believed—rightly or wrongly, it is impossible to tell—that St. Philip's mortal remains had been transferred from the tomb in the northern aisle to the subterranean chamber beneath the altar.[92] Whether or not some relics remained under the basilica at Hierapolis after the reputed transfer of Philip's remains to Constantinople and Rome in the sixth century, the basilica at Hierapolis remained a site of pilgrimage until its abandonment in the thirteenth century.[93]

:::  90. D'Andria 2003: 184–91.
91. D'Andria 2011–12.
92. As confused and contested as the evidence is, the archaeology of the earliest structures beneath the church of Agios Dimitrios in Thessaloniki seems to offer several parallels

for the reconstructed history of worship to St. Philip at Hierapolis.
93. According to tradition, Pope John III (561–74) installed some relics of St. Philip in the church of the Holy Apostles Philip and James at Rome.

It is difficult to determine precisely when Christian worshippers began to believe that the tomb beneath the Hierapolis basilica was that of St. Philip. Of more interest for now, however, are the first literary references to the whereabouts of Philip's burial. We have already had cause to discuss Gaius's claim, preserved in Eusebius's *Ecclesiastical History*, to have seen the *tropaia* of Peter and Paul at Rome (document 10.4). As Eusebius explains, the information derives from a treatise that Gaius directed against the Montanist "heretic" Proclus. But later, Eusebius tells us that while Gaius could point to the *tropaia* of Peter and Paul in Rome, Proclus himself responded by speaking of the ministry of Philip and his four daughters at Hierapolis, noting that "their tomb is there, as is that of their father" (*Ecclesiastical History* 3.31.4). Eusebius also refers to a letter written by Polykrates, bishop of Ephesos, to Pope Victor (ca. 189–99 CE), in which mention is made of Philip's burial at Hierapolis (3.31.3). This only goes to confirm the suggestion that a critical awareness regarding the material traces of apostolic traditions became especially acute towards the end of the second century CE and that it often constituted a strategy within doctrinal disputes and contested claims to primacy within the Christian faith.

## DOCUMENTS FOR CHAPTER 10

**10.1**  Simon Peter . . . continued on to Rome in the second year of Claudius (43 CE) to triumph over Simon Magus, and there he held the sacerdotal chair for twenty-five years until the last, that is the fourteenth, year of Nero's reign (68 CE). And it was on the orders of Nero that he was nailed to a cross and crowned with martyrdom, with his head towards the ground and his feet raised on high, because he asserted that he was unworthy to be crucified in the same manner as his Lord. (Jerome, *On Illustrious Men* 1)

**10.2**  After this, he was crowned with martyrdom along with Paul, thirty-eight years after the passion of the Lord. He is buried on the Via Aurelia, in the precinct of Apollo, next to the place where he was crucified—the palace of Nero in the Vatican, near the Triumphal district on June 29. (*Liber Pontificalis* 1.6)

**10.3**  But neither by human effort, nor by the benefactions of the emperor or the propitiations of the gods, did the rumour recede; rather, it was believed that the fire had been started according to orders. Therefore, to get rid of the rumour, Nero declared as guilty those who were hated for their shameful deeds—whom the populace called Christians—and he inflicted the most unusual punishments on them. Christ, from whom they took their name, had been executed during Tiberius's reign on the orders of the governor Pontius Pilate; and a destructive superstition, which was initially suppressed, then broke out again not only in Judaea, the origin of this evil, but even in the city [of Rome], where all atrocious and shameful conducts from everywhere flow together and are celebrated. So, firstly those who confessed were arrested and then, on their denunciation, a large number were convicted, not so much for the crime of arson as for hatred of the human race, and derision was added to them as they were put to death. For example, they were cloaked in the skins of wild beasts and mauled to death by dogs, or they were nailed to crosses or set on fire to serve as nocturnal illumination when daylight faded. Nero offered his own gardens for this spectacle and produced the show in the circus. (Tacitus, *Annals* 15.44)

**10.4**  It is recorded that Paul was beheaded in Rome itself and that Peter was likewise crucified at the same time. The tradition is confirmed by the names of Peter and Paul that are preserved in the cemeteries there, as well as by a cleric named Gaius, who lived when Zephyrinus was bishop of Rome. In a written discussion with Proclus, the leader of the

Montanists, Gaius says this about the places where the sacred shrines of the aforementioned apostles were placed: "But I am able to point out the *tropaia* of the apostles. For if you wish to go to the Vatican or the Ostian Way, you will find the *tropaia* of those who founded this church." (Eusebius, *Ecclesiastical History* 2.25.6–7)

**10.5**   And that both were martyred at the same time is shown by Dionysius, bishop of Corinth, in his written homily to the Romans: "By so great an admonition, you have joined together the plantings of the Romans and Corinthians by Peter and Paul. For both of them planted and taught us at Corinth, and similarly, teaching together in Italy, they both gave witness/were martyred at the same time." (Eusebius, *Ecclesiastical History* 2.25.8)

**10.6**   She who is in Babylon, one of the chosen ones, sends you greetings, as does my son Mark. (1 Peter 5.13).

**10.7**   Whichever one of you is seeking the names of Peter and Paul should know that it was here that the holy men formerly dwelled (*habitasse*). The East sent her disciples, that we willingly confess. By the merit of blood, these men followed Christ through the stars and sought the celestial recesses and the kingdoms of the pious. Since Rome is more powerful, it deserved to claim these men as its citizens. Let Damasus convey your praises to these new stars. (Diehl 1925: no. 951).

**10.8**   At this time, at the request of a certain married woman named Lucina, he [Cornelius] removed by night the bodies of the apostles, blessed Peter and Paul, from Catacumbas. And first, after he had obtained the body of the blessed Paul, the blessed Lucina buried it on her own property on the Via Ostiense, near the place where he was beheaded. But the blessed Cornelius received the body of the blessed Peter and buried it next to the place where he was crucified, among the bodies of the holy bishops, in the precinct of Apollo on the Mons Aureus, in the Vatican by the Palace of Nero, on June 29. (*Liber Pontificalis* 12.3).

# 11

# Conclusion: Classical Archaeology and the Ancient Historian

*Navigating between Textual and Material Evidence*

By way of conclusion, it may be helpful to summarize some of the lessons that can be drawn from the preceding case studies. Firstly, and most obviously, we should not assume that scattered literary notices and isolated archaeological features are the inevitable reflex of one another. This is what Snodgrass has described as the "positivist fallacy," which consists of "making archaeological prominence and historical importance . . . almost interchangeable terms" and "equating what is observable with what is significant."[1] Herodotos does not specify explicitly that the second stone temple of Apollo at Eretria was sacked by the Persians. The supposition is based on the following argument: (i) Herodotos notes that the Persians burned "the sanctuaries" at Eretria in 490 BCE; (ii) the second stone temple of Apollo was unfinished, while its sculptural decoration seems to date it to the end of the Archaic period; (iii) therefore, the second temple was a casualty of the Persian sack of Eretria. That still remains a highly plausible scenario, but there are other possible explanations. It is not, for example, completely impossible that construction was halted due to lack of funds or that the temple burned down accidentally—a not uncommon occurrence in antiquity.[2]

:::      1. Snodgrass 1987: 38.

     2. See, for example, Thucydides 4.133 on the conflagration that destroyed the temple of Hera near Argos in 423 BCE or Pausanias 10.5.5 for the fire that devastated the temple of Apollo at Delphi in the mid-sixth century.

The danger posed by the "positivist fallacy" resides in the extremely fragmentary nature of our evidence. Ancient authors were not generally interested in the mundane, and they made choices—both conscious and unconscious—as to what they saw fit to record. Furthermore, of the already limited observations that they made, only the tiniest fraction has survived in the manuscripts that are extant today. Similarly, the archaeological record is the product of a series of often random factors—some due to human design, others to natural processes or even pure chance—and cannot, in any case, ever be recovered in its entirety. Quite apart from the perishability of certain artifacts, archaeological retrieval can never be complete: costs and the availability of labour set limits on what can be excavated or surveyed. It is, then, methodologically misconceived to connect the dots between these fragmentary and often isolated pieces of information in too hasty a fashion.

The only corrective that can be employed is, first, to situate a text or an archaeological feature within its broader literary or material context and only then to consider whether there might be a relationship between the two. A comparison of the sculptural decoration on the Eretrian temple with other works of art deemed similar is probably more productive than relying excessively on a "fixed point" derived from Herodotos. The fate of the Telesterion at Eleusis cannot be related to possible historical events such as the Oath of Plataia or the Peace of Kallias until it is compared to the phases of construction at other sanctuaries in Attica. It is no good identifying the Poros Building in the Athenian agora as the state prison unless we have a clearer idea of what a fifth-century Greek prison might have looked like. Attempts to identify the couple buried in Tomb II at Vergina may be premature for as long as we suspect that other royal burials of the same period are still awaiting excavation and publication. The significance of the wall at the foot of the Palatine and what Carandini has iden-

tified as the Domus Regia cannot be judged without consideration of other developments taking place in eighth-century Rome. And the location of the House of Hortensius on the Palatine would certainly be easier to pinpoint if we had a better idea of the structures that existed on the hill in the Late Republican period.

The injunction applies no less to the interpretation of textual documents. The importance that has been given to Suetonius's description of the modest decor and dimensions of Augustus's Palatine residence neglects the fact that it is seemingly contradicted by other literary testimony; it also fails to take account of why Suetonius should have entertained this belief or how it fits into his broader programmatic agenda. Diogenes Laërtios's "biography" of Simon the Cobbler needs to be situated within the Cynic tradition that later coalesced around this semilegendary figure, just as Livy's account of Tarquinius Superbus cannot be considered independently of the stock themes and tropes that were connected with tyrannical figures generally—many of them deriving from Greek historiography. Similarly, the development of the tradition concerning the execution and burial of Peter at Rome appears less unique when juxtaposed with that related to Philip at Hierapolis.

The necessity of contextualizing individual scraps of evidence—a principle "rediscovered" by postprocessualist archaeologists (see p. 15)—appears so obvious that the reader may be surprised to learn that its methodological validity is sometimes challenged. Richard Neer, for example, has recently argued that "[c]ontext is itself the product of prior judgments—*aesthetic* judgments—and therefore offers no external check upon such judgment."[3] Now, at a very basic level, Neer is absolutely right: it is scholars who construct contexts and who make inevitably subjective assessments as to whether a certain literary notice or artifact belongs or does not belong to the larger data set that is then recast as a context. Nevertheless, the example

:::  3. Neer 2010: 10.

that Neer offers in support of his argument is the danger of using Plutarch's *Life of Perikles* as a context for understanding and interpreting the Parthenon. It would be a very poor historian indeed who used a work compiled ca. 100 CE to read a monument constructed more than half a millennium earlier, notwithstanding the fact that some of Plutarch's sources almost certainly date back to the Classical period.[4] Consequently, it is mid-fifth-century architecture, sculpture, and paintings, along with Attic tragedy, comedy, and historiography—not Plutarch's *Life of Perikles*—that constitute a more valid context for interpreting the Parthenon. Furthermore, the utility of this context is predicated on the cumulative value of multiple constituents of the data set rather than on an a fortiori argument based on a single independent datum. To take an example from structural linguistics, it is virtually impossible to understand the meaning of a sentence or utterance (*parole*) without having at least some more general knowledge of the vocabulary and linguistic rules of the language in which that statement is expressed (*langue*). The *langue* is, in many ways, an artificial scholarly construct which can never be known in its totality, but it is still the system that gives meaning to—and is recursively re-created and refashioned by—*parole*.

Secondly, both ancient historians and classical archaeologists are sometimes prone to attribute a "unidimensionality" to the other field that they would never dream of accepting for their own. Archaeologists often invoke or discount the Oath of Plataia and the Peace of Kallias in their attempts to explain the lack of monumental building in Attica in the wake of the Persian War and its resumption later in the fifth century. In both cases, legitimation is claimed by reference to a couple of ancient historians who have pronounced for one side or the other without a full understanding of the complex historiographical issues involved. Similarly, the geologists who argued that the supposed existence of cross-cutting faults beneath the temple of Apollo at Delphi "proved" the literary tradition concerning intoxicating gaseous emissions failed to take account of the fact that our literary authorities are by no means unanimous about how the oracle functioned. On the other side, historians have sometimes been guilty of appealing to archaeological evidence in support of the notion that Rome was an Etruscan city in the sixth century without considering in detail the processes by which Etruscan- and Greek-made artifacts—or their imitations—were deposited in the archaeological record of Rome or the precise relationship among material culture, ethnicity, and sociopolitical organization.

The charge of unidimensionality is especially apposite when it comes to the treatment of "tradition." Arguments that the Palatine wall and the Domus Regia prove the tradition concerning the Romulean foundation of Rome, or that the *aedicula* beneath the Basilica of St. Peter proves the tradition that tells of Peter's ministry in Rome, neglect to account for the fact that, in both cases, there is no single, unitary tradition to be proved. Rather, there is a complex web of multiple and often mutually contradictory traditions that arise from different perceptions among the various constituencies for whom figures like Romulus and Peter were important, as well as from the different and sometimes divergent functions that such figures served. The point is that both ancient history and classical archaeology are interpretive practices that can, and do, yield a variety of alternative explanations. As mentioned above, textual authorities cannot necessarily be taken at face value, but neither should the seemingly concrete and physical nature of walls, pots, or tombs occlude the fundamentally interpretive role of the archaeologist. Artifacts do not speak for themselves. It is, then, tempting but profoundly misguided to assume that either textual documentation or the archaeological record can serve as an unexamined "independent variable," against which other evidence can be interpreted.

Related to this is my third point. There often seems to be a latent unidirectionality in the causal

:::    4. See, for example, Kallet 2003: 131–37.

relationship posited between literary evidence and archaeology. Typically, though not universally, this takes the form of an argument that archaeological evidence proves or refutes textual evidence, thus perpetuating the deep-seated and long-held idea that archaeology is an ancillary discipline vis-à-vis history. So, for example, the examination of the geology of Delphi proves the literary accounts about the prophetic vapours that gave the Pythian priestess her prescience; the failure to repair Attic sanctuaries devastated by the Persians proves the historicity of the Oath of Plataia; the Palatine wall proves the veracity of the Romulean tradition; the construction of the temple of Jupiter Capitolinus proves the literary accounts which date the establishment of the Roman Republic to 509 BCE; and the systematization of Campus P proves the tradition that Peter is buried beneath St. Peter's.

In fact, however, the precise relationship between textual authority and the material record may not be as direct and, in some cases, could even be recursive. Such gaseous emissions as may have taken place at Delphi need not have been directly or mechanically connected to the pronouncements of the oracle, and the suggestion that they were could be that of ancient authors—and especially later authors—who were themselves grappling with finding an explanation for how the oracle functioned. While it is reasonable to assume that the Persian invasion played some part in the decision not to repair damaged sanctuaries, the more developed accounts of a formally sworn oath to that effect could well be the reflection of fourth-century authors who were struck by the number of decades that elapsed before monumental buildings such as the Parthenon or the Telesterion at Eleusis were restored. Rather than proving the historicity of Romulus or the location of Peter's grave, the Palatine wall and the Vatican *aedicula* could actually have been the *lieux de mémoire* around which the literary traditions crystallized and gradually adopted a greater uniformity.[5] As for the Capitoline temple, there are good grounds for suspecting that, far from proving a late-sixth-

century date for the foundation of the Roman Republic, it was itself the visible core around which, in the late fourth century, was wrapped a story about the institution of the twin consulship.

Fourthly, the textual and the material are entirely different discourses. As Stephen Dyson puts it: "[M]aterial culture has a distinct contribution to make to our understanding of a society, which may intersect with the literary sphere but also has its own distinct sphere."[6] There is a plethora of ideas and concerns in literary sources, many of which are unlikely to find their material reflection in the archaeological record. Without discounting the potential contributions of cognitive or interpretive archaeology, it is difficult to imagine many archaeological correlates to Herodotean anecdotes or Plato's theory of forms. Similarly, the archaeological record yields information on a host of issues that were simply of little or no concern to ancient authors—most obviously, agricultural practices and the rural landscape but also the more mundane, diurnal activities of ordinary men, women, children, and slaves.

This is especially apparent when it comes to the archaeology of the individual. In recent decades, many ancient historians have reacted against the traditional "great man" approach to history and have adopted more processual approaches to investigate social, cultural, and economic issues. This marks a strong contrast to ancient authors, including historians, who were often fixated on individuals. Even Thucydides, who generally prefers more materialist explanations for processes and events, concedes that individuals can make a difference—especially in his account of the Sicilian Expedition of 415–413 BCE, which occupies the sixth and seventh books of his *History*. It is not that the individual is necessarily absent from the archaeological record—especially in funerary contexts. No serious doubts attend the identification of the tombs of Mausolos at Halikarnassos (modern Bodrum) or of Augustus or Hadrian at Rome; Caecilia Metella, daughter of the consul for 69 BCE and pos-

∴  5. For *lieux de mémoire*: Nora 1996.

6. Dyson 1981: 10.

sibly the daughter-in-law of Marcus Licinius Crassus, is buried on the Appian Way; Lucius Munatius Plancus, who reputedly advised Octavian on his choice of the name Augustus,[7] occupies an impressive mausoleum on Monte Orlando, above Gaeta.

Yet there seems to be no direct or unmediated relationship between the prominence of an individual in the archaeological record and his or her status in the historical tradition. The search for the material remains of Sokrates has, for the most part, been futile, and I tentatively suggested that this may have been due to a conscious democratic ideology in fifth-century Athens that militated against individual distinctiveness—important Athenian statesmen such as Kimon, Perikles, and Kleon are similarly absent from the archaeological record. On the other hand, it is also clear that other factors, still poorly understood, govern the archaeological visibility of even important historical individuals. At Vergina, we have an impressive tomb without a name; on the Palatine, a vast residential complex without an identifiable owner. By contrast, in the Vatican necropolis, we have a name but—probably—no body.

Finally, archaeology—no less than history—is a profoundly political discipline. Sometimes, this takes an overt form. The intense and often acrimonious debate about the individuals buried in Tomb II at Vergina cannot be dissociated from ethnonationalist claims and counterclaims concerning the Greekness of the ancient Macedonians. Nor can papal pronouncements about the vestiges of SS. Peter and Paul be divorced from the Roman Catholic Church's claims to primacy within the apostolic tradition. There often exists also, however, a "softer," more ideological component to archaeological practice. Sokrates was no fan of the Athenian democracy. Yet the search for the archaeological footprints of the historical Sokrates is part of a broader project that presents—at least to the wider public—a celebration of Athenian democracy through the finds

of the Athenian agora. In practice, democracy at Athens was inherently exclusionary, and not all scholars are convinced that it offers an especially edifying model to follow.[8] Others, conversely, are convinced that the *principle* of Athenian democracy offers important lessons for democratic theory building today.[9] One is, then, entitled to wonder whether the recent focus on the archaeology of the Athenian democracy is entirely disconnected from the frequent invocation, over the past sixty years, of democratic ideals by the foreign policy makers of Western nations—at least when it suits them.

Ancient historians and classical archaeologists need to be sensitive to the politics of the past. Peremptory dismissals will neither neutralize nor negate the pathways through which constituencies construct their own, lived social reality and on which they ground their sense of community. This is especially critical when, as is so often the case, the archaeologist or historian is an "outsider" to those communities. Not so long ago, I was taken to task by a Greek-American professor who took exception to my treatment of the burials at Vergina. Her anguish was genuine: for centuries, Greece has been pillaged and exploited by foreign explorers, whether illicitly or with government approval, and now foreign scholars were threatening to undermine the important achievements that had been accomplished by Greek archaeologists. I tried to explain that I sympathized with this sentiment and that, as someone who has spent half of his career to date examining issues concerned with ethnicity, I fully understood the sensitivities involved. "How can you?" she asked. "You are not a Greek." That is true, but I was troubled by the implication—namely, that I had no right meddling in Greek history. No doubt, I should have stuck to studying the Ancient Britons, or the Scots, or the Saxons, or the Normans, or the Danes or . . . Like many other historians, I consider my mongrel ethnic heritage entirely irrelevant to my professional identity but that only makes it all the

:::     7. Suetonius, *Augustus* 7.2.

    8. For a recent discussion of the exclusionary nature of Athenian democracy, see Lape 2010.

9. E.g., Ober 2005.

more important to try to be sensitive to the politics of a history that I can hardly claim as my own.

Sensitive, but not obeisant. In the introduction to this book (p. 2), I claimed that the historical enterprise is a "profoundly humanistic project of self-knowledge." In studying the past, we also study ourselves—not in the trite sense that we necessarily re-create the past in the image of the present but rather in the consciousness that a cross-examination of a chronologically and geographically distanced society that was, in many respects, very different from our own will inevitably compel us to re-evaluate our own values and assumptions.[10] This project of self-knowledge, however, operates through a double lens—one that refracts between past and present and another that amplifies the differences between competing interpretations of the past. Those competing interpretations are often driven by theoretical preferences and ideological dispositions—both of which are, in their own right, perfectly valid ways of engaging with the past—but if we are searching for a more neutral discourse of analysis that could, at least potentially, transcend interpretive differences, then I suggest that we would do well to concentrate more on issues of methodology.[11] While theory is an explanatory tool, normally imported from contexts that are independent of the data sets to which it is applied, method depends on the nature and quality of the surviving evidence.[12] It follows, then, that methodological rigour requires a solid familiarity with the materials, both textual and material, as well as an understanding that historical documents and archaeological evidence cannot necessarily be interpreted according to the same analytical methods.[13] In this sense, and only in this sense, David Clarke was right to protest that "archaeology is not history."[14] That, however, is a message that has not yet been fully understood by many ancient historians.

## Words and Things

Ray Laurence has recently written: "I have a sense that ancient history may be becoming more open to archaeology as a discipline and has incorporated the material dimension into its historical narrative."[15] That assessment may, however, be a little optimistic. Out of curiosity, I decided to select—at random—three relatively recent issues of academic journals devoted to ancient history in order to get some sense of the extent to which archaeological evidence is currently employed by historians. Volume 42, number 1, of the American journal *Ancient World* for 2011 contains five articles, of which only one (on the Lydos painter) engages with archaeological evidence while the remaining four—including a piece on Greek colonies in Spain—are almost exclusively based on literary sources. Volume 56, number 4 (2007) of the German journal *Historia* is constituted by six articles, of which only one (on the Boiotian festival of the Daidala) truly discusses archaeological findings alongside literary evidence, although a shorter note (on the Seleucid general Achaios) employs numismatic evidence. Of the twelve articles in volume 41 (2011) of the Belgian periodical *Ancient Society*, only three—one on

:::     10. Cf. Hartog 2009: 979: "[T]he point is not to forget the present but to manage to look at it as if from a distance in order to better understand it."

11. See Chandler 2009: 733: "One might even say that the stronger the emphasis on method as such, the further we are from doxa, from belief or opinion."

12. Cf. Finley 1985: 106: "A historian must deploy different strategies according to the nature of the evidence available to him and the questions he is posing." The first, I would suggest, involves method; the second, theory. See Hall 2014: 12–15.

13. See Foxhall 2004: 82: "Despite their fraternal affinity, the history and archaeology of the classical world will continue to have a troubled relationship as long as each discipline forgets that the contexts of the other are different and not always straightforwardly complementary."

14. Clarke 1968: 12.

15. Laurence 2012: ix.

colonists in mid-Republican Italy and two on associations of merchants—engage even fleetingly with archaeological evidence.

Granted, it is a little unfair to criticize scholars for the choices that they have every right to make with regard to topic or the evidence to be studied. It is a frustration of every academic author to be taken to task for not writing the book that a reviewer would have written—or, in some cases, is writing. Nevertheless, there does seem to be a lingering notion that archaeological evidence is, at best, supplementary and, at worst, even a luxury when there is an abundance of textual documentation. Part of this, no doubt, is a consequence of training—a point to which I shall return in the final section—but part is also surely a legacy of the traditional subordination of archaeological to textual approaches within the formation of the discipline of classics.

Still interesting—and, I suspect, influential—in this respect are the views of Moses Finley, who devoted considerable thought and attention to issues of historical method. To Finley, archaeology almost seems like an irritation that he knew, deep down, he could not do without: "*The happy days are gone* when historians of antiquity . . . could relegate archaeology to a minor ancillary activity that produced picturesque information about private life and art with which to dress up the 'real' history derived from the written evidence. The ancient historian today *has to accept* that his armoury includes qualitatively different kinds of evidence which often appear mutually contradictory or at least unrelated" (my emphasis).[16] Part, but not all, of Finley's discomfort was occasioned by the manifesto of the New Archaeology (see pp. 13–14), which, in his view, ran the risk of distancing archaeology from ancient history—or, at least, "from the kinds of questions historians have *traditionally* put to archaeologists" (my

emphasis).[17] The qualification is critical, because Finley was anything but a traditional historian. As he goes on to note, "Anyone who is happy with kings and battles or with 'calling ancient things to life' . . . will find the discussion wholly irrelevant."[18] In fact, by espousing a more explicitly social and economic type of history, Finley provided ancient historians with research agendas that did speak more directly to the sorts of issues and debates that concerned archaeologists—and especially New Archaeologists—and for which the archaeological record was much better placed to make an important contribution than had been the case for the sort of *histoire événementielle* practised by political and military historians. Ultimately, what Finley objected to in New Archaeology was not its explicit formulation of hypotheses, construction of models, or focus on quantitative approaches, but its dogmatic rejection of nonmaterial contexts and historicizing narratives.[19] It is this antihistorical militancy that probably accounts for why he was so critical of the value of archaeological evidence—even with regard to topics such as the ancient economy, which many today would consider especially amenable to archaeological analysis.[20]

Finley's solution was to deny an autonomous status to archaeology as a discipline and to recast it as one type of historical evidence, alongside others: "I believe it to be false to speak of the relationship between history and archaeology. At issue are not two qualitatively distinct disciplines but two kinds of evidence about the past, two kinds of *historical* evidence. There can thus be no question of the priority in general or of the superiority of one type of evidence over the other; it all depends in each case *on the evidence available* and *on the particular questions to be answered*" (my emphasis).[21] With regard to the availability of evidence, Finley proclaimed:

::: 16. Finley 1985: 7.

17. Finley 1975: 88.

18. Finley 1975: 88. Cf. Finley 1985: 5: "If, for example, one believes it to be a misjudgment of social behaviour to seek the mainsprings in the personalities and decisions of political and military elites, then the alternative analyses and explanations of some contemporary historians represent progress."

19. Finley 1975: 88–93.

20. E.g., Finley 1985: 25: "I merely wish to make the simple point that archaeological evidence or archaeological analysis *by itself* cannot possibly uncover the legal or economic structure revealed by the Oxyrhyncus papyri or the alternative structures in Arezzo, Puteoli, Lezoux or North Africa."

21. Finley 1985: 20.

"It is self-evident that the potential contribution of archaeology to history is, in a rough way, inversely proportional to the quantity and quality of the available written sources."[22] Needless to say, for most archaeologists this professed truism is anything but self-evident. But Finley himself seems to have experienced a moment of self-doubt, because a couple of pages later, in a discussion of the "counterfeit history" of early Rome, he concedes that "it is tempting to draw the rather paradoxical conclusion that the contribution of archaeology to history becomes greater as the volume and reliability of nonarchaeological evidence increase. There is truth in that proposition, but not the whole truth."[23]

If the availability of evidence is something of a red herring, what about the sorts of questions that the historian wants answered? Here Finley is quite clear: "I should repeat that, on all available evidence, it is impossible to infer social arrangements or institutions, attitudes or beliefs from material objects alone."[24] Now, in fact, the employment by archaeological theorists of anthropological models—a practice of which, at least in principle, Finley should have approved[25]—means that it is not impossible to *infer* "social arrangements or institutions, attitudes or beliefs" even if such inferences are often difficult to test empirically. Yet Finley's attitude concerning the limited value of archaeological evidence is, I suspect, still fairly widely diffused among ancient historians. I am reminded of an interview I attended for a postdoctoral position a couple of decades ago, during which an eminent ancient historian leaned forward and said: "[T]he trouble with you and your supervisor [Anthony Snodgrass] is that you think you can use archaeology to talk about social organization and ideas. But you can't." At the time, I preferred to think that the pronouncement was deliberately intended to provoke me into mounting an articulate and robust

defence of archaeology's potential contributions— which, I am ashamed to say, I spectacularly failed to do. In retrospect, however, I am not so sure.

If, however, there is an air of misunderstanding and mistrust on the part of ancient historians with regard to archaeological evidence, the opposite is also true. In decrying the hierarchical structure of the discipline of classics, in which "the literary text stands at the top and the humble pot at the bottom," Dyson has adopted a stance that is almost diametrically opposed to that of Finley: "Of course, it should be obvious to any historian with a modern social science conscience, be he Marxist or non-Marxist, that the classical texts tell us relatively little about the ancient world, and the large sections and strata of the society of Greece and Rome are only going to be understood through archaeological investigation."[26] The charge is one that will be familiar to most ancient historians: because textual documents were almost invariably written by elite male authors, they are so subjective, skewed, and biased as to be practically useless in reconstructing the past. Two points may be made in response.

Firstly, ancient historians would indeed be guilty of the grossest form of naïveté if they were unaware of the fact that their literary sources are partial—in both senses of the word. But such an assumption is based on a misunderstanding of what it is that ancient historians actually do. They do not simply take their literary sources at face value and regurgitate them as some objective account of the past. Rather, they subject them to interrogation and cross-examination, seeking to understand the motivations behind what they say, the audiences that they target, and, when possible, confronting them with alternative and independent testimony. They recognize that authors may be biased and pursuing a specific agenda and they attempt to correct for that.[27]

22. Finley 1975: 93.
23. Finley 1975: 95.
24. Finley 1975: 93. Cf. Piggott 1972: 950: "But when we try to infer such things as social structure or in the broadest sense religious practices, such evidence becomes almost wholly ambiguous" (cited in Finley 1985: 25).

25. E.g., Finley 1985: 60–61, 66.
26. Dyson 1981: 8.
27. See generally Morley 1999: 53–95; Hall 2014: 16–21.

Secondly, while it is undoubtedly true that there are innumerable aspects of the Mediterranean world for which archaeology provides almost our only information, the belief that it is only archaeology that can offer information about the lower strata of society may be overstated. For one thing, the perishability of materials that were typically employed by poorer segments of the population means that the archaeological record is not always as socioeconomically representative as is sometimes claimed. Indeed, Morris has argued that from the eleventh through to the second quarter of the eighth century BCE, and again from the beginning of the seventh through to the end of the sixth century, subelites are practically absent from the burial record of Attica.[28] For another, there is a range of textual evidence on which ancient historians draw that is not "literary" in the high-cultural sense of the term and that was not exclusively written by the wealthy. Papyri, recording contracts and lawsuits in Hellenistic and Roman Egypt, are one example of this, as are the funerary epitaphs commissioned by ex-slaves and artisans in Rome or the graffiti scratched by shepherds on rocks in southern Attica.[29]

There is no a priori reason why historical narratives cannot, or should not, be written on the basis of archaeology alone. They would—and do—look very different from the sorts of narratives that are constructed following the textual evidence of ancient authors, but then these too are qualitatively different from the accounts of modern historians who conduct their research in archives.[30] But if texts are simply a meaningless distraction from the "real" business of reconstructing the past, why should so many archaeological theorists have turned to historical archaeology precisely because of its rich textual documentation?[31] And why should they have gone to the trouble of inventing "proxy" approaches such as "kinaesthetics," whereby the investigator hopes to reanimate the world of the past through his or her own sensory perceptions of, and bodily movement through, archaeological landscapes?[32] There is a lesson that classical archaeologists could profitably draw from this: namely, that the availability of textual documentation should be a cause for celebration rather than—as inexplicably often seems to be the case—a source of embarrassment.

## Bridging the "Great Divide"?

As already noted in chapter 1 (pp. 13–14), Colin Renfrew's call, in 1980, to bridge what he saw as a "Great Divide" between the "great tradition" of classical archaeology and the more theoretically oriented approaches of the New Archaeologists largely fell on deaf ears. In 1993, for example, Dyson could still complain that "[c]lassical archaeology continues to have relatively little place in this rapidly expanding theoretical debate."[33] Six years later, in the first edition of his introduction to archaeological theory,

Matthew Johnson published a pair of cartoons that seem to concur with Dyson's gloomy assessment.[34] The first, reproduced from Paul Bahn and entitled "Archaeology in 1988," shows three groups of people. In the centre, a bunch of archaeologists, labelled "core," trade insults such as "processualist reactionary!," "post-structuralist pseud!," and "phallocratic scum-bag!" To the right is the J. Public Family, with the subtitle "irritating distraction": "[W]hat the hell do *you* want?" yells one of the ar-

::: 28. Morris 1987.
29. For a preliminary report of the Attic graffiti, see Langdon 2005.
30. See the disparaging comment of Carr 1987: 14.
31. Johnson 2010: 120; cf. Hodder 1991: 145–46.
32. Tilley 1994. Thomas (2001: 180–81) defends the method on

the grounds that it is an "allegory" rather than a "surrogate," designed to identify differences as much as appealing to empathetic intuition. See, however, Shennan 2004: 3.
33. Dyson 1993: 204.
34. Johnson 2010: 183–84 (the first edition appeared in 1999).

chaeologists to the confused family. To the left, in a position marked "periphery," is a balding, bearded, pipe-smoking gentleman who says out loud, "I wonder what all that noise is?" His identification is assured by the "Classical Archaeology" book he reads and by the pile of volumes of the *CIL* (*Corpus Inscriptionum Latinarum*) on which he sits and the stack of Loebs in front of him. Johnson's second, "updated" cartoon, entitled "Archaeology in 1998," replicates the three groups of the original. But this time, the archaeologists are engaged in cozy discussion, muttering platitudes such as "wow . . . Foucault and feminism . . . fascinating" or "mmm . . . Darwin . . . sex for food . . . interesting." J. Public has now definitively retreated off into the sunset, but the classical archaeologist still sits in splendid solitude, reading "More Classical Archaeology."[35] The message seems clear: if some classical archaeologists think they have been invited to the party, someone neglected to inform the hosts.

Ian Morris takes exception to this characterization of the field: "Classical archaeologists have not been wondering what all the noise is. They went from despising it, to listening to it, to being part of it."[36] For Morris, the historicist turn in archaeological theory in the 1980s (see p. 15) offered the opportunity of bringing history and archaeology into a closer dialogue: "Ancient historians were already asking questions about ideology and power, and postprocessual ideas gave classical archaeologists an opportunity to join the debates."[37] He further argues that, precisely due to its exploitation of both textual and material records, "classical archaeology can play a major role in putting historical archaeology at the forefront of theoretical debates in the next generation."[38] Morris warns, though, that "if historical archaeologies are to recognize their potential, we should avoid decoupling archaeologists and historians."[39] The prescriptive tone of this agenda arises from two interrelated obstacles

that currently militate against closer integration of the two fields: one is the question of training; the other, the strong influence exerted by institutionalized disciplinary boundaries, which can often foster mutual miscommunication between ancient history and classical archaeology—a relationship that Lin Foxhall has described as a "problematic one of squabbling siblings."[40]

Ideally, since ancient historians and classical archaeologists are both presumably interested in reconstructions of the past, they would receive much of their training in common. In practice, however, quite aside from obstructionist efforts on the part of some proprietorial "gatekeepers," there are very real constraints that arise from differences in the required skill sets. In 1980, James Wiseman enumerated the range of skills with which archaeologists were expected to familiarize themselves beyond their traditional responsibility to recover, document, analyse, and interpret material evidence. These included palaeoenvironmental approaches; quantitative analysis; ground and air reconnaissance, including regional field survey; a familiarity with scientific techniques such as radiocarbon dating and provenance studies; comparative studies; and social archaeology.[41] Needless to say, the vast array of approaches and techniques with which the archaeologist should be familiar has only expanded over the past generation, as has our empirical knowledge—especially with regard to the earliest phases of prehistory, on which more attention is now being focused than ever before. Since one of the great merits of archaeology is its capacity to track change over the long term, attempts to make the knowledge base more "manageable" by demarcating chronological subdivisions can only be arbitrary and perhaps even counterproductive.

There is, then, already an unwieldy abundance of data, methods, techniques, and approaches that the classical archaeologist should ideally master,

:::     35. Both cartoons are reprinted in Morris 2004: 254–55.

36. Morris 2004: 256.

37. Morris 2004: 263.

38. Morris 2004: 265.

39. Morris 2004: 266.

40. Foxhall 2004: 76. See Bintliff 1991: 2; Dialismas 2004: 64.

41. Wiseman 1980: 279–84.

and it is unrealistic to expect that ancient historians could hope to acquire a similar in-depth familiarity with these in addition to what is already expected of them. Another potentially defining criterion is the question of languages—primarily Ancient Greek and Latin but also, where relevant, languages such as Egyptian, Hittite, Phoenician/Punic, and so on, not to mention the modern languages of scholarship such as French, German, Italian, or Modern Greek. Dyson argues that "[i]t is something of an illusion that all of these years of language study will do you much good as a field archaeologist" and notes that he would "gladly have sacrificed several semesters of Greek for some more geomorphology."[42] In fact, given that it typically takes several years to gain an easy fluency in reading most ancient languages, it is far from clear that a few semesters or so of Greek or Latin would be sufficient to reach even a functional literacy. Gone are the days when American—and increasingly British—undergraduates could be expected to have acquired sufficient expertise in Greek or Latin in high school. A possible solution would be to concentrate on language acquisition at the undergraduate level and then specialize more in archaeological skills at graduate school. But Britain has little in the way of formal instruction at the graduate level, while the typical liberal arts curriculum at American colleges, as admirable as it is, tends not to allow for a high degree of specialization—especially for students who choose their major relatively late in their undergraduate education.

Renfrew's claim that "even for one who has no great facility in reading Greek or Latin, most of the major authors are available in admirably edited bilingual editions" may be some consolation to the classical archaeologist, but it does not really help the ancient historian.[43] Firstly, while translations do indeed exist for "most of the major authors," this is not the case for the vast—and growing—corpora of

papyri and inscriptions; even the crucial fragments of the more than eight hundred historical authors collected by Felix Jacoby have only recently been translated.[44] Secondly, since the act of translation is itself as subjective as the interpretation of material artifacts, translations are of little use to the ancient historian unless s/he understands fully the translation choices that were made as well as alternative possible interpretations. To be blunt, knowledge of the ancient languages is as indispensable to the historian of the ancient Mediterranean as knowledge of Russian is to historians of the Soviet Union or of Arabic to historians of the Middle East. This, in turn, has an important disciplinary consequence: if linguistic competence is necessarily going to serve as a boundary marker between classical archaeology and other branches of classical study, then the former will continue to remain marginalized so long as it is housed in departments of classics.

This brings us to the issue of institutionalized disciplinary divisions and the impediments that they create for a sustained and engaged dialogue between ancient historians and classical archaeologists. In many British universities, the former are housed in classics departments and the latter in departments of archaeology.[45] Even where they are housed together in the same department, barriers still exist. The Faculty of Classics at the University of Cambridge is subdivided into "caucuses" based on subdisciplines: history constitutes the "C" caucus and art and archaeology the "D" caucus—needless to say, the flagship "A" caucus is dedicated to literature. Each caucus sponsors its own weekly seminar, which is one of the primary modes of graduate instruction, but it is still rare for caucuses to sponsor joint seminars or for history graduates to attend the art and archaeology seminar and vice versa.[46]

The situation in the United States is a little different—not least because archaeologists sel-

⋮ ⋮ ⋮     42. Dyson 1981: 9.

43. Renfrew 1980: 289. Renfrew is presumably thinking of the Loeb Classical Library series.

44. Online at http://www.brill.nl/publications/online -resources/jacoby-online.

45. Millett 2012: 37–39; Laurence 2012: x.

46. Dialismas 2004: 64.

dom constitute a department in their own right but are housed in departments of anthropology, which is one of the reasons why Wiseman wondered whether archaeology might be "too inherently interdisciplinary to fit into the traditional departmental structure of universities."[47] Classical archaeologists, by contrast, typically belong to classics departments, or art history departments, or both. Although—partly for reasons outlined in chapter 1—the relationship between classics and art history has not always been an easy one, the last decade or so has seen new productive alliances forged between ancient art historians and classicists, but not so much with ancient historians as with literary scholars. This is especially true of current approaches that focus on visuality, the experience of the ancient viewer and *ekphrasis*—descriptions of viewing penned by authors such as Ovid, Pausanias, or Philostratos. I certainly do not mean to imply that such approaches are less-than-legitimate ways of reading visual culture—just as works of ancient literature can be appreciated independently of their historical context. Nevertheless, it remains the case that the tendency to interpret art through a literary lens compromises the efforts of those classical archaeologists who seek an autonomous status for their field, while the focus on the erudite exercises of ancient literati holds little appeal for many contemporary ancient historians who doubt the applicability of the insights obtained to a broader cross-section of society.[48]

It is, however, worth pointing out that ancient history is often just as marginalized as classical archaeology within institutes of higher education. This is due in no small part to the fact that it is typically housed in either classics departments or history departments or occasionally both—meaning that its personnel and resources are not only dissipated but also juxtaposed with fields that are defined by different sets of practices. In departments of history, ancient historians may well share many

of the critical approaches of their colleagues—what is often called "thinking like a historian"—but they will always be differentiated from them for as long as archival research remains the dominant modus operandi within the broader discipline. In classics departments, ancient historians will at least share with their colleagues an interest in the ancient Mediterranean world, though their apparent obsession with trivial realia may put them at odds with the often ahistoricist tendencies of philologists and philosophers. And, in both departments—but especially the former—they will never constitute more than a narrow minority. Furthermore, at the national level, departmental identities are replicated and legitimated by their learned societies or professional organizations: for historians in the United States, that is the American Historical Association; for classicists, the American Philological Association. The ancient historian has to choose, and it is not an infrequent complaint of advanced graduate students that both organizations hold their annual conferences—at which preliminary interviews are held for academic positions—at exactly the same time but rarely in the same city.

One could, of course, advocate for an end to—or, at least, a reconfiguration of—institutionalized disciplinary boundaries. After all, the current departmental structure of American research universities dates back to the last decade or so of the nineteenth century and has failed to keep pace with changes in disciplinary practices and the blurring of genres. Yet that is perhaps an unrealistic aim without a complete, centralized overhaul of the university system—something that is practically unimaginable in the United States, where state legislatures militate against national conformity and where many of the major research universities belong to the private sector. The perils to academic mobility and the accreditation of students are simply too great for one institution to adopt unilateral action. As Robert Post puts it:

:::      47. Wiseman 1980: 284.

48. See Kellum 2009. For an attempt to identify a distinctively subelite way of viewing Roman art, see Mayer 2012, esp. 100–212.

As disciplines, the humanities must establish knowledge practices that create a normal science capable of reproduction and replication in university departments throughout the country. They must establish knowledge practices that yield criteria that can be used to hire, evaluate, and promote faculty in university departments and to assess the value of disciplinary work in the proceedings of disciplinary organizations and publications. Humanities scholarship cannot subvert these practices without repudiating its own disciplinarity.[49]

In short, academic departments are the—admittedly imperfect—correlates to disciplinary communities whose expertise is trusted in matters of the reproduction of knowledge (teaching and training), certification, hiring, and promotion. To dissolve disciplines would be to transfer those privileges and responsibilities to nonspecialist administrators and to surrender the right of academic freedom, which is vested in individuals only insofar as they are members of recognized academic communities.[50]

If, as looks likely, departmental structures are here to stay, then the most realistic prognosis is that ancient history and classical archaeology will remain distinct—if related—fields if they are to provide the requisite degree of training needed within each specialization. That makes it all the more critical to maintain open and mutually respectful channels of communication between the two. At the most

basic level, joint seminars, colloquia, and workshops would offer some assistance in familiarizing ancient historians with the precepts and methods of classical archaeology—and vice versa—and all ancient history graduates would benefit from a year spent abroad, ideally in one of the foreign schools of archaeology. Furthermore, an increasing number of interdisciplinary PhD programs at American universities draw on specialists from a number of different departments, which potentially offers a fruitful circumvention of outdated institutional structures—provided, of course, that faculty can be persuaded to devote time and energy to nondepartmental units that seldom pay their salaries.

The ultimate aim is to provide a discursive space for historians and archaeologists of the ancient world to communicate on equal terms and in a vocabulary that is familiar to both. As a result, ancient historians will be able to follow Finley's injunction to reflect more carefully on the questions they ought to be asking of archaeological evidence. Unlike Finley, however, we have no right to expect that classical archaeologists should adjust "their own older aims and techniques to these new demands."[51] Classical archaeologists would certainly benefit from more sustained dialogue with ancient historians—and not just for periods or areas in which literary documentation is available—but it is also incumbent upon ancient historians to gain a better understanding of what archaeological evidence can and cannot offer in reconstructions of the past.

:::     49. Post 2009: 760.
50. See generally Chandler 2009.

51. Finley 1975: 88.

# List of Ancient Authors

| | |
|---|---|
| Accius | Lucius Accius, Roman dramatist and literary scholar, 170–ca. 86 BCE |
| Aelian | Claudius Aelianus, Roman rhetorician and writer, ca. 165–ca. 230 CE |
| Aelius Aristides | Greek sophist from Asia Minor, 117–ca. 180 CE |
| Aelius Theon | Rhetorician from Alexandria, first century CE |
| Aischines | Athenian orator, ca. 397–ca. 322 BCE |
| Aischylos | Athenian tragedian, ca. 525–456 BCE |
| Alkimos | Greek historian from Sicily, mid-fourth century BCE |
| Andokides | Athenian orator, ca. 440–ca. 390 BCE |
| Androtion | Athenian historian and orator, ca. 410–340 BCE |
| Antiphon | Athenian orator, ca. 480–411 BCE |
| Apollonios of Rhodes | Greek poet from Alexandria, third century BCE |
| Appian | Greek historian from Alexandria, early second century CE |
| Apuleius | Poet, philosopher and rhetorician from Madaurus, Africa, second century CE; the attribution to him of *On the World* is not certain |
| Aristodemos | Historian, fourth century CE? |
| Aristophanes | Athenian comic poet, ca. 450–ca. 386 BCE |
| Aristotle | Northern Greek philosopher, 384–322 BCE |
| Arrian | Lucius Flavius Arrianus, Greek historian from Asia Minor, ca. 86–160 CE |

| | |
|---|---|
| Athenaios | Greek writer from Naukratis, late second/early third century CE |
| Augustine | Aurelius Augustinus, orator, philosopher and bishop from northern Africa, 354–430 CE |
| Aulus Gellius | Roman writer, second century CE |
| Calpurnius Piso | Lucius Calpurnius Piso Frugi, Roman politician and historian, later second century BCE |
| Cassius Dio | Greek senator and historian, ca. 164–ca. 230 CE |
| Cato | Marcus Porcius Cato, Roman statesman and historian, 234–149 BCE |
| Censorinus | Roman grammarian, third century CE |
| Cicero | Roman statesman and writer, 106–43 BCE |
| Cincius Alimentus | Lucius Cincius Alimentus, Roman statesman and historian, late third/early second century BCE |
| Claudius Ptolemy | Mathematician, astronomer, and geographer from Alexandria, second century CE |
| Clement of Rome | Bishop, late first/early second century CE |
| Curtius Rufus | Quintus Curtius Rufus, rhetorician and historian, late first/early second century CE |
| Damastes of Sigeion | Greek geographer and historian, late fifth century BCE |
| Demosthenes | Athenian orator, 384–322 BCE |
| Didymos Chalkenteros | Literary critic from Alexandria, first century BCE |
| Diodoros | Greek historian from Sicily, first century BCE |
| Diogenes Laërtios | Greek philosopher, early third century CE |
| Diokles of Peparethos | Greek historian, third century BCE |
| Dionysios of Halikarnassos | Greek rhetorician and historian, late first century BCE |
| Diyllos | Athenian historian, early third century BCE |
| Ennius | Quintus Ennius, Roman grammarian and playwright, 239–169 BCE |
| Ephoros | Greek historian from Kyme, ca. 405–330 BCE |
| Eratosthenes | Greek scholar from Cyrene, ca. 285–194 BCE |
| Euripides | Athenian tragedian, ca. 484–ca. 407 BCE |
| Eusebius | Church chronicler from Caesarea, ca. 260–339 CE |
| Fabius Pictor | Quintus Fabius Pictor, Roman statesman and historian, late third/early second century BCE |
| Festus | Sextus Pompeius Festus, Roman scholar, late second century CE |
| Harpokration | Valerius Harpokration, lexicographer from Alexandria, second century CE |
| Hellanikos | Mythographer and historian from Lesbos, ca. 480–395 BCE |
| Herodotos | Historian from Halikarnassos, ca. 484–ca. 427 BCE |
| Hesychios | Lexicographer from Alexandria, fifth century CE |
| Hieronymos of Kardia | Greek statesman and historian, late fourth/early third century BCE |
| Homer | Epic poet, early seventh century BCE? |
| Horace | Quintus Horatius Flaccus, Roman poet, 65–8 BCE |
| Iamblichos | Neoplatonist philosopher from Koile, Syria, ca. 245–ca. 325 CE |
| Ignatius of Antioch | Bishop, late first century CE |
| Irenaeus | Theologian and bishop, ca. 130–ca. 202 CE |
| Isokrates | Athenian orator, 436–338 BCE |
| Jerome | Eusebius Hieronymus, biblical scholar, ca. 347–420 CE |
| John Chrysostom | Bishop, ca. 354–407 CE |
| Josephus | Flavius Josephus, Greek historian of Jewish descent, first century CE |
| Justin | Marcus Iunianus Iustinus, Roman epitomizer, second–fourth century CE? |
| Kallisthenes | Greek historian from Olynthos, fourth century BCE |

| Krateros | Chronicler, early third century BCE? |
| Lactantius | Lucius Caelius Firmianus, Christian rhetorician, ca. 240–ca. 320 CE |
| *Liber Pontificalis* | Collection of papal biographies, sixth–ninth centuries CE? |
| Livy | Titus Livius, Roman historian, ca. 59 BCE–ca. 17 CE |
| Longinus | The author (probably wrongly) credited with the first-century CE literary treatise *On the Sublime* |
| Lucan | Marcus Annaeus Lucanus, Roman poet, 39–65 CE |
| Lucian | Literary scholar from Samosata, second century CE |
| Lykourgos | Athenian orator, ca. 390–ca. 325 BCE |
| Lysias | Orator resident in Athens, 459–380 BCE? |
| Marsyas | Historian from Macedonia, fourth century BCE |
| Naevius | Gnaeus Naevius, Campanian dramatist, late third century BCE |
| Origen | Origenes Adamantius, philosopher, theologian, and priest, ca. 185–ca. 254 CE |
| Ovid | Publius Ovidius Naso, Roman poet, 43 BCE–17 CE |
| *Palatine Anthology* | Tenth-century CE collection of epigrams |
| Pausanias | Antiquarian and traveller from Asia Minor, mid-second century CE |
| Philostratos | Essayist from Lemnos, third century CE |
| Photios | Byzantine scholar, ca. 810–ca. 893 CE |
| Pindar | Lyric poet from Boiotia, ca. 518–ca. 446 BCE |
| Plato | Athenian philosopher, ca. 429–347 BCE |
| Pliny the Elder | Gaius Plinius Secundus, encyclopaedist, ca. 23–79 CE |
| Plutarch | Greek philosopher and biographer from Boiotia, ca. 50–ca. 120 CE |
| Pollux | Iulius Pollux, scholar and rhetorician from Alexandria, second century CE |
| Polybios | Greek historian, ca. 200–ca. 118 BCE |
| Pompeius Trogus | Biologist and historian, late first century BCE |
| Promathion | Greek historian, third century BCE? |
| Propertius | Sextus Propertius, Roman poet, ca. 50–ca. 5 BCE |
| Pseudo-Skymnos | The author of a geographical treatise, first century BCE |
| Quintilian | Marcus Fabius Quintilianus, Roman rhetorician, ca. 35–ca. 90 CE |
| Seneca | Lucius Annaeus Seneca, Roman philosopher and tragedian, ca. 4 BCE–65 CE |
| Servius | Grammarian and commentator on the works of Vergil, fourth century CE |
| Simonides | Greek poet from Keos, late sixth/early fifth centuries BCE |
| Solinus | Gaius Iulius Solinus, geographer, early third century CE |
| Sophokles | Athenian tragedian, ca. 496–406 BCE |
| Statius | Publius Papinius Statius, Roman poet, ca. 50–96 CE |
| Stephanos of Byzantium | Greek grammarian, sixth century CE |
| Stesichoros | Greek lyric poet from southern Italy or Sicily, early sixth century BCE |
| Strabo | Greek geographer from Pontus, ca. 64 BCE–ca. 21 CE |
| *Suda/Suidas* | Lexicon, compiled towards the end of the tenth century CE |
| Suetonius | Gaius Suetonius Tranquillus, Roman biographer and administrator, ca. 70–ca. 130 CE |
| Tacitus | Publius Cornelius Tacitus, Roman historian, ca. 56–ca. 120 CE |
| Tertullian | Quintus Septimius Florens Tertullianus, Christian apologist, ca. 160–ca. 240 CE |
| Theognis | Elegiac poet from Megara, mid-sixth century BCE |
| Theokritos | Greek poet from Syracuse, early third century BCE |
| Theophrastos | Greek philosopher from Lesbos, ca. 371–ca. 287 BCE |
| Theopompos | Greek historian from Chios, ca. 378–ca. 320 BCE |
| Thucydides | Athenian historian, ca. 455–ca. 397 BCE |

| | |
|---|---|
| Tibullus | Albius Tibullus, Roman poet, ca. 50-19 BCE |
| Timaios | Greek historian from Sicily, ca. 350-260 BCE |
| Valerius Maximus | Roman writer, first century CE |
| Varro | Marcus Terentius Varro, Roman antiquarian, 116-27 BCE |
| Velleius Paterculus | Roman historian, ca. 20 BCE-ca. 30 CE |
| Verrius Flaccus | Marcus Verrius Flaccus, Roman grammarian and scholar, ca. 55 BCE-ca. 20 CE? |
| Vergil | Publius Vergilius Maro, Roman poet, 70-19 BCE |
| Vitruvius | Vitruvius Pollio, Roman architect, first century BCE/first century CE |
| Xenophon | Greek historian and philosopher, ca. 430-ca. 360 BCE |

# Glossary

| | |
|---|---|
| acropolis | The fortified "upper town" of a Greek city |
| *adyton* | A restricted area within the *cella* of a Greek temple |
| *aedicula* | A niche or small shrine |
| agora | An open space in Greek cities which served as the administrative, religious, and commercial centre |
| amazonomachy | A depiction of the mythical battle between Greeks and Amazons |
| amphiprostyle | A building with colonnaded porches at its front and rear |
| amphora | A clay storage vessel with two handles |
| *anaktoron* | A palace, temple, or shrine; the name given to the "holy of holies" in the Telesterion at Eleusis |
| Archaic period | The period of Greek history down to the Persian invasion of 480–479 BCE |
| architrave | The stone or wooden course that runs across columns |
| *archon* | The chief magistracy at Athens |
| Asklepieion | A sanctuary dedicated to the healing god Asklepios |
| *atrium* house | A house arranged around a central light well |
| Attica | The territory controlled by Athens |
| *basileus* | The Greek word for "king," "big man," or chieftain; also the name of a magistracy in several Greek cities |
| black-figure pottery | A style of decorated pottery produced from the |

seventh to early fifth centuries BCE in which silhouettes of figures are painted in black against the background of the red clay and details are rendered by incision, allowing the natural colour of the clay to show through

| | |
|---|---|
| *bucchero* | A type of pottery with a glossy black surface, typical of Etruria |
| capital | The crowning element of a column |
| *cappellaccio* | A grey, lamellar tufa used in early Roman masonry |
| caryatid | An architectural supporting column in the form of a female figure |
| catacombs | Subterranean chambers used for burials; the name derives from the area south of Rome, along the Appian Way |
| *cella* | The primary chamber of a temple, housing the cult statue |
| *chitōn* | A light Greek tunic |
| choregic monuments | Monuments commemorating the producer and sponsor (*chorēgos*) of a musical or dramatic performance |
| chryselephantine | The application of gold and ivory to a wooden core, especially used for cult statues |
| *cippus* | A small pillar, usually of stone |
| cist tomb | A tomb in which a pit, dug into the earth, is lined and covered with stone slabs |
| Classical period | The period of Greek history from the Persian invasion in 480-479 BCE to the death of Alexander the Great in 323 BCE |
| columbarium | A built structure with internal niches to accommodate cinerary urns |
| consul | The highest elected magistrate at Rome |
| Corinthian | A style of architecture, characterized by columns with acanthus capitals; also a style of pottery, manufactured in Corinth, in use from the late seventh through sixth centuries |
| cornice | A horizontal moulded projection at the top of a building |
| dendrochronology | A technique of dating by measuring tree-ring patterns in timber |
| *desmotērion* | A Greek prison |
| *didrachm* | A coin valued at two drachmas |
| *dikastērion* | A Greek law court |
| *dolium* | A large globular jar, sometimes used for burials |
| Doric | A style of architecture, characterized by metope and triglyph friezes and by tapering columns without bases |
| Early Bronze Age | The period from ca. 3000 BCE to ca. 1900 BCE |
| electrum | A natural alloy of gold and silver |
| entablature | The horizontal architectural elements above the columns of a building |
| epigraphy | The study of inscriptions |
| epistyle | The architrave of a building |
| Etruscans | A population of northern-central Italy |
| *fibula* | A metal brooch for fastening clothing |
| field survey | The plotting of surface remains and artifacts by teams of fieldwalkers |
| fixed points | Events recorded by literary sources which are used to pin stylistic chronologies to dates |
| Flavian | The period in which the Flavian imperial dynasty (Vespasian, Titus, and Domitian) ruled Rome, 69-96 CE |
| forum | The central square of a Roman settlement, housing political, religious, and commercial functions |
| Geometric | The name given to the period ca. 900-ca. 700 BCE, characterized by pottery with painted geometric patterns; the period is divided into Early, Middle, and Late phases |
| Geophysical prospection | The identification of subsurface remains by magnetometry, electric resistivity, or ground-penetrating radar |
| gigantomachy | A depiction of the mythical battle between gods and giants |

| | |
|---|---|
| *gorytos* | A case used to store the Scythian bow and arrows |
| *Grotta Oscura* | A pale, yellowish type of tufa from quarries near the Tiber, used in Roman masonry |
| *hekatompedon* | A building or structure—often a temple—measuring 100 feet in length |
| Hellenistic period | The period of Greek history from the death of Alexander the Great in 323 BCE to the Roman conquest of 146 BCE |
| *heröon* | A sanctuary dedicated to a hero |
| *hieron* | The Greek word for a sanctuary |
| *hydria* | A vessel used for carrying water |
| impasto | A coarse type of pottery, often handmade |
| *kouroi* | Standing, nude male statues, typical of the Archaic period |
| *kratēr* | A mixing bowl for wine |
| *kylix* | A drinking cup with two handles |
| *larnax* | A chest or box, sometimes used as a cinerary urn |
| Late Helladic | The Late Bronze Age on the Greek mainland, ca. 1600–1200 BCE; also known as the "Mycenaean period" |
| Late Republic | The period of Roman history from ca. 133 to 27 BCE |
| Latial culture | The archaeological culture of Latium (the region in which Rome is located) in the Early Iron Age |
| *lekythos* | A one-handled oil flask |
| *loculus* | A niche, often used for burial |
| metic | A resident alien in Athens |
| metope | A rectangular panel, framed by triglyphs, on Doric friezes |
| Minoan | The name coined by Arthur Evans to describe the civilization that flourished on Crete in the second millennium BCE |
| Mycenaean | The name given to the Late Bronze Age culture of the Greek mainland, ca. 1600–1200 BCE |
| *naiskos* | A small temple |
| *naos* | The Greek word for a temple |
| narthex | The entrance porch to a Byzantine church, typically situated at the west end of the nave |
| necropolis | A cemetery |
| Neolithic | The period from ca. 6000 BCE to ca. 3000 BCE |
| numismatics | The study of coins |
| *opisthodomos* | The back room of a temple, often serving as a treasury |
| *opus quadratum* | A style of Roman masonry with squared blocks laid in parallel courses |
| *opus reticulatum* | A style of Roman masonry in which a cement core is faced with diamond-shaped bricks |
| ossuary | A box or container holding human skeletal remains |
| ostracism | An annual procedure at Athens whereby a vote was held to exile a prominent individual for ten years without confiscation of property |
| Panathenaic amphorae | Amphorae awarded as prizes in the Great Panathenaic Games |
| papyrology | The study of papyri texts |
| patricians | Members of Roman aristocratic clans |
| Pentelic | A type of marble from Mount Pentelikon in Attica |
| *peperino* | A greyish tufa from quarries in the Alban hills, southeast of Rome |
| *peribolos* | Enclosure or precinct |
| peripteral | Surrounded by a *peristasis* or colonnade |
| *peristasis* | A peristyle or colonnade |
| peristyle | A colonnade |
| philology | The study of language and/or literature |

| | |
|---|---|
| *pithos* | A large ovoid or cylindrical storage container, sometimes used for burials |
| plebeians | Roman citizens who did not belong to the patrician class |
| polychrome | Multicoloured |
| polygonal | A style of masonry in which polygonal-shaped blocks are dressed and fitted to one another |
| Pontifex Maximus | The most important priest at Rome |
| poros | A type of limestone |
| pozzuolana | A cement made from volcanic ash |
| praetor | A Roman magistrate |
| Principate | The system of imperial succession under which the Roman Empire was ruled from 27 BCE to 476 CE |
| prostyle | A building with a colonnaded front porch |
| Protocorinthian | A style of pottery, manufactured in Corinth, in use from the late eighth through late seventh centuries BCE |
| Protogeometric | A style of pottery manufactured in various regions of Greece during the eleventh and tenth centuries BCE |
| Protovillanovan | The Late Bronze Age archaeological culture of central Italy |
| Pseudopolygonal | A type of polygonal masonry where the blocks are not dressed to fit one another exactly |
| radiocarbon dating | A method of dating organic materials by measuring residual amounts of the carbon 14 isotope |
| red-figure pottery | A style of decorated pottery, produced from the late sixth to fourth centuries BCE, in which the background is painted black while figures are depicted by reserving the red clay and by applying details in black paint with a fine brush |
| rescue excavations | Limited excavations conducted in advance of building and infrastructural development; also known as "salvage archaeology" |
| Seleucids | The dynasty that ruled over an empire stretching from Anatolia to central Asia in the third, second, and first centuries BCE |
| Severe Style | A style of sculpture typical of the early fifth century BCE |
| sima | The gutter that runs above the cornice on a building |
| *statēr* | A high-denomination coin |
| *stēlē* | A stone slab or pillar |
| stoa | A long, colonnaded portico providing shade and shelter |
| stratigraphy | The study of the superimposed settlement layers (strata) of a site |
| stucco | A plaster coating, made from lime, sand, or occasionally ground marble, applied to the surface of columns and walls |
| stylobate | The course of masonry on which columns stand |
| *tablinum* | The principal reception room in a Roman house |
| Telesterion | An initiation hall for mystery cults |
| *temenos* | A precinct, often associated with sanctuary enclosures |
| *terminus ante quem* | The absolute latest date for an archaeological artifact or attribute |
| *terminus post quem* | The absolute earliest date for an archaeological artifact or attribute |
| *terra sigillata* | Mould-made Roman pottery with relief decoration and a glossy red slip |
| tetrastyle | A room whose roof is supported by four columns |
| Thesmophoria | A festival in honour of Demeter, attended by women only |
| tholos | A name given to any circular structure; in the Athenian agora, the Tholos housed the executive committee (*prytaneia*) of the council (*Boulē*) |
| travertine | A compacted type of limestone |
| *triclia* | A funerary banqueting hall at Christian sites |

| | |
|---|---|
| *triclinium* | The dining room of a Roman house |
| triglyph | The "grooved" element that appears on Doric friezes |
| *tropaion* | A monument signifying a triumph |
| tufa | A type of volcanic stone used in Roman construction |
| *vestibulum* | The entrance porch of a Roman house |
| wiggle-match dating | A method of dating obtained by fitting a series of radiocarbon dates obtained from tree rings to the shape of the radiocarbon calibration curve |

# Bibliography

Accame, S. (1956) "Il problema della nazionalità greca nella politica di Pericle e Trasibulo," *Paideia* 11: 241-53.

Adams, W. L. (1980) "The royal Macedonian tomb at Vergina: an historical explanation," *AncW* 3: 67-72.

———— (1991) "Cassander, Alexander IV and the tombs at Vergina," *AncW* 22: 27-33.

Adams, W. L., and E. N. Borza, eds. (1982) *Philip II, Alexander the Great, and the Macedonian Heritage*. Washington DC.

Akamatis, I. M. (2011) "Pella," in Lane Fox, ed., 393-408.

Albertoni, M., and I. Damiani, eds. (2008) *Il tempio di Giove e le origini del colle Capitolino*. Milan.

Alcock, S. E., J. F. Cherry, and J. L. Davis (1994) "Intensive survey, agricultural practice and the classical landscape of Greece," in Morris, ed., 137-70.

Alcock, S. E., and R. Osborne, eds. (1994) *Placing the Gods: Sanctuaries and Sacred Space in Ancient Greece*. Oxford.

———— (2012) *Classical Archaeology*, 2nd ed. Chichester.

Alföldi, A. (1965) *Early Rome and the Latins*. Ann Arbor.

Allen, D. S. (1997) "Imprisonment in Classical Athens," *CQ* 47: 121-35.

———— (2000) *The World of Prometheus: The Politics of Punishing in Democratic Athens*. Princeton.

Allen, S.H. (1999) *Finding the Walls of Troy: Frank Calvert and Heinrich Schliemann at Hisarlík*. Berkeley.

Amandry, P. (1950) *La mantique apollinienne à Delphes: essai sur le fonctionnement de l'Oracle*, Bibliotheque des Écoles Françaises d'Athènes et de Rome 170. Paris.

———— (1980) "Sur les concours argiens, *Études Argiennes*, *BCH* suppl. 6, 211-53. Paris.

Ammerman, A.J. (1990) "On the origins of the Forum Romanum," *AJA* 94: 627-45.

———— (1996a) "The Comitium in Rome from the beginning," *AJA* 100: 121-36.

———— (1996b) "The Eridanos valley and the Athenian Agora," *AJA* 100: 699–715.

Ampolo, C. (1975) "Gli Aquilii del V secolo a.C. e il problema dei fasti consolari più antichi," *PP* 30: 410–16.

———— (1980) "Le condizioni materiali della produzione: agricoltura e paessaggio agrario," *DArch* 2: 15–46.

———— (1988a) "La nascita della città," in Momigliano and Schiavone, eds., 153–80.

———— (1988b) "Introduzione," in Ampolo and Manfredini, eds., ix–lv.

Ampolo, C., and M. Manfredini, eds. (1988) *Plutarco: le vite di Teseo e di Romolo*. Milan.

Anderson, G. (2003) *The Athenian Experiment: Building an Imagined Political Community in Ancient Attica, 508–490 BC*. Ann Arbor.

Andrewes, A. (1961) "Thucydides and the Persians," *Historia* 10: 1–18.

Andronikos, M. (1978) *The Royal Graves at Vergina*. Athens.

———— (1984) *Vergina: The Royal Tombs and the Ancient City*. Athens.

———— (1987) "Some reflections on the Macedonian tombs," *ABSA* 82: 1–16.

———— (1994a) *Vergina*, vol. 2: *The "Tomb of Persephone."* Athens.

———— (1994b) "The Macedonian tombs," in Ginouvès, ed., 144–91.

Apollonj Ghetti, B. M., A. Ferrua, E. Josi, and E. Kirschbaum (1951) *Esplorazioni sotto la confessione di San Pietro in Vaticano eseguite negli anni 1940–1949*. Vatican City.

Armstrong, G. T. (1974) "Constantine's churches: symbol and structure," *JSAH* 33: 5–16.

Auberson, P. (1968) *Eretria*, vol. 1: *Temple d'Apollon Daphnéphoros; Architecture*. Berne.

Auberson, P., and K. Schefold (1972) *Führer durch Eretria*. Berne.

Badian, E. (1968) "A king's notebooks," *HSCP* 72: 183–204.

———— (1982) "Greeks and Macedonians," in Barr-Sharrar and Borza, eds., 33–51.

———— (1993) *From Plataea to Potidaea: Studies in the History and Historiography of the Pentekontaetia*. Baltimore.

Bagatti, B., and J. T. Milik (1958) *Gli scavi del Dominus Flevit (Monte Oliveto—Gerusalemme)*, vol. 1: *La necropoli del periodo romano*. Jerusalem.

Baldwin, M. C. (2005) *Whose Acts of Peter? Text and Historical Context of the Actus Vercellenses*. Tübingen.

Balme, J., and A. Paterson (2006) "Stratigraphy," in Balme and Paterson, eds., 97–116.

Balme, J., and A. Paterson, eds. (2006) *Archaeology in Practice: A Student Guide to Archaeological Analyses*. Malden.

Barbanera, M. (1998) *L'archeologia degli Italiani*. Rome.

Barbera, M., and M. Magnani Cianetti (2008) *Archeologia a Roma Termini: Le mura serviane e l'area della stazione; scoperte, distruzioni e restauri*. Milan.

Barker, G., and R. Hodges, eds. (1981) *Archaeology and Italian Society*, *BAR* 102. London.

Barrett, J. (2001) "Agency and the archaeological record," in Hodder, ed., 141–64.

Barr-Sharrar, B. (1991) "Vergina Tomb II: dating the objects," *AncW* 22: 11–15.

Barr-Sharrar, B., and E. N. Borza, eds. (1982) *Macedonia and Greece in Late Classical and Early Hellenistic Times*. Washington DC.

Bartsiokas, A. (2000) "The eye injury of King Philip II and the skeletal evidence from Royal Tomb II at Vergina," *Science* 288: 511–14.

———— (2008) "The royal skeletal remains at Vergina," *Archaeological Institute of America: Abstracts of the 109th Annual Meeting*, 129.

Bayet, J. (1920) "Les origines de l'arcadisme romain," *MEFRA* 38: 63–143.

Beard, M. (2003) *The Parthenon*. Cambridge, MA.

Beard, M., J. North, and S. Price (1998) *Religions of Rome*, vol. 1: *A History*. Cambridge.

Beck, H., A. Duplá, M. Jehne, and F. Pina Polo, eds. (2011) *Consuls and "Res Publica": Holding High Office in the Roman Republic*. Cambridge.

Beloch, K. J. (1926) *Römische Geschichte bis zum Beginn der punischen Kriege*. Leipzig.

Bengtson, H. (1970) *Introduction to Ancient History*, trans. R. I. Frank and F. D. Gilliard. Berkeley.

Bérard, C. (1970) *Eretria*, vol. 3: *L'Hérôon à la porte de l'ouest*. Berne.

———— (1971) "Architecture érétrienne et mythologie delphique," *AK* 14: 59–73.

Bernal, M. (1987) *Black Athena: The Afroasiatic Roots of Classical Civilization*, vol. 1: *The Fabrication of Ancient Greece, 1785–1985*. London.

Bettelli, M. (1997) *Roma: la città prima della città; La cronologia delle sepolture ad inumazione di Roma e del Lazio nella prima età del ferro*, Studia Archaeologica 86. Rome.

Bianchi Bandinelli, R. (1985) *Introduzione all'archeologia*, 5th ed. Bari.

Bickerman, E. J. (1952) "Origines gentium," *CPh* 47: 65–81.

Biers, W. R. (1992) *Art, Artefacts, and Chronology in Classical Archaeology*. London.

Bietti Sestieri, A. M. (1980) "Aggiornamento per i periodi I e IIA," in *La formazione della città nel Lazio*, DArch 2, 65–71.

———— (1982) *The Iron Age Community of Osteria dell'Osa*. Cambridge.

———— (2009) "Factors of cultural and political change in ancient Lazio, 12th–8th century BC," *ScAnt* 15: 345–58.

Bietti Sestieri, A. M., and A. De Santis (2008) "Relative and absolute chronology of Latium Vetus from the Late Bronze Age to the transition of the Orientalizing period," in Brandherm and Trachsel, eds., 119–33.

Billot, M.-F. (1977) "Note sur un sime en marbre de Delphes," *Etudes Delphiques, BCH* suppl. 4, 161–77.

Binford, L. R., and S. R. Binford (1968) *New Perspectives in Archaeology*. Chicago.

Bintliff, J. (1991) "The contribution of the Annaliste/structural history approach to archaeology," in Bintliff, ed., 1–33.

Bintliff, J., ed. (1991) *The Annales School and Archaeology*. Leicester.

—— (2004) *A Companion to Archaeology*. Malden.

Bintliff, J., P. Howard, and A. M. Snodgrass, eds. (2007) *Testing the Hinterland: The Work of the Boeotia Survey (1989–1991) in the Southern Approaches to the City of Thespiai*. Cambridge.

Bloch, E. (2002) "Hemlock poisoning and the death of Socrates: did Plato tell the truth?," in Brickhouse and Smith, eds., 255–78.

Boardman, J. (1957) "Early Euboean pottery and history," *ABSA* 52: 1–29.

—— (1973) "Treading on Classic ground: new work in Greek archaeology," *Encounter* 40.4: 67–69.

—— (1975) "Herakles, Peisistratos and Eleusis," *JHS* 95: 1–12.

—— (1984) "*Signa tabulae priscae artis*," *JHS* 104: 161–63.

Bockmuehl, M. (2004) "Simon Peter's names in Jewish sources," *JJS* 40: 58–80.

Boegehold, A. L. (1995) "History and analysis," in Boegehold et al., 1–50.

Boegehold, A. L., J. McK. Camp, M. Crosby, M. Lang, D. R. Jordan, and R. F. Townsend (1995) *The Athenian Agora: Results of Excavations Conducted by the American School of Classical Studies at Athens*, vol. 28: *The Lawcourts at Athens: Sites, Buildings, Equipment, Procedure, and Testimonia*. Princeton.

Boegehold, A. L., and M. Crosby (1995) "Testimonia," in Boegehold et al., 117–241.

Boersma, J. S. (1970) *Athenian Building Policy from 561/0 to 405/4 BC*. Groningen.

Bommelaer, J.-F., and D. LaRoche (1991) *Guide de Delphes: Le site*. Paris.

Bonnechère, P. (2008–9) "Divination et revelation en Grèce ancienne," *AEHE V* 117: 386–90.

—— (2010) "Oracles and Greek mentalities: the mantic confirmation of mantic revelations," in Dijkstra, Kroesen, and Kuiper, eds., 115–33.

Borza, E. N. (1987) "The royal Macedonian tombs and the paraphernalia of Alexander the Great," *Phoenix* 41: 105–21.

—— (1996) "Greeks and Macedonians in the age of Alexander: the source traditions," in Wallace and Harris, eds., 122–39.

—— (1999) *Before Alexander: Constructing Early Macedonia*. Claremont.

—— (2008) "The royal paraphernalia of Alexander the Great?," *Archaeological Institute of America: Abstracts of the 109th Annual Meeting*, 130.

Borza, E. N., and O. Palagia (2007) "The chronology of the Macedonian royal tombs at Vergina," *JDAI* 122: 81–125.

Bosworth, A. B. (1971) "The Congress Decree: another hypothesis," *Historia* 20: 600–616.

—— (1988) *Conquest and Empire: The Reign of Alexander the Great*. Cambridge.

—— (1990) "Plutarch, Callisthenes and the Peace of Callias," *JHS* 110: 1–13.

Bosworth, A. B., and E. J. Baynham, eds. (2000) *Alexander the Great in Fact and Fiction*. Oxford.

Boudouris, K. J., ed. (1991) *The Philosophy of Socrates*. Athens.

Bowden, H. (2005) *Classical Athens and the Delphic Oracle: Divination and Democracy*. Cambridge.

Bowkett, L., S. Hill, D. Wardle, and K. A. Wardle (2001) *Classical Archaeology in the Field: Approaches*. London.

Boyd, T. (1978) "The arch and vault in Greek architecture," *ABSA* 82: 83–100.

Brandherm, D., and M. Trachsel, eds. (2008) *A New Dawn for the Dark Age? Shifting Paradigms in Mediterranean Iron Age Chronology, BAR* International Series 1871. Oxford.

Braun, K., and A. Furtwängler, eds. (1985) *Studien zur klassischen Archäologie: Friedrich Hiller zur seinem 60. Geburtstag am 12. März 1986*. Saarbrücken.

Braund, D., and C. Gill, eds. (2003) *Myth, History and Culture in Republican Rome: Studies in Honour of T. P. Wiseman*. Exeter.

Brecoulaki, H. (2006) *La peinture funéraire de Macedoine: emplois et fonctions de la couleur IV$^e$–II$^e$ s. av. J.-C.* Athens.

—— (2011) "Painting at the Macedonian court," in Kottaridi and Walker, eds., 209–18.

Bremmer, J., ed. (1987) *Interpretations of Greek Mythology*. London.

Brendel, O. (1931) *Ikonographie des Kaisers Augustus*. Nuremberg.

Brennan, T. C. (2000) *The Praetorship in the Roman Republic*, 2 vols. Oxford.

Bresson, A. (2010) "Revisiting the Pentekontaetia," in Fromentin, Gotteland, and Payen, eds., 383–401.

Briant, P. (1991) "Chasses royals macédoniennes et chasses royals perses: le thème de la chasse au lion sur la chasse de Vergina," *DHA* 17: 211–55.

Brickhouse, T. C., and N. D. Smith, eds. (2002) *The Trial and Execution of Socrates: Sources and Controversies*. Oxford.

Brilliant, R. (1984) *Visual Narratives: Storytelling in Etruscan and Roman Art*. Ithaca.

Broad, W. J. (2006) *The Oracle: Ancient Delphi and the Science behind Its Lost Secrets*. New York.

Brocato, P. (1995) "L'abitato stabile della prima età del Ferro," in Carandini and Carafa, eds., 109–18.

Brothwell, D. R., and A. M. Pollard, eds. (2001) *Handbook of Archaeological Sciences*. Malden.

Brown, K. S. (1994) "Seeing stars: character and identity in the landscapes of modern Macedonia," *Antiquity* 69: 784–96.

Bruins, H. J., A. J. Nijboer, and J. van der Plicht (2011) "Iron Age Mediterranean chronology: a reply," *Radiocarbon* 53: 199–220.

Bruit Zaidman, L., and P. Schmitt Pantel (1997) *Religion in the Ancient Greek City*, trans. P. Cartledge. Cambridge.

Brumbaugh, R. S. (1991) "Simon and Socrates," *AncPhil* 11: 151–52.

Burkert, W. (1985) *Greek Religion: Archaic and Classical*, trans. J. Raffan. Oxford.

——— (1987) *Ancient Mystery Cults*. Cambridge, MA.

Burnet, J. (1911) *Plato's Phaedo*. Oxford.

Calder, W. M., and D. A. Traill (1986) *Myth, Scandal, and History: The Heinrich Schliemann Controversy and a First Edition of the Mycenaean Diary*. Detroit.

Camp, J. McK. (1990) *The Athenian Agora: A Guide to the Excavation and Museum*. Athens.

——— (1995) "Square Peribolos," in Boegehold et al., 99–103.

——— (2001) *The Archaeology of Athens*. New Haven.

——— (2010) *The Athenian Agora: Site Guide*, 5th ed. Princeton.

Camp, J. McK., and C. A. Mauzy, eds. (2009) *The Athenian Agora: New Perspectives on an Ancient Site*. Mainz.

Carafa, P. (1995) "I reperti," in Carandini and Carafa, eds., 194–200.

——— (2005) "Il *Volcanal* e il comizio," *WACPCR* 2: 135–49.

Carafa, P., and P. Brocato (1992) "Lo scavo delle mura palatine: i reperti," *BollArch* 16–18: 129–32.

Carandini, A. (2000) *Giornale di scavo: pensieri sparsi di un archeologo*. Turin.

——— (2003) *La nascita di Roma: Dèi, lari, eroi e uomini all'alba di una civiltà*, 2nd ed. Turin.

——— (2004) *Palatino, Velia e Sacra Via: Paesaggi urbani attraverso il tempo*, *WACQ* 1. Rome.

——— (2006) "Introduzione," in Carandini, ed., xiii–lxxix.

——— (2010) *Le case del potere nell'antica Roma*. Rome.

——— (2011) *Rome: Day One*, trans. S. Sartarelli. Princeton.

Carandini, A., ed. (1992) 'Lo scavo delle mura palatine,' *BollArch* 16–18: 111–38.

——— (2006) *La leggenda di Roma*, vol. 1: *Dalla nascita dei gemelli alla fondazione della città*. Rome.

Carandini, A., and D. Bruno (2008) *La casa di Augusto dai "Lupercalia" al Natale*. Rome.

Carandini, A., and R. Cappelli, eds. (2000) *Roma, Romolo, Remo e la fondazione della città: Catalogo della mostra*. Milan.

Carandini, A., and P. Carafa, eds. (1995) *Palatium e Sacra Via*, vol. 1: *Prima delle mura, l'età delle mura e l'età case archaiche*, *BollArch* 31–34. Rome.

Carcopino, J. (1956) *De Pythagore aux apôtres: études sur la conversion du monde romain*. Paris.

Carettoni, G. (1954–55) "Tomba arcaica a cremazione scoperta sul Palatino," *BPI* 64: 261–76.

——— (1967) "I problemi della zona augustea del Palatino alla luce dei recenti scavi," *AttiPontAcc* 38: 55–75.

——— (1978–80) "La 'domus virginum vestalium' e la 'domus publica' del periodo repubblicano," *AttiPontAcc* 51–52: 325–55.

——— (1983) *Das Haus des Augustus auf dem Palatin*. Mainz.

Carney, E. D. (1991) "The female burial in the antechamber of Tomb II at Vergina," *AncW* 22: 17–26.

——— (2008) "Two royal couples and Tomb II at Vergina," *Archaeological Institute of America: Abstracts of the 109th Annual Meeting*, 129.

Carr, E. H. (1987) *What Is History?*, 2nd ed. London.

Cartledge, P. A., and F. D. Harvey, eds. (1985) *Crux: Essays Presented to G. E. M. de Ste Croix on His 75th Birthday*. Sidmouth.

Carubba, A. M. (2007) *La lupa capitolina: Un bronzo medievale*. Rome.

Cassatella, A. (2005) "Favisae capitolinae," in Comella and Mele, eds., 77–83.

Castagnoli, F. (1964) "Note sulla topografia del Palatino e del Foro Romano," *ArchClass* 16: 173–99.

——— (1974) "Topografia e urbanistica di Roma nel IV sec. a.C.," *StudRom* 22: 425–43.

Castagnoli, F., ed. (1975) *Lavinium*, vol. 2: *Le tredici are*. Rome.

Cecamore, C. (1996) "Apollo e Vesta sul Palatino fra Augusto e Vespasiano," *BullCom* 96: 9–32.

Chadwick, H. (1957) "The problem of the *Memoria Apostolorum ad Catacumbas*," *JThS* 8: 31–52.

Chambers, M. H., R. Gallucci, and P. Spanos (1990) "Athens' alliance with Egesta in the year of Antiphon," *ZPE* 83: 38–57.

Chandler, J. (2009) "Introduction: doctrines, disciplines, discourses, departments," in Chandler and Davidson, eds., 729–46.

Chandler, J., and A. I. Davidson, eds. (2009) *The Fate of Disciplines*, *CI* 35, no. 4. Chicago.

Chaney, E. (1998) *The Evolution of the Grand Tour: Anglo-Italian Cultural Relations since the Renaissance*. London.

Cherry, J. F. (1983) "Frogs around the pond: perspectives on current archaeological survey projects in the Mediterranean region," in Keller and Rupp, eds., 375–416.

Childe, V. G. (1929) *The Danube in Prehistory*. Oxford.

——— (1956) *Piecing Together the Past*. London.

Childs, W. A. P. (1994) "The date of the old temple of Athena on the Athenian acropolis," in Coulson et al., eds., 1–6.

Christidis, A.-F., ed. (2007) *A History of Ancient Greek from the Beginnings to Late Antiquity*. Cambridge.

Cifani, G. (2008) *Architettura romana arcaica: Edilizia e società tra monarchia e repubblica*. Rome.

——— (2010) "I grandi cantieri della Roma arcaica: aspetti tecnici e organizzativi," *AAEA* 57: 35-49.

Claridge, A. (2010) *Rome: An Archaeological Guide*, 2nd ed. Oxford.

Clarke D. L. (1968) *Analytical Archaeology*. London.

Clinton, K. (1986) "The date of the Classical Telesterion at Eleusis," in Φιλία ἔπη εἰς Γ.Ε. Μυλωνᾶν, vol. 2, 254-62.

——— (1993) "The sanctuary of Demeter and Kore at Eleusis," in Marinatos and Hägg, eds., 110-24.

——— (1994) "The Eleusinian Mysteries and panhellenism in democratic Athens," in Coulson et al., eds., 161-72.

Clogg, R. (2002) *A Concise History of Greece*, 2nd ed. Cambridge.

Coarelli, F. (1980) *Guide archeologiche Laterza: Roma*. Bari.

——— (1983) *Il Foro Romano*, vol. 1: *Periodo arcaico*. Rome.

——— (1993) *Dintorni di Roma*, 2nd ed. Bari.

——— (2003) "Remoria," in Braund and Gill, eds., 41-55.

——— (2007) *Rome and Its Environs: An Archaeological Guide*. Berkeley.

Cobb-Stevens, V., T. J. Figueira, and G. Nagy (1985) "Introduction," in Figueira and Nagy, eds., 108.

Coldstream, N. (2003) "Some Aegean reactions to the chronology debate in the southern Levant," *Tel Aviv* 30: 247-58.

Colini, A. M. (1938) "Notizario di scavi, scoperte et studi intorno all'antichità di Roma e del Lazio: Tra la Via del Mare e Piazza della Consolazione," *BullCom* 66: 279-82.

Collingwood, R. G. (1993) *The Idea of History*, rev. ed. Oxford.

Comella, A., and S. Mele, eds. (2005) *Depositivi votivi e culti dell'Italia antica dall'età arcaica a quella tardo-repubblicana*, Atti del Convegno di Studia, Perugia 1-4. Bari.

Connor, W. R. (1968) *Theopompus and Fifth-Century Athens*. Washington, DC.

Cook, R. M. (1989a) "The pediment of Apollo Sosianus," *AA*, pp. 525-28.

——— (1989b) "The Francis-Vickers chronology," *JHS* 109: 164-70.

Corbier, M. (1992) "De la maison d'Hortensius à la *curia* sur le Palatin," *MEFRA* 104: 871-916.

Cornell, T. J. (1977) "Aeneas' arrival in Italy," *LCM* 2: 77-83.

——— (1995) *The Beginnings of Rome: Italy and Rome from the Bronze Age to the Punic Wars (c. 1000-264 BC)*. London.

Correnti, V. (1965) "Relazione dello studio compiuto su tre gruppi di resti scheletrici umani già rinvenuti sotto la confessione della basilica vaticana," in Guarducci, 83-160.

Cosmopoulos, M. B. (2001) *The Rural History of Ancient Greek City-States: The Oropos Survey Project*, *BAR* International Series 1001. Oxford.

——— (2003) "Mycenaean religion at Eleusis: the architecture and stratigraphy of Megaron B," in Cosmopoulos, ed., 1-24.

Cosmopoulos, M. B., ed. (2003) *Greek Mysteries: The Archaeology and Ritual of Ancient Greek Secret Cults*. London.

Coulson, W. D. E., O. Palagia, T. L. Shear Jr., H. A. Shapiro, and F. J. Frost, eds. (1994) *The Archaeology of Athens and Attica under the Democracy*. Oxford.

Coulton, J. J. (1979) "Doric capitals: a proportional analysis," *ABSA* 74: 81-153.

Courbin, P. (1988) *What Is Archaeology? An Essay on the Nature of Archaeological Research*, trans. P. Bahn. Chicago.

Courby, M. F. (1915-27) *Fouilles de Delphes*, vol. 2: *Topographie et architecture: la terrasse du temple*, 3 fascicules. Paris.

Cristofani, M. (1990) "Blocco iscritto da Satricum," in Cristofani, ed., 23-24.

Cristofani, M., ed. (1990) *La grande Roma dei Tarquini: Catalogo della mostra*. Rome.

Crosby, M. (1951) "The Poros Building," *Hesperia* 20: 168-87.

Cross, T. M., and S. Aaronson (1988) "The vapours of one entrance to Hades," *Antiquity* 62: 88-89.

Cullmann, O. (1962) *Peter: Disciple, Apostle, Martyr; A Historical and Theological Study*, trans. F. V. Filson. London.

Cunliffe, B., C. Gosden, and R. A. Joyce, eds. (2009) *The Oxford Handbook of Archaeology*. Oxford.

Curran, J. (1996) "The bones of Saint Peter?," *Classics Ireland* 3: 18-46.

Damaskos, D., and D. Plantzos, eds. (2008) *A Singular Antiquity: Archaeology and Hellenic Identity in Twentieth-Century Greece*. Athens.

D'Andria, F. (2003) *Hierapolis di Frigia (Pamukkale): Guida Archeologica*. Istanbul.

——— (2011-12) "Il santuario e la tomba dell'apostolo Filippo a Hierapolis di Frigia," *RPAA* 84: 1-52.

Danforth, L. M. (1995) *The Macedonian Conflict: Ethnic Nationalism in a Transnational World*. Princeton.

——— (2010) "Ancient Macedonia, Alexander the Great and the star or sun of Vergina: national symbols and the conflict between Greece and the Republic of Macedonia," in Roisman and Worthington, eds., 572-98.

Daniel, G. (1975) *One Hundred and Fifty Years of Archaeology*, 2nd ed. London.

——— (1981) *A Short History of Archaeology*. London.

Darcque, P. (1981) "Les vestiges mycéniens découverts sous le Télestérion d'Eleusis," *BCH* 105: 593-605.

Daux, G. (1965) "Deux steles d'Acharne," in Χαριστήριον εἰς Ἀναστάσιον Κ. Ὀρλάνδον, vol. 1, 78-90. Athens.

Davis, G. M. (1952) "Was Peter buried in Rome?," *JBR* 20: 167-71.

de Boer, J., J. R. Hale, and J. Chanton (2001) "New evidence for the geological origins of the ancient Delphic oracle (Greece)," *Geology* 29: 707-10.

Degrassi, N. (1967) "La dimora di Augusto sul Palatino e la base di Sorrento," *AttiPontAcc* 38: 77-116.

de la Coste-Messelière, P. (1946) "Les Alcméonides à Delphes," *BCH* 70: 271-87.

Delivorrias, A. (1974) *Attische Giebelskulpteren und Akrotere des fünften Jahrhunderts*. Tübingen.

De Martino, F. (1972) *Storia della costituzione romana*, vol. 1, 2nd ed. Naples.

Demetriou, K. N. (2001) "Historians on Macedonian imperialism and Alexander the Great," *JMGS* 19: 23–60.

De Rossi, G. B. (1864) *La Roma sotterranea cristiana*, vol. 1. Rome.

De Sanctis, G. (1956) *Storia dei Romani*, vol. 1, 2nd ed. Florence.

De Simone, C. (2006) "I nomi Romolo e Remo come etruschi," in Carandini, ed., 455–68.

Dialismas, A. (2004) "The Aegean melting pot: history and archaeology for historians and prehistorians," in Sauer, ed., 62–75.

Dickinson, O. (2005) "The face of Agamemnon," *Hesperia* 74: 299–308.

Dijkstra, J., J. Kroesen, and Y. Kuiper, eds. (2010) *Myths, Martyrs, and Modernity: Studies in the History of Religions in Honour of Jan N. Bremmer*. Leiden.

Dinsmoor, W. B. (1932) "The burning of the opisthodomos at Athens," *AJA* 36: 143–72, 307–26.

——— (1940) "The temple of Ares at Athens," *Hesperia* 9: 1–52.

——— (1947) "The Hekatompedon on the Athenian acropolis," *AJA* 51: 109–51.

Docter, R., and E. Moormann, eds. (1999) *Classical Archaeology Towards the Third Millennium: Reflections and Perspectives; Proceedings of the XVth International Congress of Classical Archaeology, Amsterdam, July 12–17, 1998*. Amsterdam.

Dodds, E. R. (1951) *The Greeks and the Irrational*. Berkeley.

Dorion, L.-A. (2011) "The rise and fall of the Socratic problem," in Morrison, ed., 1–23.

Dörpfeld, W. (1885) "Der alte Athena-Tempel auf der Akropolis zu Athen," *MDAI(A)* 10: 275–77.

——— (1887) "Der alte Athenatempel auf der Akropolis II," *MDAI(A)* 12: 25–61.

Dougherty, C., and L. Kurke, eds. (2003) *The Cultures within Ancient Greek Culture: Contact, Conflict, Collaboration*. Cambridge.

Dow, S. (1942) "Studies in the Athenian Tribute Lists I," *CPh* 37: 371–84.

——— (1943) "Studies in the Athenian Tribute Lists II," *CPh* 38: 20–27.

Drerup, H. (1985) "Das sogenannte Daphnephoreion in Eretria," in Braun and Furtwängler, eds., 3–21.

Drews, R. R. (1993) *Basileus: The Evidence for Kingship in Geometric Greece*. New Haven.

Drougou, S. (2005) Βεργίνα· Τα πήλινα αγγεία της Μεγάλης Τούμπας. Athens.

——— (2006) "Περίπατος στον τόπο και το χρόνο," in Drougou and Saatsoglou-Paliadeli, eds., 96–207.

——— (2011) "Vergina—the ancient city of Aegae," in Lane Fox, ed., 243–56.

Drougou, S., and C. Saatsoglou-Paliadeli, eds. (2006) Βεργίνα· ο τόπος και η ιστορία του. Athens.

——— (2008) *Vergina: Wandering through the Archaeological Site*. Athens.

Drummond, A. (1978) "Some observations on the order of consuls' names," *Athenaeum* 56: 80–108.

Duchesne, L. (1886) *Le Liber Pontificalis: texte, introduction et commentaire*. Paris.

——— (1923) "La Memoria Apostolorum de la Via Appia," *AttiPontAcc (Memorie)* 1: 1–22.

Ducrey, P. (1993) *Eretria*, vol. 7: *Le quartier de la maison aux mosaïques*. Lausanne.

——— (2004) *Eretria: A Guide to the Ancient City*. Fribourg.

Dyson, S. L. (1981) "A classical archaeologist's response to 'New Archaeology,'" *BASOR* 242: 7–13.

——— (1993) "From New to New Age Archaeology: archaeological theory and classical archaeology—a 1990s perspective," *AJA* 97: 195–206.

——— (1998) *Ancient Marbles to American Shores: Classical Archaeology in the United States*. Philadelphia.

——— (2006) *In Pursuit of Ancient Pasts: A History of Classical Archaeology in the Nineteenth and Twentieth Centuries*. New Haven.

Easterling, P., and J. Muir, eds. (1985) *Greek Religion and Society*. Cambridge.

Eddy, S. K. (1970) "On the Peace of Callias," *CPh* 65: 8–14.

Eisner, R. (1991) *Travelers to an Antique Land: The History and Literature of Travel to Greece*. Ann Arbor.

Elliott, J. K., ed. (1993) *The Apocryphal New Testament: A Collection of Apocryphal Christian Literature in an English Translation based on M. R. James*. Oxford.

Erbes, C. (1901) "Petrus nicht in Rom, sondern in Jerusalem gestorben," *ZKG* 22: 1–47, 161–231.

Erdkamp, P., ed. (2007) *A Companion to the Roman Army*. Malden.

Etienne, R., C. Müller, and F. Prost (2000) *Archéologie historique de la Grèce antique*. Paris.

Etiope, G., G. Papatheodorou, D. Christodoulou, M. Geraga, and P. Favali (2006) "The geological links of the ancient Delphic Oracle (Greece): a reappraisal of natural gas occurrence and origin," *Geology* 34: 821–24.

Evans, N. A. (2002) "Sanctuaries, sacrifices, and the Eleusinian mysteries," *Numen* 49: 227–54.

Evans-Pritchard, E. E. (1937) *Witchcraft, Oracles and Magic among the Azande*. Oxford.

Fagan, B. M. (2005) *A Brief History of Archaeology: Classical Times to the Twenty-First Century*. Upper Saddle River.

Faklaris, P. B. (1994) "Aegae: determining the site of the first capital of the Macedonians," *AJA* 98: 609–16.

Fantalkin, A., I. Finkelstein, and E. Piasetzky (2011) "Iron

Age Mediterranean chronology: a rejoinder," *Radiocarbon* 53: 179-98.

Farnell, L. R. (1907) *The Cults of the Greek States*, vol. 4. Oxford.

Feeney, D. (2007) *Caesar's Calendar: Ancient Time and the Beginnings of History*. Berkeley.

Fentress, E., and A. Guidi (1999) "Myth, memory and archaeology as historical sources," *Antiquity* 73: 463-66.

Ferrari, G. (2002) "The ancient temple on the acropolis at Athens," *AJA* 106: 11-35.

Figueira, T. J., and G. Nagy, eds. (2005) *Theognis of Megara: Poetry and the Polis*. Baltimore.

Filippi, D, (2004) "La domus Regia," *WACPCR* 1: 101-21.

——— (2005) "Il Velabro e le origini del Foro," *WACPCR* 2: 93-115.

Finegan, J. (1981) *The Archeology of the New Testament: The Mediterranean World of the Early Christian Apostles*. Boulder.

Finley, M. I. (1975) *The Use and Abuse of History*. London.

——— (1985) *Ancient History: Evidence and Models*. London.

Fischer, B., and V. Fiala, eds. (1952) *Colligere Fragmenta: Festschrift Alban Dold zum 70. Geburtstag am 7.7.1952*. Beuron in Hohenzollern.

Fisher, N., and H. van Wees, eds. (1998) *Archaic Greece: New Approaches and New Evidence*. London.

Fitzmyer, J. A. (1966) "The Phoenician inscription from Pyrgi," *JAOS* 86: 285-97.

Flannery, K. V. (1973) "Archaeology with a capital 'S,'" in Redman, ed., 47-53.

Flannery, K. V., and E. J. Marcus (1993) "Cognitive archaeology," *CAJ* 3: 260-70.

Fontenrose, J. E. (1978) *The Delphic Oracle: Its Responses and Operations, with a Catalogue of Responses*. Berkeley.

Forrest, W. G. F. (1957) "Colonisation and the rise of Delphi," *Historia* 6: 160-75.

Forsberg, S. (1995) *Near Eastern Destruction Datings as Sources for Greek and Near Eastern Iron Age Chronology: Archaeological and Historical Studies; The Cases of Samaria (722 BC) and Tarsus (696 BC)*. Uppsala.

Forsythe, G. (2005) *A Critical History of Early Rome from Prehistory to the First Punic War*. Berkeley.

——— (2007) "The army and centuriate organization in early Rome," in Erdkamp, ed., 21-41.

Foxhall, L. (2004) "Field sports: engaging Greek archaeology and history," in Sauer, ed., 76-84.

Fraccaro, P. (1931) "La storia dell'antichissimo esercito romano e l'età dell'ordinamento centuriato," in *Atti II Congresso nazionale di studi romani*, vol. 3, 91-97.

——— (1957) "The history of Rome in the Regal Period," *JRS* 47: 59-65.

Francis, E. D., and M. Vickers (1983) "*Signae priscae artis*: Eretria and Siphnos," *JHS* 103: 49-67.

Frank, T. (1924) *Roman Buildings of the Republic: An Attempt to Date Them from Their Materials*, Papers and Monographs of the American Academy in Rome 3. Rome.

Frederiksen, M. (1984) *Campania*. London.

Frederiksen, R. (2011) *Greek City Walls of the Archaic Period, 900-480 BC*. Oxford.

Fredricksmeyer, E. A. (1981) "Again the so-called tomb of Philip II," *AJA* 85: 330-34.

Fridh, A. (1987) "Three notes on Roman toponymy and topography," *Eranos* 85: 115-33.

Frier, B. W. (1999) *Libri Annales Pontificum Maximorum: The Origins of the Annalistic Tradition*, 2nd ed. Ann Arbor.

Fromentin, V., S. Gotteland, and P. Payen, eds. (2010) *Ombres de Thucydide: la reception de l'historien depuis l'Antiquité jusqu'au début du XXe siècle*. Bordeaux.

Gabba, E. (1997) "Review of T. P. Wiseman, *Remus*," *Athenaeum* 85: 308-9.

——— (2000) *Roma arcaica: storia e storiografia*. Rome.

Galanakis, Y. (2011) "Aegae: 160 years of archaeological research," in Kottaridi and Walker, eds., 49-58.

Galinsky, K. (1969) *Aeneas, Sicily, and Rome*. Princeton.

Gallant, T. W. (2001) *Modern Greece*. New York.

Gallia, A. (2007) "Reassessing the 'Cumaean Chronicle': Greek chronology and Roman history in Dionysius of Halicarnassus," *JRS* 97: 50-67.

Gelsomino, R. (1975) *Varrone e i sette colli di Roma*. Rome.

Gerhard, E. (1850) "Archäologischen Thesen," *AA* 8: 203-6.

Gill, C. (1973) "The death of Socrates," *CQ* 23: 25-28. Reprinted in Brickhouse and Smith, eds., 251-55.

Gill, D. W. J. (2008) "Inscribed silver plate from Tomb II at Vergina: chronological implications," *Hesperia* 77: 335-58.

Ginouvès, R. (1962) *Balaneutike: Recherches sur le bain dans l'antiquité grecque*. Paris.

Ginouvès, R., ed. (1994) *Macedonia: From Philip II to the Roman Conquest*. Princeton.

Gjerstad, E. (1953) *Early Rome*, vol. 1: *Stratigraphical Researches in the Forum Romanum and Along the Via Sacra*. Lund.

——— (1954) "The fortifications of Early Rome," *ORom* 1: 50-65.

——— (1960) *Early Rome*, vol. 3: *Fortifications, Domestic Architecture, Sanctuaries, Stratigraphic Excavations*. Lund.

——— (1965) "Cultural history of Early Rome: summary of archaeological evidence," *ActaArch.* 36: 1-41.

——— (1966) *Early Rome*, vol. 4: *Synthesis of Archaeological Evidence*. Lund.

——— (1967) "The origins of the Roman Republic," in *Les origines de la république romaine*, Fondation Hardt Entretiens 13, 3-30. Geneva.

——— (1973) *Early Rome*, vol. 6: *Historical Survey*. Lund.

Goldman, N. (2001) "Roman footwear," in Sebesta and Bonfante, eds., 101-30.

Gomme, A. W. (1945) *Historical Commentary on Thucydides*, vol. 1. Oxford.

Goulet, R. (1997) "Trois cordonniers philosophes," in Joyal, ed., 119–25.

Grafton, A. (1993) *Joseph Scaliger: A Study in the History of Classical Scholarship*, vol. 2. Oxford.

Grandazzi, A. (1997) *The Foundation of Rome: Myth and History*, trans. J. M. Todd. Ithaca.

Graves, B. M., G. M Graves, A. K. Tsakopoulos, and J. P. Anton (1991) "Hemlock poisoning: twentieth century scientific light shed on the death of Socrates," in Boudouris, ed., 156–68.

Green, P. (1982) "The royal tombs at Vergina: a historical analysis," in Adams and Borza, eds., 129–51.

——— (1989) *Classical Bearings: Interpreting Ancient History and Culture*. Berkeley.

——— (1991) *Alexander of Macedon, 356–323 BC: A Historical Biography*. Berkeley.

Greene, K. (1986) *The Archaeology of the Roman Economy*. London.

Greene, K., and T. Moore (2010) *Archaeology: An Introduction*, 5th ed. Abingdon.

Greenwalt, W. (1994) "The production of coinage from Archelaus to Perdiccas III and the evolution of Argead Macedonia," in Worthington, ed., 105–34.

——— (1999) "Why Pella?," *Historia* 48: 158–83.

Gruen, E. (1992) *Culture and National Identity in Republican Rome*. Ithaca.

Gruen, E., ed. (2005) *Cultural Borrowings and Ethnic Appropriations in Antiquity*. Stuttgart.

Guarducci, M. (1958) *I graffiti sotto la confessione di San Pietro in Vaticano*, 3 vols. Vatican City.

——— (1960) *The Tomb of St. Peter: The New Discoveries in the Sacred Grottoes of the Vatican*, trans. J. McLellan. New York.

——— (1965) *Le reliquie di Pietro sotto la confessione della basilica vaticana*. Vatican City.

Guimier-Sorbets, A.-M., and Y. Morizot (2006) "Construire l'identité du mort: l'architecture funéraire en Macédoine," in Guimier-Sorbets, Hatzopoulos, and Morizot, eds., 117–29.

Guimier-Sorbets, A.-M., M. B. Hatzopoulos, and Y. Morizot, eds. (2006) *Rois, cités, necropolis: institutions, rites et monuments en Macédoine*. Athens.

Gurval, R. A. (1995) *Actium and Augustus: The Politics and Emotions of Civil War*. Ann Arbor.

Gusberti, E. (2005a) "Il deposito votivo capitolino," *WACPCR* 2: 151–55.

——— (2005b) "Il centro abitato dei *Quiriti* e lo spazio della prima Roma," *WACPCR* 2: 169–72.

Guthrie, W. K. C. (1971) *Socrates*. Cambridge.

Habicht, C. (1961) "Falsche Urkunden zur Geschichte Athens im Zeitalter der Perserkriege," *Hermes* 89: 1–35.

Hafner, G. (1992) "Die beim Apollotempel in Rom gefundenen griechischen Skulpturen," *JDAI* 107: 17–32.

Hale, J. R., J. Z. de Boer, J. P. Chanton, and H. A. Spiller (2003) "Questioning the Delphic Oracle," *Scientific American* 289: 67–73.

Hall, J. M. (1991) "Practising postprocessualism? Classics and archaeological theory," *ARC* 10: 155–63.

——— (1997) *Ethnic Identity in Greek Antiquity*. Cambridge.

——— (2001) "Contested ethnicities: perceptions of Macedonia within evolving definitions of Greek identity," in Malkin, ed., 159–86.

——— (2002) *Hellenicity: Between Ethnicity and Culture*. Chicago.

——— (2004) "Culture, cultures and acculturation," in Röllinger and Ulf, eds., 35–50.

——— (2005) "*Arcades his oris*: Greek projections on the Italian ethnoscape?," in Gruen, ed., 259–84.

——— (2007) "Politics and Greek myth," in Woodard, ed., 331–54.

——— (2008) "Foundation stories," in Tsetskhladze, ed., 383–426.

——— (2014) *A History of the Archaic Greek World ca. 1200–479 BCE*, 2nd ed. Chichester.

Hamilakis, Y. (2007) *The Nation and Its Ruins: Antiquity, Archaeology, and National Imagination in Greece*. Oxford.

Hammond, N. G. L. (1970) "The archaeological background to the Macedonian kingdom," *Ancient Macedonia*, vol. 1, 53–67. Thessaloniki.

——— (1972) *A History of Macedonia*, vol. 1. Oxford.

——— (1978) "'Philip's tomb' in historical context," *GRBS* 19: 331–50.

——— (1979) *A History of Macedonia*, vol. 2 (with G. T. Griffith). Oxford.

——— (1982) "The evidence for the identity of the royal tombs at Vergina," in Adams and Borza, eds., 111–27.

——— (1983) *Venture into Greece: With the Guerillas, 1943–4*. London.

——— (1991) "The royal tombs at Vergina: evolution and identities," *ABSA* 86: 69–82.

Hanell, K. (1946) *Das altrömische eponyme Amt*. Lund.

Hansen, M. H. (1991) *The Athenian Democracy in the Age of Demosthenes: Structure, Principles and Ideology*. Oxford.

Hansen, M. H., ed. (1995) *Sources for the Ancient Greek City-State*, Acts of the Copenhagen Polis Centre 2. Copenhagen.

——— (2000) *A Comparative Study of Thirty City-State Cultures: An Investigation Conducted by the Copenhagen Polis Centre*. Copenhagen.

Hansen, M. H., and T. H. Nielsen, eds. (2004) *An Inventory of Archaic and Classical Poleis*. Oxford.

Harris, W. V. (2001) Review of Steinby's *LTUR* III and IV, *JRA* 14: 539–46.

Hartog, F. (2009) "The double fate of the classics," in Chandler and Davidson, eds., 964–79.

Hatzopoulos, M. B. (1996) "Aigéai: la localisation de la première capitale macédonienne," *REG* 109: 264–69.

——— (2008) "The burial of the dead (at Vergina) or the undending controversy on the identity of the occupants of Tomb II," *Tekmeria* 9: 91–118.

Hatzopoulos, M. B., and P. Paschidis (2004) "Makedonia," in Hansen and Nielsen, eds., 794–809.

Hayashi, T. (1992) *Bedeutung und Wandel des Triptolemosbildes vom 6.–4.Jhr. v. Chr.* Würzburg.

Heid, S. (2007) "The Romanness of Roman Christianity," in Rüpke, ed., 406–26.

Heiken, G., R. Funiciello, and D. De Rita (2005) *The Seven Hills of Rome: A Geological Tour of the Eternal City.* Princeton.

Heilmeyer, W.-D. (1981) "Antike Werkstättenfunde in Griechenland," *AA*, pp. 440–53.

Heurgon, J. (1966) "The inscriptions of Pyrgi," *JRS* 56: 1–15.

——— (1973) *The Rise of Rome to 264 BCE.* Berkeley.

Higgins, M. D., and R. Higgins (1996) *A Geological Companion to Greece and the Aegean.* Ithaca.

Hill, B. H. (1912) "The older Parthenon," *AJA* 16: 535–38.

Hinard, F. (1985) *Les proscriptions de la Rome républicaine*, Collections de l'École Française de Rome 83. Paris.

Hitchens, C. (1987) *The Elgin Marbles: Should They Be Returned to Greece?* (with essays by R. Browning and G. Binns). London.

Hock, R. F. (1976) "Simon the shoemaker as an ideal cynic," *GRBS* 17: 41–53.

Hodder, I. (1991) *Reading the Past: Current Approaches to Interpretation in Archaeology*, 2nd ed. Cambridge.

——— (2001) "Introduction: a review of contemporary theoretical debates in archaeology," in Hodder, ed., 1–13.

Hodder, I., ed. (2001) *Archaeological Theory Today.* Cambridge.

Hodder, I., M. Shanks, A. Alexandri, V. Buchli, J. Carman, J. Last, and G. Lucas, eds. (1995) *Interpreting Archaeology: Finding Meaning in the Past.* London.

Holland, L. A. (1953) "Septimontium or Saeptimontium?," *TAPhA* 84: 16–34.

Holloway, R. R. (1994) *The Archaeology of Early Rome and Latium.* London.

Hölscher, T. (1988) "Historische Reliefs," in *Kaiser Augustus und die verlorene Republik*, 351–400. Berlin.

Homolle, T. (1896) "La temple delphique du IVe siècle," *BCH* 20: 677–701.

Hopkins, J. N. (2012) "The Capitoline Temple and the effects of monumentality on Roman temple design," in Thomas and Meyers, eds., 111–38.

Hornblower, S. (1991) *A Commentary on Thucydides*, vol. 1. Oxford.

Horsfall, N. (1979) "Some problems in the Aeneas legend," *CQ* 29: 372–90.

Huber, S. (2003) *Eretria*, vol. 14: *L'aire sacrificielle au nord du sanctuaire d'Apollon Daphnéphoros: un rituel des époques géométrique et archaïque.* Gollion.

Hughes, B. (2010) *The Hemlock Cup: Socrates, Athens and the Search for the Good Life.* London.

Humboldt, W. von (1903) *Wilhelm von Humboldts gesammelte Schriften*, vol. 1. Berlin.

Hunter, V. (1997) "The prison of Athens: a comparative perspective," *Phoenix* 51: 296–326.

Hurwit, J. M. (1985) *The Art and Culture of Early Greece, 1100–480 BC.* Ithaca.

——— (1999) *The Athenian Acropolis: History, Mythology, and Archaeology from the Neolithic Era to the Present.* Cambridge.

——— (2004) *The Acropolis in the Age of Pericles.* Cambridge.

Huxley, G. (1958) "Argos et les derniers Téménides," *BCH* 82: 588–601.

Iacopi, I. (1995a) "Domus: Livia," in Steinby, ed., 130–32.

——— (1995b) "Domus: Augustus (Palatium)," in Steinby, ed., 46–48.

——— (2008) *The House of Augustus Wall Paintings*, trans. J. Scott. Milan.

Iacopi, I., and G. Tedone (2006) "Bibliotheca e Porticus ad Apollinis," *MDAI (R)* 112: 351–78.

Ignatieff, M. (1978) *A Just Measure of Pain: The Penitentiary in the Industrial Revolution, 1750–1850.* New York.

Ismaelli, T. (2009) "Il *monopteros* del santuario di Apollo a Hierapolis di Frigia," *IstMitt* 59: 131–92.

Jacoby, F. (1954a) *Die Fragmente der griechischen Historiker*, vol. 3B, suppl. 1. Leiden.

——— (1954b) *Die Fragmente der griechischen Historiker*, vol. 3B, suppl. 2. Leiden.

Jameson, M. H. (1960) "A decree of Themistokles from Troizen," *Hesperia* 29: 198–223.

Jameson, M. H., C. N. Runnels, and T. H. Van Andel (1994) *A Greek Countryside: The Southern Argolid from Prehistory to the Present Day.* Stanford.

Janko, R. (1982) *Homer, Hesiod and the Hymns: Diachronic Development in Epic Diction.* Cambridge.

Johnson, M. (2010) *Archaeological Theory: An Introduction*, 2nd ed. Malden.

Johnston, S. I. (2008) *Ancient Greek Divination.* Malden.

Joyal, M., ed. (1997) *Studies in Plato and the Platonic Tradition.* Aldershot.

Kahil, L. (1980) "Contribution à l'étude de l'Erétrie géométrique," in ΣΤΗΛΗ· τόμος εις μνήμην Νικολάου Κοντολεόντος, 525–31. Athens.

——— (1981) "Erétrie à l'époque géométrique," *ASAA* 59: 165–73.

Kahn, C. H. (1996) *Plato and the Socratic Dialogue.* Cambridge.

Kaldellis, A. (2009) *The Christian Parthenon: Classicism and Pilgrimage in Byzantine Athens*. Cambridge.

Kallet, L. (2003) "Dēmos tyrannos: wealth, power, and economic patronage," in Morgan, ed., 117–44.

Karakasidou, A. N. (1997) *Fields of Wheat, Hills of Blood: Passages to Nationhood in Greek Macedonia, 1870–1990*. Chicago.

Karamitrou-Mentessidi, S. A. (2008) *Aiani: A Guide to the Archaeological Sites and the Museum*. Aiani-Kozani.

——— (2011) "Aiani: historical and geographical context," in Lane-Fox, ed., 93–112.

Kaschnitz-Weinberg, G. von (1962) *Die Grundlagen der republikanischen Baukunst*. Reinbek.

Keller, D. R., and D. W. Rupp, eds. (1983) *Archaeological Survey in the Mediterranean Area*, BAR International Series 155. London.

Kellum, B. (2009) "Review of J. Elsner, *Roman Eyes: Visuality and Subjectivity in Art and Text*," *ArtB* 91: 107–10.

Kelly, T. (1976) *A History of Argos to 500 BC*. Minnesota.

Kindt. J. (2006) "Delphic oracle stories and the beginning of historiography: Herodotus' *Croesus Logos*," *CPh* 101: 34–51.

Kirschbaum, E. (1957) *The Tombs of St Peter and St Paul*, trans. J. Murray. New York.

Klauck, H.-J. (2008) *The Apocryphal Acts of the Apostles: An Introduction*, trans. B. McNeil. Waco.

Knigge, U. (1991) *The Athenian Kerameikos: History, Monuments, Excavations*, trans. J. Binder. Athens.

Koïv, M. (2000) "The dating of Pheidon in antiquity," *SHT* 1: 1–21.

——— (2003) *Ancient Tradition and Early Greek History: The Origins of States in Early-Archaic Sparta, Argos and Corinth*. Tallinn.

Kölb, R. (1995) *Rom: Die Geschichte der Stadt in der Antike*. Munich.

Koliopoulos, J. S., and T. M. Veremis (2002) *Greece: The Modern Sequel From 1821 to the Present*. New York.

Konstan, D. (2011) "Socrates in Aristophanes' *Clouds*," in Morrison, ed., 75–90.

Konstantinou, J. (1954–55) "Aus dem Eretriagiebel," *MDAI(A)* 69–70: 41–44.

Kottaridi, A. (1999) "Βασιλικές πυρές στη νεκρόπολη των Αιγών," *Ancient Macedonia*, vol. 6, 631–42. Thessaloniki.

——— (2002) "Discovering Aegae, the old Macedonian capital," in Stamatopoulou and Yeroulanou, eds., 75–81.

——— (2004) "Η ανασκαφή της ΙΖ' ΕΠΚΑ στην πόλη και στη νεκρόπολη των Αιγών το 2003-4; νέα στοιχεία για τη βασιλική ταφική συστάδα της Ευρυδίκης και το τείχος της αρχαίας πόλης," *AEMT* 18: 527–42.

——— (2006) "Couleur et signification: l'usage de la couleur dans la tombe de la reine Eurydice," in Guimier-Sorbets, Hatzopoulos, and Morizot, eds., 155–68.

——— (2011a) "Burial customs and beliefs in the royal necropolis of Aegae," in Kottaridi and Walker, eds., 131–52.

——— (2011b) "Aegae: the Macedonian metropolis" in Kottaridi and Walker, eds., 153–66.

——— (2011c) "Appendix: the palace of Philip II in Aegae," in Kottaridi and Walker, eds., 233–36.

——— (2011d) "The palace of Aegae," in Lane Fox, ed., 297–333.

Kottaridi, A., and S. Walker, eds. (2011) *Heracles to Alexander the Great: Treasures from the Royal Capital of Macedon, a Hellenic Kingdom in the Age of Democracy*. Oxford.

Koumanoudis, S. N. (1984) "Perhaps > usually > certainly" [in Greek], *Horos* 2: 71–81.

Kourouniotis, K. (1900) "Ἀνασκαφαὶ ἐν Ἐρετρίᾳ," *Praktika*, 53–56.

——— (1935) "Das eleusinische Heiligtum von den Anfängen bis zur vorperikleischen Zeit," *ArchRel* 32: 52–78.

Kremydi, S. (2011) "Macedonian coinage before Alexander," in Kottaridi and Walker, eds., 205–8.

Krentz, P. (2007) "The oath of Marathon, not Plataia?," *Hesperia* 76: 731–42.

Kuniholm, P. I. (2001) "Dendrochronology and other applications of tree-ring studies in archaeology," in Brothwell and Pollard, eds, 35–46.

Lane Fox, R. J. (2011a) "Macedon, c. 650–336 BC," in Kottaridi and Walker, eds., 25–38.

——— (2011b) "Introduction: dating the royal tombs at Vergina," in Lane Fox, ed., 1–34.

Lane Fox, R. J., ed. (2011) *Brill's Companion to Ancient Macedon: Studies in the Archaeology and History of Macedon, 650 BC–300 AD*. Leiden.

Lang, M. L. (1978) *Socrates in the Agora*, Excavations of the Athenian Agora Picture Book No. 17. Princeton.

——— (1990) *The Athenian Agora: Results of Excavations Conducted by the American School of Classical Studies at Athens*, vol. 25: *Ostraka*. Princeton.

Langdon, M. (2005) "A new Greek abecedarium," *Kadmos* 44: 175–82.

Lape, S. (2010) *Race and Citizen Identity in the Classical Athenian Democracy*. Cambridge.

La Rocca, E. (1974–75) "Due tombe dall'Esquilino: alcune novità sul commercio euboico in Italia centrale nell'VIII sec.a.C." *DArch* 8: 86–103.

——— (1977) "Note sulle importazioni greche in territorio laziale nell'VIII secolo a.C.," *PP* 32: 375–97.

——— (1985) *Amazzonomachia: le sculture frontonali del tempio di Apollo Sosiano*. Rome.

——— (1988) "Die Giebelskulpturen des Apollo-Sosianus-Tempels in Rom," *Gymnasium* 95: 129–40.

Laurence, R. (2012) *Roman Archaeology for Historians*. Abingdon.

Lauro, C., and G. C. Negretti (1965) "Risultato dell'analisi petrografico dei campioni di terra," in Guarducci, 169–81.

Lavelle, B. M. (2005) *Fame, Money, and Power: The Rise of Pei-sistratos and "Democratic" Tyranny at Athens*. Ann Arbor.

Lawall, M. L. (2009) "The temple of Apollo Patroos dated by an amphora stamp," *Hesperia* 78: 387-403.

Leach, E. (1977) "A view from the bridge," in Spriggs, ed., 161-76.

Lehmann, P. (1980) "The so-called tomb of Philip II: a different interpretation," *AJA* 84: 527-31.

———— (1982) "The so-called tomb of Philip II: an addendum," *AJA* 86: 437-42.

Lietzmann, H. (1927) *Petrus und Paulus in Rom: liturgische und archäologische Studien*, 2nd ed. Berlin.

Lloyd, J., and G. Barker (1981) "Rural settlement in Roman Molise: problems of archaeological survey," in Barker and Hodges, eds., 289-304.

Lønstrup, G. (2008) "Constructing myths: the foundation of Roma Christiana on 29 June," *AnalRom* 33: 27-64.

Lord, L. (1947) *A History of the American School of Classical Studies at Athens, 1882-1942*. Cambridge, MA.

Lugli, G. (1946) *Roma antica: Il centro monumentale*. Rome.

Luther, A., M. Meier, and L. Thommen, eds. (2006) *Das frühe Sparta*. Stuttgart.

MacDonald, B. R. (1982) "The authenticity of the Congress Decree," *Historia* 31: 120-23.

MacDowell, D. M. (1971) *Aristophanes Wasps*. Oxford.

MacGillivray, J. A. (2000) *Minotaur: Sir Arthur Evans and the Archaeology of the Minoan Myth*. New York.

MacKendrick, P. (1962) *The Mute Stones Speak: The Story of Archaeology in Italy*. London.

———— (1981) *The Greek Stones Speak: The Story of Archaeology in Greek Lands*, 2nd ed. New York.

MacMullen, R. (2010) "Christian ancestor worship in Rome." *JBL* 129: 597-613.

Malkin, I. (1998) *The Returns of Odysseus: Colonization and Ethnicity*. Berkeley.

Malkin, I., ed. (2001) *Ancient Perceptions of Greek Ethnicity*. Washington DC.

Mallwitz, A., and W. Schiering (1964) *Olympische Forschungen*, vol. 5: *Die Werkstatt des Pheidias in Olympia*. Berlin.

Manacorda, D., and R. Tamassia (1985) *Il piccone del regime*. Rome.

Manning, S., B. Kromer, P. I. Kuniholm, and M. W. Newton (2001) "Anatolian tree rings and a new chronology for the East Mediterranean Bronze-Iron Ages," *Science* 294: 2532-35.

Manning, S. W., C. B. Ramsey, W. Kutschera, T. F. G. Higham, B. Kromer, P. Steier, and E. M. Wild (2006) "Chronology for the Aegean Late Bronze Age 1700-1400 BC," *Science* 312: 565-69.

Manoledakis, M., and E. Livieratos (2007) "On the digital placement of Aegae, the first capital of ancient Mace-donia, according to Ptolemy's *Geographia*," *e-Perimetron* 2: 31-41.

Marchand, S. L. (1996) *Down from Olympus: Archaeology and Philhellenism in Germany, 1750-1970*. Princeton.

———— (2007) "From antiquarian to archaeologist? Adolf Furtwängler and the problem of 'modern' classical archaeology," in Miller, ed., 248-85.

Marec, E., and H. G. Pflaum (1952) "Nouvelle inscription sur la carrière de Suétone, l'historien," *CRAI*, 76-85.

Marinatos, N., and R. Hägg, eds. (1993) *Greek Sanctuaries: New Approaches*. London.

Mark, I. S. (1993) *The Sanctuary of Athena Nike in Athens: Architectural Stages and Chronology*, AIA Monographs, n.s. 2; *Hesperia* suppl. 26. Princeton.

Mastrocinque, A. (1983) "La cacciata di Tarquinio il Superbo: tradizione romana e letteratura greca," *Athenaeum* 61: 457-80.

Mattingly, H. B. (1961) "The Athenian coinage decree," *Historia* 10: 148-88.

———— (1965) "The Peace of Kallias," *Historia* 14: 273-81.

Maurizio, L. (1995) "Anthropology and spirit possession: a reconsideration of the Pythia's role at Delphi," *JHS* 115: 69-86.

———— (1997) "Delphic oracles as oral performances: authenticity and historical evidence," *ClAnt* 16: 308-34.

Mayer, E. (2012) *The Ancient Middle Classes: Urban Life, Economics, and a New Aesthetic in the Roman Empire, 100 BCE-250 CE*. Cambridge, MA.

Mazarakis-Ainian, A. (1987) "Geometric Eretria," *AK* 30: 3-24.

Mazzarino, S. (1945) *Dalla monarchia alla stato repubblicano: Ricerche di storia romana arcaica*. Catania.

Mazzei, P. (2007) "L'area archeologica della Protomoteca in Campidoglio: Ricognizione preliminare e lettura della documentazione attuale come premessa al rilievo delle strutture," *BollArch* 108: 145-93.

McDonald, W. A., and G. R. Rapp, eds. (1972) *The Minnesota Messenia Expedition: Reconstructing a Bronze Age Regional Environment*. Minneapolis.

McDonald, W. A., and C. A. Thomas (1990) *Progress into the Past: The Rediscovery of Mycenaean Civilization*, 2nd ed. Bloomington, IN.

McKinley, J. I., and J. M. Bond (2001) "Cremated bone," in Brothwell and Pollard, eds., 281-92.

Medwid, L. (2000) *The Makers of Classical Archaeology*. Amherst.

Meiggs, R. (1972) *The Athenian Empire*. Oxford.

Meritt, B. D., H. T. Wade-Gery, and M. F. McGregor (1939) *The Athenian Tribute Lists*, vol. 1. Cambridge MA.

Meyer, J. C. (1980) "Roman history in the light of the import of Attic vases to Rome and South Etruria in the 6th and 5th centuries BC," *AnalRom* 9: 47-68.

Miles, M. M. (1998) *The Athenian Agora: Results of Excavations*

Conducted by the American School of Classical Studies at Athens, vol. 31: *The City Eleusinion*. Princeton.

Miller, P. N., ed. (2007) *Momigliano and Antiquarianism: Foundations of the Modern Cultural Sciences*. Toronto.

Miller, Stella G. (1986) "Alexander's Funeral Cart," in *Ancient Macedonia*, vol. 4, 401-12. Thessaloniki.

Miller, Stephen G. (1995) "Architecture as evidence for the identity of the early *polis*," in Hansen, ed., 201-44.

Millett, M. (2012) "What is classical archaeology? Roman archaeology," in Alcock and Osborne, eds., 30-50.

Mohlberg, L. K. (1952) "Historisch-kritische Bemerkungen zum Ursprung der sogenannten 'Memoria Apostolorum' an der Appischen Strasse," in Fischer and Fiala, eds., 52-74.

Momigliano, A. (1963) "An interim report on the origins of Rome," *JRS* 53: 95-121.

––––– (1966a) *Studies in Historiography*. London.

––––– (1966b) *Terzo contributo alla storia degli studi classici e del mondo antico*. Rome.

––––– (1975) "La leggenda di Carano, re di Macedonia," in *Quinto contributo alla storia degli studi classici e del mondo antico*, 425-33. Rome.

––––– (1986) "The rise of the *plebs* in the Archaic age of Rome," in Raaflaub, ed., 175-97.

––––– (1989) *Roma arcaica*. Florence.

––––– (1994) *Studies on Modern Scholarship*, ed. G. W. Bowersock and T. J. Cornell. Berkeley.

Momigliano, A., and A. Schiavone, eds. (1988) *Storia di Roma*, vol. 1. Turin.

Mommsen, T. (1859) *Die römische Chronologie bis auf Caesar*, 2nd ed. Berlin.

Morgan, C. (1990) *Athletes and Oracles: The Transformation of Olympia and Delphi in the Eighth Century BC*. Cambridge.

Morgan, C., and T. Whitelaw (1992) "Pots and politics: ceramic evidence for the rise of the Argive state," *AJA* 95: 79-108.

Morgan, K., ed. (2003) *Popular Tyranny: Sovereignty and Its Discontents in Ancient Greece*. Austin.

Morley, N. (1999) *Writing Ancient History*. Ithaca.

Morris, I. (1986) "The use and abuse of Homer," *ClAnt* 5: 81-138.

––––– (1987) *Burial and Ancient Society: The Rise of the Greek City-State*. Cambridge.

––––– (1991) "The early polis as city and state," in Rich and Wallace-Hadrill, eds., 25-57.

––––– (1994) "Archaeologies of Greece," in Morris, ed., 8-47.

––––– (2004) "Classical archaeology," in Bintliff, ed., 253-71.

Morris, I., ed. (1994) *Classical Greece: Ancient Histories and Modern Ideologies*. Cambridge.

Morrison, D. R., ed. (2011) *The Cambridge Companion to Socrates*. Cambridge.

Moscati Castelnuovo, L., ed. (2002) *Identità e prassi storica nel Mediterraneo greco*. Milan.

Mosshammer, A. A. (1979) *The Chronicle of Eusebius and Greek Chronographic Tradition*. Lewisburg.

Müller-Karpe, H. (1962) *Zur Stadtwerdung Roms, MDAI(R)* 8. Heidelberg.

Murison, C. L. (1971) "The Peace of Callias: its historical context," *Phoenix* 25: 12-31.

Musgrave, J. H. (1991) "The human remains from Vergina Tombs I, II and III: an overview," *AncW* 22: 3-9.

Musgrave, J. H., R. A. H. Neave, and A. J. N. W. Prag (1984) "The skull from Tomb II at Vergina: King Philip II of Macedon," *JHS* 104: 60-78.

Musgrave, J. H., and A. J. N. W. Prag (2011) "The occupants of Tomb II at Vergina: why Arrhidaios and Eurydice must be excluded," in Kottaridi and Walker, eds., 127-30.

Musgrave, J. H., A. J. N. W. Prag, R. Neave, R. Lane Fox, and H. White (2010) "The occupants of Tomb II at Vergina: why Arrhidaios and Eurydice must be excluded," *IJMS* 7: 1-15.

Musti, D. (1990) "La tradizione storica sullo sviluppo di Roma fino all'età dei Tarquinii," in Cristofani, ed., 9-15.

Mylonas, G. E. (1961) *Eleusis and the Eleusinian Mysteries*. Princeton.

Mylonopoulos, J., and F. Bubenheimer (1996) "Beiträge zur Topographie des Artemision von Brauron," *AA*, pp. 7-23.

Nedergaard, E. (2001) "Facts and fiction about the Fasti Capitolini," *AnalRom* 27: 107-27.

Neer, R. T. (2003) "Framing the gift: the Siphnian Treasury at Delphi and the politics of architectural sculpture," in Dougherty and Kurke, eds., 129-49.

––––– (2010) *The Emergence of the Classical Style in Greek Sculpture*. Chicago.

Negri, S., and G. Leucci (2006) "Geophysical investigation of the temple of Apollo (Hierapolis, Turkey)," *JAS* 33: 1505-13.

Newton, M., K. A. Wardle, and P. I. Kuniholm (2003) "Dendrochronology and radiocarbon determinations from Assiros and the beginning of the Greek Iron Age," *AEMT* 17: 173-90.

Nieddu, A. M. (2009) *La Basilica Apostolorum sulla via Appia e l'area cimiteriale circostante*. Vatican City.

Nijboer, A. J. (2005) "The Iron Age in the Mediterranean: a chronological mess or 'trade before the flag,' part II," *AWE* 4: 254-77.

Nilsson, M. P. (1951) *Cults, Myths, Oracles and Politics in Ancient Greece*, Skrifter Utgivna av Svenska Institutet i Athen 8, no. 1. Lund.

Noack, F. (1927) *Eleusis: die baugeschichtliche Entwicklung des Heiligtumes*. Berlin.

Nora, P. (1996) "From *lieux de mémoire* to realms of memory," in Nora ed., xv-xxiv.

Nora, P., ed. (1996) *Realms of Memory: Rethinking the French Past*, vol. 1: *Conflicts and Divisions*, trans. A Goldhammer. New York.

Oakley, S. P. (1998) *A Commentary on Livy Books VI–X*, vol. 2. Oxford.

Ober, J. (1989) *Mass and Elite in Democratic Athens: Rhetoric, Ideology, and the Power of the People*. Princeton.

——— (2005) *Athenian Legacies: Essays on the Politics of Going On Together*. Princeton.

Ober, W. (1977) "Did Socrates die of hemlock poisoning?," *NYSJM* 77: 254–58.

O'Connor, D. W. (1969) *Peter in Rome: The Literary, Liturgical, and Archeological Evidence*. New York.

Ogilvie, R. M. (1976) *Early Rome and the Etruscans*. Glasgow.

Oliver, J. H. (1957) "The Peace of Callias and the Pontic expedition of Pericles," *Historia* 6: 254–55.

Oost, S. I. (1972) "Cypselus the Bacchiad," *CPh* 67: 10–30.

Oppé, A. P. (1904) "The chasm at Delphi," *JHS* 24: 214–40.

Osborne, M. J., and S. G. Byrne (1996) *The Foreign Residents of Athens: An Annex to the Lexicon of Greek Personal Names; Attica, Studia Hellenistica* 33. Leuven.

Osborne, R. (1987) "The viewing and obscuring of the Parthenon frieze," *JHS* 107: 98–105.

——— (1994) "Archaeology, the Salaminioi, and the politics of sacred space in archaic Attica," in Alcock and Osborne, eds., 143–60.

Osborne, R., and B. Cunliffe, eds. (2005) *Mediterranean Urbanization 800–600 B.C.*, Proceedings of the British Academy 126. Oxford.

Packer, J. (1989) "Urbanism and archaeology in 'Roma Capitale': a troubled past and a controversial future," *AJA* 93: 137–41.

Palagia, O. (2000) "Hephaestion's pyre and the royal hunt of Alexander," in Bosworth and Baynham, eds., 167–206.

——— (2005) "A new interpretation of Menander's image by Kephisodotos II and Timarchos," *ASAA* 83: 287–98.

——— (2008) "Underworld and royal hunt: the wall paintings from Tombs I and II," *Archaeological Institute of America: Abstracts of the 109th Annual Meeting*, 130.

Papadimitriou, J. (1959) "Βραυρών," *Ergon*, pp. 13–20.

Papadopoulos, J. K. (1996) "The original Kerameikos of Athens and the siting of the classical agora," *GRBS* 27: 107–28.

Papazoglou, F. (1957) *Makedonski gradovi u rimsko doba*. Skopje.

Papazois, T. (2002) *Ο βασιλικός τάφος της Βεργίνας αποκαλύπτει τον Μ. Αλέξανδρο*. Thessaloniki.

Parke, H. W., and D. E. W. Wormell (1956) *The Delphic Oracle*, vol. 1: *The History*. Oxford.

Parker, R. (1985) "Greek states and Greek oracles," in Cartledge and Harvey, eds., 298–326.

——— (1996) *Athenian Religion: A History*. Oxford.

Parslow, C. (1995) *Rediscovering Antiquity: Karl Weber and the Excavation of Herculaneum, Pompeii, and Stabiae*. Cambridge.

Paspalas, S. A. (2011) "Classical art," in Lane-Fox, ed., 179–207.

Pensabene, P. (1997) "Elementi architettonici dalla casa di Augusto sul Palatino," *MDAI(R)* 104: 149–92.

Perlman, S. (1976) "Panhellenism, the polis and imperialism," *Historia* 25: 1–30.

Perret, J. (1940) *Les origines de la légende troyenne de Rome (281–31)*. Paris.

Peterson, F. P. (1960) *Peter's Tomb Recently Discovered in Jerusalem*. Fort Wayne.

Petricioli, M. (1990) *Archeologia e Mare Nostrum: Le missioni archeologiche nella politica mediterranea dell'Italia 1898–1943*. Rome.

Petrounias, E. B. (2007) "The pronunciation of Classical Greek," in Christidis, ed., 556–70.

Pfann, S. (2007) "Has St. Peter returned to Jerusalem? the final resting place of Simon Peter and the family of Barzillai," http://www.uhl.ac/Lost_Tomb/ShimonBarzillai/.

Piccardi, L. (2000) "Active faulting at Delphi, Greece: seismotectonic remarks and a hypothesis for the geological environment of a myth," *Geology* 28: 651–64.

Piccardi, L., C. Monti, O. Vaselli, F. Tassi, K. Gaki-Papanastassiou, and D. Papanastassiou (2008) "Scent of a myth: tectonics, geochemistry and geomythology at Delphi (Greece)," *JGS* 165: 5–18.

Piggott, S. (1972) "Conclusion," in Ucko, Tringham, and Dimbleby, eds., 947–53.

Pinza, G. (1910) "Il tempio di Apollo Palatino," *BullCom* 38: 3–41.

Pisani Sartorio, G. (1995) "Fortuna e Mater Matuta, aedes," in Steinby, ed., 281–85.

Plommer, H. (1960) "The Archaic acropolis: some problems," *JHS* 35: 127–59.

Pollard, A. M. (2009) "Measuring the passage of time: achievements and challenges in archaeological dating," in Cunliffe, Gosden, and Joyce, eds., 145–68.

Pollitt, J. J. (1990) *The Art of Ancient Greece: Sources and Documents*, 2nd ed. Cambridge.

Popham, M. R., L. H Sackett, and P. G. Themelis (1980) *Lefkandi*, vol. 1: *The Iron Age*. London.

Post, R. (2009) "Debating disciplinarity," in Chandler and Davidson, eds., 749–70.

Potter, T. W. (1979) *The Changing Landscape of South Etruria*. London.

Prag, A. J. N. W. (1990) "Reconstructing Philip II: the 'nice' version," *AJA* 94: 237–47.

Prag, J., and R. Neave (1997) *Making Faces: Using Forensic and Archaeological Evidence*. London.

Preisshofen, F. (1977) "Zur Topographie der Akropolis," *JDAI* 92: 74–84.

Prestiani Giallombardo, A. M., and B. Tripodi (1980) "Le tombe regale di Vergina: quale Filippo?," *ASNSP* 10: 989–1001.

Price, S. (1985) "Delphi and divination," in Easterling and Muir, eds., 128–54.

Pritchett, W. K. (1953) "The Attic stelai: Part I," *Hesperia* 22: 225–99.

Purcell, N. (1997) "Review of T. P. Wiseman, *Remus: A Roman Myth*," *BMCRev* 97.5.18.

—— (2003) "Becoming historical: the Roman case," in Braund and Gill, eds., 12–40.

Raaflaub, K. (1986a) "The conflict of the orders in Archaic Rome: a comprehensive and comparative approach," in Raaflaub, ed., 1–51.

—— (1986b) "From protection and defense to offense and participation: stages in the conflict of the orders," in Raaflaub, ed., 198–243.

—— (1998) "A historian's headache? How to read 'Homeric Society,'" in Fisher and van Wees, eds., 169–93.

Raaflaub, K., ed. (1986) *Social Struggles in Archaic Rome: New Perspectives on the Conflict of the Orders*. Berkeley.

Ramage, N. (1992) "Goods, graves, and scholars: eighteenth-century archaeologists in Britain and Italy," *AJA* 96: 653–61.

Raubitschek, A. E. (1960) "The covenant of Plataea," *TAPhA* 91: 178–83.

Reber, K. (1998) *Eretria*, vol. 10: *Die klassischen und hellenistischen Wohnhäuser im Westquartier*. Lausanne.

Reber, K., M. H. Hansen, and P. Ducrey (2004) "Euboia," in Hansen and Nielsen, eds., 643–63.

Rebuffat, M. R. (1966) "Les Phéniciennes à Rome," *MEFRA* 78: 7–48.

Redfield, J. M. (1985) "Herodotus the tourist," *CPh* 80: 97–118.

Redman, C., ed. (1973) *Research and Theory in Current Archaeology*. New York.

Renfrew, C. (1972) *The Emergence of Civilization: The Cyclades and the Aegean in the Third Millennium B.C.* London.

—— (1980) "The Great Tradition versus the Great Divide: archaeology as anthropology?" *AJA* 84: 287–98.

—— (1984) *Approaches to Social Archaeology*. Edinburgh.

—— (2001) "Symbol before concept: material engagement and the early development of society," in Hodder, ed., 122–40.

Renfrew, C., and P. Bahn (2007) *Archaeology Essentials: Theories, Methods and Practice*. London.

Rhodes, P. J. (2008) "After the three-bar sigma controversy: the history of Athenian imperialism reassessed," *CQ* 58: 501–6.

Rhodes, P. J., and R. Osborne (2003) *Greek Historical Inscriptions, 404–323 BC*. New York.

Ricci, G., P. Brocato, and N. Terrenato (1992) "Lo scavo delle mura palatine: la sequenza delle fasi," *BollArch* 16–18: 112–28.

—— (1995) "Le fortificazioni: la fase 2; le prime mura," in Carandini and Carafa, eds., 139–60.

Rich, J., and A. Wallace-Hadrill, eds. (1991) *City and Country in the Ancient World*. London.

Richard, J.-C. (1986) "Patricians and plebeians: the origin of a social dichotomy," in Raaflaub, ed., 105–29.

Richmond, O. L. (1914) "The Augustan Palatium," *JRS* 4: 193–200.

Richter, G. (1970) *Kouroi, Archaic Greek Youths: A Study of the Development of the Kouros Type in Greek Sculpture*, 3rd ed. London.

Ridley, R. T. (1980) "*Fastenkritik*: a stocktaking," *Athenaeum* 58: 264–98.

—— (2005) "Unbridgeable gaps: the Capitoline temple at Rome," *BullCom* 106: 83–104.

Riginos, A. S. (1994) "The wounding of Philip II of Macedon: fact and fabrication," *JHS* 114: 103–19.

Ritti, T. (2006) *An Epigraphic Guide to Hierapolis (Pammukale)*, trans. P. Arthur. Istanbul.

Rizzo, G. (1932) "La base di Augusto," *BullCom* 60: 7–109.

Robert, L. (1938) *Études épigraphiques et philologiques*. Paris.

Robertson, N. (1978) "The myth of the First Sacred War," *CQ* 28: 38–73.

—— (1982) "The decree of Themistocles in its contemporary setting," *Phoenix* 36: 1–44.

Robinson, D. (1945) "Where and when did Peter die?," *JBL* 64: 225–67.

Robinson, E. W. (1997) *The First Democracies: Early Popular Government outside Athens*, Historia Einzelschriften 107. Stuttgart.

Roccos, L. J. (1989) "The Augustan Apollo on the Sorrento base," *AJA* 93: 571–88.

Röllinger, R., and C. Ulf, eds. (2004) *Das Archaische Griechenland: Interne Entwicklungen—Externe Impulse*. Berlin.

Roisman, J., and I. Worthington, eds. (2010) *A Companion to Ancient Macedonia*. Malden.

Romm. J. (2011) "Who was in Tomb II?," *LRB* 33.19: 27–28.

Rotroff, S. I. (1984) "Spool salt-cellars in the Athenian Agora," *Hesperia* 53: 343–54.

—— (1997) *The Athenian Agora: Results of Excavations Conducted by the American School of Classical Studies at Athens*, vol. 29: *Hellenistic Pottery: Athenian and Imported Wheelmade Table Ware and Related Material*. Princeton.

—— (2006) *The Athenian Agora: Results of Excavations Conducted by the American School of Classical Studies at Athens*, vol. 33: *Hellenistic Pottery: The Plain Wares*. Princeton.

—— (2008) "Whose pottery? the ceramics from the Vergina tombs," *Archaeological Institute of America: Abstracts of the 109th Annual Meeting*, 129.

—— (2009) "Commerce and crafts around the Athenian Agora," in Camp and Mauzy, eds., 39–46.

Royo, M. (1999) *Domus Imperatoriae: topographie, formation et imaginaire des palais impériaux du Palatin*. Rome.

Rüpke, J. (1995) "*Fasti*: Quellen oder Produkte römischer Geschichtsschreibung?," *Klio* 77: 184–202.

——— (2008) *Fasti Sacerdotum: A Prosopography of Pagan, Jewish, and Christian Religious Officials in the City of Rome, 300 BC to AD 499*, trans. D. M. B. Richardson. Oxford.

Rüpke, J., ed. (2007) *A Companion to Roman Religion*. Malden.

Saatsoglou-Paliadeli, C. (2004) Βεργίνα· ο τάφος του Φιλίππου, η τοιχογραφία με το κυνήγι. Athens.

——— (2011a) "Το ανάκτορο των Αιγῶν: προδημοσίευση," *AEMT* 21: 127–34.

——— (2011b) "The royal presence in the agora of Aegae," in Kottaridi and Walker, eds., 193–204.

Sakka, N. (2008) "The excavation of the Ancient Agora of Athens: the politics of commissioning and managing the project," in Damaskos and Plantzos, eds., 111–24.

Salviat, F. (1977) "La dédicace du trésor de Cnide à Delphes," *Études Delphiques, BCH* suppl. 4, 23–36. Paris.

Sánchez, P. (2001) *L'Amphictionie des Pyles et de Delphes: recherches sur son role historique, des origins au IIe siècle de notre ère, Historia* Einzelschriften 148. Stuttgart.

Santi Amantini, L. (2005) "A proposito di 'pace' in Teopompo," in Santi Amantini, ed., 35–59.

Santi Amantini, L., ed. (2005) *Dalle parole ai fatti: relazioni interstatali e comunicazione politica nel mondo antico*. Rome.

Sauer, E. W., ed. (2004) *Archaeology and Ancient History: Breaking Down the Boundaries*. London.

Saunders, N. J. (2006) *Alexander's Tomb: The Two Thousand Year Obsession to Find the Lost Conqueror*. New York.

Schauenberg, K. (1960) "Aeneas und Rom," *Gymnasium* 67: 176–91.

Schmid, S. (1999) "A new millennium at Eretria (Euboea, Greece): the Roman period," in Docter and Moormann, eds., 358–61.

Schmidt, C. (1930) "Zur Datierung der alten Petrusakten," *ZNTW* 29: 150–55.

Schnapp, A. (1996) *The Discovery of the Past*, trans. I. Kinnes and G. Varndell. London.

Scott, E. M., A. Y. Alekseev, and G. Zaitseva, eds. (2004) *Impact of the Environment on Human Migration in Eurasia*. Dordrecht.

Seager, R. (1969) "The Congress Decree: some doubts and a hypothesis," *Historia* 18: 129–41.

Sealey, R. (1954–55) "The Peace of Callias once more," *Historia* 3: 325–33.

——— (1976) *A History of the Greek City States, ca. 700–338 BC*. Berkeley.

Sebasta, J. L., and L. Bonfante, eds. (2001) *The World of Roman Costume*. Madison.

Sellars, J. (2003) "Simon the shoemaker and the problem of Socrates," *CPh* 98: 207–16.

Servais, J. (1969) "Hérodote et la chronologie des Cypsélides," *AC* 38: 28–81.

Shanks, M. (1996) *Classical Archaeology of Greece: Experiences of the Discipline*. New York.

Shanks, M., and I. Hodder (1995) "Processual, postprocessual and interpretive archaeologies," in Hodder et al., eds., 3–29.

Shapiro, H. A. (1989) *Art and Cult under the Tyrants*. Mainz.

Shear, T. L., Jr. (1982) "The demolished temple at Eleusis," in *Studies in Athenian Architecture, Sculpture, and Topography Presented to Homer A. Thompson, Hesperia* suppl. 20, 128–40. Princeton.

Shennan, S. (2004) "Analytical archaeology," in Bintliff, ed., 3–20.

Shennan, S., ed. (1989) *Archaeological Approaches to Cultural Identity*. London.

Sickinger, J. P. (2009) "Ostraka from the Athenian Agora," in Camp and Mauzy, eds., 77–83.

Siewert, P. (1972) *Der Eid von Plataia*. Munich.

Smith, C. J. (1996) *Early Rome and Latium: Economy and Society c. 1000–500 BC*. Oxford.

——— (2005) "The beginnings of urbanization in Rome," in Osborne and Cunliffe, eds., 91–111.

——— (2006) *The Roman Clan: The Gens from Ancient Ideology to Modern Anthropology*. Cambridge.

——— (2011) "The magistrates of the early Roman Republic," in Beck et al., eds., 19–40.

Snodgrass, A. M. (1980) *Archaic Greece: The Age of Experiment*. London.

——— (1985) "The New Archaeology and the classical archaeologist," *AJA* 89: 31–37.

——— (1987) *An Archaeology of Greece: The Present State and Future Scope of a Discipline*. Berkeley.

——— (2006) *Archaeology and the Emergence of Greece*. Ithaca.

——— (2012) "What is classical archaeology? Greek archaeology," in Alcock and Osborne, eds., 13–29.

Snyder, G. F. (1969) "Survey and 'new' thesis on the bones of Peter," *BibArch* 32: 2–24.

——— (2003) *Ante Pacem: Archaeological Evidence of Church Life before Constantine*, rev. ed. Macon, GA.

Sommella, P. (1971–72) "Heroon di Enea a Lavinium: recenti scavi a Pratica di Mare," *RPAA* 44: 47–74.

——— (1974) "Das Heroon des Aeneas und die Topographie des antiken Lavinium," *Gymnasium* 81: 283–97.

Sourvinou-Inwood, C. (1987) "Myth as history: the previous owners of the Delphic oracle," in Bremmer, ed., 215–41.

——— (2002) "Greek perceptions of ethnicity and the ethnicity of the Macedonians," in Moscati Castelnuovo, ed., 173–203.

——— (2003) "Festivals and mysteries: aspects of the Eleusinian cult," in Cosmopoulos, ed., 25–49.

Sparkes, B. A., and L. Talcott (1970) *The Athenian Agora: Results of Excavations Conducted by the American School of*

*Classical Studies at Athens*, vol. 12: *Black and Plain Pottery of the 6th, 5th and 4th Centuries BC.* Princeton.

Sperber, L. (1987) *Untersuchungen zur Chronologie der Urnenfelderkultur im nördlichen Alpenvorland von der Schweiz bis Oberösterreich.* Bonn.

Spiller, H. A., J. R. Hale, and J. Z. de Boer (2002) "The Delphic Oracle: a multidisciplinary defense of the gaseous vent theory," *CT* 40: 189–96.

Spriggs, M., ed. (1977) *Archaeology and Anthropology*, BAR Supplementary Series 19. Oxford.

Stamatopoulou, M., and M. Yeroulanou, eds. (2002) *Excavating Classical Culture: Recent Archaeological Discoveries in Greece*, BAR International Series 1031. Oxford.

Starr, C. G. (1965) "The credibility of early Spartan history," *Historia* 14: 257–72.

Stavely, E. S. (1956) "The constitution of the Roman Republic 1940–1954," *Historia* 5: 74–122.

St. Clair, W. (1998) *Lord Elgin and the Marbles*, 2nd ed. Oxford.

Stein, M. L., and P. Malatesta (1965) "Risultato dell'esame merceologico dei frammenti di tessuto," in Guarducci, 182.

Steinby, E. M., ed. (1995) *Lexicon Topographicum Urbis Romae*, vol. 2. Rome.

——— (1996) *Lexicon Topographicum Urbis Romae*, vol. 3. Rome.

Stewart, A. (1990) *Greek Sculpture*, 2 vols. New Haven.

——— (2008) "The Persian and Carthaginian invasions of 480 BCE and the beginning of the classical style: Part 1: The stratigraphy, chronology, and significance of the acropolis deposits; Part 2: The finds from other sites in Athens, Attica, elsewhere in Greece, and on Sicily; Part 3: The Severe Style: motivations and meanings," *AJA* 112: 377–412, 581–615.

Stockton, D. (1959) "The Peace of Callias," *Historia* 8: 61–79.

Storchi Marino, A., ed. (1995) *L'incidenza dell'antico: studi in memoria di Ettore Lepore*, vol. 1. Naples.

Strasburger, H. (1968) *Zur Sage von der Gründung Roms.* Heidelberg.

Stroud, R. F. (1998) *The Athenian Grain-Tax Law of 374/3 B.C.*, *Hesperia* suppl. 29. Princeton.

Stucchi, S. (1958) *I monumenti del lato meridionale del Foro Romano.* Rome.

Syme, R. (1939) *The Roman Revolution.* Oxford.

Tarn, W. W. (1948) *Alexander the Great*, vol. 2. Cambridge.

Taylor, A. E. (1911) *Varia Socratica.* Oxford.

Taylor, R. E. (2001) "Radiocarbon dating," in Brothwell and Pollard, eds, 23–34.

Terrenato, N. (1995) "La topografia," in Carandini and Carafa, eds., 200–208.

——— (1996) "'Murus Romuli,'" in Steinby, ed., 315–17.

——— (2003) "La morfologia originaria di Roma," in Carandini, 587–94.

Themelis, P., and I. Touratsoglou (1997) Οι τάφοι του Δερβενίου. Athens.

Thomas, C. M. (2003) *The Acts of Peter, Gospel Literature, and the Ancient Novel.* Oxford.

Thomas, J. (1995) "Where are we now? archaeological theory in the 1990s," in Ucko, ed., 343–62.

——— (2001) "Archaeologies of place and landscape," in Hodder, ed., 165–86.

Thomas, M., and G. Meyers, eds. (2012) *Monumentality in Etruscan and Early Roman Architecture: Ideology and Innovation.* Austin.

Thomas, R. (1989) *Oral Tradition and Written Record in Classical Athens.* Cambridge.

Thompson, D. B. (1960) "The house of Simon the shoemaker," *Archaeology* 13: 234–40.

Thompson, D. L. (1981) "The meetings of the Roman senate on the Palatine," *AJA* 85: 335–39.

Thompson, H. A. (1948) "The excavation of the Athenian Agora twelfth season: 1947," *Hesperia* 17: 149–96.

——— (1954) "Excavations in the Athenian Agora: 1953," *Hesperia* 23: 31–67.

Thompson, H. A., and R. E. Wycherley (1972) *The Athenian Agora: Results of Excavations Conducted by the American School of Classical Studies at Athens*, vol. 14: *The History, Shape, and Uses of an Ancient Civic Center.* Princeton.

Thompson, W. E. (1981) "The Peace of Callias in the fourth century," *Historia* 30: 164–77.

Threatte, L. (1980) *The Grammar of Attic Inscriptions*, vol. 1: *Phonology.* Berlin.

Tilley, C. (1994) *A Phenomenology of Landscape: Places, Paths and Monuments.* Oxford.

Tölle-Kastenbein, R. (1993) "Das Hekatompedon auf der Athener Akropolis," *JDAI* 108: 43–75.

Tolotti, F. (1953) *Memorie degli Apostoli in Catacumbas: rilievo critico della Memoria e della Basilica Apostolorum di III miglio della Via Appia.* Vatican City.

Tomei, M. A. (1998) *The Palatine*, trans. L. Guarneri Hynd. Milan.

——— (2000) "Le case di Augusto sul Palatino," *MDAI(R)* 107: 7–36.

Tomlinson, R. A. (1972) *Argos and the Argolid from the End of the Bronze Age to the Roman Occupation.* London.

——— (1987) "The architectural context of the Macedonian vaulted tombs," *ABSA* 82: 305–12.

Touloupa, E. (1983) Τα ἐναέτια γλυπτά τοῦ ναοῦ τοῦ Ἀπόλλωνος Δαφνηφόρου στήν Ἐρέτρια. Ioannina.

Townsend, R. F. (1995a) *The Athenian Agora: Results of Excavations Conducted by the American School of Classical Studies at Athens*, vol. 27: *The East Side of the Agora: The Remains beneath the Stoa of Attalos.* Princeton.

——— (1995b) "The Square Peristyle and its predecessors," in Boegehold et al., 104–13.

Toynbee, J. M. C. (1953) "The shrine of St. Peter and its setting," *JRS* 43: 1–26.

Toynbee, J. M. C., and J. B. Ward-Perkins (1956) *The Shrine of St. Peter and the Vatican Excavations*. London.

Traill, D. A. (1995) *Schliemann of Troy: Treasure and Deceit*. New York.

Travlos, J. (1971) *Pictorial Dictionary of Ancient Athens*. New York.

Trigger, B. (1989) *A History of Archaeological Thought*. Cambridge.

Tripodi, B. (1991) "Il fregio della caccia della II tomba reale di Vergina e le cacce funerarie d'Oriente," *DHA* 17: 143–209.

—— (1998) *Cacce reali macedoni*. Messina.

Tsetskhladze, G., ed. (2008) *Greek Colonisation. An Account of Greek Colonies and Other Settlements Overseas in the Archaic Period*, vol. 2. Leiden.

Tung, A. (2001) *Preserving the World's Great Cities: The Destruction and Renewal of the Historic Metropolis*. New York.

Ucko, P. (1969) "Ethnography and archaeological interpretation of funerary remains," *WA* 1: 262–80.

Ucko, P. J., ed. (1995) *Theory in Archaeology: A World Perspective*. London.

Ucko, P. J., R. Tringham, and G. W. Dimbleby, eds. (1972) *Man, Settlement and Urbanism*. London.

Ustinova, Y. (2009) *Caves and the Ancient Greek Mind: Descending Underground in the Search for Ultimate Truth*. Oxford.

van der Plicht, J. (2004) "Radiocarbon, the calibration curve and Scythian chronology," in Scott, Alekseev, and Zaitseva, eds., 45–61.

van der Plicht, J., H. J. Bruins, and A. J. Nijboer (2009) "The Iron Age around the Mediterranean: a high chronology perspective from the Groningen radiocarbon database," *Radiocarbon* 51: 213–42.

Vanderpool, E. (1980) "The state prison of ancient Athens," in *From Athens to Gordion: the Papers of a Memorial Symposium for Rodney S. Young, Held at the University Museum, the Third of May, 1975*, 17–31. Philadelphia.

Vansina, J. (1985) *Oral Tradition as History*. Madison.

van Wees, H. (2006) "'The oath of the sworn bands': the Acharnae stela, the oath of Plataea and Archaic Spartan warfare," in Luther, Meier, and Thommen, eds., 125–64.

Veit, U. (1989) "Ethnic concepts in German prehistory: a case study on the relationship between cultural identity and archaeological objectivity," in Shennan, ed., 35–56.

Verdan, S. (2000) "Fouilles dans le sanctuaire d'Apollon Daphnéphoros," *AK* 43: 128–30.

—— (2001) "Fouilles dans le sanctuaire d'Apollon Daphnéphoros," *AK* 44: 84–87.

—— (2002) "Fouilles dans le sanctuaire d'Apollon Daphnéphoros," *AK* 45: 128–32.

—— (2012) *Eretria*, vol. 22: *Le sanctuaire d'Apollon Daphnéphoros à l'époque géométrique*, 2 vols. Lausanne.

Vernant, J.-P. (1991) *Mortals and Immortals: Collected Essays*, ed. F. Zeitlin. Princeton.

Voudouri, D. (2008) "Greek legislation concerning the international movement of antiquities and its ideological and political dimensions," in Damaskos and Plantzos, eds., 125–39.

Wade-Gery, H. T. (1940) "The Peace of Kallias," in *Athenian Studies Presented to William Scott Ferguson*, HSCP suppl. 1, 121–56. Cambridge, MA.

—— (1945) "The question of tribute in 449/8 BC," *Hesperia* 14: 212–29.

—— (1958) *Essays in Greek History*. Oxford.

Walker, K. (2004) *Archaic Eretria: A Political and Social History from the Earliest Times to 490*. London.

Wallace, R. W., and E. M. Harris, eds. (1996) *Transitions to Empire: Essays in Greco-Roman History, 360–146 B.C. in Honor of E. Badian*. Norman.

Wallace-Hadrill, A. (1983) *Suetonius: The Scholar and his Caesars*. London.

Wallace-Hadrill, A., et al. (2001) *The British School at Rome: One Hundred Years*. London.

Walsh, J. (1981) "The authenticity and the dates of the Peace of Callias and the Congress Decree," *Chiron* 11: 31–63.

Walsh, J. E. (1982) *The Bones of St. Peter: The First Full Account of the Search for the Apostle's Body*. Garden City.

Wardle, D. (2000) "Valerius Maximus on the Domus Augusta, Augustus, and Tiberius," *CQ* 50: 479–93.

Waterhouse, H. (1986) *The British School at Athens: The First Hundred Years*. London.

Weiss, R. (1988) *The Renaissance Discovery of Classical Antiquity*, 2nd ed. Oxford.

Werner, R. (1963) *Der Beginn der römischen Republik*. Munich.

Whitley, J. (1991) *Style and Society in Dark Age Greece: The Changing Face of a Pre-literate Society, 1100–750 BC*. Cambridge.

—— (1997) "Beazley as theorist," *Antiquity* 71: 40–47.

—— (2001) *The Archaeology of Ancient Greece*. Cambridge.

Whittaker, C. R. (1965) "The Delphic Oracle: belief and behaviour in ancient Greece—and Africa," *HTR* 58: 21–47.

Wilamowitz-Moellendorff, U. von (1879) "Phaidon von Elis," *Hermes* 14: 187–93.

Wilhelm, A. (1892) "Ἐπιγραφαὶ ἐξ Εὐβοίας," *AE*, 119–79.

Wilkinson, T. J. (2001) "Surface collection techniques in field archaeology: theory and practice," in Brothwell and Pollard, eds, 529–42.

Will, E. (1955) *Korinthiaka: recherches sur l'histoire et la civilisation de Corinthe des origines aux guerres médiques*. Paris.

Willey, G., and P. Phillips (1958) *Method and Theory in American Archaeology*. Chicago.

Winckelmann, J. J. (1880) *The History of Ancient Art among the Greeks*, vol. 1, trans. G. H. Lodge. Boston.

Wiseman, J. (1980) "Archaeology in the future: an emerging discipline," *AJA* 84: 279-85.

Wiseman, T. P. (1987) "*Conspicui postes tectaque digna deo*: the public image of aristocratic and imperial houses in the Late Republic and Early Empire," in *L'Urbs: Espace urbain et histoire*, 393-413. Rome.

———— (1995) *Remus: A Roman Myth*. Cambridge.

———— (2001) "Reading Carandini," *JRS* 91: 182-93.

———— (2008) *Unwritten Rome*. Exeter.

———— (2009) "The house of Augustus and the Lupercal," *JRA* 22: 527-45.

Woodard, R. D., ed. (2007) *The Cambridge Companion to Greek Mythology*. Cambridge.

Worthington, I., ed. (1994) *Ventures into Greek History*. Oxford.

Wycherley, R. E. (1957) *The Athenian Agora: Results of Excavations Conducted by the American School of Classical Studies at Athens*, vol. 3: *Literary and Epigraphical Testimonia*. Princeton.

———— (1978) *The Stones of Athens*. Princeton.

Xirotiris, N. I., and F. Langenscheidt (1983) "The cremations from the royal Macedonian tombs at Vergina," *AE* (1981), pp. 142-60.

Young, R. S. (1951) "An industrial district of ancient Athens," *Hesperia* 20: 135-288.

Zampas, K. 2001. "Ἀποκατάσταση τοῦ ἀναλημματικοῦ τοίχου στὸ προαύλιο τοῦ Φιλίππου Β," *AEMT* 13: 561-63.

Zanker, P. (1988) *The Power of Images in the Age of Augustus*, trans. A. Shapiro. Ann Arbor.

Zeller, E. (1868) *Socrates and the Socratic Schools*, trans. O. J. Reichel. London.

Zevi, F. (1995) "Demarato e i re 'corinzi' di Roma," in Storchi Marino, ed., 291-314.

Zwierlein, O. (2009) *Petrus in Rom: die literarischen Zeugnisse mit einer kritischen Edition der Martyrien des Petrus und Paulus auf neuer handschriftlicher Grundlage*. Berlin.

# Index

Note: page numbers in italics denote illustrations

Boni, Giacomo, 122, 138, 151
Boniface IV (pope), 3
Borghese, Scipio, 199
Boston Museum of Fine Arts, 8
Boupalos, 172
Bramante (Donato di Angelo di Pascuccio), 193n35
Brauron, temple of Artemis, 70, 73
British Museum, 4, 6, 7, 81, 85, 107n56
British School at Athens, 7, 9n55, 12, 13
British School at Rome, 7, 12-13
Brutus, Lucius Junius, 149, 155, 156
Brutus, Marcus Junius, 172
Bryn Mawr College, 8
buildings, dating of, 10, 37n7, 38, 73

Caere, 149, 154
Calvert, Frank, 10
Camillus, Marcus Furius, 159
Campania: Etruscans and, 162; Roman influence in, 129, 131n43
Capitoline wolf, 130
Capua, 162
Carettoni, Gianfilippo, 136, 168, 170-72, 181; house of Augustus
    (see Rome: House of Octavian)
Carr, Edward Hallett, 2n2
Carrey, Jacques, 5
Carthage, 155
caryatids, 6, 48, 49, 50-51, 68
Cassander, 102, 110, 113, 114, 115
Castel di Decima, 126
Cato, Marcus Porcius, 150
Catulus, Quintus Lutatius, 175, 176, 181
Cesnola, Luigi Palma di, 8
Chalkis, 35
charismatic authority. See status: achieved
Charles I, 4
Charles VII, 4
Chios, 153
Christianity, rise of, 3
chronology: archaeological, 11, 38-39, 40; challenges to con-
    ventional schema, 39-42, 47, 48-51, 52; generational
    dating, 134; of Latium, 134. See also dendrochronology;
    fixed points; radiocarbon dating
Cicero: on the Annales Maximi, 150; on the consular lists, 156;
    letters to Atticus, 3
Cincius Alimentus, Lucius, 150
Clarke, David, 13, 212
classical archaeology: definitions of, 3, 14; part of university
    curricula, 8, 216-19
classics: in Britain, 12, 217; in the United States, 12, 217-18
Claudius (emperor), 152
Claudius Caecus, Appius, 163
Clement VIII (pope), 188
Clement XIII (pope), 5
Cleopatra, 46, 167, 173n29

Cluvium, 149, 154
cognitive archaeology, 15, 210
coins: Limoges, 188; Macedonian, 110; Roman, 130, 178, 179
collecting, 4, 5, 6-7, 8, 15
collegia, 197-98
Collingwood, Robin, 15
colonization, Greek, 19
columbaria, 197
comitia centuriata, 157
comitium plebis, 156. See also plebeians
Congress Decree. See Perikles: Congress Decree
connoisseurship, 3, 7, 12, 15
Constantina, 200
Constantine I (the Great), 189, 192, 195
Constantinople, 5, 6, 201; capture of, 3; Ecumenical Council of,
    201
consulship: establishment of, 131, 155, 157, 158, 159-60, 210;
    lists, 155-57; opened to plebeians, 131, 156
context: archaeological, 15, 208-9; historical, 208-9
Corinth, 151; early development of, 140; excavations of, 9 isth-
    mus of, 59, 61; temple of Apollo, 37, 41
Cornelius (pope), 200, 201
corona civica, 179, 180
Correnti, Venerando, 188, 200, 203
Cosa, 10
Courbin, Paul, 14-15
Courby, M. F., 22-23
Coventry Cathedral, 42n27
Crassus, Marcus Licinius, 176n32, 211
cremation, 106-9, 115, 138, 162, 191, 197. See also inhumation
cultic dedications, 9, 18, 42, 56, 139, 146, 148
culture, theories of, 13
culture history, 13
Cumae, 46, 149, 150, 160
Curtius, Ernst, 8-9
Cynic tradition of philosophy, 82, 208
Cyprus, 63, 65, 66, 67, 72

Damastes of Sigeion, 126n23
Damasus (pope), 199, 201
Darius II, 64
de Alcubierre, Rocque Joaquin, 4
dei Pizzicolli, Ciriaco (Cyriac of Ancona), 3-4
Delian League, 42, 65
Delos, 9
Delphi: adyton, 20, 21, 22, 23; Athenian treasury, 50; chasm,
    18, 21, 22-23, 25; French excavations, 9, 18, 22-23, 25; fault
    lines, 18, 23, 24, 25-26, 209; geochemistry, 24-26, 210;
    history of, 19-20; Knidian treasury, 49-50; pneuma, 22;
    sanctuary of Apollo, 9, 23; sanctuary of Athena Pronaia,
    19, 23n42; Serpent Column, 72; Siphnian treasury, 42, 48,
    49, 50-51; temple of Apollo, 18, 19, 20, 21, 22, 23, 24, 25, 37,
    41, 207n2; Theban treasury, 50. See also Delphic Amphik-
    tyony; Delphic oracle; Pythian priestess of Apollo

Olympia: German excavations, 8–9, 10, 11; Nike of Paionios, 8; Pheidias's statue of Zeus, 46; temple of Hera, 9; temple of Zeus, 8, 9, 41; treasuries, 9; Workshop of Pheidias, 80

Olympias, 102, 104n32, 115

Olympos, Mount, 105

Olynthos, 9n55, 39

Oppé, Paul, 18

oral history, "hourglass" model of, 150

Oropos, 43

Orvieto, 132

Ossa, Mount, 105

Osteria dell'Osa, 138

Österreichisches Archäologisches Institut, 7, 9n55

Ostian Way: Basilica of St. Paul outside the Walls, 187; *tropaion*, 195, 205

ostracism, 79, 81, 83

Ottoman Turks, 4; conquest of Crete, 5

palaeoanthropology, 13

panhellenism, 65

Panopticon, 92

Paparrigopoulos, Konstantinos, 103

Paris, judgement of, 48

*patres conscripti*, 156

patricians, 153, 156; closure of, 156. *See also* struggle of the orders

Patroklos, funeral of, 115

Paul VI (pope), 188, 189, 192, 202

Paul, Saint: execution of, 194, 195, 202; ministry of, 195, 196; tomb of, 187, 199–201, 202–3, 211. *See also* Appian Way; Ostian Way

Pausanias (assassin of Philip II), 115

Pausanias (author), 8, 10, 11, 80

Peace, King's. *See* Antalkidas, Peace of

Peiraieus, 91

Peisistratids, 43, 58, 148n11, 159, 163

Peisistratos, 42–43, 56

Pelasgians, 122, 125

Pella, 97, 98, 177

Peloponnesian War, 31, 65; First, 67

Pembroke, 8th Earl of (Thomas Herbert), 4

*Penates*, 126, 127

Penthesilea, 113n88

Pentonville prison, 92

Perachora, 9n55

Perdikkas (son of Orontes), 114

Perdikkas I, 105

Pergamon, 7n36, 9

Perikles, 77, 78, 82, 211; building programme, 56, 69, 209; Congress Decree, 67, 72; Euboian revolt, 47

Persephone, rape of, 99

Persians: invasion of Greece, 6, 30, 46, 49, 50, 62, 65; peace treaties with Greeks (*see* Kallias: Peace of)

Peter, Saint: execution of, 189, 194–96, 197, 202, 203, 208; ministry of, 194, 195, 196, 201, 209; tomb of, 188, 194, 195, 199–201, 202, 208, 210, 211. *See also* Appian Way; Vatican

Petrarca, Francesco (Petrarch), 3

Phaidon of Elis, 78

Phaistos, 9n55

Phaleron, temple of Demeter, 71

Phaselis, 63

Pheidias, 5

Pheidon of Argos, 151n25

Phila (wife of Philip II), 106, 116n112

Philip II, 103, *108*, 111, 113, 115, 177; assassination, 98, 102, 110, 115; and Athens, 63; burial, 98, 115; as occupant of Tomb I, 114–16; as occupant of Tomb II, 102, 104, 106, 107, 110, 114; sack of Olynthos, 39; wounds suffered, 106, 107, 109

Philip III (Arrhidaios), 104, 109, 110, 111, 112, 113, 114; as occupant of Tomb II, 102, 106, 108, 114–15, 116

Philip, Saint, 204–5, 208

Philippi, battle of, 172n27

Phillips, Philip, 13

Phlya, 72

Phocas, 3

Phoenicians, 140, 154, 162

Phokaia, 72

Phokion, 85, 93

Phylakopi, 12n68

Picus, 126

Piso Frugi, Lucius Calpurnius, 150, 152

Pithekoussai, 35

Pius XI (pope), 188

Pius XII (pope), 188, 202

Plancus, Lucius Munatius, 211

Plataia, 62; battle of, 41, 59, 60, 61, 72; Oath of, 42, 59–60, 61, 62, 63, 67, 69, 72–73, 208, 209, 210; temple of Athena, 72

plebeians, 156. *See also* consulship: opened to plebeians; struggle of the orders

Pliny the Elder, 5n24

Plutarch: and Delphi, 20–22, 24, 25, 29; and Perikles, 209

Polykleitos, 179

Polykrates of Ephesos (bishop), 205

Polykrates of Samos, 48

*pomerium*, 134, 136, 141

Pompeii, 4, 11; House of Pansa, 176; styles of painting, 168, 170

Pompeius Magnus Pius, Sextus, 171, 173, 178

Pontifex Maximus, 121, 136n79, 150, 152, 153, 176

Poplios Valesios. *See* Valerius Publicola, Publius

positivist fallacy, 207–8

postprocessual archaeology, 15, 208, 216

pottery: Attic black-figure, 9; Attic red-figure, 9, 81, 110n67, 159; *bucchero*, 148, 151; Corinthian, 39, 124; in Etruria, 126; Geometric, 39; impasto, 133, 136, 139; Italo-Geometric, 133; Panathenaic amphorae, 110; *terra sigillata*, 39

Praeneste (Palestrina), 130; calendar, 179

Praetor Maximus, 158, 159

Pratica di Mare, 127, 128, 129